Victims of Ireland's Great Famine

Bioarchaeological Interpretations of the Human Past:
Local, Regional, and Global Perspectives

UNIVERSITY PRESS OF FLORIDA

Florida A&M University, Tallahassee
Florida Atlantic University, Boca Raton
Florida Gulf Coast University, Ft. Myers
Florida International University, Miami
Florida State University, Tallahassee
New College of Florida, Sarasota
University of Central Florida, Orlando
University of Florida, Gainesville
University of North Florida, Jacksonville
University of South Florida, Tampa
University of West Florida, Pensacola

2

Victims of Ireland's Great Famine

The Bioarchaeology of Mass Burials
at Kilkenny Union Workhouse

JONNY GEBER

Foreword by Clark Spencer Larsen

University Press of Florida
Gainesville · Tallahassee · Tampa · Boca Raton
Pensacola · Orlando · Miami · Jacksonville · Ft. Myers · Sarasota

This book may be available in an electronic edition.

First cloth printing, 2015
First paperback printing, 2018

23 22 21 20 19 18   6 5 4 3 2 1

Library of Congress Cataloging-in-Publication Data
Geber, Jonny, author.
Victims of Ireland's great famine : the bioarchaeology of mass burials at Kilkenny Union
Workhouse / Jonny Geber ; Foreword by Clark Spencer Larsen.
pages cm — (Bioarchaeological interpretations of the human past: local, regional, and
global perspectives)
Includes bibliographical references and index.
ISBN 978-0-8130-6117-7 (cloth)
ISBN 978-0-8130-6467-3 (pbk.)
1. Famines—Ireland—Kilkenny (County—History—19th century. 2. Mass burials—
Ireland—Kilkenny (County—History—19th century. 3. Workhouses—Ireland—
History—19th century. 4. Ireland—History—Famine, 1845–1852. 5. Starvation—
History—19th century. 6. Poor—Ireland—History—19th century. I. Larsen, Clark
Spencer, author of introduction, etc. II. Title.
DA950.7.G43 2015
941.5081—dc23
2015019365

The University Press of Florida is the scholarly publishing agency for the State University
System of Florida, comprising Florida A&M University, Florida Atlantic University,
Florida Gulf Coast University, Florida International University, Florida State University,
New College of Florida, University of Central Florida, University of Florida, University
of North Florida, University of South Florida, and University of West Florida.

University Press of Florida
15 Northwest 15th Street
Gainesville, FL 32611-2079
http://upress.ufl.edu

This book is dedicated to the hundreds of thousands of men, women, and children who experienced the workhouse institutions of Ireland.

Contents

Figures

Tables

Foreword

The story of the great Irish potato famine is one of remarkable demographic disruption involving the deaths of some 1 million persons and the emigration of another million (mostly to the United States) in the period 1845–1852. Estimates range widely but indicate that at least one-eighth of Ireland's men, women, and children succumbed and died in an eyeblink of history. Many of the 1 million victims of the famine died while serving as inmates of the dreaded workhouses, not directly from starvation but from infectious disease. The likelihood of dying was strongly influenced by the poor living conditions prior to the famine, which resulted in a population rife with compromised immune systems because of poor nutrition and deprivation generally. Virtually all who entered a workhouse had likely requested shelter and food only as a last resort, especially when they had reached a point of not being able to purchase or raise food for their families.

The story of the famine and its outcome for most communities is known today mostly from mortality statistics and county records, which account for the nameless and faceless people who confronted challenges and underwent hardships. One of the communities hard hit by the famine was Kilkenny City, where a workhouse was established for the very poor and destitute. An associated intramural mass burial discovered 160 years after the famine was unknown to the local community until commercial development began to expose human remains. Following national guidelines, a team of archaeologists commenced excavation, recovering nearly 1,000 of the workhouse deceased and providing Geber and his colleagues the opportunity to give us a picture of the people and the biological costs they incurred during some of the roughest times in modern human history. Although the story they uncovered is one of perseverance, ultimately it is a story of collapse.

In the following pages, Jonny Geber provides us with a new perspective on the Kilkenny City workhouse people as they are represented by their mortal remains. As Geber so eloquently articulates, skeletons provide a fundamental retrospective story of life and living, of distress, and ultimately of the circumstances surrounding death. The skeletons from the Kilkenny City workhouse mass burials tell us of the remarkably poor quality of living conditions both before and during the famine. The bioarchaeological record is a rich one, in part because it presents a viewpoint not well represented in the traditional politicized framework of nineteenth-century Ireland, in the ledgers listing the dead, or in historical sources. Rather, his study provides the biocultural context from the archaeology and the historical record, including work and labor practices, foods eaten, nutrition, and living circumstances. Geber successfully portrays the power of bioarchaeology and how the study of skeletal remains gives an essential platform for reconstructing and interpreting a period of time and its tragic outcome. The skeletal series—the largest mass burial ground excavated and studied in Ireland—is unique, reflecting the conditions those who were already ill and depleted before entering the workhouse had endured.

Prior to Geber's investigation, surprisingly little was known about the workhouse funerary context. The archaeological record indicates that a burial pit was prepared on weekly basis. The 63 burial pits found at the Kilkenny workhouse cemetery contain an average of sixteen wooden coffins. Contrary to general perceptions deriving from folklore, bodies were not thrown willy-nilly into hastily dug pits. Rather, the body was prepared, placed in a carefully prepared wooden coffin, and carefully placed in the ground. All the victims were from the lower social classes of Ireland, yet in death they were clearly treated with a certain degree of respect.

The skeletons display a considerable record of pathology reflecting poor conditions. What struck me was the skeletal signature of work life, one that involved highly demanding physical labor. Indeed, the elevated prevalence and severity of degenerative joint disease is consistent with the rule that anyone admitted to the workhouse was required to perform physical labor. Perhaps most arresting about those who lived in the workhouse was the record of injury from accidental causes and interpersonal violence. Indeed, at least some of the periosteal bone responses seen in so many of the skeletons likely reflect injuries. Some diseases will not be reflected in the skeletal record, especially those that kill quickly, such as cholera. No doubt some of the deceased met their end during the horrific cholera epidemics that swept the world in the middle nineteenth century. On the other hand, chronic deficiency diseases are well represented in these skeletons—some two-thirds of the children and adolescents and half of the adult population displayed skeletal evidence of scurvy. The remarkably high prevalence of lesions relating to vitamin C deficiency is among the highest reported in any archaeological skeletal series that has been studied.

The bioarchaeological study presented in this important book provides the reader with a picture of a highly stressed subpopulation of Irish society in the mid-nineteenth century. The fear that entering a workhouse during the famine meant that one might leave in a pine box was well founded. Most important, Geber's study provides a new and much-needed perspective on a group that has largely been forgotten. The combination of the record from historical sources and his findings reveal the consequences of severe famine and suffering for a community and its individual members. The skeletons help us remember the lives and livelihoods that vanished in the face of disaster. Their remains and the record they provide remind us of the perils of focus on a limited range of foods, certainly the especially narrow range that is unsuited for long-term sustainability and well-being.

Clark Spencer Larsen
Series Editor

Preface

With this book, I have made an attempt to tell the story of almost 1,000 victims of the notorious Great Famine in Ireland who died in the union workhouse in Kilkenny City from 1847 to 1851. Anonymously and without ceremony, they were buried in simple pine coffins stacked on top of each other in large mass burial pits dug into the ground within the boundary walls of the institution. Their physical skeletal remains were discovered about 160 years later, and if it had not been for the consequential archaeological excavation, historical research, and scientific analysis of their bones, very little would have been known about them. In the surviving archival sources relating to the Kilkenny workhouse, they are generally referred to as mere mortality statistics written down in tables in the minute books. But behind these statistics were once living people: men, women, and children who endured lives of hardship and struggle and who met their untimely deaths during one of the worst famines in recorded history. Relatively little is known about them, and it is not possible to historically identify any of the individuals in the workhouse mass burials. But they nevertheless deserve to be acknowledged for the lives they lived, the struggles of poverty they endured, and the tragedies they suffered in the period leading up to their deaths. To "deanonymize" these statistics, primarily through the study of their physical remains, has perhaps been the most important goal for the research that is presented in this book.

It may be difficult to comprehend the horrors of the Great Famine and what the workhouse inmates in Kilkenny had to go through, but archaeology—and bioarchaeology in particular—has exposed a very approachable and quite tangible insight into both their collective and individual experiences. Site archaeologists felt this very much as they excavated and recorded the burials, and I felt this as I analyzed the remains and contemplated what the skeletons revealed about the people they once were part of. I have therefore felt a huge responsibility throughout this project to treat the remains of these people with the greatest respect. Although, from my impression, the local reaction in Kilkenny to the research project has been one of great interest, never a feeling of any real controversy, there was a voiced opinion that the remains should be returned to Kilkenny and reinterred after the skeletal analysis was completed. This eventually took place during a multidenominational ceremony attended by representatives of the local community and the general public (see chapter 6).

This monograph is based on research I conducted while at Queen's University Belfast from 2008 to 2012. It does not include all aspects of the study that has been undertaken, and the study of this population is ongoing. The book begins with an introductory chapter that outlines the aims, objectives, and theoretical background of the research project to date. It continues in chapter 2 with historical background that contextualizes the mass burials and the skeletal population. Chapter 3, the first part of the analytical aspect of the research, describes the skeletal characteristics of the population interpreted within its social and historical context. Chapter 4, the second part of skeletal analysis, focuses on the paleopathological findings relating to the physical experience of famine and mortality and institutionalization at the Kilkenny Union Workhouse. Chapter 5 discusses research findings and asserts the value of an archaeological perspective for research about the Great Famine period. Chapter 6 provides my concluding remarks about the Kilkenny Union Workhouse and the people who were interred in its intramural burial ground.

Acknowledgments

This book began at the School of Geography, Archaeology and Palaeoecology at Queen's University Belfast in 2008. However, my involvement in the original project began in the summer of 2006, when I was employed as the project osteoarchaeologist during the post-excavation phase of the archaeological investigation at Macdonagh Junction, Kilkenny City, where the burials were excavated. The excavation was undertaken by Margaret Gowen & Co. Ltd. and directed by Brenda O'Meara under license from the National Museum of Ireland (license no: 05E0435). The site and post-excavation archaeologists were (with apologies to those whose names I may have missed) Vicki Herring, Brid Kirby, Eileen McKenna, and Adam Slater (supervisors); Olivia Bergin, Alan Buckley, Malin Crona, Niall Fitzpatrick, Lisa Hartzell, Catherine Hawkes, Grzegorz Kudła, Phil Kavanagh, Danielle Lyons, Aoife McCarthy, Miriam McDermott, Mats Nilsson, Kristina Olli, Mats Pettersson, Meredith Robertshawe, Sean Rooney, and Daniel Seaver (assistants); and Kevin Crennan, John Dumecz, Ciarán Fox, Richard Hetherington, Laura Kennedy, Stuart Martin, Johnny McCabe, Damien Mippel, Margaret Murphy, Elaine O'Toole, Jason Phelan, Tomasz Pokorny, Jonathan Quinn, Jason Ryder, Mark Slattery, and Wojciech Stuczuk (general operatives).

Although the progression of the post-excavation research project was halted due to the Irish economic downturn in 2008, the project was completed thanks to support and help from many people to whom I am profusely grateful. I would especially like to thank Eileen Murphy, Colm Donnelly, and Mark Gardiner for providing support, advice, and encouragement and thereby making my research experience immensely rewarding. I am also extremely thankful to Margaret Gowen, as this project would not have been possible without her continuous backing and support. I would also like to thank Audrey Horning of Queen's University

Belfast and Simon Mays of English Heritage and the University of South-ampton for their comments and constructive criticism. I am also very grateful to Clark Spencer Larsen of Ohio State University and Meredith Morris-Babb of the University Press of Florida for supporting the book proposal and for accepting it as part of the series Bioarchaeological Inter-pretations of the Human Past: Local, Regional, and Global Perspectives. I would also like to thank press readers Charles E. Orser Jr. of Vanderbilt University and Della Collins Cook of Indiana University for their con-structive criticism of the submitted manuscript. They considerably helped to improve the final version presented in this book.

Thanks are also extended to my parents, Josef and Agneta Geber, to Siobhán Scully, Brenda O'Meara, Margaret Gowen, Claire Murphy, Fredrik Fahlander at Stockholm University, to Alexander Portch, Lorna Gray, Elin Ahlin Sundman, Laureen Buckley, Barra Ó Donnabháin at University College Cork, and to Damien Brett at the Local Studies sec-tion of Kilkenny County Library for all their help and support. Particular thanks are due to Géza and Elsa Géber. I also thank Maarten Blaauw of Queen's University Belfast and Thomas Svensson of Chalmers Univer-sity of Technology for help with statistical queries. I would also like to thank my employers during these years, Margaret Gowen & Co. Ltd. and Cotswold Archaeology Ltd., for granting me flexibility at work and per-mission to take time off when required. I am also grateful to the staff at the Irish Antiquities Section of the National Museum of Ireland for granting export licenses, to the National Library of Ireland for permission to use copyrighted photos (figures 2.1–2), to Ordnance Survey Ireland for allowing the use of the historical maps in figures 2.5 and 2.10, and to Karyn Deegan via the Local Studies section of Kilkenny County Library for permission to use the photo in figure 1.6. I would also like to thank Małgorzata Kryczka for her stunning illustrations of the skulls depicted in figures 4.19 and 4.21. Finally, I wish to acknowledge my teacher, the late Ebba During (1937–2007) of Stockholm University, whose contagious en-thusiasm for osteology led me to study the discipline in the first place, and Berit Sigvallius formerly of the Swedish National Heritage Board (Riksan-tikvarieämbetet), who provided great support and advice to me when I started my career as a bioarchaeologist.

Generous funding for this research was received from Johan and Ja-kob Söderberg's Foundation (Johan och Jakob Söderbergs Stiftelse), the

Wellcome Trust (Grant Ref: 096435/Z/11/Z), Margaret Gowen & Co. Ltd., Kilkenny County Council, Macdonagh Junction Shopping Centre, the Emily Sarah Montgomery Travel Scholarship, and the School of Geography, Archaeology and Palaeoecology of Queen's University Belfast.

Go raibh milé maith agaibh!

1

Setting the Stage for a Bioarchaeology of the Great Irish Famine

> One poor woman, whose cabin I visited, said, "There will be nothing for us but to lie down and die." I tried to give her hope of English aid, but, alas! her prophecy has been but too true. Out of a population of 240, I found 13 already dead from want. The survivors were like walking skeletons; the men stamped with the livid mark of hunger; the children crying with pain; the women in some of the cabins too weak to stand.
>
> Society of Friends, *Transactions of the Central Relief Committee of the Society of Friends during the Famine in Ireland, in 1846 and 1847* (1852)

Kilkenny City (figure 1.1) is located in the southeast of Ireland (52°39"N, -7°15"W) within the province of Leinster and is one of the best preserved medieval cities in Ireland. It is also one of the most historically important cities. In 2005, while an archaeological evaluation was taking place on a plot of land adjacent to the former union workhouse located just at the outskirts of the city center, an unexpectedly large amount of human remains was exposed from the ground. The evaluation work was undertaken by the local heritage consultants Kilkenny Archaeology as a prior requirement for commercial development of the area into a shopping center and residential complex (Ó Drisceoil 2005). The next year, a full archaeological excavation of the area took place. This was undertaken from January to June by Margaret Gowen & Co. Ltd. and revealed a completely unknown mass burial ground for nearly 1,000 individuals. The skeletons of these individuals were found positioned in layers on top of each other in subrectangular pits arranged in rows and spaced less than a meter apart (O'Meara 2010). Later archival research was able to confirm that these burials relate to mass deaths that occurred during the notorious Great Famine (1845–1852), an event that represents a watershed in Irish

Figure 1.1. Drawing of the castle and city of Kilkenny, *London Illustrated News*, November 1845.

history and that had a significant effect in other nations around the world because of mass emigration from Ireland during these years.

As there was no local awareness of any burials at the workhouse, the scale of the archaeological discovery was unanticipated. These factors contributed to an early decision that the best option would be to relocate the burials and acknowledge these people with a formal and consecrated grave elsewhere. The Kilkenny burials are the largest mass burial ground ever to have been excavated and studied in Ireland and as such have significant archaeological and historical value. In addition to providing a contextualization of historical mass burials undertaken at Victorian institutions, they made possible a unique perspective into life as it was experienced by the poor and destitute in mid nineteenth-century Ireland and the physical experience of the Great Famine itself.

The Great Famine—also sometimes referred to as the Great Hunger (An Gorta Mór)—left a large and substantial legacy, and this is a contributing factor to why it is generally considered to be one of the most important episodes in Irish history. The famine is also very much part of Irish national and cultural identity today, not just in Ireland but also in descendent and Irish diaspora communities all over the world. Despite this notion, it was only relatively recently that the period of the famine received proper interest from Irish historians and other scholars. In fact, the relatively limited attention given to the period by researchers in the past illustrates how much there still is to learn about this calamity. For example, the topics of the social, economic, and ideological background; the human experience of the famine; and the true short- and long-term consequences would benefit from further investigations (see Gray 1995; Kinealy 2006, xli).

The Great Famine is considered to have ended completely in 1852. By then, the potato blight—which was the primary cause of the disaster—had virtually disappeared and relief schemes initiated by the government had ended (Kinealy 2006, xxii). Ireland (figure 1.2) was recovering from a seven-year period of continuous privation that had led to a considerable demographic and sociocultural shift. During these years, Ireland had lost about a quarter of its population (about 2 million people), half as the result of mass deaths and half as the result of large-scale emigration.

The Irish Famine is among the best recorded historical events of severe food shortage with catastrophic consequences. There are numerous shocking and rather frightening narratives of the conditions people endured and descriptions and sketched images of the extremely famished physical state of their bodies and faces. These were widely published by newspapers, philanthropists, and relief organizations and feature in numerous official government paper reports. Plentiful recollections and narratives also survived in the folklore that was passed on from those who survived to the generations that followed. It is, however, necessary to acknowledge the fact that these descriptions and reports, and even the folklore, are products of their time. To be fully able to assess these sources, it is essential to take the cultural tradition and ideological perceptions that dominated Victorian society in Ireland and Britain into account. These cultural, ideological, social, and political contexts greatly influenced the thoughts and actions that, for instance, determined the nature and organization of the government relief schemes to Ireland and the implementation of the 1838 Poor Law that had such a significant impact on the outcome of the famine. The often demeaning way that the poor and other unfortunates were treated in Victorian society is quite upsetting to contemplate today. At the same time, people from all social classes and

Figure 1.2. County map of Ireland. Based on template by Alan O'Rourke
(©www.toodle.com), used by permission.

followers of all religions and communities in both near and distant countries recognized the suffering of Ireland and tried to help in the best way they could (see Kinealy 2013).

When considering the historiography of the Great Famine it is quite clear that contemporary cultural traditions have been very influential in how the research of the period has been undertaken and presented. For example, the often-sensitive Irish political context has been very conspicuous, particularly in relation to the situation in Northern Ireland and the relationship between Ireland and Britain. This has led to an often politically charged writing of famine history—both intentionally and unintentionally—that has focused on the questions of cause and blame (Davis 1997; Donnelly 2001, 209ff; Keenan 2000, 67–68; Kinealy 2006, xv–xlii). During the period of the famine, Ireland was a constitutional part of the United Kingdom and thus governed by a British government from Westminster, London. The early Irish descriptions of the famine tended, therefore, to be very nationalistic in the way they morally condemned the response of the two governments in office during the period (Whelan 2004, 195–99). The famine was described as a politically designed and artificial event. As one observer commented, "the Almighty, indeed, sent the potato blight, but the English created the Famine" (Mitchel 1876, 219). These Anglo-phobic opinions were also anti-Protestant and the famine was described as an intentional attempt to diminish Catholic devotion in Ireland (O'Rourke 1902). These early descriptions, which became foundation stones in a popular narrative construction of the Great Famine, were formulated in a decisive period of Irish history that eventually led to the formation of the Irish Free State in 1922 and later the declaration of the Republic of Ireland (Éire) in 1948.

It was criticism against these unrivalled perceptions that led Irish historians in the 1930s to enter a period of conservative revisionism that became the prevailing line of thought for six decades. The revisionists contested the traditional populist interpretation of the famine as a watershed in Irish history (Whelan 2004). Instead, they described the famine as a consequence of indirect internal factors such as a considerable population increase, a poorly managed agricultural economy, and underlying widespread poverty and destitution (Daly 1986; Green 1956; McDowell 1956; O'Neill 1956). Amid this period of general academic revisionist consensus, the book *The Great Hunger* was published by English historian Cecil Woodham-Smith (1964). It received a negative response from established scholars but became very popular with the public. Woodham-Smith's rhetoric challenged the views of the revisionists and was closer to the nationalistic populist line from which established academics were trying to distance themselves. Historian Christine Kinealy (2006, xxi) has pointed out that the success of Woodham-Smith's book exposed "the tension between the prevailing academic orthodoxy and the popular memory of the Famine."

Nonetheless, the Great Famine did not receive wide genuine interest and attention from the academic research community until around the time of the sesquicentenary of the first appearance of the potato blight during the 1990s. These scholars, who later came to be labeled as postrevisionists, conducted their research during a period of the advancement of the peace process in Northern Ireland and improved Anglo-Irish relations. The postrevisionists began to criticize the objectification and simplification of the work of the revisionists. Through their research, postrevisionists have exposed areas that had been ignored by both the preceding nationalistic and revisionist historians. These included topics such as how the famine struck Northern Ireland, how the Protestant community was affected, the role of Catholic landlords and trade merchants, the role of the Catholic Church, the ideological background of the famine, and the true long-term consequences of the famine for the economy, demography, social structure, and folk culture of the island (Kennedy et al. 1999; Kinealy 2006; Morash and Hayes 1996; O'Boyle 2005). The research of postrevisionists and the debate they initiated has helped us gain a much better understanding of the variability of the famine experience and how the disaster progressed on the local, the regional, and the national levels. There is still much scope for further exploration of these and other aspects of the famine, particularly if multidisciplinary approaches from a wider range of perspectives are considered (see Crowley, Smyth, and Murphy 2012).

Archaeology has great potential for providing a perspective that would give not only new insights but also new knowledge of the period and how it was experienced by the Irish population. As archaeologists study past societies and people through the remains of their material culture (Welinder 1992), it not only offers a different viewpoint but is also particularly beneficial when attempting to study the history of the poor, disenfranchised, or illiterate, who are largely invisible in the historical record (Little 2007, 29; Orser 1996, 77) (figure 1.3). Through the application of

RETURN of PAUPERS who were Admitted into, or Discharged from, the Workhouse; and of the number of Sick, and the number Born, or who Died therein, during the Week ended SATURDAY, 27th day of Feby, 184 7

	ADMITTED						BORN		DISCHARGED						DIED					
	Males, aged 15 and upwds.	Females aged 15 and upwds.	Boys under 15.	Girls under 15.	Children under 2.	TOTAL.	Males.	Females.	Males, aged 15 and upwds.	Females aged 15 and upwds.	Boys under 15.	Girls under 15.	Children under 2.	TOTAL.	Males, aged 15 and upwds.	Females aged 15 and upwds.	Boys under 15.	Girls under 15.	Children under 2.	TOTAL.
During the Week ended as above,	67	79	65	48	31	1	1		24	47	23	26			0	8	17	6	14	50
Remaining on the previous Saturday, as per last Return,	440	722	444	345	130															
TOTAL,	480	801	487	440	177															
Deduct Discharged and Died during the Week ending as above,	34	60	30	32	29															
REMAINING ON THE ABOVE DATE,	448	746	424	444	442															

RETURN OF SICK AND LUNATIC PAUPERS.

		OBSERVATIONS
No. of Pauper in Hospital on the above date.		In case of any unusual number of these classes of Paupers.
No. of Lunatics and Idiots in Workhouse on the above date.		
	In separate Wards.	In Wards with other inmates.
In Work house,		4	6
In Fever Hospital.			10
	Total,	

Number of Inmates that the Workhouse is calculated to contain, 1300

NEXT MEETING of Guardians to be held on Thursday the 11th day of March 184 7

COPY of MINUTES of Proceedings of the Board of Guardians, at a Meeting held on Thursday, day, the 4th day of March 184 7 archaeology to studies of historical periods, new perspectives on the life experiences of the recent past can potentially even contest documentary history (e.g., Horning 2007), or as archaeologist Charles J. Orser Jr. (1996, 80) described it, "historical archaeology has the ability to lift the curtain of silence and peek behind history, revealing what might otherwise never be known." The archaeological study of the Kilkenny workhouse mass burials has been able to do just that, and the unanticipated discovery of the burial ground gives rise to several big questions: how much is there yet to be uncovered in the soil and what new and unique insights into the famine might these potential discoveries yield?

Orser was the first to fully recognize the potential value of using an archaeological approach for research on the Great Famine in Ireland. Archaeological studies of historical periods developed independently in the 1960s in the United States and Britain. In the former, it came to be defined as "historical archaeology," while in the latter it is known as "post-medieval archaeology." While historical archaeology in the United States is very much founded on an anthropological tradition, the discipline of post-medieval archaeology in Britain initially developed from pure artifact studies and has been more influential in Ireland (Orser 2006a). Orser has used the U.S. perspective in his famine studies and his study of abandoned cottiers' homesteads in Gorttoose townland in County Roscommon. Orser highlighted the potential for comparative analyses of the material culture found in head-tenant and subtenant houses and addressed the issue of whether there would be any contrast between the archaeological evidence and the historical nineteenth-century description of the material scarcity that was characteristic of poor Irish tenant farmer families at that time. In addition to studying the material culture, as represented by artifacts, he explored the daily life of a small nineteenth-century settlement by assessing the size and orientation of the cabins. He also looked at how the archaeological evidence in this specific homestead, in conjunction with historical records, might reveal information about the tenant-landlord relations that had resulted in eviction in 1847 (Orser 1996, 1997).

After Orser's articles, further acknowledgement of the potential contributions of archaeology followed. Recommendations included looking at the physical remains left behind from relief works, workhouses, abandoned buildings, and mass burials (Fewer 1997). Patrick O'Sullivan (1997, 4) identified the potential in paleopathological research with the question "Can the dead be allowed to speak for themselves?" With the

Figure 1.4. The Cherryfield famine graveyard outside Callan in County Kilkenny. This burial ground was used by the Callan Union Workhouse and is one of well over 100 known famine-period graveyards across Ireland. Photo by author.

exception of the Kilkenny workhouse burials, analyses of human remains from famine victims have so far been limited to only a few cases. This is likely a reflection of the fact that many of these famine burial grounds are known locally and therefore very unlikely to be impacted by development (figure 1.4). Some of the archaeological investigations that have been undertaken include excavations at Old Donard School in Banbridge, County Down, which was undertaken in the winter of 2005–2006, which revealed a mass burial containing eight interred individuals (Porteus 2006). These burials are associated with the Banbridge Union Workhouse that used to occupy the site. Dating to the mid-nineteenth century (McKee 2006), they are likely the remains of workhouse inmates who died during the famine. Other famine period skeletons used for comparative purposes in this study include seventy-three burials excavated from the burial ground associated with the former union workhouse in Manorhamilton, County Leitrim (Fibiger 2003; Lynch 2002; Rogers et al. 2006) and six coffined burials of former inmates of the Thurles Union Workhouse in County Tipperary (Fibiger 2010; Sutton 2010). More recently, famine period burials relating to the Tuam Union Workhouse in County Galway and Clones Union Workhouse in County Monaghan have been discovered (Finn Delaney, pers. comm.; Edmond O'Donovan, pers. comm.). Institutional burials, which are likely to have primarily accommodated the poorer classes of society, were also excavated at the St. Brigid's Hospital in Ballinasloe, County Galway, in 2002. The burial ground, from which twelve skeletons of mid-nineteenth-century date were excavated and analyzed, is associated with the former Connaught Lunatic Asylum that was established on the site in 1833 (Fibiger 2002; Rogers et al. 2006).

Nineteenth-Century Skeletal Populations

For comparative purposes, this book will also be considering data from other analyzed contemporaneous nineteenth-century populations across Ireland, Britain and North America. In addition to the populations mentioned above, the Irish record also includes middle- and upper-class nineteenth-century populations that have been analyzed from the city of Cork and Sligo Town. These include a group of burials belonging to the old cemetery associated with St. Anne's Shandon Protestant Church in Cork City (Lynch 2004). The Sligo population, which was buried at St. John the Baptist Cathedral, belonged to the Church of Ireland Protestant community and was comprised of members of a higher social class. A total of forty-nine burials were discovered, of which thirty-two were subjected to a thorough skeletal and paleopathological analysis (Lynch 2001).

Several large-scale excavations of nineteenth-century burial grounds have been undertaken in Britain in recent decades, of which the results of the analysis and research of the majority of the largest projects have been published. Many of these, however, are of middle- and upper-class populations buried in urban cemeteries, and much of the British data is thus biased toward these social groups. Nineteenth-century burial grounds for the poor and lower class communities have been excavated on several occasions within the City of London. These include burials associated with the Catholic Mission of St. Mary's and St. Michael's in Whitechapel, London, which had a substantial Irish community at the time (Henderson et al. 2013; Walker and Henderson 2010). Excavations and studies of the burials and skeletons of poor and disenfranchised population groups in London have also been undertaken at the City Bunhill Burial Ground at Golden Lane in South Islington (Connell and Miles 2010) and at the burial ground associated with the former union workhouse at Cross Bones in Southwark (Brickley, Miles, and Stainer 1999). The comparative populations also include skeletons from burial grounds of middle-class groups buried in the City of London. These involve burials at St. Luke's Church in Islington (Boyle, Boston, and Witkin 2005) and at St. Benet Sherehog (Miles, White, and Tankard 2008; White 2008). Other middle-class population burial grounds that have been excavated and analyzed in recent years include the Quaker cemetery in Kingston-upon-Thames in Surrey (Start and Kirk 1998) and the Tanyard and Quaker burial ground in Bromyard in Herefordshire (Brickley 2004).

Several of the most substantial excavations of nineteenth-century cemeteries in recent years have included those of upper-class populations. The most famous of these are the excavations at Christ Church in Spitalfields in London (Molleson et al. 1993; Waldron 1993; Whittaker 1993), which has also generated several in-depth research articles (e.g., Heuzé and Braga 2008; Kerr 1994; Liversidge and Molleson 1995, 1999; Loth 1995; Whittaker, Griffiths et al. 1990; Whittaker, Jones et al. 1990). Other important archaeological projects from London include the recording and analysis of crypt burials at St. George's Church in Bloomsbury (Boston et al. 2009); St. Marylebone Church (Miles, Powers et al. 2008); St. Pancras (Powers 2011; White 2011); the Baptist burial ground at Bow Baptist Church (Henderson et al. 2013); Sheen's Burial Ground, a private cemetery in Whitechapel (Henderson et al. 2013); and the New Bunhill Fields burial ground in Southwark (Miles and Connell 2012). One Scottish population of upper-class association is also included for comparative purposes in this study, which includes burials from Glasgow Cathedral that were excavated in the 1980s and 1990s (Driscoll 2002).

In addition to these socially selective burial grounds, some cemeteries included all strata of contemporaneous society. In these locations, it has been difficult to differentiate economic and social group association based on the archaeological evidence. For example, the poor and the rich were all buried in the cemetery associated with St. Peter's Collegiate Church in Wolverhampton, Staffordshire/West Midlands in the middle of the nineteenth century (Adams and Colls 2007; Arabaolaza, Nerin, and Oris 2007). This is also the case in the cemetery at St. Martin's-in-the-Bull Ring in the middle of the city of Birmingham (Brickley et al. 2006). The last two comparative populations from the British bioarchaeological record include middle- to upper-class individuals buried at the cemeteries of All Saints, Chelsea Old Church, in London (Bekvalac and Kausmally 2008; Cowie et al. 2008) and St. Peter's Church in Barton-upon-Humber in North Lincolnshire (Waldron 2007).

I have also included the published results of the osteological and paleopathological analyses of a few contemporaneous skeletal populations from North America for comparative purposes in this study. These are of particular interest, as many are likely to include burials of first-generation immigrants of the laboring poor classes in Europe, of which many were from Ireland. The only Canadian cemetery among these is the burial ground of St. Thomas' Church in Belleville, Ontario, which includes graves of poor and middle-class sections of society (Saunders, De Vito, and Katzenberg 1997). The studies of nineteenth-century American populations I selected are all of the poorer sections of society. They include inmates belonging to the Monroe County Almshouse in Rochester, New York (Higgins et al. 2002), patients of the Eastern State Hospital in Lexington, Kentucky (Favret 2006), burials in the Legion of Honor Cemetery in San Francisco (Buzon et al. 2005) and early nineteenth-century burials in Cincinnati, Ohio (Murray and Perzigian 1995).

Exploring the "Human Experience" of the Great Irish Famine

In the introduction to her book *This Great Calamity*, Christine Kinealy called for a greater attention to the "human experience" of the Great Famine in Ireland (Kinealy 2006, xli). This has been the primary objective of this research, which has aimed to explore and study the actual experience of the Great Famine based on the human skeletal remains from the Kilkenny Union Workhouse mass burials in conjunction with the archaeological evidence and the available historical sources. The first theme has focused on the osteological and paleopathological analysis of the skeletal remains of a mid-nineteenth-century disenfranchised and socioeconomically marginalized community. Because these individuals belonged to the lowest social classes, they were severely constrained by political, social and economic factors that did little to help improve their situation. The nature of poverty in mid-nineteenth-century Ireland was frequently reported on at the time but rarely directly described by those who themselves suffered it. The known social and historical provenance of the Kilkenny workhouse population therefore gives it particular importance; it provides insight into the physical life experience of the poor, an aspect of nineteenth-century Ireland that is largely unknown. An objective of this theme has therefore been to answer the question of whether—and if so, how—social and economic background influenced population health in Ireland during this period, which was characterized by extreme poverty and destitution in areas where famines and disease epidemics were commonly taking place.

A second theme has explored the physiological impact of famine on an archaeological skeletal population, as illustrated through skeletal pathological changes and mortality structure. This theme aims to answer the question of how those who died during the Great Famine might have experienced the event, both on an individual and on a community level, based on the analysis and interpretation of their skeletons. The third and final theme investigated the response to the famine crisis by the workhouse institution. This theme aims to answer the question of how the crisis was managed on a microlevel, using evidence from the archaeological and bioarchaeological record, which I have contextualized within the historical setting of the period.

Human Skeletal Remains as Interpretative Bodies of the Past

The skeleton is a physical part of the human being, and living patterns and experiences are potentially permanently manifested as osseous and dental responses and adaptations. This biological expression of the human physical condition can also be interpreted as a social agent, as the body is important for social reproduction, order, and control (Freund 1988). However, what we can learn from the body—or the skeleton, in this particular study (figure 1.5)—is limited when it is studied in isolation. To acquire insight into life experiences through skeletal and paleopathological analyses, it is essential to acknowledge the sociocultural frame within which the individual and individuals lived. This is the biocultural approach, which has been recognized by anthropological disciplines since the late 1960s (Bindon 2007). Biocultural research in physical anthropology and bioarchaeology evolved from the processual thinking of the "New Archaeology" debate (Binford 1962; Binford and Binford 1968; Willey and Phillips 1958), and its goals are problem-solving and discussion rather than the traditional goals of data description and quantification by themselves (Armelagos and van Gerven 2003; Buikstra 1977; Buikstra and Beck 2006; Larsen 1990, 2000). The biocultural approach recognizes

Figure 1.5. In situ photograph of the skeleton of a late middle adult male (DCCXLIV) as he was discovered in the mass burial pit. His remains revealed several dental ailments, clay-pipe facets, and degenerative joint disease in his spine and left foot. Photo by Margaret Gowen & Co. Ltd.

the relationship and interaction between biological and cultural entities in human social constructions. As such, it is positivistic and also more inclusive of subjective realities. While the skeletal and archaeological data represent the physical and materialistic, the cultural and social contexts that can be acquired from the disciplines of history and sociology provide an understanding of the generalist frame within which these materialities functioned. The mass burials from the Kilkenny workhouse will tell little on their own—they are merely the physical imprint of past actions. However, their cultural and historical contexts serve to emphasize the human effort and reaction to a greater issue—in this case the famine crisis—thereby revealing the true significance and meaning of these burials and the life and death experiences of the individuals who were interred at this location.

In this research, the skeletal remains, the historical sources, and the material culture are viewed as equal participants in a dialogue of evidence (see Tarlow 1999, 2–5) and are all used to tell the story of these unfortunate victims of the Great Famine. While the physical skeletal remains primarily tell the story of those who died, the historical and archaeological data reveal insight into the experience of those who were not buried in the mass burial pits. The creation of the mass burial ground was the product of a conscious decision that was made by a person or persons living in a societal structure and was essentially an effort to deal with the disposal of corpses during an event of mass deaths and prevent the spread of disease (see Morgan 2004). But these pits had also to be physically excavated, the corpses had to be handled and coffins had to be interred, and these efforts might have resulted in unforeseen psychological consequences to those who performed them (see McCorkle 2010). These actions were therefore part of an experienced reality that continued long after the famine had come to an end. The trauma of the famine is evident in the folklore of the period, and it may even have been archaeologically manifested in the Kilkenny workhouse mass burial ground (see chapter 5).

Paleopathology and the Experience of Disease

Human skeletal remains provide a physical testimony of the living individual they once belonged to. The concept of how human skeletal tissue responds to outer stress and influences, usually referred to as Wolff's Law (Wolff 1892), has been used as a basis for the reconstruction of past lifestyles and life experiences (see Pearson and Lieberman 2004). With a few notable exceptions (e.g., Brickley and Ives 2008), the paleopathological diagnostic literature noticeably lacks discussion about the experience and sensory consequences of disease. This perspective has often characterized bioarchaeological research, which generally focuses on reports of the skeletal nature and characteristics of specific pathological changes rather than on the experience of disease. This traditional approach is in many ways unfortunate, as it objectifies human skeletons (see Cornell and Fahlander 2002b, 3–4; Sofaer 2006) rather than making use of their potential as interpretative bodies of life in the past. This potential in paleopathological research within a bioarchaeological setting can be effectively explored on an individual level; for example when considering the experiences of pain, disability, and stigma (Geber 2013; Kjellström 2010). It can also be assessed on a greater communal level, for example in the societal response to periods of stress, including the management of infectious disease and care of disabled and diseased individuals (Lorentz 2008, 291; Tilley and Oxenham 2011), especially when these data are combined with the archaeological record. The paleopathological evidence of disease can reveal aspects of social stigma relating to certain diseases, a society's care and treatment of individuals of poor health, the medical treatment of the desperately ill, and the social valuation of people subjected to physical scientific research, such as the autopsies and dissections that were commonly undertaken in workhouses in both Ireland and Britain during the nineteenth century. All these aspects are clearly reflected in the Kilkenny mass burials. While the archaeology reveals the treatment of the dead, the osteology reveals the treatment of the living.

However, a recurrent debate in the discipline of paleopathology has been whether the skeletal reflection of disease in a population is a valid representation of the overall presence of disease. This discourse is based on the question of the presence of the "osteological paradox" and is a critical assessment of interpretations of paleopathological data (Sofaer 2006, 46; Wood et al. 1992). Because individuals have varying underlying levels of health and strength, the survival rate for some may not have been long enough for skeletal lesions to appear when they were attacked by a particular disease process, and they would therefore be invisible in the paleopathological record. This poses the question of whether the skeletons that display the most advanced skeletal pathological changes are in fact the strongest and, in a way, "healthiest" individuals. This is a complicating factor, particularly when assessing skeletal health in individuals who died as a consequence of famine or other events that led to catastrophic death instead of death by attrition. The high mortality rates characteristic of famines are in most cases due to infectious diseases, and these are induced from a depressed immune response in populations suffering from severe malnutrition. Because individuals are malnourished, they are less likely to survive long enough for infectious diseases to become chronic and thereby potentially affect the skeleton (see Ortner 2003, 115). The paleopathological record is also limited by the disease processes that by their nature leave skeletal lesions, and the impact of skeletally invisible diseases cannot be directly assessed or studied.

Microarchaeology: Assessing the Generic from a Local Perspective

The idea of a structural entity within which the specific operates is encompassed in the microarchaeological[1] line of thought that has evolved and been defined from the relatively recent works of Swedish archaeologists Per Cornell and Fredrik Fahlander (Cornell and Fahlander 2002a, 2002b; Fahlander 2001, 2003). They have highlighted the value of breaking down the dependence of the discipline of archaeology on structures and models of data interpretation and instead seek a focus on the opposite relationship in which the material culture decides the direction of the research (Cornell and Fahlander 2002b, 45–46). This theoretical discussion is perhaps best explained as recognition of the particular and local as representatives of the greater whole, hence meaning that each individual archaeological site—even when studied in isolation—will tell something about the wider society.

The disciplines of history and sociology have long used a microperspective. In Peltonen's (2001) discussion and descriptive review of the evolution of microhistory from the 1970s to the 1990s, he recognized how a focus on the "typical exception" has introduced a center of attention on the previously marginalized aspects of past societies in historical research. Microhistory argues for the value of scaling down the research to expose diversity in social thought abstractions and offers the alternative route of interpreting historical sources through existing "evidential paradigms" (Muir 1991, viii). Cornell and Fahlander (2007, 7) do, however, make a distinction in the microarchaeological perspective, wherein the main focus is not to describe small-scale variations or particularities but rather to identify the large scale through a focus on the small scale through their entwined relation as the general and the particular.

Just as microhistory is, microarchaeology is optimistic. It is permissive and inclusive in its acceptance of local variations and characteristics of material culture (Cornell and Fahlander 2002b, 45). Its theoretical foundations are influenced by the later works on existentialism by philosopher Jean-Paul Sartre (1905–1980), in particular his social analysis in *Critique of Dialectical Reason* (1976 [1960]). Sartre discussed the relationship between individual intentions and the greater collective and recognized a fundamental social structure of fluid homogeneity that he referred to as series (Sartre 1976 [1960], 256–341). Fahlander (2003) uses this notion of "serial action" as a tool to understand processes of social plurality in archaeological materialities. Following Fahlander, I view material culture as part of a process of social structuralization (see Latour 2005) that integrates serial actions. Each archaeological unit—or excavation—represents a series of the greater generic but is defined and visible only through recognition by a third party: the "others" who constitute the structural entity of the overall society or context. In summary, by acknowledging that each individual archaeological site is a part of a greater entity, it is possible to gain insight into the wider society it formed a part of.

Microarchaeology is particularly beneficial as a way of explaining the representative value of the Kilkenny Union Workhouse mass burials as a valid reflection of the human experience of the famine. Fahlander (2003, 16) described microarchaeology as neither processual nor postprocessual but instead as an attempt to combine theory, methodology, and practice of different origins. This notion is an important consideration in multidisciplinary approaches, such as biocultural interpretation, in which archaeology, osteology, and—in the case of this research—historical evidence are included.

The microarchaeological concept of social structuralization is validated through the application of its fundamental line of thought to the analysis of the archaeological and human remains from the Kilkenny workhouse, as these are clearly defined and easily recognized through the available historical evidence. While the mass burials are a local reflection of the famine, their very existence is a product of societal structure, culturally and ideologically as well as physically. It is apparent that because of the implementation of the 1838 Poor Law (see chapter 2), each union

Figure 1.6. Aerial photograph of the Kilkenny Union Workhouse complex, ca. early 1960s. Virtually all workhouses in Ireland followed this architectural design. Courtesy of Karyn Deegan via the local studies section of the Kilkenny County Library.

workhouse in Ireland was a product of a greater structural entity that was defined by the social attitudes and perceptions of contemporary society. The Poor Law was therefore a rigid reference point that all poor law unions adhered and related to, although local variations would have taken place. Even the workhouse buildings themselves were identical, as the vast majority of them were built during the same period and followed the same architectural design (figure 1.6). It is therefore reasonable to claim that the scenes and actions that took place at the workhouse in Kilkenny City during the Great Famine are a valid representation of the Irish workhouse regime in the period 1845–1852.

2

"An entire nation of paupers"

Contextualizing Poverty and Famine
in Mid-Nineteenth-Century Ireland and Kilkenny

The kind of instinctive and hereditary contempt which the rich feel in Ireland for everything that is poor and beneath them,—the prejudice which even amongst Catholics makes this contempt a sign of fashion and elegance,—the opinion so generally diffused, that the rich man has a right to oppress the poor man, and trample him under foot with impunity,—such are the traditions.

Gustav de Beaumont, *Ireland: Social, Political, and Religious* (2006 [1839])

Victorian Ireland was, in general, a rural and strongly hierarchical society with a complex social scale divided into several strata, from the ruling nobleman and gentleman classes to the middle class and the working classes and, at the absolute bottom of the scale, the destitute. The upper classes included aristocrats and gentlemen; the latter, except for wealthy landowners, also included some high-ranking and upscale professionals who had a university degree, such as barristers and lawyers. The middle class was predominantly comprised of well-to-do farmers but also included land agents, doctors, clergy, and military officers. This class also included those who were referred to as shoneens, buckeens, or half-sirs, farm holders who lived on the rental or produce income of their properties but who did no work themselves. The working classes included small tenant farmers who leased land from which they could both feed and financially support their families. Master tradesmen, such as weavers and carpenters, were also classified as less than middle class. At the lower scale within the working class were the cottiers, penniless smallholders who paid their rent by means of day labor, and the hired day laborers and servants who made their living through both temporary short-term and long-term employment (Keenan 2000, 18–35; Mokyr and Ó Gráda 1988).

The large size of the destitute class—which was comprised of the members of Irish society at the lowest end of the social scale—was a feature of Ireland that was so pronounced that it often was described as a characteristic of the nation. French sociologist, statesman, and aristocrat Gustave de Beaumont (1802–1866), who traveled through Ireland in the decade before the famine, famously described it as "an entire nation of paupers" (de Beaumont 2006 [1839], 130). The destitute had no source of income and were poorly nourished and clothed; many had no other choice than to resort to begging. Those who were able to rent a small patch of ground on which they could grow potatoes would pay for this by either day labor or a share of their crop. Their living conditions were those of utmost misery and deprivation, to such an extreme degree that de Beaumont—in an often-quoted remark—stated: "I have seen the Indian in his forests, and the negro in his chains, and thought, as I contemplated their pitiable condition, that I saw the very extreme of human wretchedness; but I did not then know the condition of unfortunate Ireland" (de Beaumont 2006 [1839], 130).

Numerous other accounts of Irish destitution and poverty were given in contemporary reports and newspapers. In 1845, it was reported that in the parish of Tullaghobegley in County Donegal, the community of 4,000 inhabitants possessed only one plough, ninety-three chairs, and seven table forks (Killeen 1995, 21). Poverty and pauperism in County Kilkenny were not as severe as in the west of Ireland, which was constituted of relatively infertile land (Green 1956, 89), yet living conditions were much poorer there than in the neighboring eastern counties (Jordan 2003). Kilkenny was nevertheless still a relatively industrialized city and region, and the local textile industry at the Ormonde Woollen Mills by the banks of the River Nore and the famous "Kilkenny marble" that was quarried at Black Quarry on the southeast outskirts of the city provided employment and income. Coal was also quarried in the north of the county, at Castlecomer, and coach building, boot and shoe manufacturing, printing businesses, and several breweries and distilleries contributed to the local economy (Bradley 2000; Egan 1884; Halpin 1989; Somerville 1994, 44). During the early decades of the nineteenth century, the shops in Kilkenny were regarded as among the most fashionable in the country (Neely 1989, 173–210; Walsh 1966, 53–54).

Figure 2.1. Late nineteenth-century photograph of cottage buildings in Kilkenny City, taken from the northwest. The Black Abbey and St. Mary's Cathedral are in the background. Courtesy of the National Library of Ireland.

Several long-established educational institutions were also present in the city; these included Pococke College, founded in 1763; St. John's College, founded in 1684; and St. Kieran's College and Kilkenny College. In 1849, during the famine, the Museum of the Kilkenny Archaeological Society was founded (Bassett 1884, 45, 50; Egan 1884 259–60). In the late eighteenth century and early nineteenth centuries, the city theatre, which was a particular source of local pride, reached national fame (Egan 1884, 80–96; Plumptre 1817, 226–27). The Kilkenny Races, which took place each spring and autumn in the townland of Danesfort, were also famous nationwide (McEvoy 1981). Visitors made note of the impressive buildings and paved streets made from the local marble, and gas lighting had been introduced in 1838 (Neely 1989, 178). Nonetheless, this was a city (figure 2.1) in which two-thirds of the dwellings were mud cabins and that had become desperately overcrowded. Many of the houses contained four or more families, and this high concentration of several people in small spaces plus the old medieval layout of the city, which included narrow lanes and streets, created problems of poor sanitation and filth, which unavoidably resulted in the spread of infectious disease from time to time (see Neely 1989, 231–33).

Culturally and economically, Kilkenny showed more similarities with the counties in Munster than those in Leinster. While the middle and upper classes spoke English as their first language, the main bulk of the population were predominantly Irish speakers (Nic Eoin 1990, 465–66). There was also a regional geographical divide in the county in terms of its social, cultural, and economic organization. The north was a sparsely populated region influenced by an English culture that had emerged through immigration during the seventeenth century. In contrast, the central lowlands, including the city, were densely populated. This area was of particular commercial importance and included many prosperous tillage farms. The upland areas in the south were characterized by a conservative Irish social and cultural structure, and it was here that the most severe expressions of poverty and destitution were seen (Cullen 1990). This poverty and destitution, as in most of Ireland, was a key feature of the local social fabric. A pre-famine and early nineteenth-century survey of County Kilkenny, instigated by former Irish MP William Tighe (1766–1816), who was also a prominent local estate owner, described "the condition of the labouring poor . . . to be wretched in the extreme" (Tighe 1802, 473). In another comment about the poor, Tighe remarked that

it is surprizing how in the cheapest times, they can struggle for existence, unaided as they are by many little helps they meet with in the country: and in fact we find them, on such wretched diet, curtailed of that necessary article milk, during great part of the year, and using salt in its stead, of sometimes herrings to give a relish to their food; scantily supplied with potatoes, cloathed with rags, and famished with cold in their comfortless habitations: nor can they, though sober, frugal and laborious, which from my own knowledge I assert, provide against infirmity, and old age, any other resource than beggary, or dependence, than the precarious relief of charity; extremities which many are constantly reduced to; none can better tell than the member of the charitable societies here what numbers of wretched, miserable objects, depend on the distribution of their county for existence, and how inadequate language is, to convey a just idea of their poverty and suffering. (Tighe 1802, 474–75)

The poor of Kilkenny were reported to constantly suffer from bad health and to frequently be afflicted with rheumatism and subject to pleurisy, "of which from the manner they are constantly exposed to cold and damp, they have often successive relapses" (Tighe 1802, 481). In the parish of Fiddown, the poor slept "on a wad of straw, or perhaps heath laid on a damp clay floor. . . . Through the scanty thatch, the rain sometimes descends upon their beds, and bringing down the sooty substance lodged there by the smoke of the cabin, wets and stains the bed itself and those who are stretched upon it" (Tighe 1802, 480–81). Descriptions of the conditions in the outskirts of the town of Callan told how "their cabins were mere holes, with nothing within them (I speak of two which I entered) excepting a little straw, and one or two broken stools. And all the other outskirts of the town, are in nearly a similar condition:—ranges of hovels, without a ray of comfort or a trace of civilization about them: and people either in a state of actual starvation, or barely keeping body and soul together" (Inglis 1835, 98–99).

Why not just parts of County Kilkenny but virtually the whole of Ireland was plagued by such extreme and widespread poverty during a time when Ireland was in union with Great Britain and therefore part of the richest and most dominant and powerful empire in the world has been the subject of scholarly debate (e.g., Dunn 1992; Kinealy 2006; Woodham-Smith 1964). The Act of Union (Acht an Aontais) of 1801 that had made Ireland constitutionally a part of the United Kingdom gave Irish merchants access to the wider British market, but Ireland remained overall economically inferior with an income per capita of less than half of that in Great Britain (Kinealy 2006, 6–11; Ó Gráda 2006, 8). Much of the British political line about Ireland focused on solving the issues related to Irish nationalism and nationalistic groups—the so-called Irish question. In addition to its political aspects, the issue included economic and religious considerations that had often been the root of conflict between the countries (Boyce 2005, 105; Heyck 2008, 281–85). The cultural relationship between Ireland and England had been hostile for centuries, and for various reasons a clear anti-Irish and anti-Catholic consensus was often expressed in nineteenth-century England (Paz 1992). The most recent major Irish rebellion had taken place from May to September in 1798 (McDowell 1986), and violence had broken out between 1830 and 1836 during the Tithe War, a rebellion against the forced payments of tithes to the Church of Ireland despite the fact that the vast majority of the population were Catholic

(Boyce 2005, 63–104). Within a twelve-month period during the latter conflict in the county of Kilkenny alone, thirty-two murders or attempted murders took place, thirty-four houses were burned down, cattle from thirty-six farmers were stolen and slaughtered, and 519 burglaries and 178 serious assaults had been committed (Locker-Lampson 1907, 148–79).

For a long period, the large Irish estates had been outmoded and badly managed compared to their English equivalents. The relationship between the landlord and his tenants was also reportedly poor, and this was often pointed out as one of the main causes of Irish economic underdevelopment. Many of the Irish landlords, the majority of whom were part of a Protestant dominating elite of mainly English cultural identity, often took limited interest in their estates and properties and spent most of their time and income abroad (Woodham-Smith 1964, 21). In addition, Ireland had experienced a rapid population growth, from 2.6 million in 1750 to 8.5 million in 1845. This increase had put pressure on land values, which had led to higher rents. Unlike other countries in Europe where population had increased significantly during the same period, strong industrialization did not take place in Ireland (Donnelly 2001, 3–6). An additional persistent feature of Irish society at this time was the high unemployment rate. As a consequence of this, large-scale seasonal movement of the rural population looking for work was a common phenomenon. This was particularly true for the rural populace in the west. For example, workers and laborers regularly traveled from County Clare to Kilkenny to find work (Robins 1995, 42).

Local unemployment in Kilkenny was also comparatively high. In 1834, it was estimated that more than 2,000 people were without work in the city, which at that time had a population of about 25,000 (Inglis 1835, 91). Much of the local unemployment was the result of the steady decline of the textile industry. This industry had been of particular local importance ever since the middle of the eighteenth century and it had mainly produced blankets for the army. The protective duties imposed under the Act of Union were gradually withdrawn from the 1820s onward, and this inevitably resulted in an influx of cheaper goods and products from England into the Irish market. In 1800, about 3,000 people were steadily employed in the Kilkenny blanket manufacturing industry, but in 1841 there were only 925 workers left (Locker-Lampson 1907, 183). Similarly, in 1821 between 3,000 and 4,000 people were working in the local wool industry, but by 1837 only 600 employees remained (Jackson 1974, 53). Another example was the local carpet industry, which had formerly employed 200 workers but was completely wiped out by 1840 (Walsh 1966, 53).

The 1838 Poor Law and the Introduction of the Union Workhouse

Unlike England and Wales, which had been practicing a universal poor law since the sixteenth century, no such policy existed in Ireland prior to 1838. Nor did Ireland share the same tradition of charity that constituted a large component of English, Welsh, and Scottish poor relief. The poor and destitute of Ireland had instead traditionally relied on relief from the resident elite (Bailey 2006, 457; Kinealy 2006, 18). Yet the ordinary Irish man and woman were famously noted for their hospitality and helping nature (Inglis 1835, 246–47). One such observation was given by the French politician, journalist, and writer Paschal Grousset (1844–1909) about four decades after the famine. Grousset noted that the poor and destitute in Dublin "try to help and comfort one another in their misery. [It was] remarked . . . long ago: let an Irishman be as poor as you like; he will always contrive to find another Irishman poorer still, whom he will serve and oblige, and make the partaker of his good or bad luck. And it is absolutely true" (pseud. Daryl 1888, 40). Another account of how the poor helped the poor, in this case relating to the poor of County Donegal, was given in a report by His Majesty's Commissioners for Enquiring into the Condition of the Poorer Classes in Ireland a decade before the famine:

> Susan M'Lafferty, a blind beggarwoman, says, "that the middling houses are as good as the rich ones; and often much better. A good grouping (three to six potatoes, or a handful of meal, etc.) is always sure to the beggar from the poorest farmer." And Kitty Hegarthy, a poor widow beggarwoman, states, "I always find the poor man's door open; and his hand is never backward, when there is aught in the creel." (His Majesty's Commissioners 1835, 411)

In Kilkenny, several charities had been established from the eighteenth century onward. These included the Charitable Society, which was founded in 1740, and the Benevolent Society, which was established in 1785. The local aristocracy in Kilkenny had also recognized their duty to help the impoverished population of the county for generations (Neely 1989, 233–37), and several poorhouses and asylums had long existed in the city. The earliest institution was the Shee's Alms House, established in the late sixteenth century at Rose Inn Street in the middle of the city, near the castle. The Ormonde Poor House was another old institution, founded in the early seventeenth century at Gallow's Green, east of the River Nore. Other almshouses were Father Tobin's Poor House on Walkin Street, the poorhouse at St. Canice's Cathedral, St. James' or Switzer's Asylum on the southeast outskirts of the city, Lee's Lane Poor House, and Evan's asylum for destitute orphans at John's Street (Birthistle 1964; Carrigan 1905, 63–73; Egan 1884, 170; Lewis 1837, 113–14; Neely 1989, 233–37). Another institution was the House of Industry, the precursor of the union workhouse, which opened in 1814 on Kells Road. The inmates were occupied by spinning yarn and manufacturing cotton wicks (Birthistle 1964). During the cholera epidemic of 1832–1833, which claimed more than 300 lives throughout the county (Law 1996), the institution functioned as the cholera hospital.

As a measure to deal with the seemingly chronic pauperism in Ireland, a poor law was introduced in July 1838. It was based on the new Poor Law that had been introduced in England four years earlier. It was clear from the very beginning that the application of the English model to the Irish situation would be problematic, and the British government's determination to go through with the reform met with much political opposition (Boyce 2005, 76; Gray 2009, 219–80; Kinealy 2005, 51; O'Connor 1995, 58–67; Powell 1965, 3). The Poor Law, which was designed to provide a "more effectual Relief of the Destitute Poor in Ireland" (O'Connor 1995, 68), was based on the belief that people had a natural passion for idleness and that discouraging incentives were needed to help the poor evade poverty (see de Tocqueville 1835, 27–28). This was a perception that existed in both Britain and Ireland; members of the elite in both societies differentiated between the deserving and the undeserving poor (the buccoughs; from the Irish word *bacach*, meaning "lame"). This view was shared across the social scale but was defined differently depending on which economic level people belonged to (Ó Ciosáin 1998).

The Poor Law introduced a new workhouse institution in Irish society that was genuinely hated throughout its existence. Indoor relief in the workhouse was to become the only form of government poor relief for those who were considered to be impoverished due to no fault of their own; these people were referred to as the "deserving poor" (figure 2.2). The scheme was based on the so-called workhouse test theory, which was formed on the basis of the ideas of philosopher Jeremy Bentham

Figure 2.2. Early twentieth-century photograph of inmates from an unknown work-house in Ireland. Courtesy of the National Library of Ireland.

(1748–1832). This theory was based on the notion that the workhouse applicant would have "weighed the 'pleasures' of staying outside the workhouse with the 'pain' of entering it" (May 2003, 8), meaning that only the truly destitute would accept relief while the able-bodied would be encouraged to find work and improve their situations by themselves. The rather socially demeaning attitude toward the poor, which is reflected in the action of subjecting them to forced institutionalization when they were in desperate need of help, must nevertheless also be acknowledged as an effort of the time to improve their prospects. This was particularly true for children, who were given some education and were taught practical skills that—it was hoped—would benefit them later in life.

The implementation of the new system included the establishment of poor law commissioners who organized a system division of 163 administrating unions, each of which was centered on a major market town. The unions in turn were administered by a Board of Guardians, which followed directions laid out by the commissioners (O'Connor 1995, 69–72). Set rules on which type of applicants were to be considered most entitled for relief regulated admission into the workhouse. The individuals who were given first consideration were those who were not able to support themselves due to old age, infirmity, or physical or mental disabilities. Destitute children were also considered to be in this category. The second tier were those who were considered to be destitute and unable to make their own living by their own industry or other lawful means. It was also stated that preference should be given to applicants who belonged to the local administration union over applicants from elsewhere in Ireland (*Kilkenny Journal* 1842b). Those who were admitted were segregated; boys from girls, men from women, and children over the age of two years from their mothers. The women's side was on the left half of the workhouse and the men's side on the right. These divisions meant that family structures were destroyed when the family entered the workhouse (Kinealy 1995, 106; O'Connor 1995, 81–84).

A total of 163 workhouses were constructed in Ireland from 1841 to 1853. Most of them followed the standard plans drawn by architect George Wilkinson (1814–1890). Wilkinson, a young Englishman from Oxfordshire, had devised two standard designs; one for 800 and one for 1,000 pauper inmates. His designs were limited by the need to construct these buildings as cheaply and as durably as possible; construction materials were taken from local resources (Powell 1965). The typical workhouse layout consisted of an entrance block that housed the administration, separate H-shaped ward buildings and, in the back part of the building, the infirmary (figures 2.3–2.4). The administration building included a board room in which the weekly meetings of guardians took place, the clerk's office, and the applicants' waiting hall. There was also a room for the porter, male and female probationary wards, bathhouses, washing rooms, fumigation closets for disinfecting the clothes of the inmates, privies, and refractory wards, which consisted of cells with compact earthen floors (Powell 1965, 8; Raftery 1995). A long single-story building linked the front to the back of the complex. This part of the workhouse contained stores, the kitchen, the laundry, and the large dining hall, which also functioned as a chapel during mass. The back buildings of the workhouse were used as an infirmary and an "idiot's" ward. Further beyond this building was a small mortuary block generally referred to as the "dead house" (Raftery 1995). The deterring purpose of the workhouse was imitated in the architecture, which had no plastered walls, bare rafter ceilings, bare rough floors, small windows, and narrow stairways. Their appearance was described as "gloomy, narrow and repulsive" (Driver 1993, 61) and the

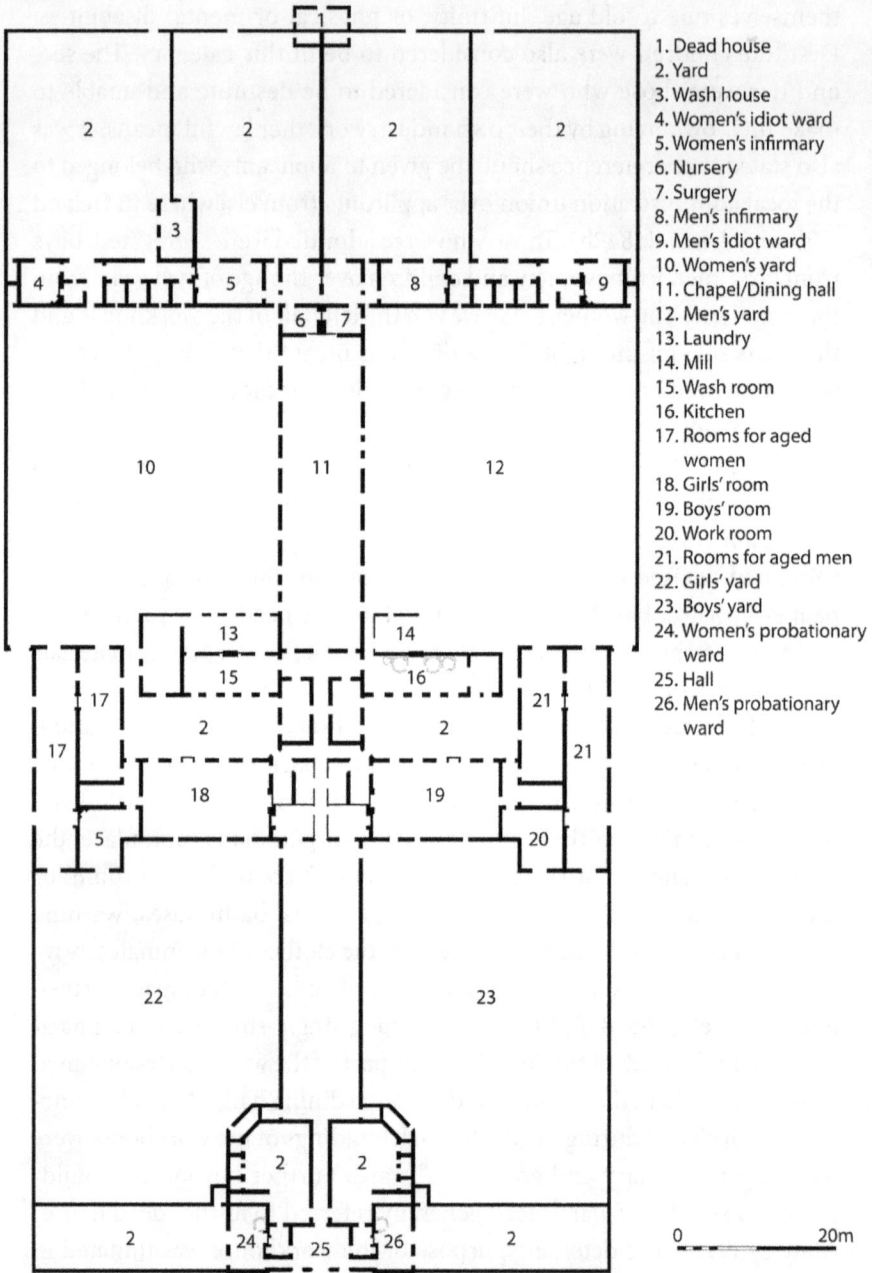

1. Dead house
2. Yard
3. Wash house
4. Women's idiot ward
5. Women's infirmary
6. Nursery
7. Surgery
8. Men's infirmary
9. Men's idiot ward
10. Women's yard
11. Chapel/Dining hall
12. Men's yard
13. Laundry
14. Mill
15. Wash room
16. Kitchen
17. Rooms for aged women
18. Girls' room
19. Boys' room
20. Work room
21. Rooms for aged men
22. Girls' yard
23. Boys' yard
24. Women's probationary ward
25. Hall
26. Men's probationary ward

Figure 2.3. Plan of the ground floor and layout of the Kilkenny Union Workhouse, redrawn from the original plan by George Wilkinson.

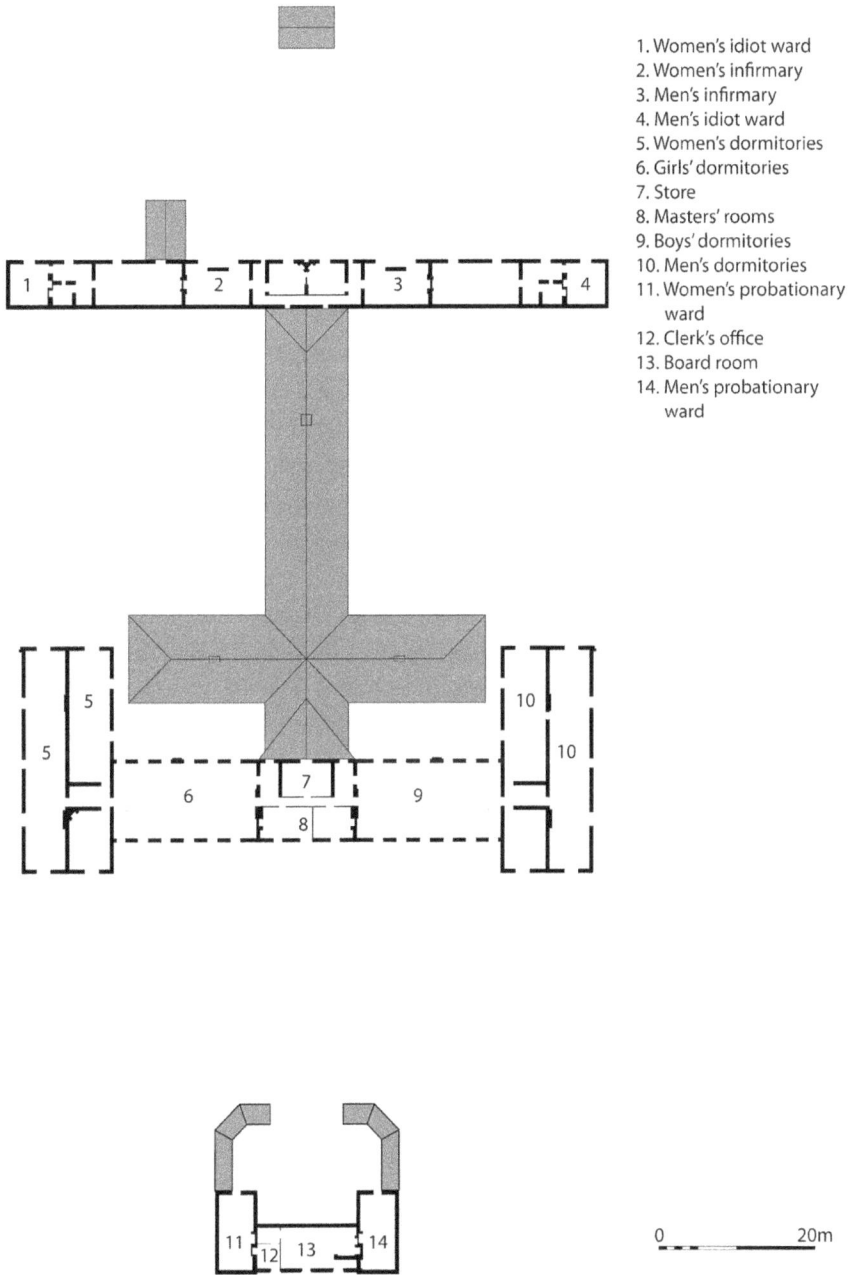

1. Women's idiot ward
2. Women's infirmary
3. Men's infirmary
4. Men's idiot ward
5. Women's dormitories
6. Girls' dormitories
7. Store
8. Masters' rooms
9. Boys' dormitories
10. Men's dormitories
11. Women's probationary ward
12. Clerk's office
13. Board room
14. Men's probationary ward

0   20m

Figure 2.4. First-floor plan and layout of the Kilkenny Union Workhouse.

sleeping quarters as "large, draughty, and unceiled, and the boards are so badly laid that you can see down between them into the room below" (Lough 1896, 164). Segregation of workhouse inmates from the rest of society was imposed by the buildings themselves and by eight-foot-high stone walls (Raftery 1995).

The first meeting of the Board of Guardians of the newly formed Kilkenny Union took place on 15 August 1839, in the courthouse on Parliament Street in the center of the city (Crotty 1996, 8). The Kilkenny Union Board of Guardians consisted of forty-seven members (Gray 2009, 290). Meetings were held weekly every Thursday at noon, and a summary of the minutes was published in two local newspapers, the *Kilkenny Journal* and the *Kilkenny Moderator*. The union was the largest in the county and included the three electoral divisions of the city (St. Canice, St. John's, and St. Mary's) and twenty-one divisions from the county. The second union in the county was Callan and the southern region of the county was served by unions in other counties: Carrick-on-Suir in County Tipperary, Waterford in County Waterford, and New Ross in County Wexford (Crotty 1996). Later, in 1853, Kilkenny Union was divided into the three additional unions of Castlecomer, Thomastown, and Urlingford (O'Connor 1995).

The construction of the workhouse began in 1840. It was erected on the eastern outskirts of the city, between Hebron Road and William's Lane and east of Dublin Road in Pennefatherslot townland in the parish of St. John's (figure 2.5). Like many of the other union workhouses built during this period, it was constructed on high ground, probably for the purpose of creating fear among prospective applicants. The cost of the construction was £9,700, which proved to be the fourth most expensive after the building of the workhouses in Cork, Cavan, and Limerick. It came to be the fifth largest workhouse institution in Ireland. It had allocated space for 1,300 inmates and an accommodation block of four floors. In total, the whole complex occupied an area of nine acres, three roods, and twenty-one perches, the equivalent of four hectares (O'Connor 1995, 261). The first admissions took place on 21 April 1842, when thirty applications were accepted (*Kilkenny Journal* 1842b).

Four ways of being granted admission were recognized: first, by a ticket from a warden on the recommendation of at least three rate payers; second, by order of the guardians during their weekly meetings; third, by the clerk if authorized to do so by the guardians; and fourth, by the master "if the applicant was in such a state of distress as to be likely to die before

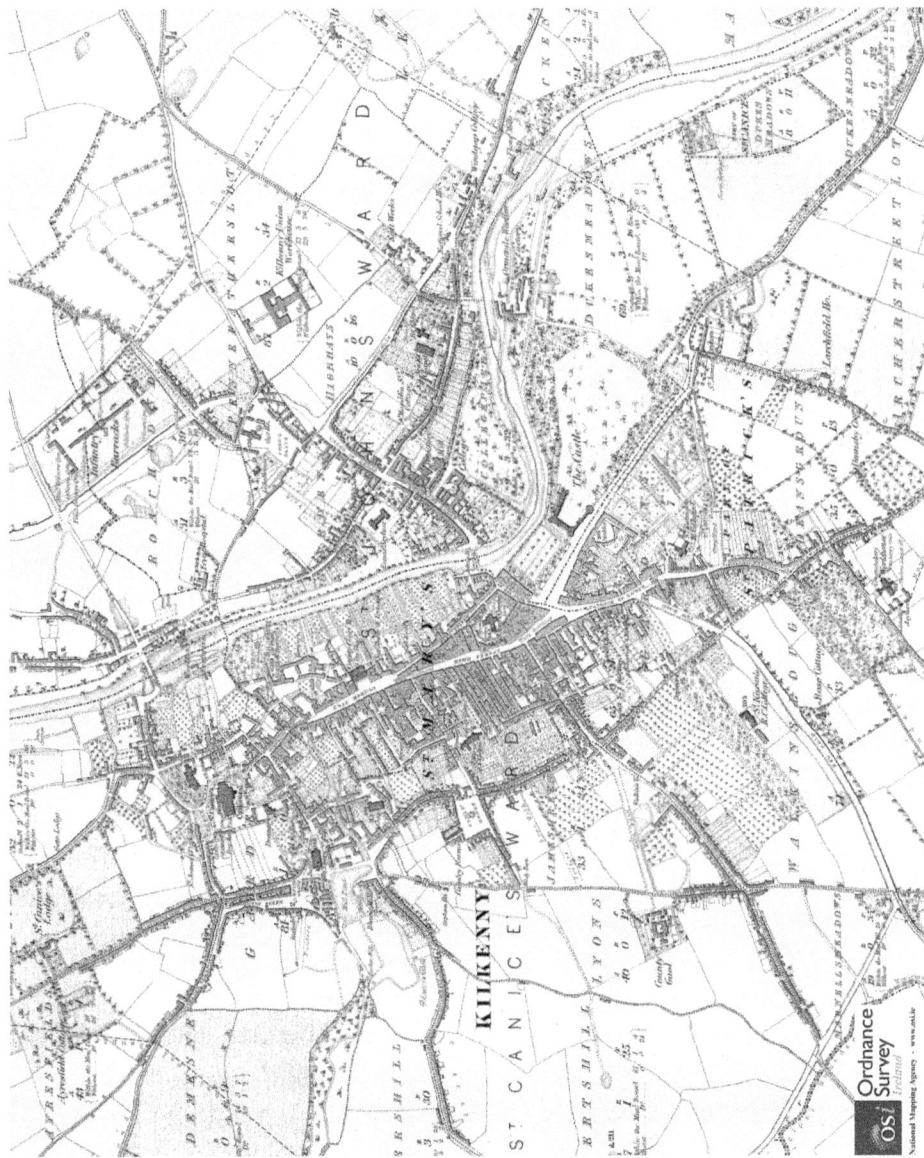

Figure 2.5. Ordnance Survey map of Kilkenny, 1829–1841. © Ordnance Survey Ireland, Government of Ireland, copyright permit no. MP 001613.

the next meeting of the board" (*Kilkenny Journal* 1844f). The processing of applicants into the workhouse was occasionally vividly described by the local newspapers in their weekly report of board meetings. One such account provides insight into the social views of the members of the board but also a distressing description of the experience of poverty.

> Several decent women with large families, who had been deserted by their husbands, some of them so long as six months, were refused admission by the Board, on the ground that desertion should not be encouraged. One poor woman, with four or five children, exclaimed, as the tears streamed from her eyes—"What am I to do? Am I to lie down in the streets and die because I cannot find my husband. For all I know, he might be in Cork, or Dublin, or anywhere else." A Guardian asked—How did you manage before this? The woman replied that before the house was opened she got a bit for God's sake, but she could no longer get anything, for every body said you have the poor house to go to. Several county guardians said "that was the truth." It was admitted by all that was a case of individual hardship, but it was contented on the other hand that the reception of such cases would tend to the greatest abuses. (*Kilkenny Journal* 1842c)

The industrial activity in the workhouse reflected the traditional local economy. The inmates produced blankets, clothes, and pins. Boys were being taught the skill of shoemaking. Several weavers were employed in the house (*Kilkenny Journal* 1844e, 1844g). Inmates were also kept occupied by breaking stones and working in the agricultural plot of lands attached to the workhouse (*Kilkenny Journal* 1845a). In February 1845, it was reported that twenty-nine male paupers had left the house rather than undertaking their assigned task of breaking stones (*Kilkenny Journal* 1845b). Any kind of idleness was not accepted. For example, four able-bodied male inmates were brought before the board in June 1848 for refusing to work when told to do so as a protest against not having been given enough to eat. All were severely punished: two of the men were sentenced to one month of hard labor in jail, while the other two were sent to do hard work in the prison for three weeks (*Kilkenny Journal* 1848d). Even though strict discipline was a key component of the management of the workhouse establishment, there was a limit to what even the guardians would consider acceptable. In June 1846, the *Kilkenny Journal* reported an incident involving the schoolmaster and some of the boy pupils:

The Master begs leave to report to the Board that ten or twelve of the children had been beat by Mr. John Magennis last night in the dormitories with a stick. . . . The children, whose number amounted to eighteen, were brought before the Board and, being undressed, exhibited several severe marks of bruises and contusions on several parts of their bodies. . . . Several broken fragments of sticks were exhibited which had been used in the infliction of the punishment. . . . It was finally moved . . . that Mr. John Magennis be immediately suspended from his situation, and that a strong recommendation be addressed to the Commissioners for his dismissal from office. (*Kilkenny Journal* 1846a)

An Gorta Mór (The Great Hunger), 1845–1852

The reasons why there was such a severe famine in Ireland in the mid-1840s and early 1850s have been the subject of discourse among generations of scholars. It is a charged debate that continues to this day. It is clear, nonetheless, that it began with a potato blight that first appeared in Ireland in 1845. The blight (*Phytophtora infestans*) originated in the Americas but spread through Europe via Belgium after arriving in an import of new potato breeding material in 1844 (Zadoks 2008, 6). The fungus spread with the wind, and in August of the following year it reached Ireland, where the counties of Waterford, Antrim, Monaghan, and Clare were particularly affected (Daly 1986, 53). The first signs of the infestation were brown and rotting patches of the leaves and foliage. When the potato tuber itself was affected, it turned into a dark and brownish rotting mass that produced a pungent odor. The blight made the potato crop completely inedible, and initial attempts to battle the murrain by scientific means proved unfruitful. A successful antidote was first developed in the 1880s, long after the end of the famine (Kinealy 2006, 33–34).

From the eighteenth century onward, due to mainly economic reasons, the diet of the Irish poor had become increasingly monotonous, consisting of mainly potatoes and dairy products. It has been estimated that the bottom third of the population relied entirely on the potato crop for sustenance in the early 1840s (Ó Gráda 2006, 7). Fish was a seasonal food source that consisted mostly of herring during the late summer. Oatmeal was consumed mainly in the northeast, and wheat bread was considered a luxury and was barely eaten at all (Bourke 1968; Crawford 1988, 282; Crawford 1995; Kennedy et al. 1999, 68–75; Sexton 2012). The potato was popular among all social classes in Ireland, but for those with limited or no financial means it was an essential crop for their very subsistence. The potato grew well in the Irish climate and was very productive. Of the several varieties that were grown—such as the black potato, the "Irish apple," the kidney potato, the red potato, and the cup variety—the poor preferred the high-yielding "Irish lumper" (Green 1956; Kennedy et al. 1999). Agriculture in County Kilkenny was varied, but opinions were expressed that the land was mismanaged and that crops were not cultivated to their full potential. Much of the land was used as pasture and for growing wheat and oats ("D" 1838), but for the poorest people the potato remained the main source of food.

It has been estimated that an adult Irish male consumed about 12 pounds (5½ kg) of potatoes a day, a woman about 10 pounds (4½ kg), and children aged less than eleven years about 4 pounds (2 kg). The lower classes depended the most on the crop; cottiers, laborers, and smallholders accounted for about 75 percent of the total human consumption of potatoes. A high dependency on the potato in a single family was therefore always a direct reflection of social class. The potato was also an important food stock for farm animals, particularly pigs, but it was also used for feeding cattle, horses, and poultry. About 40 percent of the crop was used for this purpose. One small proportion of the crop was also used for making farina, starch, and alcohol and about 13 percent for seeding for the next season (Bourke 1968). The potato was cultivated by the householders themselves, making families virtually self-sufficient, and a very small proportion of the total crop was traded commercially (Daly 1986, 57). A diet consisting mainly of potatoes and buttermilk was very nutritious; it provided more than enough of the required daily intake of proteins and vitamins (Crawford 1988). On the other hand, the potato could not be stored from season to season, which inevitably resulted in a situation in which a large proportion of the moneyless population starved annually during the "meal months" in the summer, between the exhaustion of the old crop and the arrival of the new yield (Woodham-Smith 1964, 35–36).

The extent of the blight in County Kilkenny was first reported in the

Kilkenny Journal on 22 October 1845, when it was estimated that one-third of the crop had already been destroyed throughout the county (*Kilkenny Journal* 1845d). Five days earlier, the Irish constabulary had reported to the government that the "crop [in Johnstown was] more or less diseased throughout the district: on some farms nearly half quite rotten" (qtd. in Tóibín and Ferriter 2001, 45). Nationwide, the seriousness of the situation had been quickly realized, and at the end of October the Mansion House Committee was established. A couple of weeks later, an official temporary national Irish Famine Relief Commission was formed. Plans for relief measures were immediately made, as the authorities were well aware that a crisis would inevitably follow the next spring (Kinealy 2006, 33). A month later, one-third of the potato crop of Ireland had been lost (Donnelly 2001, 43).

Part of the initial relief program by the government under Tory prime minister Sir Robert Peel (1788–1850) was the establishment of food depots, particularly in the west of Ireland, and the purchase of food supplies from abroad. These consisted of cheap Indian corn and meal (maize) from the United States and oatmeal from Britain (Daly 1986, 70; Donnelly 2001, 49; Gray 2012). Initiatives were also made by local relief committees across Ireland, who also organized food depots (Daly 1986, 71). The blight reappeared in 1846, arriving much earlier than in the previous year due to a warm and damp summer, and three-quarters of the crop consequently failed (Crawford 1995, 61; Daly 1986, 55). Because of the blight of the previous year, only about 80 percent of the usual acreage was planted in 1846 (Donnelly 2001, 58). As expected, the real tragic consequences of the blight began to appear in that year, and by autumn roadside deaths of wandering beggars had become a common sight, along with rising crime rates, unattended funerals, rampant infectious disease, and an increasing panic among the population (Ó Gráda 1999, 39). Throughout 1846, the pressure on workhouses increased significantly; at the beginning of the year, the nation's workhouses housed 40,000 inmates, a figure that increased to almost 100,000 people a year later (Ó Gráda 1999, 52).

The lack of potatoes made people dependent on wages to buy other foods, and the widespread refusal by large tenant farmers to make cash payments forced many laborers to surrender their plots and try to find income in the public works or, as the last resort, relief in the workhouse (Donnelly 2001, 58–59). Large-scale public works schemes that had been introduced in the spring of 1846 were designed to provide laborers with enough wages to purchase food by themselves. Such schemes had traditionally been the response to previous distresses, but their success proved to be limited during the Great Famine. It has been calculated that more than 700,000 people with over 3 million dependents were working in the public works scheme at its peak, and the scheme eventually became a massive expense for the government (Donnelly 2001, 72; Ó Gráda 1999, 52). In County Kilkenny alone, it is estimated that in the winter of 1846–1847 about 20,000 people, including women and boys, were employed through the public works scheme (O'Neill 1958, 2). Following the same ideology that underlay the Poor Law, the public works scheme was designed to function as a deterrent, and it was therefore felt necessary to give lower wages than normal for equal labor, at least 2 pennies less a day (Griffiths 1970, 642).

The absence of market regulations meant that food prices kept increasing, and eventually a public works wage became insufficient to purchase food. As the famine progressed, relief workers became too malnourished and weak for heavy labor that was often undertaken in harsh conditions of cold weather (Daly 1986, 73–87; Dunn 1992). The lack of money and escalating food prices meant that alternative foods were out of reach for the poorest tenant farmers and cottiers, who were then forced to eat the remaining healthy potatoes that had been saved for seeding, which meant that a further deepening of the crisis would occur the following year (Daly 1986, 60–63; Donnelly 2001, 59).

In June 1846, the government fell and was replaced by a new Whig government under the leadership of Lord John Russell (1792–1878). The ultimate cause of the downfall was the repeal of the Corn Law that month. The Corn Law had been enacted in 1815 as a means to protect the British and Irish markets against competition from cheap foreign cereal products through import restrictions. Even before the appearance of the blight, the need for reform to abolish the Corn Law had become increasingly apparent to the Tory government, and the famine in Ireland provided an opportunity to realize this goal (Daly 1986, 69; Kinealy 2006, 36–37; Lengel 2002, 63). They argued that a repeal of the Corn Law would make the Irish less dependent on only one staple food, which in turn would improve "their social and therefore [also] political habits" (qtd. in Gray 1999, 116). The new government adopted relief measures purely on the laissez faire policy strongly advocated by Charles Trevelyan (1807–1886), the assistant secretary to the treasury who had in reality become the organizer of relief to Ireland. It was believed that a free home market, through its private merchants, would be able to sort out the food crisis (Donnelly 2001, 65). Trevelyan, who was knighted by Queen Victoria (1819–1901) in 1848 for his administration of Irish famine relief, has remained controversial to this day in Ireland for these policies. While some scholars have explained both his response and that of the British government as a reflection of the laissez faire economic ideology of the time (Haines 2004; Wilson 2003), others have asked if Trevelyan used the famine, emigration, and mass deaths as a tool for a socioeconomic and cultural reform of Irish society and whether he believed that God had inflicted the famine upon the Irish people to teach them a lesson (Kinealy 2006, 249; Woodham-Smith 1964).

By the end of 1846, food had become scarce all over Britain and Europe, and Trevelyan expressed doubts about whether the famine in Ireland should be battled at the expense of the actions against the crises that were also emerging in England and Scotland (Daly 1986, 72). While some of the governments in mainland Europe had imposed restrictions and bans on food export in 1845–1847 (Vanhaute, Paping, and Ó Gráda 2007), Trevelyan remained convinced of the soundness of the laissez faire policy and minimal market interventions. The export of grain from Ireland to Britain continued and in fact increased significantly during 1846 (Donnelly 2001, 61; Zadoks 2008). To deal with the increasing crisis, the government enacted the Temporary Relief Act in February 1847. Soup kitchens replaced public works and were made fully available for free to the destitute but were to be paid for by wage earners (Kinealy 1995, 113). However, some expressed concern that distributing free food to the poor would pauperize the Irish population even further. Constant appeals for relief by the Irish, which later coincided with a severe financial crisis in England, had hardened British public opinion (Lengel 2002, 82–87), and by August 1847 the decision was made to make the Poor Law fully responsible for relief and the soup kitchen scheme was terminated (Daly 1986, 113; Donnelly 2001, 101; Kinealy 1995, 114; Ó Gráda 1999, 43). By this time, large crowds of poor and destitute people were gathering outside the gate of the union workhouse in Kilkenny, and in December 1847 it had become necessary to station the police and a group of able-bodied workhouse inmates outside the establishment to keep order (*Kilkenny Journal* 1848a).

Mistrust among politicians in Britain of the inefficient and poorly managed Irish estates made them increasingly blame the landholding system for much of the consequences of the potato blight, and the consensus was that the Irish landowning class bore primary responsibility for the financial burden of the disaster. The responsibility taken by Irish landlords varied throughout the country; some estate landowners went through great economic difficulties to provide relief, while others refused to do so (Boyce 2005, 117). The often harsh and cruel eviction of tenant farmers, almost a quarter of a million people, is one of the strongest narratives of the harsh realities of the famine years that have survived to the present day. From 1849 to 1852, a total of 1,837 evictions of families, affecting 9,420 individuals, took place in County Kilkenny alone (Walsh 2008, 137).

The failed potato harvest in 1848 coincided with a poor grain yield and eventually forced many of the small farmers to use what means they had left and emigrate. From 1849 to 1852, over 200,000 people emigrated annually, reaching a peak in 1851, when a quarter of a million people left Ireland (Ó Tuathaigh 2007, 183–84). From Kilkenny, emigration reached its highest numbers in 1852, when 6,513 persons departed (Walsh 2008, 21). It is estimated that about 1 million people emigrated during the famine years, equivalent to the number who had left Ireland during the entirety of the three decades prior to 1845 (Boyce 2005, 113). The agony and suffering would by no means be over for those who were able to flee the famine. Mortality on "famine ships" was high due to fever and other infectious diseases, and these diseases followed with the emigrants as they reached their new lands. When they arrived, they were initially placed in quarantine, and many were moved to makeshift fever wards and institutions in which thousands of them would die before having a chance to start their new lives (Keneally 2012; Laxton 1996; McGowan 2012a, 2012b; Shrout 2012).

Both mortality and admissions in the workhouses peaked in early 1847, and, because of pressure of demand, many workhouses erected temporary accommodations (Daly 1986, 93; Ó Gráda 1999, 51). The blight never appeared in 1847, but by then inadequate planting of healthy potato crops during the previous year led to a food scarcity just as dire as—or even worse than—before (Donnelly 2001, 59). The year was remembered as "Black '47."

Disease, famine fever in particular, spread vigorously that year, affecting all strata of society. In Kilkenny, the fever epidemic became very severe. Throughout 1845 and until December 1846, the average number of patients in the Kilkenny Fever Hospital had been between five and forty individuals. Then the statistics drastically changed: in December 1846, more than 100 patients were reported, in January 1847 there were almost 300, and between February and May there were between 400 and 500 patients. In April 1847, the workhouse chaplain, the schoolmistress, and the assistant master, Mr. Pratt, all succumbed to fever.[1] The number peaked in late June 1847, when more than 600 patients were suffering from fever. Thereafter, the numbers fell quickly, and by August less than 100 patients were being treated for fever (Patterson 1997). Applicants and inmates were very aware of the health risks in the workhouse and weighed this factor against the prospect of starving outside the institution. *The Kilkenny Journal* tells of one such case in Kilkenny. "A man . . . said he could not get his health in the house, and therefore would not stay. His wife was willing to remain, and said her children would starve if her husband persisted in refusing to enter the institution. The Vice-Guardian lectured the father on the impropriety of his conduct, but he was determined and went away with his wife and children" (*Kilkenny Journal* 1848d).

Famine distress continued to increase during 1848, and in the summer of the same year the blight reappeared in many parts of the country. It became clear that the Poor Law was not sufficient to cope with the situation, and many unions were in increasingly dire financial circumstances. The treasury reluctantly continued to provide additional financial relief for the most desperate cases, although the intention had been to have that policy terminated (Kinealy 2006, 227–31; O'Neill 1956, 248). At the end of 1848, Ireland was once again ravaged by cholera in an epidemic that continued until the summer of the following year. It has been noted that County Kilkenny, along with Galway, Limerick, Waterford, Clare, Dublin and Cork, suffered most from the 1849 cholera epidemic (Cousens 1963), although an article published in the *Kilkenny Journal* in June of that year indicated that "only" 172 local deaths had been attributed to the epidemic (*Kilkenny Journal* 1849d).

Mortuary Practice and Burial at Kilkenny Union Workhouse

Traditional practices related to death and burial in nineteenth-century Ireland were culturally explicit and included several ritual expressions. The various traditions and customs relating to the Irish funeral were described by American ethnographer James Mooney (1861–1921) in an article published in 1888. He described how shortly after a death had occurred, the neighboring women would wash, dress, and lay out the corpse on a board frame, such as a table or a door, covered with a white sheet. Plates containing pipes and tobacco for the wake attendants were placed next to the corpse, along with lit candles (Mooney 1888). The wake would normally last three days, during which the corpse of the deceased was never left alone; the men sat up all night, and the women took over in the morning. Friends would enter the house, help themselves to pipes and tobacco and sometimes to whiskey or *poitín* (a traditional Irish distilled beverage, often made from potatoes), and say a short prayer before sitting down and joining in conversation and laughter. Music was played for dancing, and people sang and played cards and games. The immediate family would sit or stand near the corpse with a group of women who were keening, led by the *bean caointe* (Eng. "crying woman"). The keeners—who were sometimes hired—traditionally followed the coffin to the cemetery and were present as it was lowered into the grave, all the time maintaining a passionate wailing chorus (Connolly 2001, 152–66; Mooney 1888; Ó Súilleabháin 1969).

The traditional Irish wake, which was a clearly festive gathering, has sometimes been interpreted as a reflection of a callous and fatalistic attitude to death in a period when mortality was high (Connolly 2001, 154). Other interpretations have focused on the function of the tradition, which would have helped to deal with the psychological and emotional needs of the mourners. Folklorist Seán Ó Súilleabháin (1969, 166–74) interprets the wake as a concentration of "sympathy for the dead, not for his relatives" in an attempt to "heal the wound of Death, and to do final justice to the deceased while he was still physically present." The wake was therefore a "great occasion" in "honour of the deceased," whose importance and membership in the community was expressed through the wake. The ceremonies and rituals associated with death and a proper wake and burial were therefore deeply valued elements of Irish culture. James Mooney elaborated on this aspect of Irish death rituals:

The Irishman obeys the injunction to remember his last end, and his constant prayer is to be deliverd "from a sudden or unprovided death," and to have a "decent funeral." The poorest old woman wil hoard up year after year from her slender means in order that she may be buried respectably when life's struggle is over, and above all, that she may not have a pauper's funeral, while the most poverty-stricken family wil strain every nerv to perform the same office for the departed father, mother, brother or sister. (Mooney 1888, 265)

The excessive number of deaths and mass burials that took place across Ireland during the Great Famine and the inability of many families to provide a wake or a decent burial for loved ones and friends due to poverty and fear of contracting fever must have been an enormous personal and social tragedy to both witness and endure. This could explain why so much of the folklore of the famine concentrates on the treatment and burial of those who died (see Lysaght 1996; Quinlan 1996). A substantial amount of the recorded folklore tells how some people on the verge of death were buried alive in grave pits, how mothers carried their dead children in sacks or sheets to their graves, and how boys were seen wheeling their dead parents in barrows (McHugh 1956, 419–27). Numerous recollections of decomposing and putrefying corpses alongside roads and in fields were recorded by the Irish Folklore Commission in the mid-1940s, some of utmost horror. One such story offers a harrowing example: "One day Stephen Regan met a dog dragging a child's head along. He took the head from the dog and buried it and set a tree over it. The family to whom the child belonged were getting relief for the child and for that reason did not report its death" (McHugh 1956, 421). A similar event evidently occurred in Kilkenny City in March 1848, when the newspapers reported that the corpse of an eight-day-old infant half-eaten by dogs had been found in an old house opposite the workhouse. The body was said to be "frightfully mutilated," and an inquest by the constable was initiated. The remains of the newborn child were brought in to the workhouse (*Kilkenny Journal* 1848c) and presumably were buried on the premises.[2]

The prospect of a pauper's burial in a workhouse coffin was despised, but for hundreds of thousands of people in Ireland during the famine, there was no other alternative. The notion that even a workhouse pauper deserved a decent burial was very much appreciated by wider society. This concept was expressed in the local papers in Kilkenny in February 1844, when to public disdain it was reported that

Thirteen of the paupers had been punished by the Master for improper conduct while bearing the bodies of two other paupers to the grave.

Mr. Martin said the conduct of the persons who had been punished, was most reprehensible; in carrying the corpses to the grave, they had placed one coffin on the top of the other, and the indecency of the act had shocked all the spectators. He thought a proper person ought to be delegated on all similar occasions, to see that the bodies of such persons as died in the house were properly interred and then such disgusting scenes would no longer be witnessed by the people. (*Kilkenny Journal* 1844b)

To not have been buried in a coffin was considered to be the ultimate disgrace, more so than having to endure a life of poverty and utter destitution (Bartoletti 2001, 100). There are numerous examples in contemporary newspapers of earnest yearnings for a coffin for deceased loved ones. A well-known article in the *Illustrated London News* told of a scene where a woman in Clonakilty in West Cork who was carrying the corpse of her small child made a distressing appeal to the passengers of a passing coach for some money "to enable her to purchase a coffin and bury her dead little baby" (figure 2.6) (Mahoney 1847). The wish for a coffined burial was manifested in other ways. It was noted that in Lurgan, County Armagh, people's desire to be buried in a coffin outweighed their great dislike of entering the workhouse, and many who sought refuge were nearing death and often passed away within twenty-four hours of admission (Cohen 2002, 125). However, some unions found it difficult to guarantee coffins for the deceased in their workhouses because of severe financial stress. For example, in January 1847, the coffin contractor for Castlebar Union Workhouse in County Mayo refused to supply coffins because of unpaid bills (Ó Gráda 1993, 129), and the dead were presumably buried in shrouds only.

Intramural Mass Burials

As with most of the new Irish union workhouses, no designated burial plot was assigned to the Kilkenny institution when it was constructed. However, the need for a paupers' cemetery associated with the workhouse in Kilkenny was recognized early. In January 1844, parishioners complained in the *Kilkenny Journal* about the interment of deceased workhouse paupers in the graveyard at St. Patrick's. The cemetery was clearly overcrowded at this stage, and local residents demanded that a new burial

Figure 2.6. Drawing of a destitute woman in Clonakilty, West Cork, begging for money to buy a coffin for her dead child. *Illustrated London News*, 13 February 1847.

ground be established at a convenient distance from the city (*Kilkenny Journal* 1844a). St. Patrick's cemetery, which is located in the southern district of the city, thus appears to have been the first burial ground used by the workhouse. In March 1844, notice was given that a designated portion of land attached to the workhouse was to be enclosed as a burial ground and that the land would eventually be consecrated (*Kilkenny Journal* 1844d). The enclosure and consecration never took place, and it appears that intramural burials at the workhouse began around this time. In late June 1845, Mr. Handcock, one of the Poor Law commissioners, gave strict instructions to the guardians that "no more deceased paupers be buried within the workhouse grounds" (*Kilkenny Journal* 1845c).

After the complaints by Mr. Handcock, it appears that workhouse inmates were once again interred at St. Patrick's. In March 1846, the guardians received a highly critical letter from Dean Charles Vignoles (1798–1877), who protested against the interment of paupers in the churchyard who had no claim as parishioners, referring to the increasing and critical

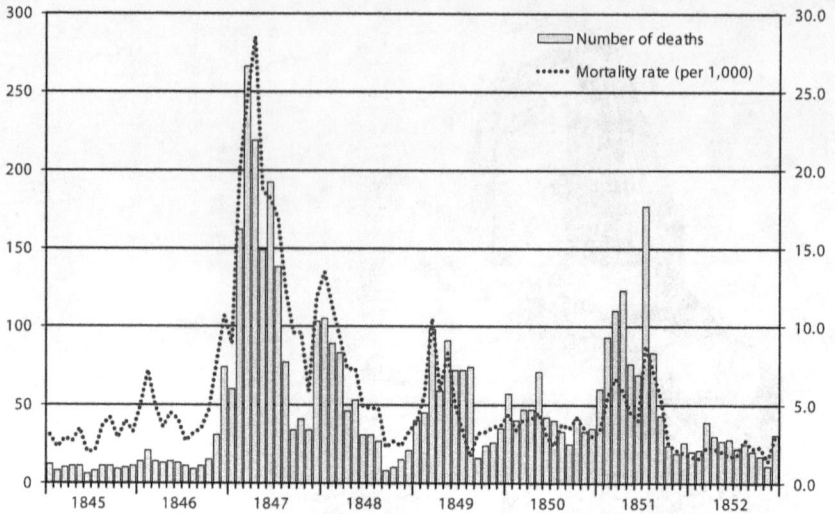

Figure 2.7. Number of recorded monthly deaths in the workhouse and fever hospital in Kilkenny, 1845–1852, based on weekly mortality statistics in the original Poor Law Union minute books, *Kilkenny Journal* and *Kilkenny Moderator*. In cases where no data are available, an estimation of the mean value from the preceding four weeks is given.

overcrowding of the cemetery (*Kilkenny Journal* 1846b). After this complaint, the St. Maul's cemetery, which was located by the fever hospital, was used for burial instead. Shortly after this time, the mortality rate in the workhouse reached its peak (figure 2.7) and by early March 1847, St. Maul's had become too crowded as well. The mayor had received complaints from residents in the area and from Dean Vignoles and a colonel, who noted that about ten corpses were carelessly buried in the burial ground every day. Considering the number of interments and the fact that St. Maul's cemetery was located on a hill, it is reasonable to presume that residents in the northeast area of the city were subjected to a constant odor of putrefying flesh from decomposing corpses interred in shallow graves when burials took place there.

The board therefore reserved £10 to be used to buy a plot of land adjoining this cemetery.[3] The board had ordered that at least three feet of earth should cover the interred coffins and an additional three feet over the original ground level, but this had not been adhered to and some graves were reportedly even left open. The interments had been taking place in large mass burial pits of several coffins that were then only covered with a few shovels of earth (*Kilkenny Journal* 1847c). In April, it was noted in the minute books that "the new plot of burial ground had been taken by the Sheriff, and the workhouse-men turned off the ground, and threatened with law proceedings" (*Kilkenny Journal* 1847d). This implies that some of the workhouse dead had been buried illegally on a plot adjacent to St. Maul's at a time when it was reported that the mortuary building was full with corpses. Negotiations with the landowner—a Mr. H. J. Loughnan—about purchasing the land had been delayed due to unsolved legalities regarding the previous land tenant (*Kilkenny Journal* 1847e). As a consequence, the workhouse once again resorted to using St. Patrick's cemetery for burial, and later in August Dean Vignoles yet again voiced his complaints to the Board of Guardians about the number of dead buried there (*Kilkenny Journal* 1847g). It is clear that from this point, there was no other alternative than to return to burying the dead within the grounds of the workhouse.[4] The minutes of the Board of Guardians' meeting in the last week of October read that "the Commissioners notified their desire that the Guardians should consider the propriety of obtaining a burial ground at a proper distance from the Workhouse; as they considered it most desirable that burials in the Workhouse grounds should be discontinued" (*Kilkenny Journal* 1847h).

The archival and archaeological evidence suggests that the mass burials of individuals from Kilkenny Union Workhouse that have been excavated were starting to take place sometime during the late summer of 1847. No single grave cuts that could be interpreted as deriving from the first period of intramural burial dating to 1844–1845 were found. It is possible that these early burials were placed either in the most northeastern corner of the workhouse grounds—where the famine burial ground was located but within the area that was beyond the limit of the archaeological excavation (see figure 2.9)—or that they were interred elsewhere within the workhouse grounds. Perhaps the most feasible explanation is that these burials would have been shallow interments and would therefore have been destroyed and lost through later horizontal truncation. Considering the difference in the weekly death rates at the workhouse before and during the famine (see figure 2.7), the early burials are very unlikely to have been mass interments.

Local papers did not include any articles or notes from the Board of Guardians minutes regarding the workhouse burials until early January 1850. Mr. Lanigan, one of the guardians, had told the board during the first weekly meeting of that year that "it was most desirable that ground

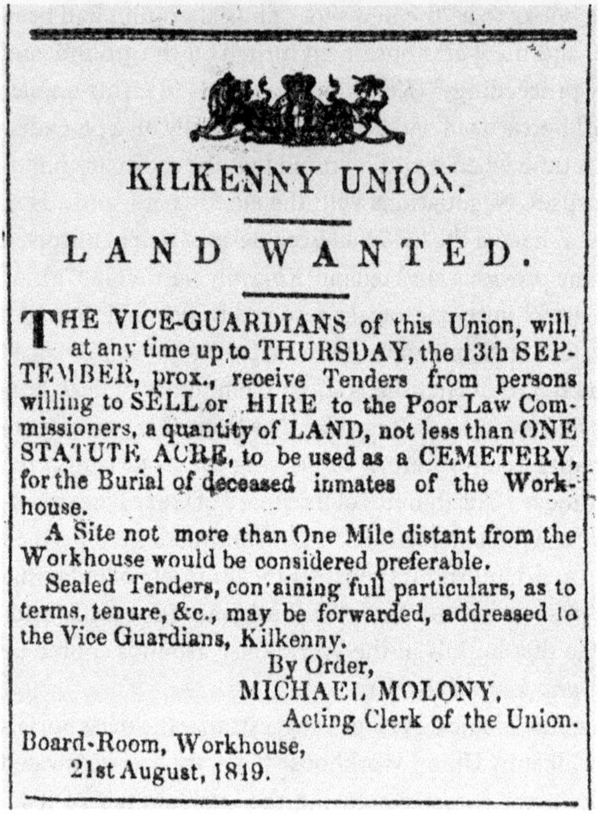

KILKENNY UNION.

L A N D   W A N T E D .

THE VICE-GUARDIANS of this Union, will, at any time up to THURSDAY, the 13th SEP-TEMBER, prox., receive Tenders from persons willing to SELL or HIRE to the Poor Law Commissioners, a quantity of LAND, not less than ONE STATUTE ACRE, to be used as a CEMETERY, for the Burial of deceased inmates of the Workhouse.

A Site not more than One Mile distant from the Workhouse would be considered preferable.

Sealed Tenders, con·aining full particulars, as to terms, tenure, &c., may be forwarded, addressed to the Vice Guardians, Kilkenny.

By Order,
MICHAEL MOLONY,
Acting Clerk of the Union.

Board-Room, Workhouse,
21st August, 1819.

Figure 2.8. Advertisement placed in the *Kilkenny Journal* on 21 August 1849 by the vice-guardians of the Kilkenny Poor Law Union, requesting a plot of land to use for a workhouse cemetery.

should be obtained at once for a cemetery" (*Kilkenny Journal* 1847a). The same week, an advertisement was placed in the paper for a portion of land of not less than one acre (figure 2.8). The advertisement sparked a response from two readers who wrote letters that were published in the following edition of the paper.

INTRAMURAL BURIAL—KILKENNY. The following letter, which we received yesterday, refers to two or three matters of very great local interest. It is most desirable that the Vice-Guardians should, if at all practicable, select ground for cemeterial purposes which lie out of town. The mischievous influence of intramural interment has been long an acknowledged evil.

In London, Liverpool, Dublin and Belfast—in fact in any town where attention is paid to sanatory [*sic*] regulations—the practice has altogether disappeared. It is impossible that any place can be free from a vitiated atmosphere where the dead are housed almost among the living; and in times of epidemic the evil is lamentably increased by the neglect invariably paid to burial in such cases, because seldom anything beyond mere surface burial is obtained, from a want of proper officers to see that all graves are sunk to a proper depth.

It is a very great abuse that the poor people who die in the hospital are not buried in consecrated ground. To whom is this to be attributed? Once the ground was procured, where was the difficulty in having it consecrated? This is, indeed, a matter that requires explanation.

Our correspondent's suggestion that there should be a town meeting to deal with the general question is an excellent one. It is for the people themselves, who are the parties most interested, to make a move in the matter. It concerns the health of themselves and their families; and a very little exertion will suffice to obviate a great and growing evil. (*Kilkenny Journal* 1849f)

A second letter was published immediately underneath this letter:

TO THE EDITOR OF KILKENNY JOURNAL. Kilkenny, August 23, 1849. Sir—I have seen in yesterday's number of your paper, an advertisement from the Vice-Guardians, for an acre of ground, for a cemetery. I trust it is their intention that in future no interments shall be allowed at the rear of the Fever Hospital, or on the Workhouse grounds. It is for many other reasons also, most desirable, that they may succeed in procuring a suitable place of interment, and one in particular which will relieve the inhabitants of Blackmill, Vicar, and Green-Street, from a repetition of the scenes of outraged decency they were frequently obliged to witness during the last year. It is also a cause of complaint that the poor people who die in the Hospitals or Work-house, unless claimed by their friends, are not buried in consecrated ground; and such has been the case with regard to one place for the last three years.

In connexion with this matter I think it would be well if the citizens of influence and position, both clergy and laity, would come together and consult about the grave yards within the town, with a view to ascertaining if the opinions of some are correct as to the great necessity that exists for a new cemetery, and whether it would be advisable to enlarge the present ones or establish a new one. (*Kilkenny Journal* 1849g)

The published letters reveal that the public was very aware of the intramural burials at the workhouse and that there were sincere concerns from both a sanitary and ethical point of view. In February 1850, negotiations started between the guardians and a Mr. Greene regarding a piece of land by the military barracks that potentially could be either bought or rented as a burial plot for the workhouse (*Kilkenny Journal* 1850c). Although the guardians offered Mr. Greene £75 for an acre of land, he rejected the offer (*Kilkenny Journal* 1850d).

In June 1850, the guardians became aware of a suitable plot of land just northeast of the workhouse, by Hebron Road, that had previously been used as a sand pit. The owner, Major Helsham, was willing to sell the piece of land for only £30. The land was purchased in the first week of July (*Kilkenny Journal* 1850f). The new workhouse cemetery, which later came to be referred to locally as Shank Yard, was of such a substantial size that the Board of Guardians permitted the burials of ordinary Kilkenny citizens within it, thereby probably acknowledging the still-current problem of overcrowding in the city's cemeteries (*Kilkenny Journal* 1850h). This act of goodwill should perhaps be interpreted as an act of gratitude by the guardians toward the city for previously allowing deceased paupers to be buried in the already crowded city cemeteries. An iron gate was erected at the burial ground in December 1850, and work on the enclosing wall, which was a prerequisite for having the burial ground consecrated, began in the same month.

A report of the weekly meeting of the Board of Guardians in the *Kilkenny Moderator*, published on 3 March 1851, records a discussion among the members of the board about how the contractors who were building the cemetery wall had asked for permission to continue the work, as the task had been postponed due to bad weather during the winter. The discussion that followed highlighted the need to discontinue the practice of intramural burial, not only at the workhouse but also at the Fever Hospital. The board decided that the new cemetery was to be brought into use immediately in a seemingly light-hearted atmosphere: "Mr. Burke thought they might use a portion of the new cemetery at once. Sir Wheeler Cuffe—Yes, let them stop the burials . . . immediately and begin to bury in the new cemetery to morrow. The Mayor—Tomorrow!

Wouldn't you wait if they have no corpse to bury Sir Wheeler? (laughter.)" (*Kilkenny Moderator* 1851).

A last indirect reference to the intramural burials at the workhouse dates to the second week of March 1851, when it was written down in the minutes from the Board of Guardians' weekly meeting that the enclosing wall of the burial ground was to be completed and that all future interments were to be made "in the new cemetery."[5] Burials within the grounds of the workhouse ceased at that time.

The Archaeological Evidence

The archaeological excavation at Kilkenny Union Workhouse revealed a minimum of sixty-three pits located in the northeast corner of the original workhouse grounds (figure 2.9). All but one contained human remains. The pits measured approximately 1.5–2 m long and 1.5 m wide. Their depth varied to a maximum of 1.2 m, and the features were dug into the natural subsoil to an underlying level of free draining gravel (O'Meara 2010). The burial ground extends beyond the limit of the excavation, and it is estimated that a further eight to eleven pits are still present in situ. All the pits were located within a defined area between the inner face of the northeast corner of the boundary wall and a cinder path to the west. The path, of which only patches were discovered during the excavation, is visible on the section of the Kilkenny City 1897–1913 Ordnance Survey map that depicts the workhouse area (figure 2.10), and the archaeological evidence suggests that the path was present at the time of the burials. It is likely to have been used for carrying coffins from the workhouse mortuary to the burial ground.

The location of the burial ground suggests that it was intentionally placed as far away as possible from the workhouse complex and the residential areas of Kilkenny City. The earliest pits are therefore most likely to be those positioned in the most northeastern corner, and the burial ground thereafter expanded first westward and then south. The pits were placed close to each other, roughly arranged in rows with a southwest to northeast alignment. The fact that each pit respected those near it and that no truncation had occurred is further evidence that these features date to within a relatively short time frame. The often very close proximity between two adjacent features—between 30 cm and 80 cm (O'Meara 2010)—also indicates that two pits were never opened at the same time, at least not if they were placed next to each other. The probable scenario

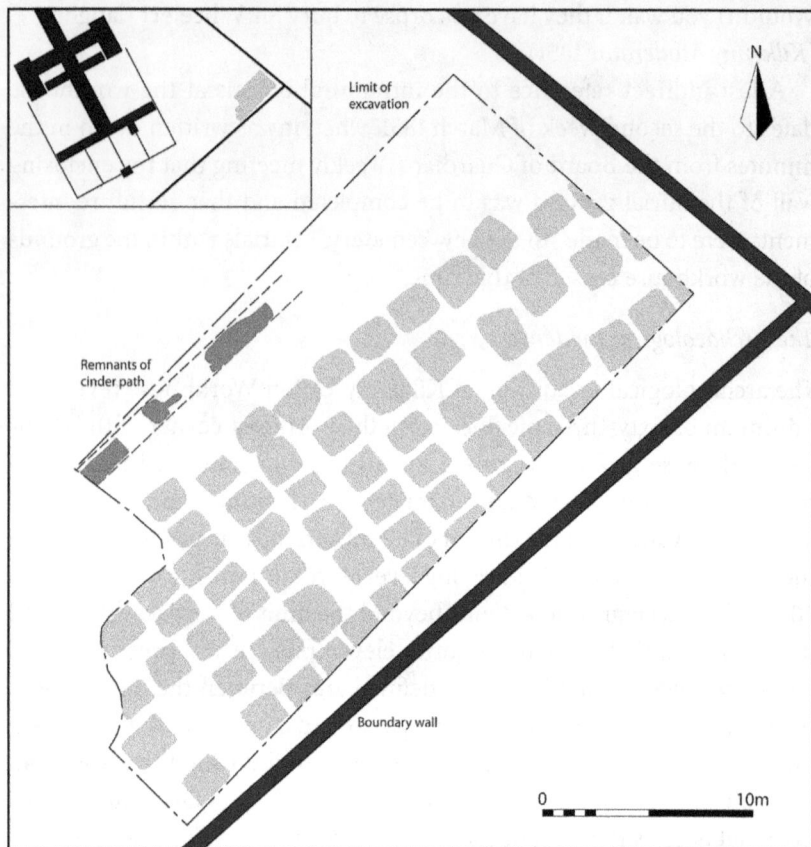

Figure 2.9. Plan of the famine mass burial ground at the Kilkenny Union Workhouse and its location in relation to the main building.

is that the pits were dug, filled with interments, and backfilled one after another in sequence. The presence of an empty pit is interesting, as it suggests that after a burial pit had been backfilled, a new one was dug in anticipation of further deaths. The burials were conducted by a Mr. John Dowling, who was paid £0.18.4 for "attending Burials" in April 1847. Fourteen days later, he was paid £1 for "twelve days Burials."[6]

There was a variation in the number of individuals buried in each pit within the burial ground. Excluding the empty and only partially excavated pits, they all contained a range of six individuals in four pits to twenty-seven individuals in one pit. The mean number in each mass burial feature was sixteen individuals, and the majority contained somewhere

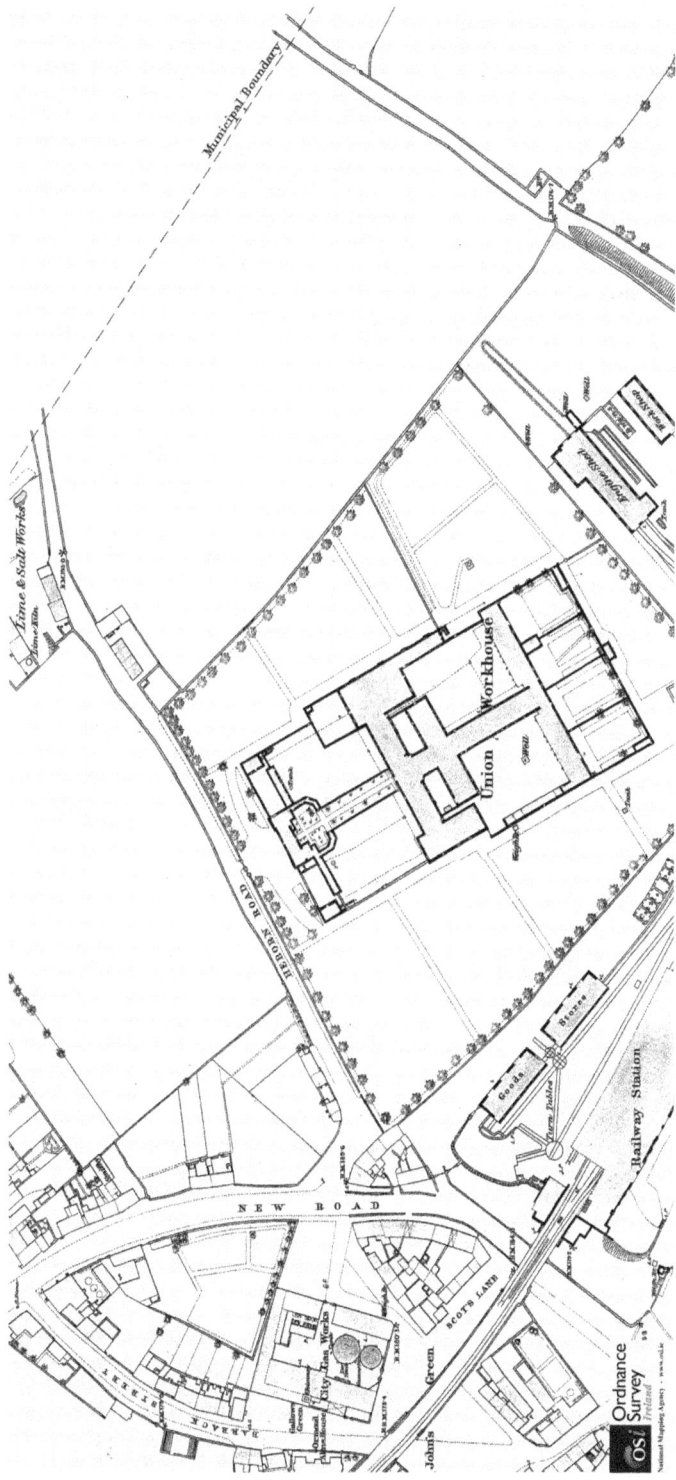

Figure 2.10. Section of the union workhouse complex in Kilkenny from the Ordnance Survey map of 1897–1913. The map makes no reference to the mass burial ground, which was positioned in the northeast corner of the boundary wall. © Ordnance Survey Ireland, Government of Ireland, copyright permit no. MP 001613.

between fourteen and twenty-two interments. The mortality tables, as available from the minute books, suggest that each pit probably represents about one week's worth of deaths. Both adults and children and males and females were buried in each pit; the rigid segregation of the living that was made in the workhouse was evidently not upheld in death.

The folklore and historical accounts of the Great Famine tell of the notorious "sliding coffin" that could be reused since the corpse within it would have been emptied into the grave at the burial ground (McHugh 1956, 422–23). The archaeological evidence for the famine burial ground at Kilkenny Union Workhouse indicates, however, that this practice most likely never took place there. In fact, it appears as if all individuals were interred in coffins. The evidence for these was mainly represented by soil stains in a clear hexagonal shape outlining the skeletons. In some cases, preserved wood fragments were also found that anatomical analysis identified exclusively as pine (*Pinus* spp.) (O'Donnell 2010). Coffin nails were also found outlining the skeletons, the majority of which were short nails with flat circular heads and rectangular tapering shanks (Scully 2010). The coffins were of simple construction that conformed to three standardized sizes: about 6' (183 cm) long for adults, 4' (122 cm) for children, and 2½' (76 cm) for infants. They were bought by the union from a Mr. John Brennan, among others, and eventually became a significant expense. In March to June 1846, the Board of Guardians received a bill of £108 for delivered coffins, based on a price of a £0.0.9 a foot.[7] A year later, a bill of £80.1.5 was paid.[8]

It appears as if the chief nurse at the fever hospital, Mrs. Hamilton, on occasion donated coffins the union had purchased for burials outside the institution. The board disapproved of this action, and eventually in the spring of 1848 it directed her "not to give coffins or any other property now under her charge to any person" unless the master had ordered her to do so.[9] Shrouding material was also a considerable expense and had to be bought at large quantities. In the second week of April 1847, a total of 500 yards of shrouding had been ordered.[10] Only four weeks later, an additional 1,000 yards had to be ordered.[11] No textile traces of the shrouds themselves were found in the mass burials, but they would traditionally have been made out of linen (Mooney 1888, 267). The coffins in the mass burials had been stacked on top of each other in varying numbers of levels depending on the depth of the pit. The majority of the coffins were oriented southwest to northeast, following the alignment of the eastern boundary of the workhouse grounds. In some pits, it was apparent that as many coffins as possible were interred, and sometimes it was evident that a coffin had been slotted into the pit on its side between a previously placed coffin and the inner side of the pit. After the placing of the coffins was complete, the pit was immediately backfilled with the material from its excavation, which consisted of a mixture of topsoil, silty subsoil, and gravel. Intentional inclusions of lime and sulfur (brimstone) were also noted in this backfill (O'Meara 2010).

It was clear in ten cases that two individuals had been placed in the same coffin. These were usually burials of adult females with a neonate (less than 4 weeks old) or an infant child (1–12 months old) placed between the legs. In one case, an infant had been placed in the crook of the right arm of a female (figure 2.11). In only one case was the adult a male. Three coffins contained two children in each, and in one case an adolescent (13–17 years old) female and a neonate had been placed in one coffin. It is not possible to determine whether there might have been a genetic link between skeletons buried in the same coffin, and the reason for the practice is likely to have been primarily economic (see Kinealy 2006, 201). In late July 1847, the *Kilkenny Journal* reported on a discussion of the guardians during one of the weekly board meetings that mentioned that two children were sometimes buried in the same coffin. There was also a discussion about the unnecessary cost of burying children in coffins that were too large, as each coffin was priced by foot length (*Kilkenny Journal* 1847f).

It was the custom in nineteenth-century Ireland to sometimes include inanimate objects with the corpse in the coffin, for "greater comfort in the other world" (Mooney 1888, 295). In the mass burials at Kilkenny Union Workhouse, evidence of this custom included two finger rings, four rosaries, and four religious medals. There is a possibility that other objects made of organic materials had originally been deposited with the burials but then disintegrated completely in the ground prior to the archaeological excavation. Nevertheless, when considering the large number of individuals interred in the mass burials, there were surprisingly few artifacts found in association with the remains. This is possibly a reflection of the poverty endured by these individuals or possibly a reflection of the fact that most inmates had sold anything they had of value before entering the workhouse. Any possession of value by an inmate might also have been sold by the Board of Guardians to cover the cost of burial. In June 1847,

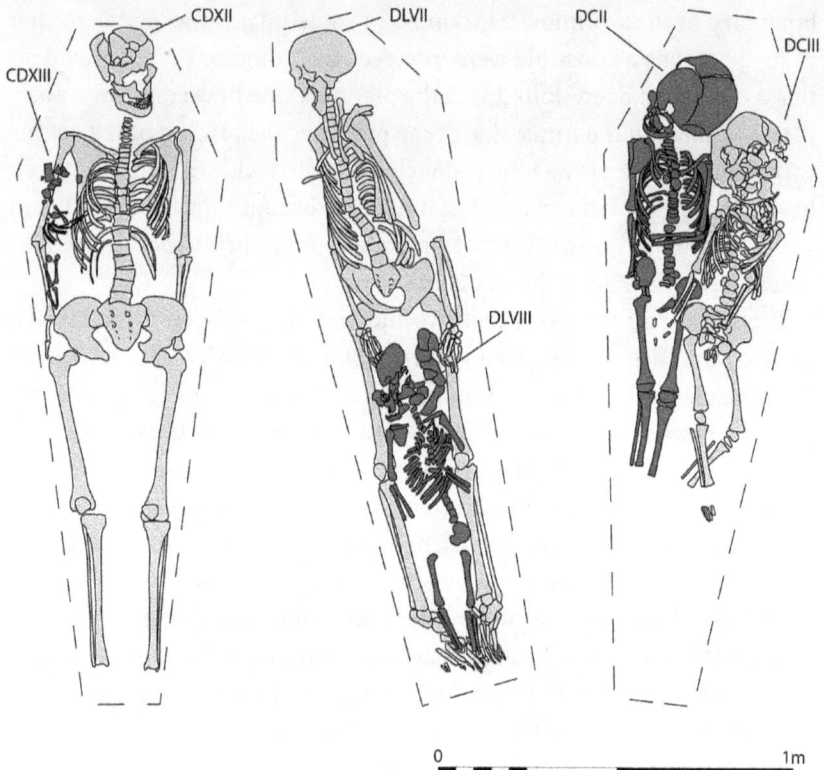

Figure 2.11. Three instances of coffins containing two individuals: a late middle adult female (CDXII) with a newborn child (CDXIII) placed in the crook of her right arm; a late middle adult female (DLVII) with the remains of a two-year-old child (DLVIII) placed between her legs; and two children aged between three and four years (DCII and DCIII) buried together in a single adult coffin.

for example, a woman died in the workhouse with £1.12.6 in her pocket, of which £0.6.3 were used to pay for her shroud and coffin.[12] In the year before the famine, a poor woman had applied to obtain the clothes of her son who had died in the workhouse and been supplied with a coffin at the expense of the union. However, the clerk stated that "the rule had been made that when the union supplied a coffin, the clothes of the deceased person should not be given to his relatives" (*Kilkenny Journal* 1844c). The same was probably true for any personal possessions that belonged to the dead inmates.

The finger rings were found with two mature females and were made out of copper alloy. One of them showed evidence of gilding (Scully 2010).

Four individuals were buried with rosaries (figure 2.12) and four with religious medallions. A May 1846 entry in the minute books mentions that "one gross of beads [were] bought for inmates who can not read."[13] Although these are usually considered as merely symbols of devotion, the comfort that these religious objects might have given the people they were found with should not be underestimated. A personal and deep religious belief might have been the reason why these objects were placed with the deceased in the coffin. The rosaries consisted of simple beads made of glass and wood and were found with females only. In addition, small textile fragments of what is believed to have been a pouch were recovered with the remains of a small child. The Christian rosary tradition is considered to originate from a Dominican practice dating to the fifteenth century, and its use within the Catholic Church was encouraged by several Vatican papacies. The rosary consists of beads that represent recitations of vocal and mental prayers of fifteen decades (mysteries) of "Hail Marys" preceded by an "Our Father" and followed by a "Glory Be to the Father" (Beinert 1992; Hinnebussch 1969).

Figure 2.12. A set of rosaries, including a copper alloy crucifix and wooden beads, found with the skeleton of an early middle adult female individual (CCXCVII). Photo by author.

One heart-shaped and three oval-shaped religious medallions were found in two mass burials. Two medallions could be associated with skeletons: one adolescent of unknown sex and one late middle adult (36–45 years old) female. All were made out of copper alloy in varying states of preservation. Religious medallions have a long tradition within the Catholic Church and have been used since the sixteenth century. They originate from devotional medals that were in use from at least the fourth century AD. Attributions of intrinsic powers to religious medals was (and is) severely condemned by the Church, which sees it only as a symbol of devotion "that recalls to the believer his faith and his religious duties" (Mulhern 1969, 547). The oval medals were so-called miraculous medals that bore an image of a vision of the Blessed Virgin Mary granted to St. Catherine Labouré, a novice Daughter of Charity of St. Vincent de Paul in Paris on 27 November 1830. In her vision, she saw the Virgin standing upon a globe and crushing a serpent beneath her feet, with rays of light streaming from her outstretched hands. In her vision, Labouré also saw the prayer "O Mary, conceived without sin, pray for us who have recourse to thee" written around her. The reverse aspect of the medal revealed an *M* surmounted by a bar and a cross, with the hearts of Jesus and Mary underneath, and twelve stars encircling the whole (Dirvin 1969).

Miraculous medals were first struck in Paris on 30 June 1832, and received papal approval on 20 January 1842, after the instant conversion of the "hostile Jew" Alphonse Ratisbonne in Rome (Dirvin 1969). The medal received its name from stories of numerous miracles all over the world that came to be attributed to it in the nineteenth century, including conversions of people from other faiths and accounts of people who were cured of typhoid and gastric fever, dropsy, consumption, fever, chronic coughs, paralysis, gout, rheumatism, epilepsy, blindness, and stammering (Aladel 1880, 94–260). The comfort some individuals presumably derived from the miraculous medals during the famine might have been based on a sincere belief in their healing power, and that perhaps explains why some individuals were buried with them. They were possibly also placed with the deceased by mourning friends or family members. For example, it was common in France for mothers to give the miraculous medal to their children as a New Year's present (Aladel 1880, 68). The heart-shaped medal is identical to one found with a famine-period burial adjacent to Manorhamilton Union Workhouse in County Leitrim (Rogers et al. 2006).

3

A Life Endured in Poverty

A Social Bioarchaeology of the "Deserving Poor"

The poor cringing laborer, touching his hat to the haughty lord, who never looked manfully in the face of him he served, has a soul burning within him capable of all that is praiseworthy, of all that is godlike. And would justice be allowed to lift her voice in his behalf, that soul would look out, and speak, "I, too, am a man."

Asenath Nicholson, *Ireland's Welcome to the Stranger, or an Excursion through Ireland in 1844 and 1845* (1847)

The skeletal remains from the mass burials at Kilkenny Union Workhouse are the physical remains of individuals who belonged to a social stratum in nineteenth-century society about which relatively little is known. Bioarchaeological studies and paleopathological analyses of nineteenth-century skeletal populations from this societal class are therefore of great importance and value, as they enable us to learn about these people and gain greater insight into the diversity of life experienced by the poor in this century. It is nevertheless important to acknowledge that the archaeological excavation and osteological study of human skeletons could be a controversial subject (Mays 2010, 331–48). When burials are encountered and excavation is the only option, it is essential to acknowledge the lives of these individuals and treat the remains with the greatest respect. It is important that the analysis of the remains acknowledge that the excavated bones and teeth are in fact remains of people and not just merely skeletal material. Each skeleton reveals a unique story; each skeleton was a person.

The archaeological excavations of the mass burials recorded 846 articulated skeletons and a large amount of disarticulated remains, from a total of sixty-one complete and two truncated pit features (O'Meara 2010).

Figure 3.1. The skeleton of a late middle adult female (LXXV) that had fallen out of place in the ground due to a postdepositional collapse of the coffin in the burial pit. This individual suffered from dental disease, joint disease, and osteoarthritis with several fractures, including a severe but healed injury of the left hip. There are also skeletal lesions indicating that she suffered from scurvy. Photo by Margaret Gowen & Co. Ltd.

The disarticulation occurred as a result of subsequent phases of coffin collapse (figure 3.1) in each pit that had led to a disturbance of the original burial stratigraphy. Skeletons were disturbed when they collapsed into the coffin layers and probable voids in the soil compacting below, and many of the skeletons in the upper layers were anatomically incomplete when they were found and recorded in situ. Following the completion of the osteological analysis of the articulated contexts, the disarticulated elements were quantified, fully analyzed, and reassociated with their original skeletons when possible. Another 130 additional skeletons were revealed from the disarticulated remains, giving a final minimum number of 970 individuals. In addition, five separate burials postdated the mass burial events; these are discussed separately (see chapter 5). Most of the articulated skeletons were virtually complete, while the majority of individuals retrieved from the disarticulated material were incomplete. The bones were occasionally fragmented but generally displayed a very good state

of preservation. Even soft tissues survived in a few cases. These were predominantly small cerebral fragments in the lower-level interments of the
pits, but they were not made the subject of any scientific analysis and were
reburied with the skeletal remains.

Because of the fact that individuals were selectively admitted to the
workhouse, the age-group bias of mortality during the famine, and the
fact that the bodies of some of the deceased inmates in the workhouse
are likely to have been claimed by friends and families outside the institution, the demographic composition of the skeletal population buried in
the Kilkenny mass burials is different from that of skeletons identified
in other nineteenth-century burial grounds. A comparison of the demographic profile of the Kilkenny sample with that of samples from a selection of formal cemeteries reveals that non-adult mortality at the Kilkenny
Union Workhouse was disproportionally high (figure 3.2). This disparity
further illustrates the uniqueness of the skeletal population in this study
and suggests that children suffered the most during the famine. Another
rather unique aspect of this population is the fact that it is a snapshot of

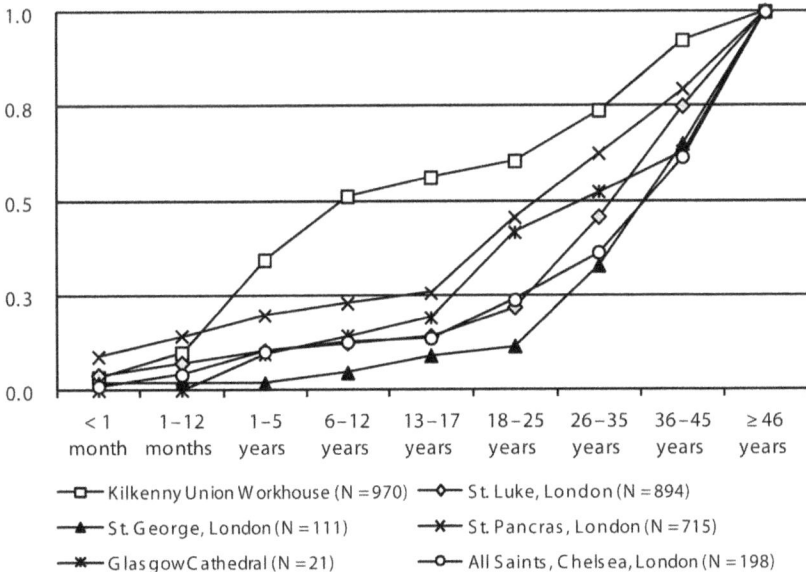

Figure 3.2. Cumulative age-group distribution of the Kilkenny Union Workhouse skeletal population compared to the age-group distribution of contemporaneous nineteenth-century populations from formal cemeteries, illustrating the disproportionally
high prevalence of non-adults in the Kilkenny burials.

the inmates who resided in the Kilkenny workhouse during the height of the famine. As they all died around the same time, it can be concluded that they must have lived around the same time. These types of chronologically defined and contextualized burial grounds are rarely available for bioarchaeological study.

Adult Stature as a Reflection of Socioeconomic Background

The obtained maximum height of an individual is one of the most variable measures in humans; it is influenced by a wide range of factors such as ancestry, environment, secular changes, sex, and social background (Floud, Wachter, and Gregory 1990, 16; Rösing 1988; Wells 1969, 454). The variation in height or stature in a population is therefore also a descriptive characteristic and is a particularly useful parameter in comparative studies. When such data are used to compare contemporaneous populations, they can reveal aspects of socioeconomic standing. In comparative studies based on chronology, it may shed light upon the progression or regression of general population health and living conditions through time.

Several studies have focused on the potential correlation between stature and socioeconomic background. Steckel (1995, 1908) describes stature as "a function of proximate determinants such as diet, disease, and work intensity" and as "a function of access" to adequate and beneficial nutrients. The correlation between height and income (i.e., a more nutritious diet) that we observe in present-day societies was not likely as strong in the mid-nineteenth century. This is because people who were economically better off would not necessarily have had adequate knowledge about how to improve their health (Steckel 1995, 1927). Secular changes in stature are likely the result of a variety of factors, both dependent and independent of each other. Floud, Wachter, and Gregory (1990) recognized four main factors: nutritional status, social and geographical inequalities, urbanization and disease environment, and rising or falling real wages.

Around 1815, Irish recruits in the British Army were between about ½ to 1" (1–2 cm) taller than English soldiers and were slightly shorter than their Scottish counterparts (Floud, Wachter, and Gregory 1990, figure 5.2). Some have attributed this fact to the relatively beneficial nutrition the Irish diet of almost exclusively potatoes and buttermilk provided (Mokyr and Ó Gráda 1994; Ó Gráda 1991). However, as a number of scholars speculate, the relatively taller stature of the Irish might have been the result of other factors. Ireland was predominantly a rural society and did not undergo the same social changes as populations in urban environments in England. During the early nineteenth century, a decrease in stature was recorded among the British urban working classes. This has been explained as a result of a decline in nutrition and welfare status and an increase in social inequality that was evident from the 1820s onward (Floud, Wachter, and Gregory 1990, 216–24). Differences in occupations among rural and urban communities are also likely to have played a role. For instance, a comparative study of the stature of nineteenth-century populations from Bavaria showed that army conscripts from a farming background had an overall taller stature than the average Bavarian (Lantzsch and Schuster 2009, 49).

The estimated stature of the adults in the Kilkenny mass burials was calculated from long bones, using the equations of Trotter and Gleser (1952, 1958) and Sjøvold (1990). The Trotter and Gleser method yielded an estimated mean height of 171 cm (5' 5½") for males and 158 cm (5' 2½") for females. The Sjøvold method yielded similar values; 169 cm (5' 6½") for males and 158 cm (5' 2") for females (table 3.1). Both methods provided very similar estimates of female statures, while the Sjøvold equations yielded shorter stature estimates for male bones. The Sjøvold equations also suggested a wider range of statures for males than the estimated results based on the Trotter and Gleser method. The greatest differences in the results the two methods yielded was in the short stature estimates based on humeri in males, and the least difference was seen in the mean stature of radii in females. Mean stature varied slightly between age groups for both sexes, but no significant differences were observed. It appears as if the younger adults had achieved the same maximum general stature as the older adults (≥46 years old) and that there were no differences in height between the generations.

Stature estimations of various nineteenth-century skeletal populations from Ireland, Britain, and the United States have provided mean heights of between 167 cm (5' 6") and 176 cm (5' 9") for males and 155 cm (5' 1") and 164 cm (5' 5") for females (table 3.2). The stature estimates obtained from the Kilkenny workhouse population fall within this range. This would suggest that the Kilkenny workhouse inmates did not exhibit a shorter stature because of their social and economic background. The mean statures of the Kilkenny population were in fact higher than the mean statures of the Christ Church Spitalfields population in London,

Table 3.1. Two methods of estimating living stature (cm) of male and female adults in the Killkenny workhouse mass burials from long-bone measurements (greatest length)

	Trotter and Gleser (1952, 1958)						Sjøvold (1990)						
	x̄	min.	max.	SD	±	n	n	x̄	min.	max.	SD	±	n
MALE													
Humerus	172.91	159.31	184.60	5.20	4.57	153	153	170.79	148.45	189.93	8.53	4.94	153
Radius	170.47	155.79	187.06	5.24	4.66	145	145	166.80	151.16	184.41	5.56	4.98	145
Ulna	173.51	157.14	185.34	5.37	4.72	151	151	169.14	148.87	183.74	6.63	4.96	151
Femur	171.09	155.55	183.15	5.67	3.94	133	133	169.63	152.00	183.30	6.42	4.52	133
Femur 2	--	--	--	--	--	--	--	168.92	148.48	185.37	7.92	3.85	132
Tibia	170.30	158.28	184.66	5.27	4.00	131	131	169.22	154.22	187.14	6.58	4.11	131
Fibula	168.88	158.83	181.58	5.39	3.86	63	63	165.91	151.30	184.37	7.83	4.06	63
Humerus + radius	171.36	155.79	186.73	5.62	4.31	120	--	--	--	--	--	--	--
Humerus + ulna	171.77	155.62	185.26	5.57	4.37	127	--	--	--	--	--	--	--
Femur + fibula	169.52	158.88	182.26	5.57	3.62	53	--	--	--	--	--	--	--
All	171.40	155.55	183.15	5.41	--	186	186	169.41	148.48	185.37	7.47	--	186
FEMALE													
Humerus	158.64	146.00	174.90	5.58	4.45	136	136	157.16	139.45	180.21	7.89	4.94	136
Radius	158.80	146.41	178.64	6.48	4.24	121	121	158.24	147.74	175.14	5.51	4.98	121
Ulna	159.42	147.43	173.90	5.51	4.30	123	123	158.62	145.61	174.44	6.01	4.96	123
Femur	157.76	146.11	171.43	5.25	3.72	124	124	160.29	147.93	174.89	5.60	4.52	124
Femur 2	--	--	--	--	--	--	--	157.73	143.99	177.00	6.50	3.85	128
Tibia	--	--	--	--	--	--	--	160.68	136.40	180.95	6.70	4.11	110
Fibula	157.96	146.92	175.49	6.30	3.57	45	45	157.04	142.79	179.65	8.13	4.06	45
All	158.22	146.11	178.64	5.59	--	160	164	157.97	143.99	177.00	6.82	--	164

Notes: Femur 2 = bicondylar length of femur. The "All" categories are based on a single estimation for each individual, where the equation most correlated to the femora formulae are chosen.

Table 3.2. Estimated living statures (cm) by sex, nineteenth-century skeletal populations

	Male					Female				
	x̄	min.	max.	SD	n	x̄	min.	max.	SD	n
IRELAND										
Kilkenny Union Workhouse, Kilkenny	171.40	155.55	183.15	5.41	186	158.22	146.11	178.64	5.59	160
Clones Union Workhouse, Clones	169.24	168.54	169.93	0.98	2	160.80	– –	– –	– –	1
Hospital of the Assumption, Thurles	175.60	– –	– –	– –	1	154.60	– –	– –	– –	1
Manorhamilton Union Workhouse, Manorhamilton[1]	174.50	n/a	n/a	n/a	n/a	155.20	n/a	n/a	n/a	n/a
Our Lady's Hospital, Manorhamilton[1]	167.40	n/a	n/a	n/a	n/a	159.00	n/a	n/a	n/a	n/a
St. Anne's Shandon, Cork	170.60	n/a	n/a	n/a	n/a	157.70	n/a	n/a	n/a	n/a
St. Brigid's Hospital, Ballinasloe	169.31	160.70	176.60	5.04	7	155.78	147.40	160.70	6.41	5
St. John the Baptist, Sligo	172.30	n/a	n/a	n/a	n/a	162.30	n/a	n/a	n/a	n/a
BRITAIN										
All Saints, Chelsea Old Church, London	170.30	158.10	179.70	n/a	37	159.60	152.40	169.20	n/a	35
Bow Baptist Church, London	169.70	157.60	182.10	4.90	55	158.30	148.00	166.00	4.10	68
Christ Church Spitalfields, London	170.27	154.62	187.79	6.16	211	157.11	139.81	173.65	6.25	206
Cross Bones, London	168.50	153.00	180.00	n/a	16	158.20	142.00	172.00	n/a	19
New Bunhill Fields Burial Ground, London	168.00	156.00	181.00	n/a	52	161.00	152.00	173.00	n/a	48
St. Benet Sherehog, London	174.10	160.80	183.20	n/a	30	156.40	144.50	164.00	n/a	28
St. George's, Bloomsbury London	172.00	152.00	185.00	n/a	15	160.00	149.00	172.00	n/a	20
St. Mary and St. Michael, London	169.80	159.50	186.40	5.40	99	160.50	151.40	169.50	4.50	62
St. Marylebone Church, London	170.00	154.00	182.00	5.61	76	159.00	145.00	169.00	5.44	62
St. Pancras, London	171.00	150.00	188.00	n/a	168	157.00	143.00	177.00	n/a	138
St. Luke's, London	171.00	149.00	194.00	n/a	295	158.00	139.00	174.00	n/a	238

(continued)

Table 3.2—*Continued*

	Male					Female				
	x̄	min.	max.	SD	n	x̄	min.	max.	SD	n
Sheen's Burial Ground, London	169.00	156.80	181.80	5.70	24	162.40	151.40	176.10	5.90	31
City Bunhill Burial Ground, London	168.00	145.00	177.00	6.20	39	160.00	151.00	172.00	4.90	38
Glasgow Cathedral, Glasgow	181.70	n/a	n/a	n/a	2	157.10	n/a	n/a	n/a	6
St. Martin's, Birmingham	171.90	156.00	185.00	5.59	173	159.10	139.00	170.50	5.65	124
St. Peter's, Barton-upon-Humber	171.00	158.00	185.00	n/a	n/a	159.00	147.00	170.00	n/a	n/a
St. Peter's, Wolverhampton	171.00	161.70	181.30	5.37	30	160.60	150.40	173.00	5.20	25
Tanyard Quaker Burial Ground, Bromyard	172.20	169.89	174.50	3.26	2	160.01	152.72	168.10	6.01	5
Quaker Burial Ground, Kingston-upon-Thames	168.70	154.50	190.00	n/a	n/a	160.30	139.50	174.50	n/a	n/a
UNITED STATES										
Eastern State Hospital, Lexington, Kentucky	173.68	168.09	184.74	6.65	5	163.50	151.48	177.06	9.37	6
Legion of Honor Cemetery, San Francisco	170.97	n/a	n/a	4.60	45	161.36	n/a	n/a	7.90	20
Monroe County Almshouse, Rochester, New York	171.70	n/a	n/a	6.10	94	160.50	n/a	n/a	6.20	64
"Music Hall," Cincinnati, Ohio	172.10	159.30	175.50	n/a	13	157.60	149.30	162.40	n/a	4

[1] Remains from two excavations at this cemetery were analyzed by two osteologists, and the data are not collated.

which was comprised of middle- to upper-class individuals. As Table 3.2 shows, on average, the Irish populations were taller than their English counterparts but shorter than contemporary U.S. populations. The latter are presumed to have been more ethnically and culturally diverse, which could explain their wider range and standard deviation values.

Much of the recorded living statures from nineteenth-century sources derive from military height data (Floud, Wachter, and Gregory 1990, 30–83), and thus these data are biased toward males. In addition, we cannot be sure that these heights were recorded in a consistent way; it is not always clear whether heights were recorded while individuals were wearing shoes or not (Inwood and Roberts 2010, 829). The osteological method of assessing stature is less subjective because individuals of both sexes, from all age groups, and belonging to several social classes can be assessed. However, the social status and chronological period usually cannot be fully determined from archaeological materials, since we often do not know the exact date of a burial and the social background of the interred individual.

Other factors that are not necessarily relating to social standing would also have the influenced the maximum obtained heights of individuals in nineteenth-century populations. Studies of the impact of industrialization on variations in secular change and differences in stature during the Victorian period have observed noticeable changes, particularly during the first half of the nineteenth century, when a negative trend occurred (Alter, Nerin, and Oris 2004; Floud, Wachter, and Gregory 1990, 287–306; Komlos 1998). As mentioned in Chapter 2, the level of industrialization differed significantly in Irish and English societies and is therefore likely to have been a contributing factor to the disparities which were apparent in the average stature of their male populations. Other research has pointed to the correlation between secular changes in mean stature and infant mortality in a given population (Maat 1990). The increased general mortality recorded in Scotland during the 1840s—an expression of the subsistence crisis and famine that also took place there—was, for instance, clearly reflected in a significant decrease in average adult heights among survivors who were children at the time of the crisis, from 173 cm in the period 1847–1850 to 167 cm in the period 1858–1860 (MacLennan 2003, 50). However, the mean stature for both male and females increased in post-famine Ireland. This change has been explained as a result of the considerable decrease in population, which would have led to greater access to resources and an overall increased general standard of living (Young, Relethford, and Crawford 2008). This further accentuates the difficulty with using short stature as an indicator of deprived health and a poor standard of living in nineteenth-century societies.

The Teeth of the Poor: Oral Health Status as a Potential Marker of Socioeconomic Status

Dental disease can greatly affect the general well-being of a person. Decayed teeth are potentially a serious health risk because they can provide the entry point for infections that can have very negative consequences. Periodontal disease and tooth loss may also affect the ability to consume certain foods and could thus restrict the dietary intake of certain nutrients essential for maintaining good health (Geissler and Bates 1984). Oral health is related to diet, personal oral hygiene, and access to dental treatment, all of which were linked to socioeconomic status in nineteenth-century Ireland. No evidence of dental treatment was noted in any of the dentition in the skeletal population from the Kilkenny mass burials. This is not surprising, as surgical dentistry was available only to those with adequate economic means in nineteenth-century Ireland. The only option for the lower classes in Victorian society would have been extraction of decayed and diseased teeth by a tooth-puller who was not necessarily a skilled practitioner (see Richards 1968).

Dental Caries, Abscesses, and Consequential Loss of Teeth

Caries, also known as tooth decay, is one of the most prevalent chronic diseases worldwide and the primary cause of oral pain and tooth loss (Selwitz, Ismail, and Pitts 2007). Caries is a destruction of the enamel, dentine, and cement of the tooth due to the production of bacterial acid in dental plaque (Hillson 1996). Dental plaque, an accumulation of microorganisms on the tooth surface (Hillson 1996), facilitates the metabolism of fermentable carbohydrate products that causes a reduction in localized pH values. This results in the demineralization of dental tissues in the form of diffusion of calcium, phosphate, and carbonate, which eventually might result in a carious cavity (Selwitz, Ismail, and Pitts 2007). However, the demineralization process is constrained by the saliva, which acts as a buffer by neutralizing oral acidity levels (Featherstone 2000, 888). Caries

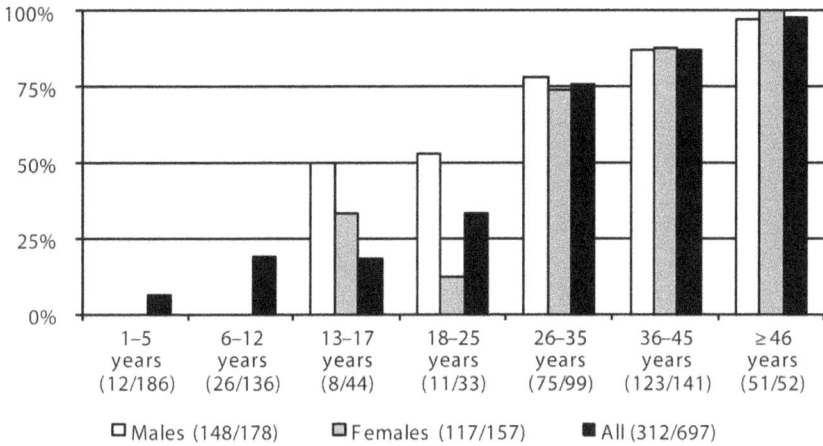

Figure 3.3. Observed frequencies of individuals affected by carious teeth by age groups and sex.

frequencies are related to lifestyle and behavioral patterns, including factors such as poor oral hygiene, a carbohydrate-rich diet, and, in the present day, socioeconomic background (Featherstone 2000, 53).

The analysis recorded the severity and surface location of cavities in the dentition of the Kilkenny skeletons (Hillson 2001). It was evident that dental caries was the most common ailment of the workhouse inmates; it was identified in individuals from all age groups with developed dentition (figure 3.3). It increased in frequency by age and was particularly common in late middle adults and older adults, more than 87 and 98 percent (respectively) of whom were affected by at least one decayed tooth. Overall, 13 percent of non-adults, 80 percent of adults, and 45 percent of all individuals were affected. The increase by age was statistically significant.[1] The same pattern was present in the frequencies of number of teeth affected by caries by total tooth count[2] (figure 3.4) and molar teeth counts only (figure 3.5).[3] However, an anomaly exists between the older child (6–12 years old) and adolescent age groups; 0.74 percent fewer number of teeth were affected in the later age group. This likely relates to the replacement of carious deciduous teeth with unaffected permanent teeth after the age of approximately six years. The adolescent age group had a lower rate of caries in molar teeth than the older child group, although this difference was not statistically significant.[4]

The most destructive carbohydrate foodstuff with regard to the risk of developing caries is refined sugar. Sugar had become increasingly

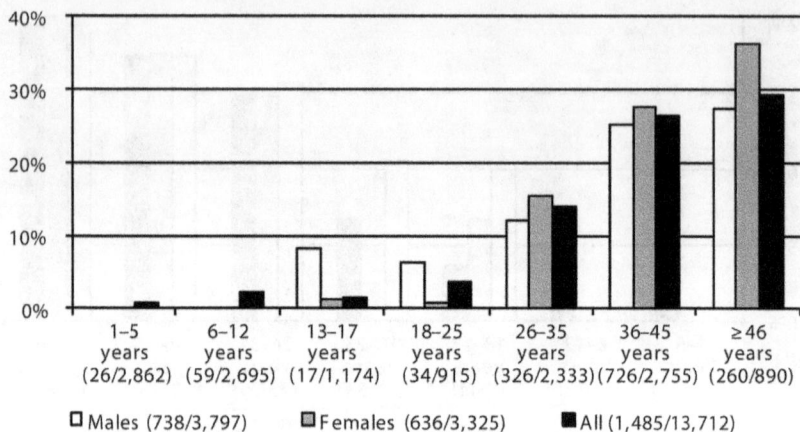

Figure 3.4. Frequency of total teeth affected by caries by age groups and sex.

available in the nineteenth century from British plantations in the West Indies, and the consumption per capita in Great Britain more than quadrupled during the eighteenth century. The price of imported cane sugar fell significantly during the first years of the nineteenth century. After that it fluctuated until it reached an all-time low in the period 1828–1832 of 26–43 shillings per hundredweight (approximately 112 pounds) (Curtin 1990, 178; Reed 1866, 142–67). However, sugar did not constitute a significant commodity on the Irish market compared to the markets in England and

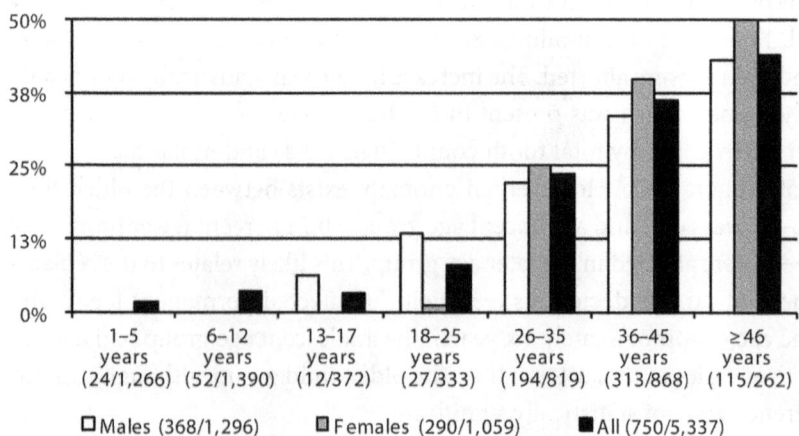

Figure 3.5. Frequency of caries on molar teeth by age groups and sex.

Scotland, and it was mainly used in Ireland for preserving food. Refined sugar was primarily used for making punch (Stanley 1833, 166–67). The poor of Ireland, including the inmates who died in the Kilkenny work-house, are therefore unlikely to have consumed sugar to the same degree as the middle and upper classes. However, a diet consisting almost exclusively of potatoes would not necessarily have been beneficial from an oral health point of view. A major proportion of the carbohydrate in potatoes is starch, which constitutes approximately 17 percent of the vegetable in uncooked weight (Woolfe 1987, 23). Studies have also shown that boiling or frying potatoes causes a reduction in the pH value of dental plaque (Lingström et al. 1989), which hinders the neutralization of natural acidity by saliva. It is, however, unclear whether the influence of starch alone is significantly cariogenic (Lingström et al. 2000). Studies of the dental effects of unprocessed wheat and corn starch have shown that they are not cariogenic when they are uncooked but that various molecular changes occur during the cooking process such as denaturation, gelatinization, and retrogradation (Grenby 1997).

As a marker of potentially differential health between social groups during the nineteenth century, dental caries is an interesting variable to consider. For example, modern population studies have indicated a close correlation between high frequencies of caries in deciduous teeth and low socioeconomic background. A state of chronic malnutrition in childhood may delay the eruption and exfoliation of the teeth, meaning that temporary teeth are exposed for a longer time and are therefore at a greater risk of developing caries (Alvarez and Navia 1989). Of the individuals in the young child age category (1–5 years old) in the Kilkenny workhouse population, 6 percent (12/185) had caries in their deciduous teeth, while the older child category exhibited a significantly higher rate of 19 percent (26/136).[5] No significant difference was noted, however, in the frequency of caries by total tooth count. Young children displayed a caries frequency of 1 percent (26/2,862) and older children a rate of 2 percent (59/2,695).[6] The frequency of caries in molar teeth only was 2 percent (24/1,266) in the young child population and 4 percent (52/1,390) in the older child population, a difference that was not statistically significant.[7] A comparison of the frequency of caries by sex among the adults also failed to give conclusive results. The caries rates in males by individual count ranged from 53 percent in young adults (18–25 years old) to 97 percent in older adults ($\bar{x}$ = 83.91 percent); in females the range was from 13 percent in young adults to 100 percent in older adults ($\bar{x}$ = 75.33 percent). Although males were 1.12 times more likely to have carious teeth than females, there was no statistically significant overall difference between the sexes),[8] except for in the young adult age group.[9]

Because caries generally increase in frequency with age, the sex of the individual can influence access to types of food and hence to the risk of caries, and anatomical and taphonomical factors must be taken into consideration, analogies of caries rates between populations are problematic unless all these factors are taken fully into account (see Wesolowski 2006). Unfortunately, because of inconsistency in how caries frequencies are reported in the published literature, it was not always possible to conduct a valid comparison in caries rates between the Kilkenny workhouse population and contemporaneous populations. However, the available data suggest that the frequency of dental caries in the Kilkenny workhouse population is relatively normal for the period. In addition, caries rates do not appear to be a reflection of socioeconomic standing in this comparison (table 3.3). Similar overall rates were observed in the populations buried at St. Marylebone Church and Christ Church Spitalfields in London; at St. Peter's in Wolverhampton, which includes individuals from lower to upper strata of nineteenth-century society; and at the Catholic Mission of St. Mary and St. Michael in Whitechapel, London, where primarily Irish Catholics were buried.

There were no evident differences in the frequency of periapical lesions of the upper and lower jawbone between the Kilkenny workhouse population and populations comprised of higher social groups (figure 3.6). Compared with contemporaneous adult skeletal populations, the prevalence rates of periapical lesions in the Kilkenny workhouse population are relatively low (see table 3.4) and are similar to frequencies observed in the middle- to upper-class populations buried at St. Pancras; All Saints, Chelsea Old Church; and St. Luke's in London. Periapical lesions include granulomae, dental cysts, and chronic abscesses, which are generally discussed as a collation in paleopathological studies (see Dias and Tayles 1997 for discussion on these). Granulomae were the most common type in the Kilkenny workhouse population; they were present in 0.5 percent (2/393) of the non-adults and 16 percent (61/381) of the adults. These are an accumulation of granulation tissue surrounding the root apices of the teeth and are usually asymptomatic (Hillson 2005, 308). Dental cysts, which are

Table 3.3. Frequency and rate of caries (total number of teeth), nineteenth-century adult skeletal populations

Population	n/total	%
Kilkenny Union Workhouse, Kilkenny	1,383/6,981	19.81
Banbridge Union Workhouse, Banbridge	9/58	15.52
Hospital of the Assumption, Thurles	18/48	37.50
All Saints, Chelsea Old Church, London	184/1,432	12.85
Bow Baptist Church, London	641/2,951	21.72
Christ Church Spitalfields, London	311/1,627	25.58
Cross Bones, London	161/621	25.93
New Bunhill Fields Burial Ground, London	319/2,743	11.63
St. Benet Sherehog, London	189/2,003	9.44
St. George's, Bloomsbury, London	669/1,632	40.99
St. Luke's, Islington, London	1,762/4,883	36.10
St. Mary and St. Michael, London	987/4,890	20.18
St. Marylebone Church, London	510/2,211	23.07
St. Pancras, London	583/5,956	9.79
Sheen's Burial Ground, London	207/1,617	12.80
City Bunhill Burial Ground, London	87/1,065	8.17
St. Martin's, Birmingham	468/4,227	11.07
St. Peter's, Wolverhampton	171/910	18.79
St. Thomas,' Belleville, Ontario	1,434/4,605	31.14

Table 3.4. Frequency and rate of periapical lesions (alveoli count), nineteenth-century adult skeletal populations

Population	n/total	%
Kilkenny Union Workhouse, Kilkenny	156/10,195	1.53
Hospital of the Assumption, Thurles	11/129	8.53
All Saints, Chelsea Old Church, London	41/2,629	1.56
Bow Baptist Church, London	72/5,685	1.27
Cross Bones, London	28/1,216	2.30
New Bunhill Fields Burial Ground, London	88/4,524	1.95
St. Benet Sherehog, London	6/2,617	0.23
St. George's, Bloomsbury, London	46/1,632	2.82
St. Luke's, Islington, London	87/4,883	1.78
St. Mary and St. Michael, London	194/7,400	2.62
St. Marylebone Church, London	141/4,316	3.27
St. Pancras, London	114/8,549	1.33
Sheen's Burial Ground, London	63/3,114	2.02
City Bunhill Burial Ground, London	66/3,178	2.08
St. Martin's, Birmingham	213/7,445	2.86
St. Peter's, Wolverhampton	33/1,091	3.02

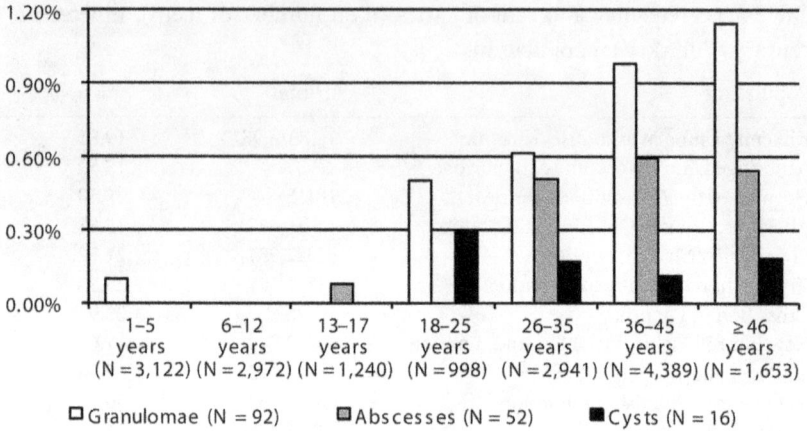

Figure 3.6. Frequency of periapical lesions on the alveoli by age group and type.

commonly a progressive but slow-paced continuation of granuloma, are also usually painless (Reichart and Philipsen 2000, 215–18), and were only identified in sixteen tooth sockets from 3 percent of the adult dentitions.

Chronic abscesses provide the greatest insight into health complications from periapical lesions and thus provide much better information about quality of life. Abscesses occur after an accumulation of pus around the apex of the root eventually breaks through the bone through a fistula and are often caused by progressed granuloma (Hillson 1996, 285). These are potentially felt as a sharp, aching, or throbbing pain that can range from mild to very severe (Burchiel 2002, 279). In the Kilkenny workhouse population, abscesses were noted in the dentition of 0.3 percent of young children and adolescents (1/393), 0 percent of young adults (0/33), 10 percent of early middle adults (26–35 years old) (11/109), 11 percent of late middle adults (18/161), and 14 percent of older adults (9/65). It is clear that dental ailments and pain due to abscesses would have been part of the experience of the older generation of this population in particular.[10] Periapical abscesses were present in 13 percent (25/196) of the dentitions in adult males and 7 percent (13/178) of adult females, but this difference was not statistically significant.[11]

Dental caries and abscesses are the likely causes of the tooth loss observed in the Kilkenny skeletons. While many factors lead to tooth loss, caries is the most common cause today, although additional factors such as progressive periodontal disease, trauma, and considerable tooth wear

Table 3.5. Frequency and rate of male and female adult individuals who lost at least one tooth prior to death, Kilkenny workhouse population

Age group	Male n/total	%	Female n/total	%	All[1] n/total	%
18–25 years	1/17	5.88	5/16	31.25	6/33	18.18
26–35 years	18/42	42.86	35/62	56.45	54/105	51.43
36–45 years	61/87	70.11	54/69	78.26	117/159	73.58
≥ 46 years	35/43	79.07	20/20	100.00	55/64	85.94
>18 years	3/3	100.00	6/6	100.00	10/11	90.91
Total	118/192	61.46	120/173	69.36	242/372	65.05

[1] Includes unsexed individuals.

may also result in a loss of teeth. With the exception of a pathological case relating to probable tuberculosis (see chapter 4), tooth loss was identified only in adult individuals. The frequency by individual counts of dentition with at least one lost tooth ranged from 18 percent in young adults to 86 percent in older adults (table 3.5). This connection between advancing age and tooth loss was confirmed statistically.[12] There was a significant difference in tooth loss frequencies among all age groups but less so between the late middle and older adult age categories.[13] This is likely because the highest risk of tooth loss occurred during late middle adulthood. The only significant difference between males and females was noted in the older adult age category; 80 percent of all males and 100 percent of all females in that age group had lost at least one tooth prior to death.[14] Two late middle adult males had no upper teeth, while six late middle adult to older adult males and five early middle adult to older adult females had lost all their mandibular teeth.

Overall, the available skeletal evidence from the Kilkenny workhouse and other populations suggests that toothache due to dental decay would have been an experience shared equally across the social scales in the nineteenth century. The diet and lifestyle of the Irish poor evidently did have a negative impact on oral health. Poor dental health was experienced across all age groups, increasing significantly with advanced age. The impact tooth loss could have had on the health of the affected individuals should not be underestimated. Other than restricting the type of foods that can be consumed, studies of modern populations have confirmed that edentulous individuals have a higher risk of mortality than those with full or partial sets of teeth. This is due to the higher risk of choking because mastication is inhibited and larger pieces of food are generally swallowed (Basker and Davenport 2002, 15). Poverty and poor oral health might not have been directly related to each other in the mid-nineteenth century, but they contributed to a life of discomfort and significant hardship for those who were at the lower end of the social scale.

Enamel Defects and Hypoplasia: Permanent Markers
of Childhood Stress

Enamel hypoplasias are manifested as linear or pitted bands across the crowns of teeth (figure 3.7). They indicate periods of childhood stress that usually occurred during the first seven years of life. During these periods, the formation of the enamel matrix is interrupted and consequently defects are formed on the tooth surface. Various etiologies are identified as causes of stress, such as fever, starvation, infection, and low birth weight (Lewis and Roberts 1997, 581–82). Studies have been able to link widespread occurrences of enamel hypoplasias in living populations to particular historical events, such as the Chinese "Great Leap Forward" famine of 1959–1961 (Zhou and Corruccini 1998). Based on that finding, it is feasible that many of the child survivors of the Great Famine in Ireland would have displayed these dental defects as permanent reminders of the catastrophe. Enamel hypoplasia in the dentitions of the Kilkenny skeletons was primarily recorded macroscopically under both a natural and artificial light source with the aid of an angular seeker. Hypocalcifications, defects that manifest as opaque white patches in the tooth enamel (Hillson 1996), were omitted from the data analysis because of the difficulties of diagnosis due to postdepositional staining and other factors.

The frequency of enamel hypoplasia in the Kilkenny workhouse population ranged from 10 percent (19/185) in young children to 36 percent (16/45) in adolescent skeletons. The defect was present in 21 percent (78/364) of all adult dentitions; the highest rates were noted in the early middle adult age category (table 3.6). Among these skeletons was an infant skeleton (twelve months or less) that displayed severe enamel hypoplasia of the mandibular incisors and cuspal deformities, so-called mulberry molars, in the maxillary dentition. These lesions may have been the result of a treponemal infection (see below). In adults, for whom the periods of childhood stress would have occurred long before the famine,

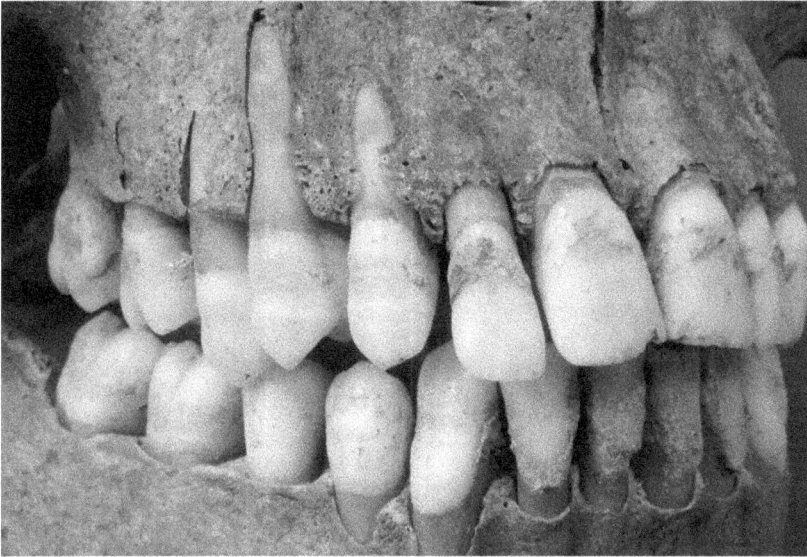

Figure 3.7. Linear enamel hypoplasia visible on the left canine and premolar teeth in the dentition of a thirteen-year-old adolescent (XLIII). Photo by author.

females were slightly more affected than males, although this result is not statistically significant.[15]

It is evident that childhood in pre-famine Ireland involved periods of stress severe enough to leave permanent markers in the dentition of many of the individuals in this population. This is possibly due to previous

Table 3.6. Frequency and rate of individuals displaying enamel hypoplasia in dentition by sex, Kilkenny workhouse population

Age group	Male		Female		All[1]	
	n/total	%	n/total	%	n/total	%
1–12 months	––	––	––	––	1/1	100.00
1–5 years	––	––	––	––	19/185	10.27
6–12 years	––	––	––	––	26/142	18.31
13–17 years	2/4	50.00	0/3	0.00	16/45	35.56
18–25 years	4/17	23.53	4/16	25.00	8/33	24.24
26–35 years	8/42	19.05	18/63	28.57	26/106	24.53
36–45 years	15/83	18.07	14/69	20.29	29/154	18.83
≥ 46 years	8/40	20.00	5/19	26.32	13/60	21.67
>18 years	0/3	0.00	2/5	40.00	2/11	18.18
Total	37/189	19.58	43/175	24.57	140/737	19.00

[1] Includes unsexed individuals.

regional famines, which were common in nineteenth-century Ireland, and disease epidemics such as the cholera that severely affected the population in Kilkenny in 1832 and 1833. It may also reflect the previously mentioned "meal months" (see chapter 2) that would have resulted in annual periods of starvation for many during childhood. It is also evident that the stress the Great Famine imposed did not result in an increased manifestation of enamel hypoplasia in the children who did not survive (Geber 2014). More than likely, these children were too weak to endure long enough for any enamel defects to form in their teeth.

Smoking Habits: Clay Pipe Notches on Teeth

Clay pipes were a common commodity in the nineteenth century, and circular-shaped abrasions of the dental crowns due to habitual smoking are frequently identified traits in dentitions of archaeological skeletons dating to this period. These abrasions would have been clearly visible in the teeth of those who smoked clay pipes. Smoking a pipe was thus a characteristic personal feature for many of these individuals (figure 3.8).

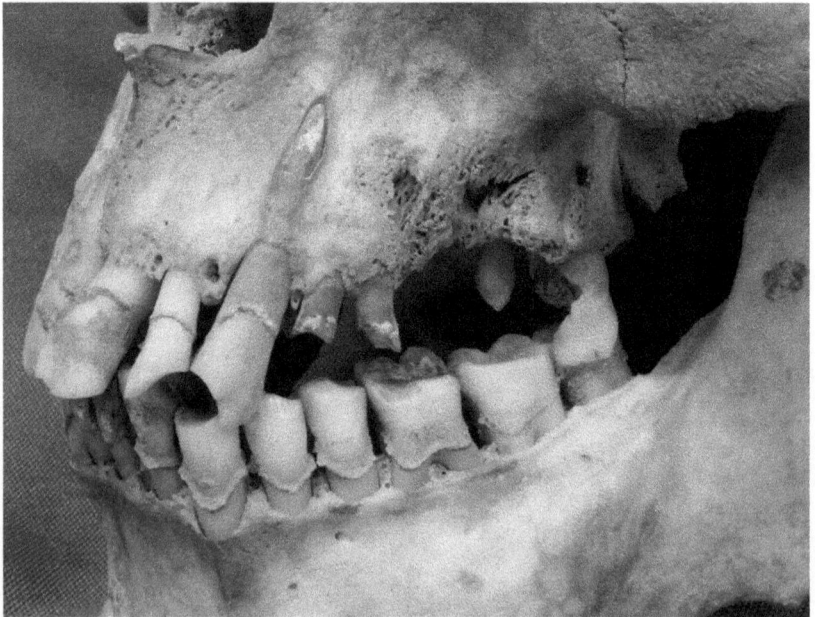

Figure 3.8. Dentition of an early middle adult male (CCLXXXV) displaying evidence of caries, antemortem tooth loss, dental calculus, periodontal disease, and a clay-pipe facet involving the left second incisors and canine teeth. Photo by author.

Table 3.7. Frequency and rate of male and female adult dentition with clay-pipe abrasions, Kilkenny workhouse population

Age group	Males n/total	%	Females n/total	%	All[1] n/total	%
18–25 years	4/17	23.53	0/16	0.00	4/33	12.12
26–35 years	20/38	52.63	11/53	20.75	31/91	34.07
36–45 years	47/73	64.38	23/59	38.98	70/133	52.63
≥ 46 years	28/35	80.00	6/12	50.00	35/48	72.92
>18 years	2/2	100.00	1/2	50.00	3/5	60.00
Total	101/165	61.21	41/142	28.87	143/310	46.13

[1] Includes unsexed skeletons.

In total, clay-pipe facets were identified in 46 percent (143/310) of all adult dentitions. This prevalence is based on dentitions where at least three out of five front teeth (incisors, canines, and premolars) were present for analysis. Additionally, one possible shallow abrasion was noticed on the left mandibular deciduous canine and first molar tooth in the dentition of a nine- to ten-year-old child (XCVI). This case may suggest that some people started smoking clay pipes when they were very young, or perhaps this particular child imitated older family members or other adults of his community by biting on the stem of a clay pipe.

Adult male dentition displayed clay-pipe facets 2.12 times more often than the dentition of females, a difference that was statistically significant.[16] Adult men were evidently the most habitual smokers. There is an increase in the frequency of individuals with abraded teeth by age group in both males and females,[17] irrespective of the degree of abrasion. No young adult females displayed clay-pipe facets, a result that suggests that males started smoking clay pipes at an earlier age than female smokers did (table 3.7). It may also suggest that there was a generational difference among the females regarding smoking habits.

The majority of the abrasion facets (57.00 percent, 293/514) in both males and females were present on teeth from the left side of the mouth. This is likely to reflect right-handedness, as it would make it possible to work and smoke simultaneously, using the right hand for labor and the left hand for holding the clay pipe. This was also evident in cases when continuous abrasion resulted in pulp exposure on some teeth that would have resulted in oral pain. In such instances, it was not uncommon to observe several clay-pipe abrasions of varying depths in the same dentition, indicating that the smoker changed the position of the clay pipe because

Table 3.8. Frequency and rate of male and female adult dentition with clay-pipe abrasions, nineteenth-century skeletal populations

Population	Male		Female		All	
	n/total	%	n/total	%	n/total	%
Kilkenny Union Workhouse, Kilkenny	101/165	61.21	41/142	28.87	143/310	46.13
Bow Baptist Church, London	2/86	2.33	0/?	0.00	2/202	0.99
Cross Bones, London	3/?	n/a	1/?	n/a	4/39	10.26
St. Mary and St. Michael, London	55/139	39.57	3/102	2.94	58/248	23.39
St. Marylebone, London	1/105	0.95	0/86	0.00	1/223	0.45
St. Martin's, Birmingham	?/?	n/a	?/?	n/a	11/302	3.64

of tooth pain. The dentition with the most number of clay-pipe facets present belonged to four males: one early middle adult (CDI), two late middle adults (LXXXV and CCCXXXIII), and an older adult individual (CCLXXXVII), all of whom displayed a minimum of four abrasions with two separate facets on each side of the mouth.

In comparison with contemporaneous skeletal populations, the rate of adult dentition displaying clay-pipe facets appears to be exceptionally high among the adult inmates of the Kilkenny workhouse (table 3.8). The highest rate of the comparative skeletal populations from England was observed in the populations buried at the cemetery of the Catholic Mission of St. Mary and St. Michael in Whitechapel, London, which were individuals primarily from the Irish Catholic community (Walker and Henderson 2010). A more pronounced habit of smoking clay pipes among the immigrant Irish and working-class population in London was also observed in the nineteenth century (Walker and Henderson 2010), and the skeletal evidence suggests that smoking clay pipes was particularly common among lower social classes during the nineteenth century. In Ireland, smoking clay pipes was an integral part of rural folk life in the nineteenth century; this was manifested in the various customs associated with the funerary wake tradition (see chapter 2). Fragments of clay-pipe stems were identified in the backfill of the workhouse mass burials (Doyle

2010), but they are unlikely to relate to any funerary practice as they are very common as inclusions in postmedieval archaeological deposits in general.

Joint Disease and Osteoarthritis

Joint disease is commonly noted in archaeological human skeletons. A majority of the adults in the Kilkenny workhouse population suffered to some degree from a degenerative ailment affecting their joints. Degenerative diseases of the joints are classified as primary (idiopathic) or secondary (e.g., due to trauma, obesity, or infection). Another secondary cause of joint disease that has received considerable attention from paleopathologists is the loading of joints related to repetitive movement. This type of evidence has been widely used to reconstruct activity patterns in past populations (e.g., Larsen 1997, 161–94; Merbs 1983; Radin, Paul, and Rose 1972; Tainter 1980). Yet the most current general consensus is that there is no clear correlation between osteoarthritis and degenerative changes to joints and activity alone, as studies have shown that individuals who are more accustomed to performing certain activities are less prone to develop osteoarthritis than those who are not. At the same time, other factors such as obesity and body mass will influence the degeneration of certain individual joints (Bridges 1994; Jurmain 1999; Knüsel 2000; Knüsel, Göggel, and Lucy 1997; Roberts and Manchester 2005, 143–54; Sandmeier 2000; Waldron and Cox 1989; Weiss 2006).

Osteoarthritis in the Nonspinal Joints

Schwartz (1995, 238) defined osteoarthritis as "a result of interruption of, or interference with normal, joint function and stability, which is brought about primarily by injury to the joint cartilage and the bone beneath the cartilage." The primary skeletal changes noted in osteoarthritis are bone buildup (osteophytes) and contour changes at the joint margins and porosity and pitting of the articular surface and/or polishing of the surfaces due to bone-to-bone contact (eburnation) (Aufderheide and Rodríguez-Martín 1998, 94; Rogers 2000). These changes occur as a response to remodeling of the articular cartilage due to wear and tear of the joint (Hough 2007, 57). However, recent medical research has revealed a more complex etiological background for the disease that involves genetics

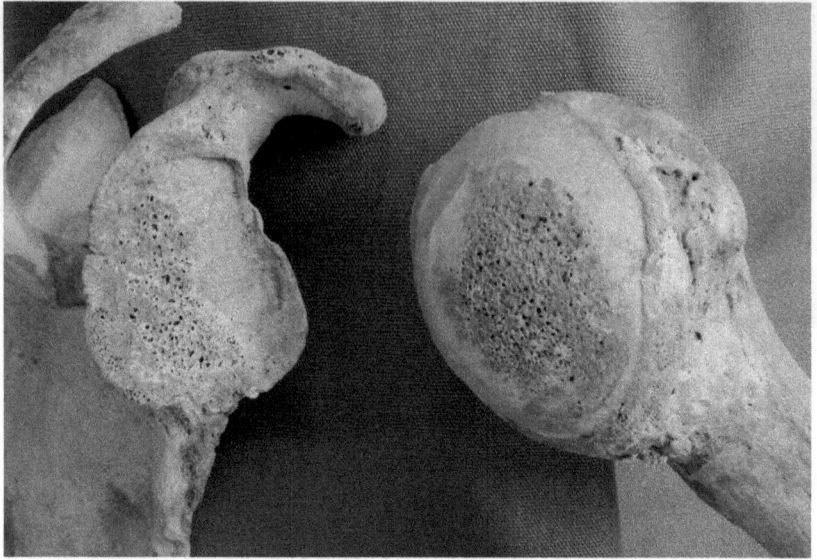

Figure 3.9. Severe degeneration with a large eburnated surface, indicating osteoarthritis of the right shoulder joint in the skeleton of an older adult male (CDXXII). Photo by author.

related to factors such as anatomy and body mass (see Weiss and Jurmain 2007). Eburnation is an indicator of severe osteoarthritis that occurs when extensive narrowing of joint space has led to direct contact between bony surfaces, resulting in a polished and smooth surface that is almost always reciprocal (Rogers and Waldron 1995, 13).

Clinically, osteoarthritis is diagnosed based on observations such as the experience of the patient (e.g., pain, swelling, morning stiffness of joints, and sensitivity) and radiographic confirmations of osteophyte formation, subchondral cysts, and narrowing of joint spaces (Moskowitz et al. 2007, 5). In contrast, a paleopathological diagnosis is generally restricted to the existence of eburnation (figure 3.9) and/or the presence of marginal osteophytosis, pitting of the surface of a joint, or alteration of the contour of a joint (Rogers and Waldron 1995). Because archaeological materials are limited to skeletal hard tissues and the clinical criteria are inapplicable, making direct analogies of the prevalence rate of osteoarthritis between populations from ancient and present-day societies is problematic (see Dieppe et al. 2006, 80; Ortner 2003, 545; Rogers 2000, 166). The genetic background of the disease also poses difficulties in comparative studies of populations. Twin and sibling studies have, for instance, shown that the genetic influence on the occurrence of osteoarthritis can range from 39 percent to 65 percent (Spector et al. 1996). Also, it has been noted that the link between genetic liability and osteoarthritis is greater in females than in males (Kaprio et al. 1996).

In the Kilkenny workhouse population, osteoarthritis was diagnosed in 17 percent (71/414) of all adult skeletons. There was a clear association between the occurrence of osteoarthritis and an advancing age. While only 6 percent (2/35) of all young adults were affected, that proportion increased to 40 percent (26/65) of all older adults. This advancement was confirmed statistically.[18] Overall, males were marginally more frequently affected than females, although this difference was not statistically significant (figure 3.10).[19] There were however some interesting differences between males and females in which joints were affected. Males were twice as prone to be affected by osteoarthritis in the elbow (2.49 percent; 5/201) than females (1.07 percent; 2/187) where the condition was noted in the skeletons of early middle to older adult individuals. Among the females, only one late middle adult (CCCXCIII) and an adult where no precise age

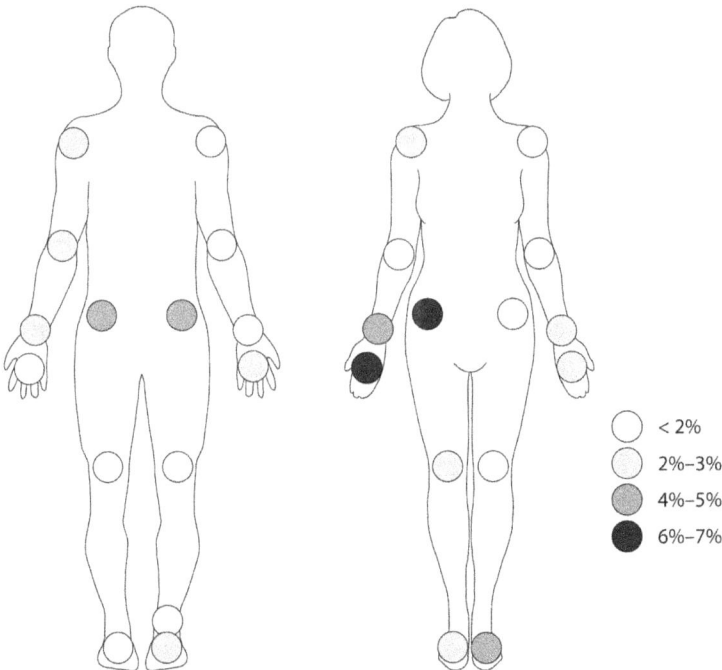

Figure 3.10. Frequencies of extraspinal joints affected by osteoarthritis in adult males (*left*) and females (*right*).

estimation could be given (DCCCLXXXVIII) was diagnosed with osteo-arthritis in the elbows.

Osteoarthritis in the elbow typically occurs as a secondary consequence of occupational and traumatic factors (Doherty and Preston 1989), and the presence of osteoarthritis in the Kilkenny workhouse population is likely to be primarily due to the former. Two individuals did, however, display a clear traumatic etiology: a late middle adult male had developed septic arthritis of the left elbow due to a fracture of the ulnar coronoid process, and an adult female displayed osteoarthritis of the right elbow that had formed secondary to a crush fracture of the joint.

After hips and hands (see below), the wrists were the third most common joints affected by osteoarthritis in both males (3.70 percent; 7/189) and females (4.94 percent; 8/162). Both sexes suffered from the condition at relatively equal prevalence rates, although slightly more females than males were affected in the middle adult age categories and more males than females were affected in the older adult age category. A notable observation in both sexes is a higher rate of osteoarthritis in the wrists of early middle adults (4.17 percent; 4/96) than in the wrists of late middle adults (2.03 percent; 3/148), although this difference was not statistically significant.[20] This trend has also been noted in studies of osteoarthritis in the wrists of living populations (e.g., Bagge et al. 1991). The hands were the joints most commonly affected by osteoarthritis in the upper limbs; 5 percent (17/326) of all adults were affected. Females were more than twice as likely to be affected (6.92 percent; 11/159) than males (3.01 percent; 5/166). However, this difference was statistically significant only in the right hand of older adult individuals.[21]

The hip joints displayed the highest frequencies of osteoarthritis in both males and females; 7 percent (27/377) of all adults were affected. In modern populations, osteoarthritis of the hip is among the most common joint abnormality in middle-aged and elderly individuals (Murray 1965, 810), and this finding is also reflected in the Kilkenny workhouse population. The condition was first identified in late middle adult male individuals and in early middle adult females. In the older adult age categories, there was a significant increase of occurrence of osteoarthritis of the hip joints; 25 percent (10/44) of all males and 25 percent (5/20) of all females were affected, compared to only 3 percent (5/163) in the previous age category. No statistical significance among males and females was noted in the rate of osteoarthritis in the hip.[22] Females, however, displayed a bias

Table 3.9. Frequency and rate of osteoarthritis of the knee (joint count), nine-teenth-century skeletal populations

Population	n/total	%
Kilkenny Union Workhouse, Kilkenny	12/671	1.79
Bow Baptist Church, London	2/387	0.52
Christ Church Spitalfields, London	22/480	4.58
St. Mary and St. Michael, London	3/463	0.65
St. Marylebone Church, London	2/273	0.73
St. Pancras, London	n/a	6.40
Sheen's Burial Ground, London	1/241	0.41
St. Martin's, Birmingham	27/591	4.57
St. Peter's, Wolverhampton	1/82	1.22

toward the right hip when tested in a McNemar test.[23] This was the only case in the appendicular skeleton when a statistically significant differ-ence was noted between left and right sides.

The only cases of osteoarthritis in young adult individuals were noted in the knee joints of one male (CCXXIV) and one female (CLXXVIII) skeleton. In total, 3 percent (5/181) of all adult males and 4 percent (7/170) of all adult females were affected, and there was no significant difference in rates between the sexes.[24] Several studies of present-day populations have identified a correlation between high body mass and osteoarthritis of the knee (e.g., Ambrose et al. 2010; Coggon et al. 2001; Davis et al. 1989; Manek et al. 2003); this pathological marker is therefore an interest-ing variable for interpopulation analogies in paleopathological studies. The rate noted in contemporaneous populations varies, and the Kilkenny workhouse population displays a middle value in comparison (table 3.9). The highest prevalence rates are present in higher-status burial grounds, such as Christ Church Spitalfields in London and the Church of St. Martin in the Bull Ring in Birmingham. It is possible that this reflects a greater proportion of individuals with a heavier and larger build in those populations.

Degenerative Joint Diseases of the Spine

Degenerative diseases of the various joints and facets of the vertebral col-umn are common pathological changes in archaeological skeletons. These are usually attributed to normal wear and tear of the joint facets and sur-faces and are thus more frequently noted in individuals of advanced age.

This was the case in the Kilkenny workhouse population. One of these pathological markers was eburnation of the Luschka's joints of the cervical vertebrae, the small joint surfaces of the uncal processes that connect the vertebrae. This was identified in thirty-five individuals. The observed osteoarthritis in these joints suggests that the affected individuals probably suffered from chronic pain in the neck. Degeneration of this joint is rarely discussed in paleopathological literature, although neck pain is a common ailment in people today and most likely was common in the past as well.

Eburnated facets in the Luschka's joints were more commonly identified in males than in females, although the difference was not statistically significant.[25] The highest prevalence was found between the fourth and fifth vertebrae in males and between the fifth and sixth in females. Sager identified the same distribution of what he called *arthosis uncovertebralis* in Danish postmortems conducted in 1963–1965, but he did not make a distinction between eburnation and other degenerative conditions such as marginal osteophytosis (Sager 1969, 91–94). Chronic neck pain, as indicated by eburnation of the Luschka's joints, appears to have been primarily initiated in early middle adulthood in both males and females and increased with advanced age,[26] a further indication of the degenerative background of this pathological condition (see table 3.10).

Clinically, the most common spinal joint disease is vertebral osteophytosis, which is characterized by marginal bone proliferation or osteophytosis of the vertebral bodies primarily seen in the mid- and lower cervical, upper thoracic, and the lower lumbar vertebrae. In severe cases, the osteophytes fuse with an adjacent vertebra and result in a so-called ankylosis. Herniation of the intervertebral disc at the perimeter of the vertebral body is often seen in association with this condition, although it is not visible skeletally (Aufderheide and Rodríguez-Martín 1998, 96; Rogers 2000; Schwartz 1995, 239–40). In the Kilkenny workhouse population, the condition was present in early middle to older adult individuals only (see table 3.10; figure 3.11), and a clear progression in prevalence with advancing age was confirmed statistically.[27] Overall, males (53.33 percent; 104/195) were slightly more affected than females (46.96 percent; 85/181), although the latter displayed a slightly higher prevalence rate of vertebral osteophytosis in middle adult age categories. However, none of these frequency differences between the sexes were statistically significant. The severity of bone buildup (Snodgrass 2004) increased with advancing age for

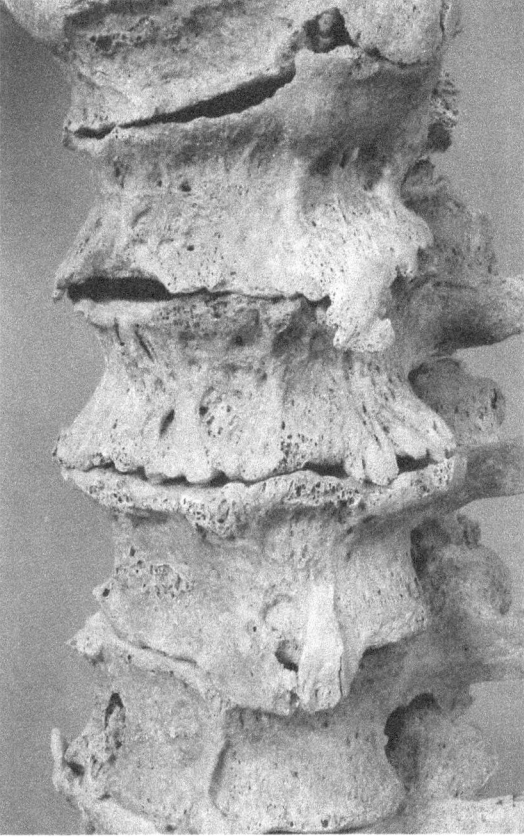

Figure 3.11. Vertebral osteophytosis with marginal lipping of the lumbar vertebrae in the skeleton of an older adult male (XXVI). Photo by author.

both sexes. Males displayed a statistically significantly higher proportion of severe lesions in the thoracic[28] and lumbar vertebrae[29] than females, while no significant difference was noticed in the cervical vertebrae (table 3.11). The standard deviation values also indicated a greater variation in lesion severity in males than in females. Although the overall prevalence between the sexes was not significantly different, the higher frequency of more severe lesions in the thoracolumbar spine of males may again suggest differential labor practices between the sexes. Whether this would have resulted in more back pain ailments for the males is less certain. Vertebral osteophytosis can be asymptomatic, and care must therefore always be taken when interpreting the presence of the condition in archaeological populations (Arcini 1999, 86–87). It is present today in between 60 percent and 80 percent of individuals over the age of fifty years, and is generally considered a normal and expected variation.

Table 3.10. Frequency and rate of spinal degenerative joint diseases in adult skeletons by sex and age group, Kilkenny workhouse population

	Uncal eburnation		Vertebral osteophytosis		Spinal osteoarthritis	
	n/total	%	n/total	%	n/total	%
MALE						
18–25 years	0/17	0.00	0/17	0.00	3/17	17.65
26–35 years	1/42	2.38	10/43	23.26	11/43	25.58
36–45 years	9/77	11.69	55/87	63.22	38/86	44.19
≥ 46 years	11/42	26.19	38/44	86.36	24/44	54.55
Total[1]	21/180	11.67	104/195	53.33	77/193	39.90
FEMALE						
18–25 years	0/16	0.00	0/16	0.00	2/16	12.50
26–35 years	5/63	7.94	17/67	25.37	13/70	18.57
36–45 years	6/67	8.96	50/73	68.49	27/73	36.99
≥ 46 years	2/18	11.11	16/20	80.00	15/20	75.00
Total[1]	13/168	7.74	85/181	46.96	59/185	31.89
ALL						
18–25 years	0/33	0.00	0/33	--	5/33	15.15
26–35 years	6/105	5.71	27/110	24.55	24/113	21.24
36–45 years	15/145	10.34	106/162	65.43	65/161	40.37
≥ 46 years	14/61	22.95	55/65	84.62	40/65	61.54
Total[1]	35/351	9.97	188/370	50.81	137/382	35.86

[1] The "Total" category includes generically aged adults (>18 years).

A total of 137 individuals also exhibited generalized osteoarthritis of the spine, which involves the apophyseal joint facets that articulate with adjacent vertebrae. As with other cases of joint disease in this population, the prevalence rate of osteoarthritis in the spine increased significantly with age;[30] 15 percent (5/33) of all young adults and 62 percent (40/65) of all older adults were affected (see table 3.10). Males displayed higher prevalence rates than females overall and in all age groups, with the exception of the older adult age category, in which 75 percent (15/20) of all females and 55 percent (24/44) of all males were affected. Males were marginally more affected in the cervical and thoracic spine than females, while the opposite was true for lumbar vertebrae. None of these differences, however, proved to be significant when tested statistically (table 3.12). Both sexes displayed higher prevalence rates in the thoracic segment than in the cervical and lumbar vertebrae. The highest prevalence

Table 3.11. Mean values of severity scores[1] of vertebral osteophytosis by spinal segment in male and female adults, Kilkenny workhouse population

	Male			Female			All[2]		
	x̄	SD	n	x̄	SD	n	x̄	SD	n
18–25 YEARS									
Cervical	0.00	--	14	0.00	--	14	0.00	--	28
Thoracic	0.00	--	17	0.00	--	16	0.00	--	33
Lumbar	0.00	--	16	0.00	--	15	0.00	--	31
26–35 YEARS									
Cervical	0.06	0.22	34	0.13	0.41	48	0.10	0.34	82
Thoracic	0.05	0.22	30	0.02	0.07	44	0.03	0.15	74
Lumbar	0.13	0.40	35	0.23	0.46	49	0.19	0.44	84
36–45 YEARS									
Cervical	0.24	0.36	59	0.25	0.33	55	0.25	0.34	114
Thoracic	0.28	0.36	46	0.11	0.17	54	0.19	0.28	100
Lumbar	0.65	0.80	59	0.31	0.46	55	0.49	0.67	114
≥ 46 YEARS									
Cervical	0.62	0.69	35	0.55	0.53	11	0.62	0.65	47
Thoracic	0.55	0.46	19	0.13	0.15	9	0.42	0.43	28
Lumbar	1.08	0.86	23	0.70	0.69	12	0.95	0.82	35
TOTALS[3]									
Cervical	0.27	0.48	142	0.21	0.39	131	0.24	0.44	275
Thoracic	0.22	0.37	112	0.07	0.13	123	0.14	0.28	235
Lumbar	0.51	0.76	133	0.28	0.48	131	0.40	0.65	264

[1] See text for definitions.
[2] Includes unsexed adults.
[3] Includes generically aged adults (>18 years).

rates in all segments were identified in older adult females, for whom 45 percent (9/20) of all cervical, 63 percent (12/19) of all thoracic, and 32 percent (6/19) of all lumbar segments were affected. Spinal osteoarthritis is more likely to have been an experienced ailment than vertebral osteophytosis in this population. Even though the differences in rates between the sexes could not be confirmed statistically, a considerably higher proportion of females in the older adult age category is likely to reflect the known greater risks of acquiring osteoarthritis after menopause (Issa and Sharma 2005), a fact that highlights the biological risk factor for the development of this condition. However, this trend was not visible in the osteoarthritis in the joints of the appendicular elements (see above).

Table 3.12. Frequency and rate of osteoarthritis in the apophyseal joints of the vertebral column (individual count) by spinal segment in male and female adults, Kilkenny workhouse population

	Male		Female		χ^2	df	p
	n/total	%	n/total	%			
Cervical	32/182	17.58	29/174	16.67	.053	1	.819
Thoracic	59/187	31.55	42/171	24.56	2.154	1	.142
Lumbar	16/175	9.14	23/166	13.86	1.868	1	.172
Any	77/193	39.90	59/185	31.89	2.627	1	.105

A Possible Case of Rheumatoid Arthritis

The skeleton of a late middle adult female (CCCXCIII) displayed pathological changes consistent with a possible diagnosis of rheumatoid arthritis. This erosive arthropathy is a relatively rare condition that mainly affects the metacarpophalangeal and proximal interphalangeal joints of the hands but is sometimes also noted in the joints of the wrists, elbows, shoulders, ankles, and cervical vertebrae. While the articular surfaces typically display eroded irregular pitted features, the affected bones are also often porotic (Goldring and Polisson 1998, 622–26; Rogers et al. 1987, 192). The conditions associated with long-standing rheumatoid arthritis include osteoporosis, periodontal disease, and tooth loss (Kennedy et al. 1975; de Pablo et al. 2008).

The skeleton in question was fragile and very poorly preserved. It displayed considerable erosive lesions of the synovial joints of the right elbow (figure 3.12a), the phalangeal joints of both hands, a proximal phalanx of the right foot (figure 3.12b), the tarsal bones of the right foot (figure 3.12c–d), the right calcaneus, and the second and fifth metatarsals of the right foot. The skeleton was also severely affected by probable osteoporosis, which was noted in all the major long bones and in the spine. The disease had caused a forward anterior collapse of the thoracic spine, and a so-called codfish vertebra was observed in the eight thoracic vertebrae.[31] She had lost at least eighteen of her teeth in life, and she also suffered from considerable periodontal disease. The only tooth present with her skeleton was affected by a carious cavity of the distal surface of the root. Other pathological changes noted were chronic maxillary sinusitis, considerable degeneration of the temporomandibular joints, degenerative joint disease

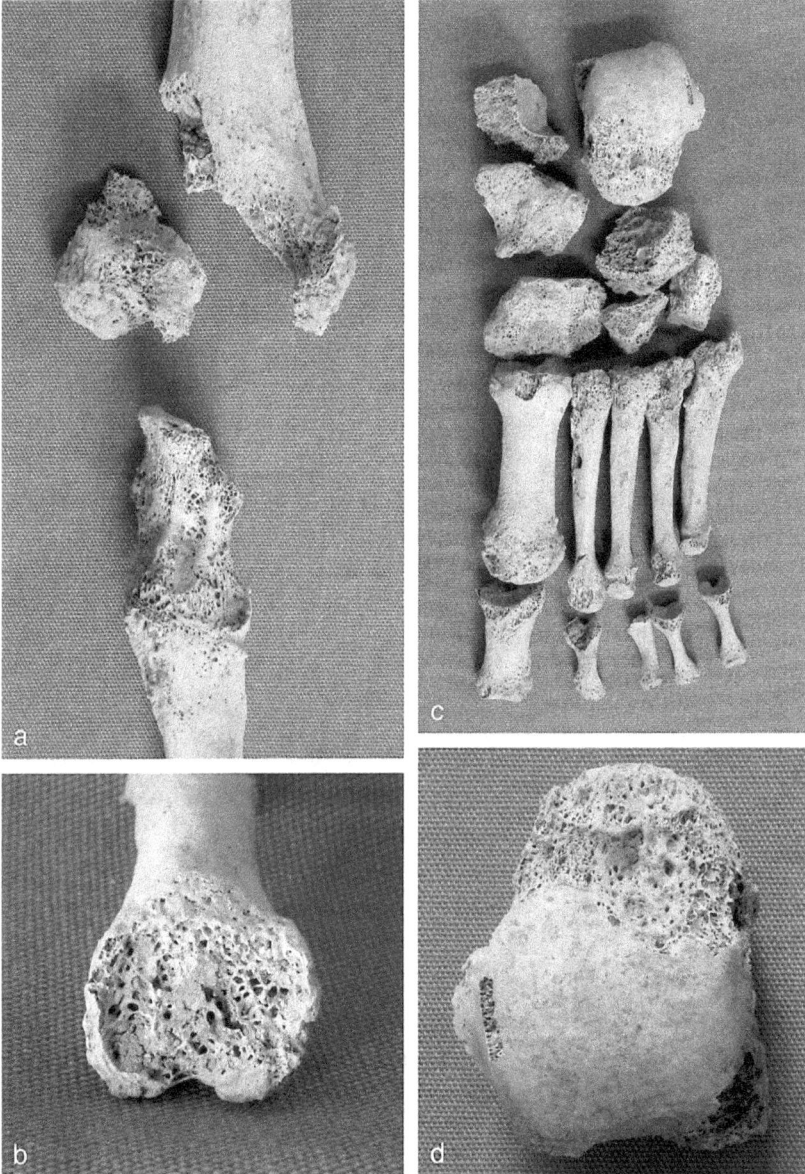

Figure 3.12. Considerable arthritic lesions, possibly due to rheumatoid arthritis, in a late middle adult female skeleton (CCCXCIII): (a) right elbow joint; (b) proximal foot phalanx; (c) joints of right foot; (d) left talus. Photo by author.

and osteoarthritis of the shoulders and spine, and new bone formation on the visceral surface of two right ribs, indicating a pulmonary infection (see below).

Rheumatoid arthritis can be a very debilitating condition (see Kobelt 2009), and the presence of this case in the context of the workhouse as an institution for the "deserving poor" makes it interesting. This unfortunate individual is likely to have been classified as not able-bodied and possibly qualified as a recipient of indoor relief on the basis of her health. Being poor and having a physical disability while suffering from malnutrition and disease is an aspect of the human experience of the Great Hunger that is worth reflecting upon. The workhouses were often the only place the poorer classes could obtain medical care, both before, during, and after the famine. Whether a physical ailment was a strong enough reason for granting indoor relief would ultimately have been a decision for the Board of Guardians, which also had to consider the financial and economic challenges of providing indoor relief for thousands of people during an escalating crisis.

Diffuse Idiopathic Skeletal Hyperostosis

Five males displayed skeletal lesions consistent with or suggestive of diffuse idiopathic skeletal hyperostosis (DISH): three late middle adults (CC, CCCXVI, and DCCLXXXVIII) and two older adults (CDLXVII and DCVIII). This condition is usually characterized skeletally by massive right anterolateral vertical osteophytes on the bodies of the thoracic vertebrae, which are commonly fused into a "candle-wax" appearance (figure 3.13). The condition might be asymptomatic, but consequences such as a marked deficit in joint function, spinal rigidity, decreased mobility, and back pain are reported (Cammisa et al. 1998; Ortner 2003, 559; Resnick et al. 1976). The location of the osteophytes to the right of the vertebral bodies is believed to be due to the pulsations of the descending aorta, which inhibits their development on the left side. Other common skeletal features are enthesophytic bony projections at the sites of tendon and ligament attachment (Resnick, Shaul, and Robins 1976; Rogers and Waldron 1995, 47–54; Rogers et al. 1987, 186–88).

The condition is currently of unclear etiology. Some evidence has suggested that abnormal metabolism of Vitamin A might be a factor that causes DISH (Malone, Carisco, and Baldwin 1999, 600). It is twice as

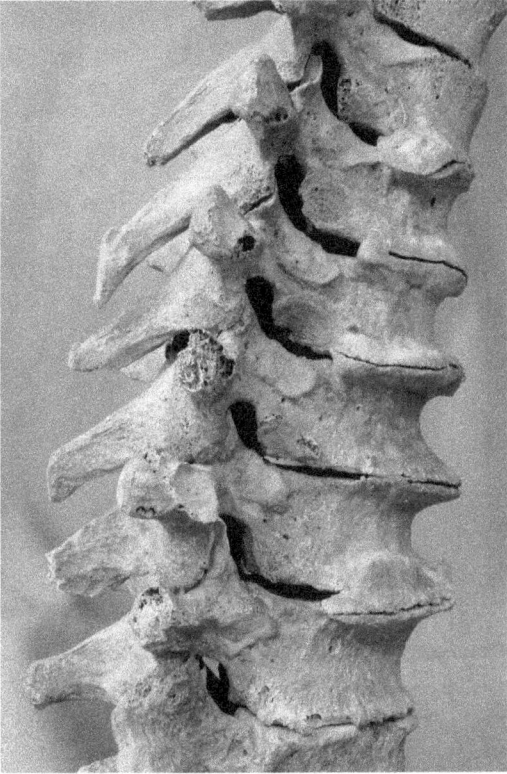

Figure 3.13. Vertical osteophytes that produce the so-called candle-wax appearance indicative of DISH along the right aspect of the lower thoracic vertebral bodies in the spine of a late middle adult male (DCCLXXXVIII). Photo by author.

common in males as in females and is more prevalent with increasing age. The occurrence of DISH has often been discussed in the bioarchaeological literature as an indirect indication of an affluent lifestyle, as it has been found to be frequent in the skeletons of high-status individuals (Giuffra et al. 2010; Jankauskas 2003; Verlaan, Öner, and Maat 2007). Compared to other nineteenth-century skeletal populations, individuals in high-status burial grounds such as those at All Saints, Christ Church Spitalfields, and St. George's in London exhibited higher prevalence rates of DISH (table 3.13). The reason for this might be the possible influence of diabetes and obesity on the occurrence of the condition; this has been discussed in the clinical literature (see Coaccioli et al. 2000; Kiss, Szilágyi Paksy, and Poór 2002; el Miedany et al. 2000). Based on that supposition, the occurrence of DISH in the Kilkenny workhouse skeletons is interesting.

Although the Kilkenny workhouse population exhibits a relatively low prevalence of DISH, the fact that it is present at all distinguishes it from the workhouse population of the Cross Bones burial ground in London.

Table 3.13. Frequency and rate of DISH, nineteenth-century adult skeletal populations

Population	n/total	%
Kilkenny Union Workhouse, Kilkenny	5/355	1.41
All Saints, Chelsea Old Church, London	10/165	6.06
Bow Baptist Church, London	6/416	1.44
Christ Church Spitalfields, London	56/968	5.79
Cross Bones, London	0/35	0.00
New Bunhill Fields Burial Ground, London	3/157	1.91
St. Benet Sherehog, London	2/174	1.15
St. George's, London	3/72	4.17
St. Luke's, Islington, London	5/219	2.28
St. Mary and St. Michael, London	2/705	0.28
St. Marylebone, London	6/223	2.69
St. Pancras, London	6/715	0.84
City Bunhill Burial Ground, London	3/117	2.56
Sheen's Burial Ground, London	4/166	2.41
St. Martin's, Birmingham	8/331	2.42
St. Peter's, Wolverhampton	1/47	2.13

If obesity is accepted as one of the causes of the disease in the Kilkenny cases, its presence might indicate that some individuals had been of better economic standing earlier in their lives but were forced into hardship as the famine crisis escalated. However, it seems more feasible that the etiological background of DISH is too varied and complex to be used as a marker of social status in archaeological skeletons.

Syphilis: A Bioarchaeological Reflection of Social Stigma

Syphilis was a particularly feared and common disease in Europe and North America during the nineteenth century. It was associated with much social stigma and embarrassment (Parascandola 2008). It could eventually cause severe physical ailments and mental disorders that would have made it difficult for a sufferer to conceal their affliction from the wider community. Syphilis is a chronic infectious disease caused by spirochetes microorganisms of the *Treponema pallidum* bacteria. It is primarily a sexually transmitted disease; the risk of infection during sexual contact is 30 percent (Woods 2005, 247). Males are more commonly affected, and they often display more severe lesions than females (Csonka and Oates 1990, 232). The disease develops slowly and in approximately 20 percent of all untreated cases may persist for several decades before it results in death (Gjestland 1955). Throughout much of the nineteenth century, mercury continued to be the preferred method of treatment (Parascandola 2008, 29; Quétel 1990, 116–20). It was generally believed that mercury was able to force the "poison" of the disease out of the patient through bodily fluids because the application of mercury caused profuse sweating and the production of copious amounts of saliva. These consequences of the treatment eventually came to be misunderstood as symptoms of the disease itself. Further, and much more serious, consequences of the mercury treatment included gum and palate ulcerations, tooth loss, skeletal deterioration, and gastrointestinal disturbances (Brandt 1993, 565–67).

The course of acquired syphilis follows a particular pattern of stages with different characteristics. The early stage of the disease follows about twenty-five days after the initial infection through sexual intercourse when skin lesions or chancres appear on the genitalia. A secondary stage begins at usually around six to twelve weeks after the initial infection when a generalized spread and multiplication of the *T. pallidum* bacteria results in a widespread occurrence of various skin lesions and rashes throughout the body. This stage also includes symptoms such as fever; headache; malaise; pain in the muscles, joints, and bones; and a sore throat. A latent stage then follows that can last for several years and even up to a decade after the initial infection. Eventually approximately 40 percent of affected individuals will enter the tertiary stage of the disease.

This tertiary stage is characterized by gumma growth lesions of inflammatory necrosis and fibrous scarring. Tertiary syphilis can affect any organ, and it is during this stage that skeletal tissues are involved. This typically involves significant formation of new bone layers (periostitis) on the long bones, especially the tibiae—often referred to as "sabre shins"—and fibulae. This condition is often painful and usually worsens at night (Csonka and Oates 1990, 243). Joint involvement is sometimes also seen, most commonly observed in the knees. Gumma lesions due to necrosis and destroyed bone tissue can also be noted, as can severe periosteal lesions. Lesions also occur on the skull, where they are usually present on the frontal bone. These cranial lesions can thereafter form severe and destructive irregular lesions that result in thickened and sclerotic bone and are collectively known as caries sicca. These are pathognomonic of the disease. Facial bones can also be affected, and the nasal structures are often destroyed (Hackett 1975; Rogers and Waldron 1989, 618–23).

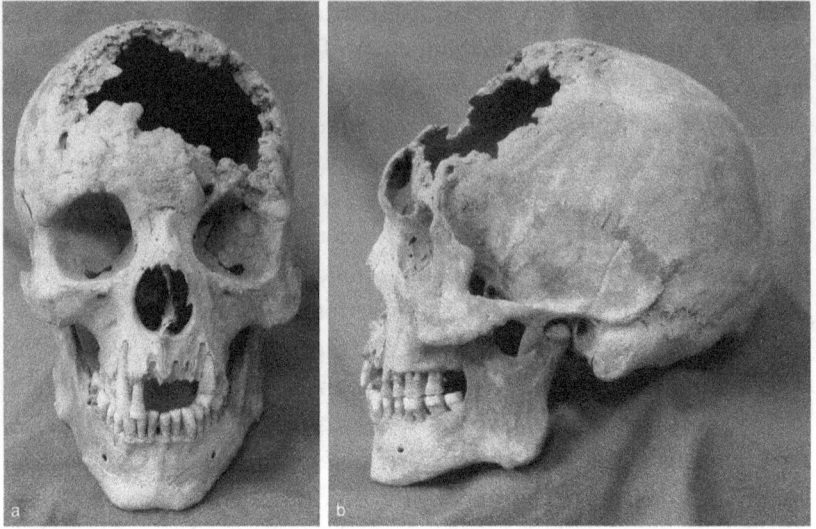

Figure 3.14. Skull of a late middle adult male (DCXI) displaying a severe case of caries sicca due to syphilis: (a) anterior view; (b) left lateral view. Photo by author.

A case of the most extreme manifestation of tertiary syphilis was diagnosed in one of the male skeletons from the Kilkenny mass burials. This was a late middle adult (DCXI) who displayed a remarkably severe caries sicca lesion that covered the entire forehead, involving the squama of the frontal bone and the forward portions of the left parietal bone (figure 3.14). Nodular cavitations were present around the margins of an exceptionally large open cavity that covered 90 percent of the entire area affected by gummata. The frontal gummata extended into the left eye socket, deformations of the nasal margins were observed, and a possible complete destruction of the ethmoid and inferior nasal conchae in the nasal cavity was also noted. Likely related postcranial lesions included semi-sclerotic patches of striated dense periosteal new bone on the forward anterior surface of the lower portion of the right femur and a complex periosteal reaction of the proximal diaphysis of the same bone, which exhibited osteitis and lobulated and speculated lesions on the dorsal surface. Considerable bilateral new bone formation was present on the entire shafts of the tibiae, where it was most severely manifested on the right bone. The severity of his tertiary lesions would suggest that he had suffered the consequences of syphilis for many years, possibly even decades, before his death.

Two other individuals interred in the workhouse mass burials displayed dental deformities indicative of possible congenital syphilis. This form of the disease originates when a fetus becomes infected from its mother through transplacental transmission or occasionally during birth by contact with an infected lesion. In utero infection can occur from nine to ten weeks after gestation and throughout pregnancy and occurs more frequently during the pre-latent stages of the disease. Late-term stillbirth occurs in 30 percent–40 percent of all cases; for the neonates who survive, about one-third show clear signs of infection. In the majority of cases these consist of various skin lesions that are most severely manifested in the palms and soles of the hands and feet (Csonka and Oates 1990, 258–65; Woods 2005). Further deformities are noted in the dentition, and this constitutes the diagnostic feature generally studied in paleopathology. The defects include Hutchinson's incisors, which are peg-shaped and notched, and mulberry and Moon's molars, or crown and cusp deformities of the first molars in the permanent dentition. In deciduous teeth, enamel malformation due to a prenatal syphilitic infection will be noted in the second molars, which often display characteristic hypoplasia at the base of the cusps. Narrowing of the root just below the cementoenamel junction of the deciduous first incisors is another deformity that has been ascribed to congenital syphilis (Hillson, Gribson, and Bond 1998).

The youngest individual with possible congenital syphilis from the Kilkenny burials was an infant aged between eighteen and twenty-four months at the time of its death (DXLI) whose skeleton was poorly preserved but virtually complete. Severe hypoplastic defects were noted on the second deciduous molars and on the first maxillary molars from the unerupted permanent dentition. Hutchinson's incisors were also observed on the first and second unerupted permanent maxillary incisor teeth. This skeleton also displayed proliferated layers of new bone of the femora and tibiae and forward bowing of the legs, although these lesions seem more likely to be scorbutic and/or rachitic rather than syphilitic in origin. The mortality rate for infants born with syphilis is high, and it is likely that the disease influenced the premature death of this child. Other than the characteristic skin lesions, the infant might have suffered from rhinitis, difficulties with feeding, and pseudoparalysis; these are other common symptoms of the disease for this particular age group (Tedberg and Hodgman 1973).

The second case of congenital syphilis was diagnosed in the skeleton of a young adult female (CDXCV). This woman displayed characteristic mulberry molar deformities of the first molar teeth and severe linear enamel hypoplasia of all the front teeth. Notches were also present on the occlusal surfaces of the maxillary incisors, although these may be extra-masticatory in origin. A small blunt osteolytic crater of about 6×6 mm was also noted on the surface of the right half of the forehead portion of the frontal bone and is tentatively diagnosed as a healed gumma lesion. She might also have had characteristic facial deformities, such as a bull-dog jaw, a flat face, and a saddle-nose feature; these are common features among those who survive congenital syphilis as small children (Csonka and Oates 1990, 258–65). However, these features could not be confirmed because of bone fragmentation. She is unlikely to have died as a result of the condition, but it might have caused her to suffer a multifocal pain in addition to the stress she must have endured as a consequence of the fam-ine (Rauh et al. 1990). Additional symptoms she may have suffered from include impaired vision and hearing and neurological problems that may have resulted in some mental deterioration (Csonka and Oates 1990, 262).

As skeletal manifestations of acquired syphilis are noted only during the tertiary stage in adults and with congenital syphilis in the children of affected mothers, the cases from Kilkenny Union Workhouse are probably a considerable underrepresentation of the prevalence of the disease in this population. It has been suggested that venereal syphilis is underestimated by as much as 90 percent in the bioarchaeological record (Roberts and Manchester 2005, 210), and based on that assumption there might be an additional twenty-five to thirty individuals in the workhouse population who suffered from syphilis but did not display any skeletal indications of the disease. The understanding that syphilis is a sexually transmitted disease dates to the eighteenth century (Csonka and Oates 1990, 227). The social stigma associated with syphilis is likely to have resulted in further unnecessary spread of the disease by people who made the utmost effort to keep their illness a secret. Severe physical deformities would eventually have made this impossible.

The spread of syphilis during the nineteenth century was often closely associated with the military and an increasing sexual commerce (see Para-scandola 2008, 27–46). Marital infidelity was often to blame for the spread of disease in wider society. Kilkenny had a long history of a military pres-ence, but this became a permanent element of the social fabric of the city with the establishment and erection of military barracks on Ballybought

Street in 1800–1803. The strict regime of the military practically forbade soldiers to marry, as marriage was seen as a hindrance to the mobility of soldiers. As a result, prostitution grew in Kilkenny (Ó Bolbuidhir 2006). The workhouse provided accommodation and relief for many of these "improper females," although the Board of Guardians attempted to implement policies that would discourage prostitutes, who were often accompanied by their illegitimate children, from entering the workhouse (Mahfoud 2009, 16–19). During the height of the famine, these women were accommodated separately in an enclosed area in one of the temporary sheds that had been erected on the workhouse grounds (*Kilkenny Journal* 1847b). One of the purposes of gender segregation in the workhouses—to prohibit sexual relations—was evidently unsuccessful at least once in the Kilkenny institution. A letter written by Thomas Ryan, at the time the Master of the workhouse, and published in the *Kilkenny Journal* in February 1850 revealed that "two years ago it was discovered that one pauper was affected by a disease 'only consequent upon the intercourse of the sexes in the workhouse.' It occurred in the hospital, and immediately on its discovery male nurses were substituted for female nurses in the wards where male paupers only are under treatment" (*Kilkenny Journal* 1850b).

It is noteworthy that when the skeleton of the late middle adult male (DCXI) who suffered from extreme tertiary syphilis was discovered during the archaeological excavation, it was found lying in an angled supine position on its back and leaning to the right (figure 3.15). This may indicate that he had been placed in the pit in a shroud only, although the apparent deviant position of his skeleton may be the result of coffin collapse in the ground. The possibility that he was not awarded a coffined burial should not be fully discarded. His skeleton displayed the most horrendous pathological changes, and it can be assumed that his disease and his apparently severely deformed body and face may have led his contemporaries to distance themselves from him; perhaps this was reflected in the treatment of his corpse. At the time of his death, he would most likely have suffered from neurological complications involving personality changes, emotional instability, memory impairment, and hallucinations. Optic nerve damage sometimes resulting in blindness is also noted as a consequence of tertiary syphilis, and as the caries sicca lesions extended into his left eye socket (see figure 3.14) this was probably the case for him. He is likely to have died from heart failure, the primary cause of death from syphilis in

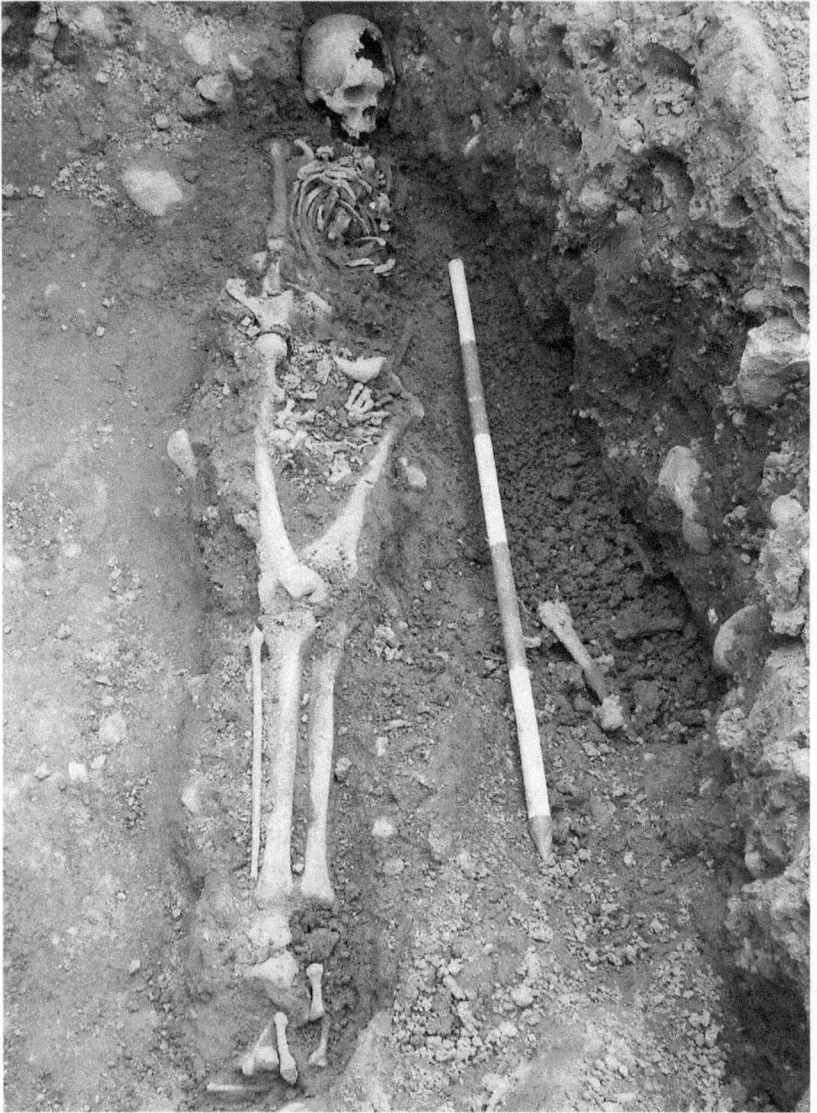

Figure 3.15. Position of skeleton DCXI, a late middle adult male who suffered from tertiary syphilis, as it appeared in the mass burial pit when discovered during the archaeological excavation. Photo by Margaret Gowen & Co. Ltd.

the majority of cases (Csonka and Oates 1990; LaFond and Lukehart 2006, 30–32; Robertson et al. 1989, 112–13; Woods 1994, 247–48).

Skeletal Trauma and Bone Fractures: Accidents and Violence

Evidence of skeletal trauma was identified in 135 individuals (13.92 percent; 135/970), of which nine cases were non-adults (1.65 percent; 9/545) and the rest were adult individuals (29.65 percent; 126/425). Most of the fractures in non-adult skeletons were due to indirect trauma and stress. Among the adults, direct and indirect traumas were the primary causes of skeletal injuries. Dislocations of joints were the least commonly observed type of skeletal trauma in the population (figure 3.16). The prevalence rates of trauma in the adults increased with age; 11 percent of all young adults, 24 percent of all early middle adults, 39 percent of all late middle adults, and 45 percent of all older adults were affected (figure 3.17). This increase is statistically significant.[32] Interestingly, the frequency of trauma in older adult females was less than in the preceding age group. However, no statistically significant difference was noted between these age groups,[33] and the observed difference likely simply reflects an uneven data set. Among the adults more generally, more males were affected (37.74 percent; 80/212) than females (22.84 percent; 45/197), a difference that was statistically significant.[34]

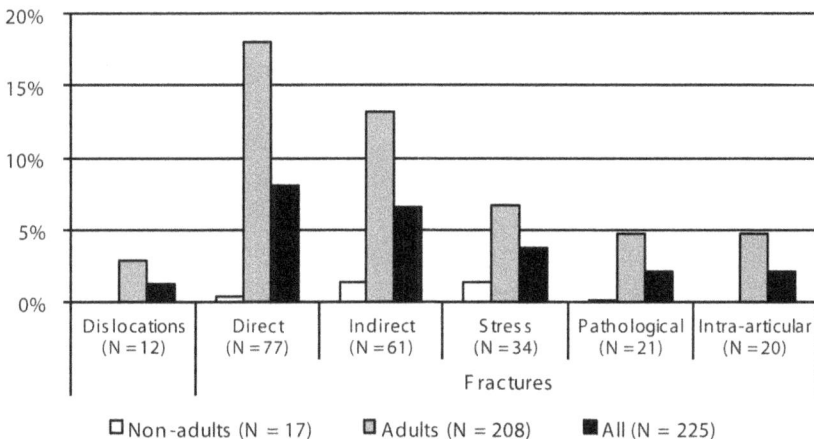

Figure 3.16. Frequency of skeletal trauma by type.

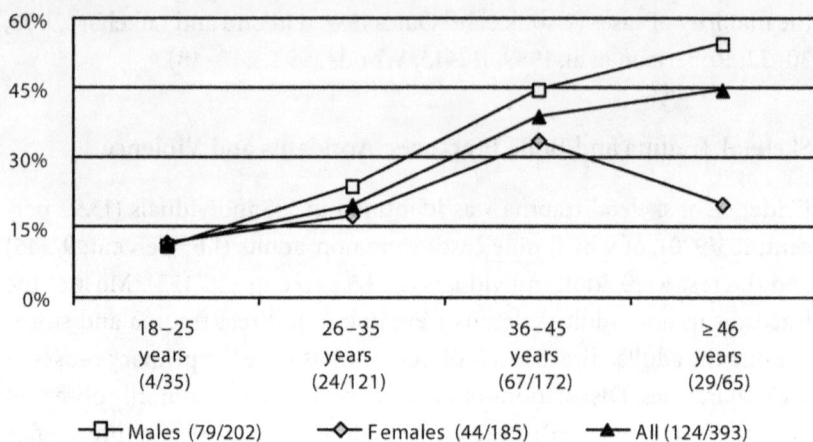

Figure 3.17. Prevalence of trauma (joint dislocations and bone fractures) in the adult population by age groups and sex.

The occurrence of trauma in a skeletal population can reflect occupational hazards, violence, and disease, and it is not always possible to determine its true etiology (see Larsen 1997, 109–60). The working and laboring classes of Ireland in the nineteenth century would undoubtedly have been exposed to hazards both as agricultural and industrial workers. Males and females would have been exposed to different types of danger. Poverty and socioeconomic standing is also a factor that influences high rates of violence (see Whitman, Coonley-Hoganson, and Desai 1984). Both metabolic and degenerative diseases increase the risk of a brittle bony structure and the consequent fractures. In comparison with contemporaneous populations, the skeletal trauma rate in the adult population at Kilkenny Union Workhouse is among the highest, particularly among females (table 3.14); it is similar to rate of the urban populations of St. Marylebone in London and St. Martin's in Birmingham. However, the comparison is complicated by the fact that the age profiles of the contemporaneous populations are not known. In addition, it is possible that the data from Kilkenny may be skewed since they include a notably low proportion of young adult individuals in the group (see table 4.11).

Table 3.14. Crude prevalence rates of trauma by sex, nineteenth-century adult skeletal populations

	Male		Female		All	
	n/total	%	n/total	%	n/total	%
Kilkenny Union Workhouse, Kilkenny	80/212	37.74	45/197	22.84	126/425	29.65
Bow Baptist Church, London	33/86	38.37	16/115	13.91	62/214	28.97
Christ Church Spitalfields, London[1]	34/358	9.49	16/348	4.59	51/753	6.77
Cross Bones, London	n/a	n/a	n/a	n/a	15/45	33.33
New Bunhill Fields Burial Ground, London	25/85	29.41	2/72	2.78	25/157	15.92
St. George's, London	16/54	29.62	4/41	9.76	20/95	21.05
St. Luke's, London	26/118	22.03	13/101	12.87	39/219	17.81
St. Mary and St. Michael, London	68/143	47.55	36/105	34.29	108/268	40.30
St. Marylebone, London	41/106	38.68	22/86	25.58	69/223	30.94
St. Pancras, London	48/231	20.78	25/224	11.16	69/715	9.65
St. Martin's, Birmingham	75/180	41.67	23/130	17.69	107/346	30.92
St. Peter's, Barton-upon-Humber	n/a	18.70	n/a	10.00	n/a	14.35

Note: Data include juveniles.

Dislocation of Joints

Eight male (3.77 percent; 8/212) and four female skeletons (2.03 percent; 4/197) displayed evidence of joint subluxations; no statistically significant frequency differences were noted between the sexes.[35] All individuals were either late middle adults or older adults. The only axial element displaying clear subluxations was the coccyx of an older adult male (DCCXI) that had resulted in a sacrococcygeal fusion that was fixed in a slight forward anterior angle (for further discussion about this particular skeleton, see chapter 5). Of the upper limbs, the most noticeable case was a traumatic and seemingly long-standing dislocation of the left elbow of another older adult male (DLXXVII). The origin of the injury appears to have been a fracture of the lateral condyle of the humerus. A second elbow dislocation was tentatively noted in the skeleton of a late middle adult female.

This injury was likely secondary to progressed rheumatoid arthritis (see above) (CCCXCIII). Also, a dislocation of the left wrist secondary to a Barton fracture of the wrist (see below) was noted in the skeleton of an older adult male (DCCXXVI) and a subluxation of metacarpal bones in the right hand was observed in an older adult female (LXXIX).

The bones of the lower extremities were most commonly affected, especially the hip joint. Subluxations of this joint were present in four males (2.06 percent; 4/194) and two females (1.10 percent; 2/181). Of these cases, one was bilateral and the remainder unilateral; the left side was affected in three cases and the right in one. The unilateral hip dislocation observed in the skeleton of a late middle adult male was likely secondary to a tuberculous infection of the affected joint (see chapter 4). The only other joint subluxation noted in limb elements was a lateral plantar displacement of the interphalangeal joints of the first metatarsal of the left foot of a late middle adult male (DCCXI).

Bone Fractures

In total, 8 percent of all skeletons (76/953) displayed evidence of direct trauma, including transverse (6.17 percent; 57/924) and crush fractures (2.83 percent; 27/953). Seven individuals (0.76 percent; 7/923) displayed both of these fracture types. No likely examples of penetrating or comminuted fractures were identified in the Kilkenny workhouse population. Fractures due to direct trauma occur at the point of impact (Lovell 1997) and were the most common fracture type in the population. Two nonadult skeletons displayed evidence of direct trauma (0.37 percent; 2/538), a two-year-old (DCXCIV) and a three- to four-year-old child (XL). The first case displayed transverse fractures of the sternal end (at the chest) of two left and four right ribs that are likely related to a rachitic rosary (see chapter 4). The second case involved the left forearm, which displayed a healed transverse fracture of both the radius and ulna (figure 3.18). In clinical literature, this type of fracture reportedly occurs in 45 percent of all pediatric fractures. Eighty percent of all cases occur over the age of five years, and it is three times more commonly reported in boys than in girls (Koval and Zuckerman 2002, 338). As was the case with the two-year-old child (DCXCIV) with rib fractures, this skeleton displayed indicative features of rickets (see below), and it is possible that the fracture also relates to an underlying poor health condition. It might also be related to

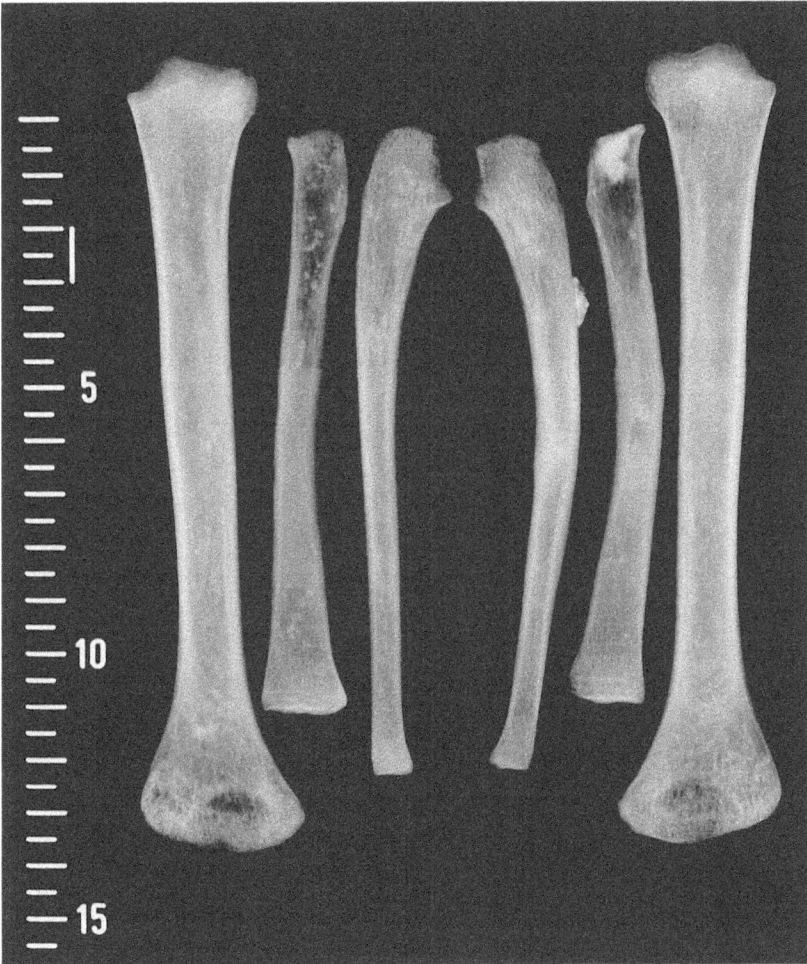

Figure 3.18. Radiograph of the arm and forearm bones of a three- to four-year-old child (XL), displaying a well-healed transverse fracture of the bones in the left forearm. Radiograph by School of Geography, Archaeology and Palaeoecology, Queen's University Belfast.

a scenario involving corporal punishment or even abuse of children, such as that of the excessive violence inflicted on the boy pupils of the Kilkenny workhouse by the schoolmaster Mr. Magennis during the summer of 1846 (see chapter 2).

Of the adults, 18 percent (76/415) displayed fractures due to direct trauma; the male rate was 24 percent (49/208) and the female rate was 13 percent (26/195), a difference that was statistically significant.[36] Transverse fractures were the most prevalent type and the ribs were most commonly affected. A significant difference between the sexes in rib fractures was observed; where males (13.79 percent, 24/174) were affected three times as often as females (4.38 percent, 7/160).[37] Another significant difference in transverse fracture frequencies between the sexes was observed in the hands; almost 4 percent (7/166) of all males were affected, but no female skeletons (0/159) displayed trauma to the hand bones.[38] This difference is probably related to a sociocultural dimension and is discussed further below.

Among the adults, 8 percent (16/208) of all males and 6 percent (11/195) of all females displayed crush fractures. Depressed fractures of the cranial vault were observed in 6 percent (12/190) of all males and 5 percent (9/175) of all females. No statistically significant difference was observed between the sexes,[39] which suggests there was no gender discrepancy in terms of risk of head trauma in this population. The frontal bone was most commonly affected; seven males and five females displayed depressed fractures. Two males (XVI and DCCLXXXVII) displayed blunt force trauma to the occipital bone.

The most severe of the cases of depressed fractures was located on the frontal bone of a late middle adult male. The depression was a large triangular-shaped indentation in the middle of the forehead that extended across part of the nose and the left eye socket (figure 3.19). Although the injury was well healed, the fracture lines were very distinct and the inferior portion of the injury included at least two portions of bone that were not fused to the rest of the skull vault: the medial portion of the left supraorbital margin and a fragment of the glabella near the eye socket. The depression is 1–7 mm deep and had caused considerable damage to the frontal sinus, and the endocranial plate of the frontal bone had been pushed 1–2 mm inward. The consequence of this injury is difficult to assess due to fragmentation, but it may have resulted in loss of the left eye. The location and nature of the fracture suggests that the individual may have been subjected to intentional directed violence. This skeleton also displayed a fracture of the left elbow and one right rib.

Other considerable depressed fractures were noted on the parietal bones of the skull vault of three individuals; two females (CXVIII and CDIV) displayed round depressions on the superior portions of the bones caused by blunt force trauma. The contours of the injuries suggest that they were caused by spherical objects. A depression fracture of a left pa-

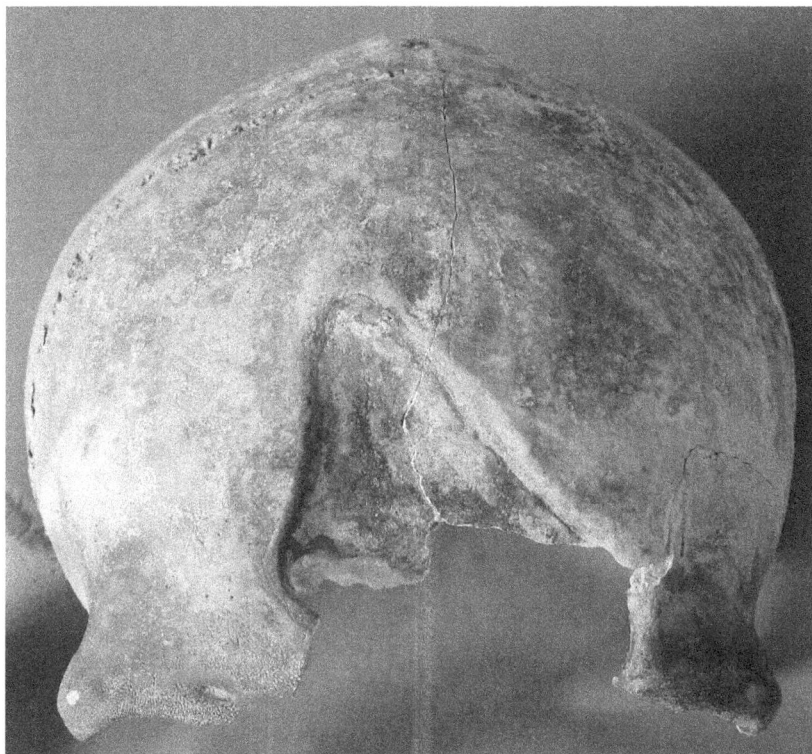

Figure 3.19. Healed depression fracture of the frontal bone of a late middle adult male (XVI). Photo by author.

rietal bone in an older adult male individual (CCCLXXVIII) was oval-shaped and had a transverse depression along the axis of the depression. This injury is likely to have been caused by impact from a blunt but angled object; a potential scenario is that this person fell backward and hit his head against an object with a horizontal edge such as a table. Among the postcranial injuries, a crush fracture was observed on the left proximal humerus of an older adult male and the right distal humerus of an adult female. Both were depression fractures and indicate direct trauma to the shoulder and elbow.

The only cases of compression fractures were identified in the wrists of three individuals: the scaphoid in the left wrist was fractured in an early middle adult male (XC), the right lunate was fractured in a late middle adult female (DCXV), and both the lunate and scaphoid bones were fractured in the right wrist of an older adult male (DCCXXVI). A healed compression fracture was also observed in the first metacarpal of the left hand of a late middle adult male (CCX).

Fractures due to indirect trauma occur at locations other than the point of impact (Lovell 1997) and were present in 1 percent (7/518) of the non-adult population and 13 percent (54/411) of the adults. Adult males were more commonly affected than females. Only males displayed spiral fractures; these were identified in the hands of two individuals (CDLIX and DCCXXII), the femur of one individual (CCLV), and the fibulae of two individuals (XXVI and DXLVII). Ten oblique fractures were identified in male skeletons and in one female skeleton, where it was observed in the left clavicle in a late middle adult individual (DCXC). Statistically significant differences were observed between the sexes in frequencies of oblique fractures of the hands.[40]

Vertebral burst fractures were more evenly distributed between the sexes; about 3 percent of both the male (6/182) and female (5/170) adult populations exhibited such fractures in the thoracic spine. In addition, a late middle adult male skeleton (DXXXIII) displayed a burst fracture of the second lumbar vertebra. No lumbar vertebrae were fractured in the adult female population. No statistically significant difference was observed between the sexes with regard to frequencies of avulsion fractures.[41] A total of four cases were identified in male skeletons and only one in a female skeleton, a fracture of the calcaneus.

One of the male cases (DCCLXXXV) involved the spinous process of the fifth thoracic vertebra. This relatively low level of the spine is atypical of the so-called clay shovelers' fracture that generally affects the spine at the level between the sixth cervical to third thoracic vertebra (Feldman and Astri 2001). This fracture type was described by orthopedic surgeon Reginald Dalton McKellar Hall, who frequently observed it in males employed in digging drains through heavy clayey soils in Western Australia during the 1930s (Hall 1940). Even though the Kilkenny case cannot be diagnosed as a clay-shovelers' fracture, the mechanism responsible for this injury was likely to have been the same: excessive muscle pull that put strain on the supraspinous ligaments of the spine. This may have occurred during physical labor when this man, who was in his late thirties or early forties at the time of death, was exposed to strain that affected his back in particular.

In both the non-adult and adult populations, the most common type of indirect fractures was spondylolysis; 3 percent (7/264) of young children

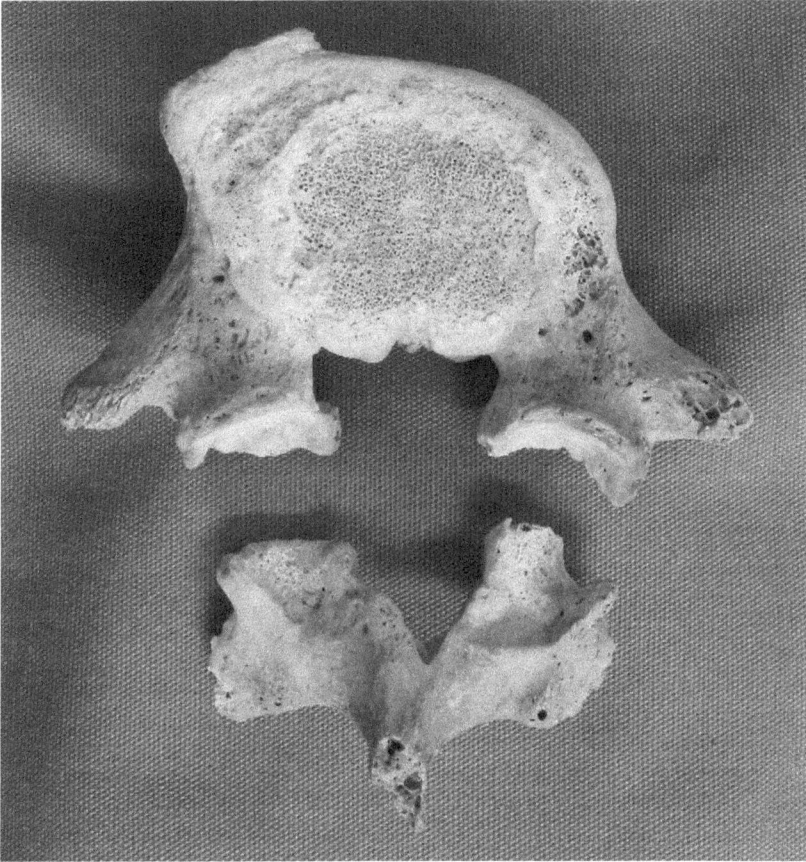

Figure 3.20. Bilateral spondylolysis of the fifth lumbar vertebra of an older adult male (DIV). Photo by author.

to adolescents and 8 percent (25/304) of adults were affected. This type of stress fracture involves the neural arch of primarily lower vertebrae (figure 3.20); the fourth and fifth lumbar vertebrae are most frequently affected. The third lumbar vertebra was affected in two cases, the fourth in five cases, and the fifth in nineteen cases. In one early middle adult male individual (DCCLXXXIII), both the fourth and fifth lumbar vertebrae displayed complete bilateral spondylolysis. Assessment of prevalence rates by age groups suggests that the primary onset of this type of fracture occurred during adolescence. Males (8.70 percent; 14/161) were only marginally more affected than females (8.00 percent; 12/150), especially in the late middle adult and older adult age categories. It has been suggested that spondylolysis has a hereditary background (Lester and Shapiro 1968).

The clinical literature has given general prevalence rates of spondylolysis in modern populations of 2 to 10 percent (Lowe et al. 1987). A survey of the prevalence rate of the anomaly in British archaeological populations gave frequencies from 1 to 17 percent; this range is likely greatly influenced by inconsistencies in the recording of the condition in various studies (Fibiger and Knüsel 2005) and by unequal sample sizes. Despite these caveats, the prevalence rate of spondylolysis in the Kilkenny workhouse population does not appear to be abnormal.

Probable Cases of Interpersonal Violence

A total of ten adult skeletons displayed evidence of trauma that is likely due to physical abuse and interpersonal violence, as they appear to conform to fracture patterns of such etiology where the face is often afflicted (see Walker 1997). Facial bone fractures were noted in six of these cases; nasal bone fractures were present in four males (XC, CXLI, CLXXV, and DCLXXXIII) (figure 3.21), the left maxilla in an early middle adult male (CCXLI), and the supraorbital margin of the left eye socket in a late middle adult male (XVI). The latter skeleton also displayed a severe depressed fracture of the frontal bone (see above) that may relate to an act of violence. A typical so-called boxer's fracture of the fifth metacarpal was noted in the right hand of an older adult male (CCXCVIII). These are common locations for fractures in a hand which, while clenched in a fist, may have struck a hard surface. Another male among these individuals displayed a metacarpal fracture of the left hand, which may also have occurred for this reason. It is also noticeable that among all fracture types affecting the hand bones, males were more frequently affected than females (see above). Although some fracture patterns, such as the boxer's fracture, would suggest interpersonal violence as a likely etiology, these might also be related to manual labor which was gender specific to males. It should also be acknowledged that the facial bone fractures could have occurred while playing sport.

The only female skeleton among these individuals that exhibited fracture patterns that possibly indicate interpersonal violence was a late middle adult (CLXII). Her skeleton displayed a left forearm fracture (a so-called parry fracture involving the ulna), a fracture of the midbody of a left rib, and a fracture at the angle of six right ribs. This distribution of rib fractures could indicate that she had been trying to shield herself against

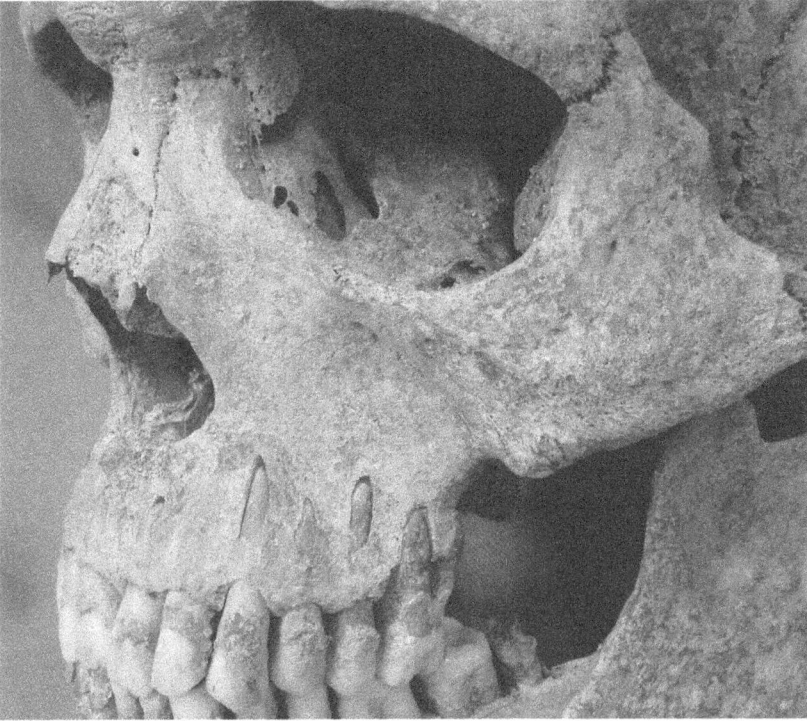

Figure 3.21. Healed nasal fracture on the cranium of an older adult male (CXLI). Photo by author.

an aggressor with the left arm and that she might have been kicked in the back while lying down on her side. No craniofacial fractures were noted in this skeleton, though; in the clinical literature this is the predominant fracture pattern that is characteristic of domestic violence (Arosarena et al. 2009). The skeleton was poorly preserved, which may have caused subtle fractures to be unidentifiable. Several teeth in the individual had also been lost in life, and only the roots remained of the lower central incisors. Whether these were lost as a result of trauma to the mouth is unclear, as the individual also displayed several considerable carious cavities in the remaining teeth that indicate poor dental health that could have resulted in loss of teeth.

Osteochondritis Dissecans

The condition known as osteochondritis dissecans is the result of fragmentation of the subchondral bone of the joint surface. It most commonly

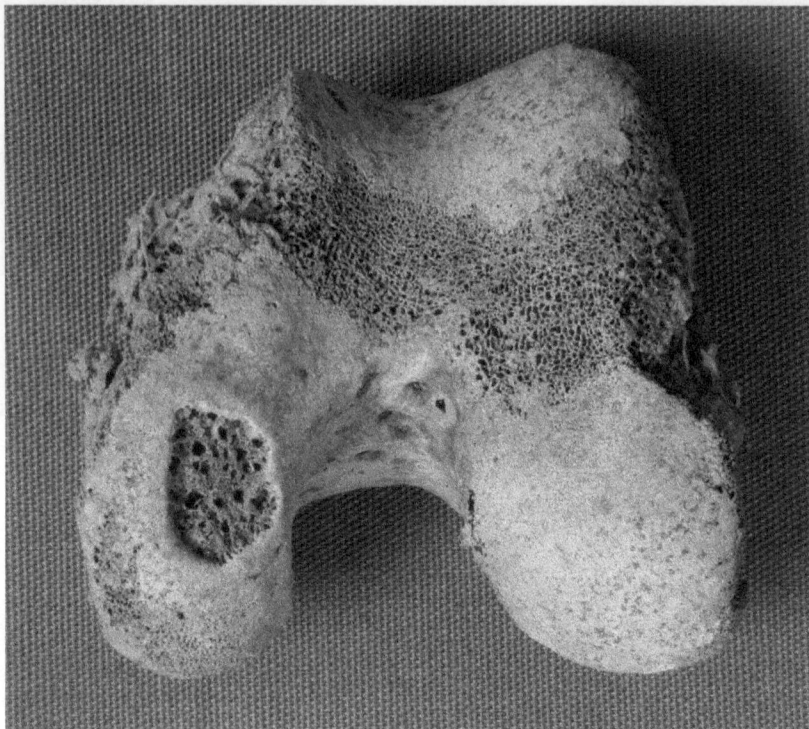

Figure 3.22. Osteochondritis dissecans on the inferior aspect of the medial condyle of the femur in the left knee joint in a sixteen- to seventeen-year-old adolescent (CCCLXXIII). Photo by author.

affects adolescents and is usually caused by trauma, but defective blood flow is a likely underlying background. This results in a segment of necrotic dead bone tissue that often separates from the surrounding bone and remains in the joint as a separate intra-articular body (Aufderheide and Rodríguez-Martín 1998, 81–83; Ortner 2003, 351–53). The lesion is generally identified as a pit in the articular surface of a joint. When symptomatic it may result in pain, limitation of motion, clicking and locking of the joint, and swelling (Resnick and Goergen 2002, 2689–708). The presence of osteochondritis dissecans in the skeletons was diagnosed only on convex surfaces, following the instructions by Rogers and Waldron (1995).

Twelve individuals displayed pathological joint lesions diagnosed as osteochondritis dissecans. These included seven adult females, two adult males, and two adolescents of unknown sex. The number of females is interesting, as osteochondritis dissecans normally appears mostly in males (Ortner 2003, 351). The most common location was the knees (75 percent; 9/12), on the medial or lateral condyles of seven femora (figure 3.22) and on the medial articular surfaces of two patellae. Osteochondritis dissecans of this joint has a particular family genetic background (Resnick and Goergen 2002, 2689). Some relatively unusual locations were also noted, such as on the heads of the femora in an adolescent individual, the head of a left humerus in a female, and the left occipital condyle in another adult female.

Slipped Femoral Capital Epiphysis

Three adult males (CCXXVII, CDLIX, DCCXCV) and one adult female (LXXXI) displayed unilateral cases of slipped femoral capital epiphyses. This is clinically a relatively common hip disorder characterized by an in-fero-posterior slippage of the capital epiphysis of the femur (figure 3.23). The condition is the result of a stress fracture of the metaphyseal junction

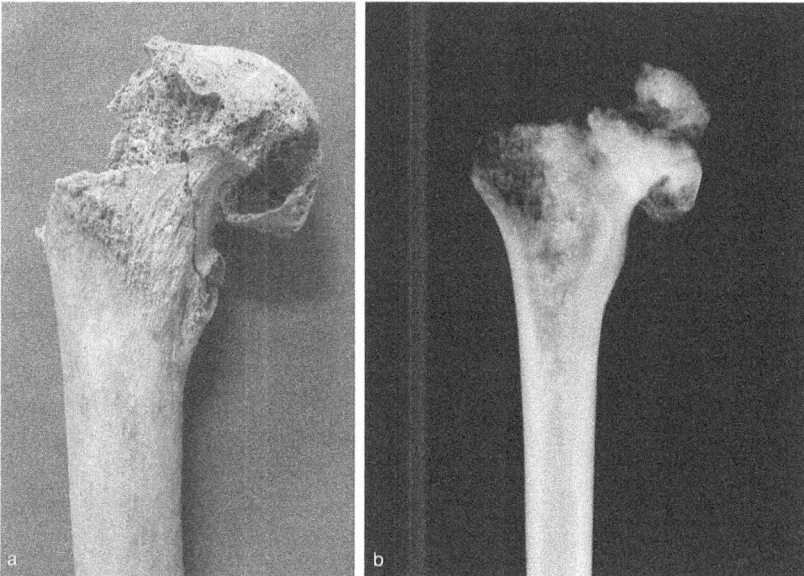

Figure 3.23. Two cases of slipped femoral capital epiphysis affecting the right hip: (a) right femur of an older adult male (DCCXCV); (b) radiograph of the right femur of a late middle adult individual of unknown sex (CDLIX). Photo by author; radiograph by School of Geography, Archaeology and Palaeoecology, Queen's University Belfast.

between the neck and the head of the femur and occurs in juveniles before epiphyses of the bones are fully fused. It manifests most frequently between ten to sixteen years of age in males and eleven to fourteen years in females. It is about two to five times more likely to occur in males than in females (Aufderheide and Rodríguez-Martín 1998, 90; Ortner 2003, 347; Resnick and Goergen 2002, 2729–734), and this sex discrepancy is reflected in the Kilkenny cases.

In the Kilkenny workhouse population, 2 percent of all male adults (4/191), 1 percent of all adults (4/370), exhibited slipped femoral capital epiphyses. The right hip was affected in three of the four cases (the exception was CCXXVII). All individuals were of advanced age and displayed secondary degenerative joint disease and osteoarthritis in the hips and knees. It therefore seems probable that these males suffered an apparent physical disability associated with chronic pain in the hip throughout most of their adult lives. The etiology of the disorder is still largely unknown, and there is currently a discourse regarding whether the condition is initiated by trauma. It is likely to be influenced by growth-related hormonal change, as it is most often observed in individuals with a delay in skeletal maturation or during a recent growth spurt. Other suggested causes include ischemia, thinning of the perichondrial ring, and collagen deficiency; genetics and obesity may also be contributing factors (Cush, Kavanaugh, and Stein 2005, 354; Pizzutillo 1992).

4

Institutionalization as the Last Resort

Famine Diseases, Mortality, and Medical Interventions

The wretched inmates had no shoes, and sadly complained of want of fire, and presented, indeed a melancholy spectacle of misery. . . . I saw groups of shivering creatures stand close together to keep themselves warm, and sitting on pavement; others were lying in beds. The dampness and cold of the place, even to a person in health, were almost intolerable.

"The Nenagh Brewery Workhouse—A Picture of the Poor Law in Nenagh," *Kilkenny Journal*, 10 January 1849

The severely overcrowded situation in the Kilkenny Union Workhouse and all the other workhouses in Ireland during the famine was a reflection of how inadequately the institutions created by the Poor Law were able to deal with the crisis. However, the fact that the workhouse institutions were generally the last option for people who must have been genuinely desperate is one way the law succeeded. Deterring the poor from seeking help was one of its goals, based on the conviction that the able-bodied could be forced to improve their "character" and escape poverty with their own industry (see chapter 2). Yet the rigid class system did little to enable the poor to advance on the social and economic ladder. Tenants feared that if they improved their farms and plots too much, their landlords would raise their rents (Keenan 2000). Many believe that this is one of the reasons why the Irish economy was underdeveloped during this period.

Contemplating the physical and emotional state people must have been in when they felt they had no other choice than to apply for indoor relief is disheartening. Many applicants would most likely have given up their rented plots and sold or pawned off any of their possessions before they entered the workhouse. As regulated by the Poor Law, relief would not be administered to those who occupied more than a quarter of an acre of land (Donnelly 2001), and it is presumed that many inmates in the Kilkenny workhouse had been forced to give up their land. They would have been well aware of the fact that they had nothing to go back to if they left the workhouse. The high risk of acquiring an infectious disease or dying in these institutions would have been a calculated risk that each applicant would have had to consider. A very high prevalence of disease due to nutritional deficiencies was evident in the Kilkenny workhouse population, and some of the infectious pathological markers identified in their skeletal remains were extreme and very severe. This provides a poignant reminder of the level of exhaustion and poor health inmates must have endured during the months and weeks before their deaths.

Famine Diseases in Ireland, 1845–1852

Many diseases became widespread and prevalent in Ireland during the Great Famine. The medical history of this period has been the focus of interest of many scholars (e.g., Crawford 1988; Kennedy et al. 1999, 104–24; MacArthur 1956). However, relying entirely on the historical sources is problematic since they are a reflection of the understanding of disease at that time (Roberts and Cox 2003, 290). It can be difficult to accurately discuss the prevalence rates of certain diseases during this period based solely on the written record. Despite the fact that they reveal which diseases were recorded and were likely most prevalent, it might not be possible to detect exactly how common these were and how they were manifested in the population. The available statistical data on causes of death are also almost exclusively from institutions such as the workhouses and fever hospitals and thus are not accurate for the population as a whole.

While the diseases caused by nutrient deficiencies struck the poor population hard during the Great Famine, infectious diseases did not discriminate and were feared by both the rich and poor. In 1847, for example, smallpox and dysentery became epidemic in Belfast after they were spread from the workhouse to the General Hospital (Killeen 1995, 163). The death rate among the infected wealthy is said to have been ten times greater than the rate among the poor (Kennedy et al. 1999, 118). This is because they had not been exposed to these diseases before and had a presumably weaker immune defense. "Famine fever," dysentery and "famine diarrhoea," cholera, smallpox, and tuberculosis were common during the

Great Famine and were the primary cause of death for the vast majority of its victims.

"Famine fever" was a nineteenth-century term for various conditions that primarily included epidemic typhus, typhoid fever, and relapsing fever; at the time of the famine, it was not always possible to differentiate between these three illnesses (Hardy 1988, 408). These were greatly infectious diseases that spread across the malnourished and weak population of Ireland, especially in the crowded and poorly ventilated workhouses and hospitals. Epidemic typhus was a familiar disease to the populace of Great Britain and Ireland during the nineteenth century, particularly in urban areas (Hardy 1988). It is caused by the *Rickettsia prowazekii* bacteria, which is spread among humans through lice. The epidemic typhus in Ireland during the famine was further spread with the emigrants to Britain and North America, where it came to be called "Irish typhus." It was transmitted from people scratching their skin and sometimes through inhaling living bacteria and was due primarily to poor sanitation and inadequate hygiene. The incubation period is from seven to twenty-one days. The disease resulted in a rash, muscle pains, and the characteristic high fever (Tubbs 1992, 13.15–17). Mortality in the nineteenth century is estimated to have been between 20 and 45 percent (Hardy 1988).

Typhoid fever was endemic. It is caused by the *Salmonella enterica* bacteria and was transmitted through water contaminated by feces from infected individuals. The disease progressed through stages and involved an increasing fever and additional symptoms such as malaise, headaches, and coughing. It can progress to delirium, diarrhea, and intestinal hemorrhage and perforation; the latter often proves fatal (Farrar 1992, 4.13–16). As with typhus, the spread of typhoid fever was heightened by poor living conditions and poor sanitation. The disease was present in the Kilkenny Union Workhouse during the famine years (Lalor 1848). Finally, relapsing fever, which was spread via lice or ticks, is likely to have caused a large number of deaths (Kennedy et al. 1999, 104–24; MacArthur 1956). The disease is a bacterial infection caused by the *Borrelia* genus. In addition to the characteristic fever, symptoms include joint pain, coughing, shortness of breath, jaundice, skin rashes, and conjunctivitis (Tubbs 1992, 13.14–15).

Dysentery, cholera, smallpox and tuberculosis were also widespread infectious diseases during the famine years. Dysentery is believed to occasionally have been diagnosed under the more general description "famine diarrhoea." It is an inflammation of the intestine that results in a characteristic blood- or mucus-textured diarrhea and was known by its alterative name, bloody flux. As with typhus and typhoid fever, the spread of this disease was related to hygiene and sanitation. It is estimated to have been the cause of one in seven deaths in the year 1847 alone (Kennedy et al. 1999, 119). Cases described as "famine diarrhoea" may also have included pellagra, a disease that was not diagnosed during the famine even though it likely was very common. This disease frequently occurs in famine-struck and displaced populations today. It is caused by inadequate intake of nicotinic acid and tryptophan and results in weight loss, skin lesions, gastrointestinal disturbances, and mental conditions. Severe chronic cases can result in damage to the nervous system that produces sensory disturbances and muscle paralysis. It is endemic in populations that rely heavily on maize as a staple food (Wing and Brown 1979, 38), and the dependence of many people in Ireland on Indian meal during the 1840s and early 1850s may have contributed to its spread. Few people in Ireland knew how to grind or store maize, and some physicians believed that the poor quality of food made from this grain was the cause of dysentery (Anonymous 1849, 367–68).

Smallpox was also common during the famine years. More than 7,000 people died of it in 1849; mortality was particularly high in the southwest of the country (Kennedy et al. 1999, 121–23). Smallpox is a highly contagious disease caused by the *Variola* virus, which is airborne. The disease was primarily transmitted from person to person through inhalation of droplets. It produces severe scabs, fever, and agonizing backaches, among other symptoms (Bartlett 2004, 119–20). It attacks the respiratory system, often resulting in fatal pneumonia. Although smallpox can also manifest skeletally as osteomyelitis variolosa, no diagnostic occurrences of this type of osteomyelitis were identified in the Kilkenny workhouse population (see below). However, it is clear from the available Kilkenny Poor Law minute books and local newspapers that the disease was diagnosed and treated in the workhouse infirmary and fever hospital in Kilkenny during the famine years (see *Kilkenny Journal* 1847i).

Tuberculosis became prevalent during the period of the Great Famine, and mortality was high. This was especially true in eastern counties, particularly in King's County (County Offaly), Queen's County (County Laois), County Kildare, and County Dublin (Kennedy et al. 1999, 112–21). In the nineteenth century, the generic term for tuberculosis was consumption or phthisis, names that suggest either pulmonary tuberculosis or a primary lung infection. It cannot be said with any certainty that patients diagnosed with consumption were in fact suffering from tuberculosis, as they may have been affected by bronchitis or pneumonia instead. The etiology of the disease and the bacteria responsible for it were not identified until 1882; physicians were not able to properly diagnose tuberculosis before that (Roberts and Manchester 2005, 183–84). Typical symptoms of the disease included coughing, often in the form of hemoptysis, and pleurisy. Early signs would also have been fatigue and weakness, a husky voice, insomnia, weight loss, and night sweats (Carman 1937).

The arrival of Asiatic cholera in Ireland in 1848 has been described as the "final assault" on the population during the famine (Kennedy et al. 1999, 123), as it struck the survivors who had overcome the worst of the crisis. The epidemic spread quickly across the country after it arrived via the harbor in Belfast during November that year. It reached Kilkenny a few months later. Cholera is caused by the *Vibrio cholera* bacteria, which is spread through water contaminated with feces from infected individuals. It causes excessive diarrhea and profuse vomiting that produces severe dehydration and had an exceptionally high fatality rate in the nineteenth century. In Kilkenny, a sanitary committee was set up in February 1849 in response to the epidemic (*Kilkenny Journal* 1849b). It was believed that "the poisonous effluvia discharged from the monster cess pool of the female part of the [work]house" (*Kilkenny Journal* 1849c) was one of the sources of the disease in the city. The risk of acquiring cholera from the workhouse continued to be a worry throughout the famine. In February 1850, the *Kilkenny Journal* reported an incident in which the guardians reprimanded one of the male inmates for exposing the workhouse and the city to the disease. He had been caught eating rotten roots that he had picked out of the manure he was supposed to be depositing outside; this was presumably on the workhouse farm or garden plot. He responded that he felt forced to do so because of hunger (*Kilkenny Journal* 1850a).

Many people died from illnesses caused by nutritional deficiencies. These included marasmus and dropsy (kwashiorkor), diseases caused by protein-energy malnutrition. Observations of the health and condition of those starving during the famine made several references to symptoms that likely related to these conditions. Marasmus, which is caused by a calorie deficiency, can result in the cessation of physical growth in children. It is most likely to occur in infants who are not being properly breast fed, which often happens because the mother is unable to lactate properly (Wing and Brown 1979, 35). Hunger edema—or dropsy, as it was called at the time—develops gradually in an individual suffering from severe malnutrition, and it thus becomes most apparent in the final stages of starvation (Anonymous 1953). During the famine period, the term is likely to have been used to describe a variety of illnesses and ailments, of which kwashiorkor probably was the most prominent. It is caused by protein deficiency, and its characteristic diagnostic feature is edema that develops across the body. This is caused by an expansion of extracellular fluid related to abnormally low levels of serum albumin in the blood (Waterlow 1992). During the famine, edema first occurred in the feet and ankles (MacArthur 1951, 6), while in modern famine-struck populations, it develops first around the eyes and the legs (Anonymous 1953).

Many people during the famine suffered from scurvy (scorbutus). We see evidence of this in the human remains from the Kilkenny mass burials (see below). For a long time, scurvy was associated with the seafaring professions, and at the time of the Great Famine a distinction was made between "sea scurvy" and "land scurvy" (Curran 1847). This terminology illustrates that the nature and cause of the disease was poorly understood at the time. A cure for scurvy was famously described by the Scottish naval physician James Lind (1716–1794) in the mid-eighteenth century (Lind 1753), who found that citrus fruits provided the best remedy. However, before the 1840s, those in the medical professions showed only limited interest in the disease and its treatment. Cases that occurred at sea were mainly explained as the result of inadequate food supplies for the ships' crews while the majority of land-based cases occurred in prisons and jails (Carpenter 1986, 98–132) and, perhaps viewed through a socially critical lens, were given a relatively low priority. While there was general knowledge of various anti-scorbutic types of foods that could be used for treatment (of which potatoes were one), the lack of full comprehension of the etiology of the disease meant that other causes were also suggested. These included the consumption of salted meat, cold weather, impure air, and drinking bad water. Scurvy was sometimes described as a contagious disease (Cook 2004, 227; Eberle 1831, 493–94).

Another disease caused by nutritional deficiencies that was commonly reported during the famine years is xerophthalmia, which at the time was known as "famine blindness." It is caused by lack of Vitamin A and affects the retina, the conjunctiva, and the cornea of the eye. Initial symptoms develop because the light-sensitive rod cells in the retina are impaired, resulting in night blindness. In the later stages of the disease, the cornea dries up, causing structural damage to the eye surface (Wing and Brown 1979, 36–37).

People also died from starvation, although not to the extent that is often believed in the popular narrative. The 20,402 deaths that were attributed directly to starvation (Mokyr and Ó Gráda 1999) account for only about 2 percent of the total number of deaths. This implies that victims of severe starvation often did not live long enough to die directly from that cause; other diseases that starvation made them vulnerable to were likely to kill them sooner. Starvation occurs as an acute consequence of severe deficiency of nutrients and is the most severe form of malnutrition. The U.S. Army studied the human physiological response to starvation in the Minnesota Starvation Experiment during the last years of World War II so it could gain a better understanding of how to treat starving and deprived people in Nazi-occupied Europe as the Allied invasion progressed (Kalm and Semba 2005). Other than the obvious physical consequences of considerable loss of weight and energy, the thirty-six young male subjects who participated in the study also became increasingly irritable and impatient and displayed hatred toward others. They became increasingly introverted and began showing an obsession with anything relating to food (Keys et al. 1950). Today these psychosocial effects of starvation are viewed clinically and socially as a consequence of extreme malnutrition. They are frequently reported in modern famine-struck populations and often result in a breakdown of family and community structures (Jelliffe and Jelliffe 1971). These effects of starvation on the Irish population during the famine are probably reflected in the numerous accounts of violence that occurred all over the country, stories of people who, without any hesitation, stole food from others and stories of how the emotional bond between parents and children was completely broken (Kennedy et al. 1999, 107).

The Kilkenny Union Workhouse Medical Officers: Dr. Lalor and Dr. Cane

In the nineteenth century, the medical profession was not always held in the highest regard in terms of social status (see Anonymous 1896; Reader 1966). Victorian physicians were often idealists with a passion for medical science. Their profession was not without risk; they were constantly exposed to diseases and they had a relatively low life expectancy (see Woods 1996). The immense workload and stress put upon the physicians of Ireland during the Great Famine cannot be overstated. Many physicians fell victim to the very diseases they were battling, and many died of famine fever (Cusack and Stokes 1848; Froggatt 1999).

Dr. Joseph Lalor and Dr. Robert Cane were the medical officers of the workhouse in Kilkenny during the most critical years of the famine. Lalor (1811–1886) had been awarded his MD at Glasgow in 1839 (McKeogh 1996). Cane (1807–1858) was born in Kilkenny and obtained his MD in Dublin in 1836. After he returned home, Robert Cane became a prominent local figure; he was elected mayor of Kilkenny in 1845 and 1848. He was a staunch nationalist and was jailed for five months in 1848 for his political convictions during the Young Irelander Rebellion. This uprising, which was inspired by the European revolts for freedom that same year, was fueled by austerity and the difficulties caused by the blight-induced subsistence crises on the continent (Patterson 1998).

Lalor and Cane were in constant struggle with the guardians regarding the management of the workhouse and the medical treatment of the patients in the infirmary and fever hospital. These medical officers played an enormously important role in Kilkenny during the famine years through their ongoing battle against the spread of infectious disease (see *Kilkenny Journal* 1849e).

The Physical Condition of the People: The Paleopathology of the Human Experience of the Great Irish Famine

With the exception of the diagnosed cases of syphilis (see above), the manifestations of other infectious diseases and metabolic disorders in the Kilkenny workhouse skeletons could relate to the stress of the Great Famine on this population. The skeletal manifestations of metabolic and infectious diseases are limited to only a few ailments and conditions. It is generally the case that pathological markers are not formed on the skeleton until the chronic stage. However, difficulties remain with the process of diagnosing these diseases, as many of the pathological markers they generate are nonspecific and are not pathognomonic for a particular disease.

Both infectious and metabolic diseases would have been very common in nineteenth-century Ireland, and they increased in frequency and severity during the years of the famine crisis. This was evident in the Kilkenny skeletons; relatively few individuals displayed inactive cases of infectious or metabolic diseases; instead, active cases were widespread across all age groups. On a general level, non-active cases are most probably representative of health ailments that occurred *before* the famine. While it must be recognized that many of the active infectious and metabolic diseases identified may have originated from factors unrelated to the famine, they would still have been a part of the experience of those who endured the Great Famine. Also, they would have greatly influenced how individuals were able to cope with famine-induced stress and ultimately their chances of survival.

How well the skeletal manifestations of disease in the Kilkenny workhouse population represent a true insight into the health of the poor in mid-nineteenth-century Ireland is less clear. This is partly due to the bias introduced by selective nature of which inmates were deemed eligible for indoor relief; the workhouse population does not constitute a representative cross-section of the overall Irish population. The skeletons do represent a mortality bias in the weakest and most vulnerable individuals. For example, because the skeletal manifestation of infectious diseases generally represents an advanced and chronic stage, when it is noted in adults it might have occurred years after the initial infection took place. Because of this, a high prevalence of infectious diseases in skeletal populations could be an indication of particularly poor health conditions. However, high prevalence rates may also be a representation of the osteological paradox (see chapter 1) and could reflect a population with sufficient health to survive a disease process long enough to leave permanent marks on skeletal tissue.

In addition to the diagnosed cases of acquired and congenital syphilis, the infectious diseases and conditions observed in the workhouse skeletons were tuberculosis, respiratory disease, and osteomyelitis. A significantly high proportion of the population displayed layers of periosteal new bone formation on their bones, changes that are often a pathological response to infection. However, some have criticized the common paleopathological definition of nondiagnostic inflammatory periosteal reactions as "non-specific infection" (Birkett 1983; Powell 1988; Weston 2012). In this population, most such cases probably relate to metabolic disorders, of which scurvy is the most likely condition. I do not discuss new bone formation as evidence of infectious disease processes unless I have been able to definitely diagnose them as such.

Metabolic disease due to a nutritional deficiency is likely to have occurred seasonally throughout much of the lives of the individuals who died in the Kilkenny workhouse. Because the bulk of the population was entirely reliant on their own agricultural produce for subsistence, poverty and unfavorable weather conditions would have placed the population at high risk when there was a poor harvest. As a consequence, famines frequently occurred in Ireland in the seventeenth and nineteenth centuries (see Dickson 2012). Although in general, only a few metabolic diseases are potentially diagnosable in the skeleton (Brickley and Ives 2008), the diseases identified in the Kilkenny workhouse population have revealed that deficiencies in vitamins and possibly iron were some of the conditions from which the inmates suffered considerably during the height of the famine period.

Tuberculosis

Tuberculosis was a widespread malady, and throughout much of the nineteenth century it was the most common cause of death of all single diseases (Aufderheide and Rodríguez-Martín 1998, 130; Roberts and Cox 2003, 338). It has been estimated that without any antibiotics, the mortality rate would have been 35–40 percent within five years of contracting the disease (Aufderheide and Rodríguez-Martín 1998, 132). Bizarrely enough, many Victorian poets, artists and novelists romanticized death by consumption, which was often referred to as "the white plague" (Jalland 1996, 40). The poor, who were painfully familiar with the disease, did not romanticize it. This familiarity was expressed in the folklore and traditions of the people. For instance, it was customary in Connemara in the west of Ireland to hang a bundle of cloth containing unsalted butter above the dying because it was believed that this would cause the consumption to leave the body and enter the butter. The bundle would then be taken down and buried to prevent the spread of the disease (Mooney 1888, 267).

Tuberculosis disease is an acute or chronic bacterial infection, caused by the *Mycobacterium* species. It is transmitted between humans through droplets in the form of *Mycobacterium tuberculosis* or from contaminated bovid products such as milk and meat or directly from these animals as

Mycobacterium bovis (Aufderheide and Rodríguez-Martín 1998, 118–19; Ortner 2003, 227). The pathogenesis of the disease depends to a great deal on the resistance of the host. Inadequate nutrition of course impairs the immune response (Aufderheide and Rodríguez-Martín 1998, 119; Ortner 2003, 227). Recent research has recognized the accelerated risk of obtaining active tuberculosis in individuals suffering from protein malnutrition; the disease in these cases is limited to the pulmonary type. This combination leads to a relatively rapid death (Wilbur et al. 2008, 967). This could explain why tuberculosis became so prevalent in Ireland during the 1840s and early 1850s.

The paleopathological and skeletal evidence of tuberculosis is well described, although there is still a debate about which lesions are reliable diagnostic indicators of the disease (Aufderheide and Rodríguez-Martín 1998, 121–24; Brothwell 1961, 325; Brothwell 1981, 132; Hershkovitz et al. 2002; Ortner 2003, 227–63; Roberts and Manchester 2005, 187–93; Rogers and Waldron 1989; Schwartz 1995, 233; Wilbur et al. 2008, 964–65). Typical skeletal indicators are bony erosions and osteolysis, which can affect both the outer cortex and interior spongiosa of bone (Schwartz 1995, 234). Researchers have also focused on pulmonary lesions noted on the ribs (see below) (Kelley and Micozzi 1984; Roberts, Lucy, and Manchester 1998), on endocranial lesions on the internal surface of the skull vault (Hershkovitz et al. 2002; Lewis 2004, 85–86), and on the osteological evidence identified through biomolecular and aDNA techniques (e.g., Mays et al. 2001; Murphy et al. 2009; Salo et al. 1994). Typical locations for skeletal tuberculous lesions are the vertebral column, the coxae, and the knee joints. It is estimated that from 25 to 50 percent of all cases of skeletal tuberculosis affect the spinal column. Only 5–7 percent of infected individuals display bony changes (Steinbock 1976, 175). This is why the paleopathological evidence of tuberculosis in many cases must be seen merely as evidence of the presence of the disease in a particular population and not as a valid representation of the frequency of the disease.

Tuberculosis was diagnosed in seven skeletons from the Kilkenny mass burials: two children, one adolescent, and four adults. One of the cases, that of a late middle adult female (DLVII), was not active at the time of death. This individual also displayed evidence of a severe case of Pott's disease involving an infection of the lower thoracic spine. It was well healed and long standing and would have occurred many years before the famine. Her condition had resulted in a complete collapse of the

Figure 4.1. Collapse of the lower thoracic spine due to tuberculosis in a skeleton of a late middle adult female (DLVII). Photo by author.

eleventh thoracic to the second lumbar vertebral segments, which caused a severe anterior kyphosis (curvature of the spine) of approximately 90°. She would have been severely disabled by a considerable hunchback (figure 4.1). Her skeleton also displayed thickened laminae at the base of the spinous processes of the seventh cervical to the ninth thoracic vertebra, osteophytosis, and osteoarthritis (eburnation) of the articular processes of the eighth to tenth thoracic and fourth and fifth lumbar vertebrae. These are most likely secondary reactions due to muscle strain and compression of the spine from her attempts to walk upright. Considerable osteoarthritis was noted on the head of the first metatarsal of the left foot which is likely related to additional anatomical loading from attempting to walk with this abnormal posture. This individual presents a parallel case to that of the female who potentially suffered from rheumatoid arthritis (see chapter 3) and provides insight into which workhouse inmates may have been granted indoor relief on the basis of disability.

A second individual was a young adult male (CXXXIX) who displayed osteolytic destruction of the bodies of the fourth and fifth lumbar vertebrae in the lower back and reactive periosteal new bone formation on the latter vertebra. A large so-called psoas abscess had destroyed approximately half of the body of his fifth lumbar vertebra. Active new bone formation was present on the anterior surface of the sacrum at the medial base of the second segment. Layers of new bone with oval osteolytic lesions were noted on the visceral surface at the neck of four left ribs and one right rib. Of lesser severity, although they were active at the time of death, were cases of tuberculous spondylitis identified in the skeleton of an early middle adult male (CCCXCVI) and a young adult female (DLXIV). Active new bone formation, osteolysis, and psoas abscesses were observed in the lumbar vertebrae of both skeletons. The male individual also displayed active new bone on the visceral surface of a left rib and on the pubic bones of the pelvis (figure 4.2). This could indicate a tuberculous infection of both his lungs and gut. Murphy et al. (2009) described the osseous changes due to bovine tuberculosis that manifest as proliferated lesions of the vertebral

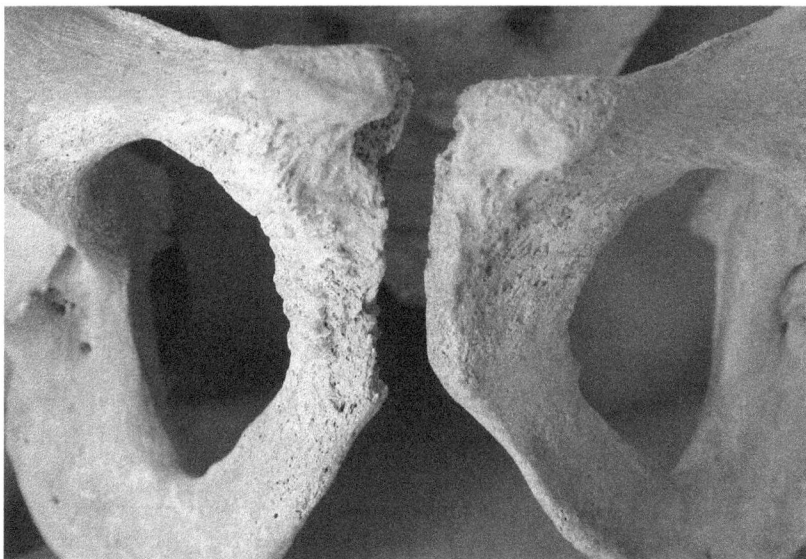

Figure 4.2. Active periostitis due to a tuberculosis infection on the pubic bones of an early middle adult male (CCCXCVI). Photo by author.

or pelvic bones; they confirmed such associations through aDNA analysis even when diagnostic psoas abscesses were absent.

Cranial tuberculosis was noted in one case: the skeleton of a nine-year-old child (XV) displayed a large active crater on the frontal bone, just superior of the right eye socket (figure 4.3a). This is the most common location for a tuberculous lesion of the skull and is primarily seen in infants and children less than ten years of age (Ortner 2003, 247–48). The lesion had extended into the middle diploë layer of the skull vault but had not penetrated through the internal table. The margins were sharp, and bony projectiles were present on the floor in the middle of the lesion. Active and fine new bone depositions were noted just inferior of the crater. A similar cortical lesion was also present on the ectocranial surface of the tuber of the right parietal bone. Lytic lesions were also observed on the manubrium, and considerable new bone formation was present on the diaphysis of the second metacarpal of the left hand. This is an indication of a form of tuberculosis referred to as tuberculous dactylitis, or spina ventosa. New bone formation was also present on the right pubic bone that probably relates to an infection of the gut.

A severe likely case of tuberculosis was diagnosed in a five- to six-year-old child (CCCLXIV). A large lytic lesion was present on the anterior portion of the mandible that had destroyed the cortex and exposed the unerupted permanent teeth and caused premature loss of the deciduous front teeth (figure 4.3b). Gross osteomyelitic infectious lesions were also present on the diaphyses of the arm bones, with the exception of the right ulna (figure 4.3c). The severest lesion was noted in the radius of the left forearm, at the level of the mid- to proximal diaphysis toward the elbow, which displayed a substantial expansion of the bone that had affected all surfaces. Multiple cloacae were noted around the lesion, and the original diaphysis was exposed by the abscesses, revealing a complete destruction of the cortical bone that had transformed it into an extremely porotic and fragile bone surface. An alternative diagnosis of this case is typhoid fever, which can also result in these severe osteomyelitic infections (see below). This skeleton also displayed lesions indicative of scurvy or Vitamin C deficiency.

Finally, a case of a probable tuberculous infection was noted in the left hip joint of the skeleton of an adolescent female (DCCLXXVIII). The lesions displayed severe subchondral destruction of the articular surface of the joint. An identical lesion was observed on the head joint of the femur.

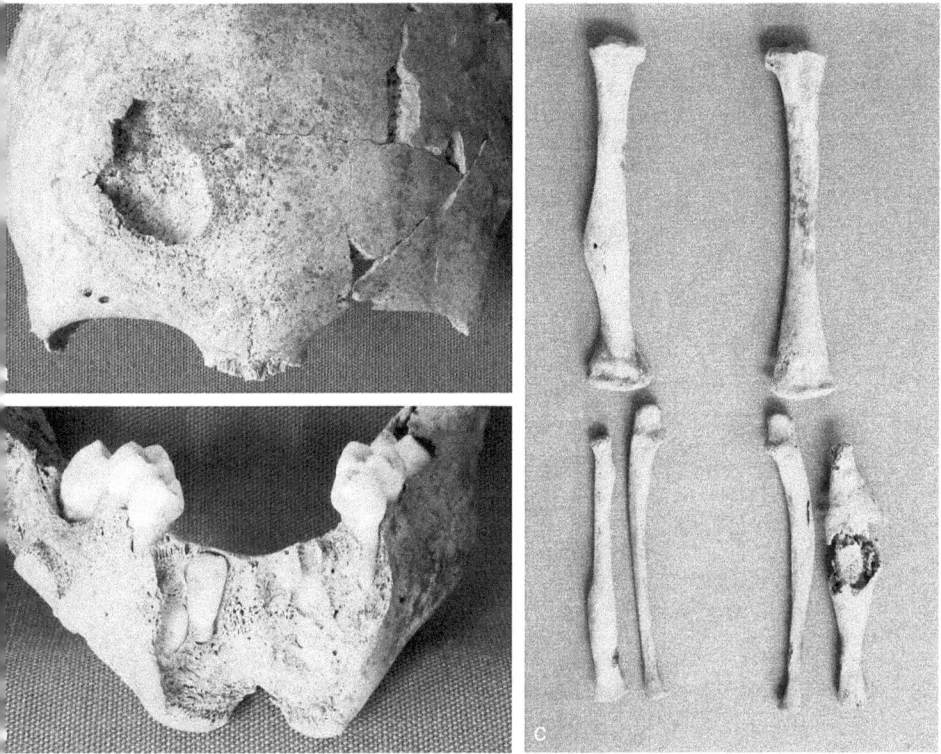

Figure 4.3. Identified cases of tuberculosis in non-adult skeletons: (a) osteolytic crater on the frontal bone of a nine-year-old child (XV); (b) osteolytic crater on the anterior aspect of the mandible of a five- to six-year-old child (CCCLXIV); (c) osteomyelitis of the arm bones of the same child. Photo by author.

The right acetabulum was also considerably enlarged and the head of the femur was slightly deformed. The changes to the hip joint appear to be secondary to the infection and are likely more directly the result of a different body posture as a consequence of the disease.

Throughout history tuberculosis has primarily affected the poor (Roberts and Buikstra 2003, 55–59). Tuberculosis is likely to have caused numerous deaths in the workhouse in Kilkenny during the Great Famine, although the skeletal evidence reflects only a few cases in individuals who managed to survive the disease for a long time. In comparison with the frequencies observed in contemporaneous skeletal populations (table 4.1), the rates observed in the Kilkenny workhouse are not particularly high, but this may indicate that most who died from tuberculosis did so before any skeletal manifestations had taken place. The presence of the disease

Table 4.1. Crude prevalence rates of tuberculosis, nineteenth-century skeletal populations

Population	n/total	%
Kilkenny Union Workhouse, Kilkenny	7/970	0.72
Hospital of the Assumption, Thurles	2/9	22.22
All Saints, Chelsea Old Church, London	2/198	1.01
Bow Baptist Church, London	8/416	1.92
Christ Church Spitalfields, London	2/968	0.21
Cross Bones, London	0/148	0.00
New Bunhill Fields Burial Ground, London	5/514	0.97
St. Benet Sherehog, London	1/177	0.56
St. George's, London	1/111	0.90
St. Luke's, Islington, London	7/503	1.39
St. Mary and St. Michael, London	5/705	0.71
St. Marylebone Church, London	4/301	1.33
St. Pancras, London	4/715	0.56
Sheen's Burial Ground, London	2/254	0.79
City Bunhill Burial Ground, London	2/239	0.84
St. Martin's, Birmingham	3/505	0.59
St. Peter's, Wolverhampton	1/150	0.67

in this population illustrates a reality for the poorer classes in Ireland during this time; for many tuberculosis sufferers, the workhouse provided the only available medical help. The individuals with active tuberculous skeletal lesions are likely to have been treated in a separate ward at the workhouse infirmary in an attempt to contain the infection. Poor nutrition and a reduced immune defense undoubtedly limited the chance of survival of these individuals considerably.

Respiratory Diseases

Tighe's survey of Kilkenny in the early nineteenth century referred to the constant suffering from pleurisy of the poor, which he related to extremely poor living conditions (see chapter 2). An article in the *Quarterly Journal of Agriculture* in 1838 attributed the cause of pulmonary disease in Kilkenny to the "contaminated atmosphere" in the cabins, which were often heated by coal that produced sulfurous gases ("D" 1838). The quality of housing at the time was assessed by four class types, of which the lowest, Class 4, consisted of a one-room mud cabin (Kennedy et al. 1999). On the eve of the famine, there were reportedly 7,778 fourth class houses in County Kilkenny that provided accommodation for 8,281

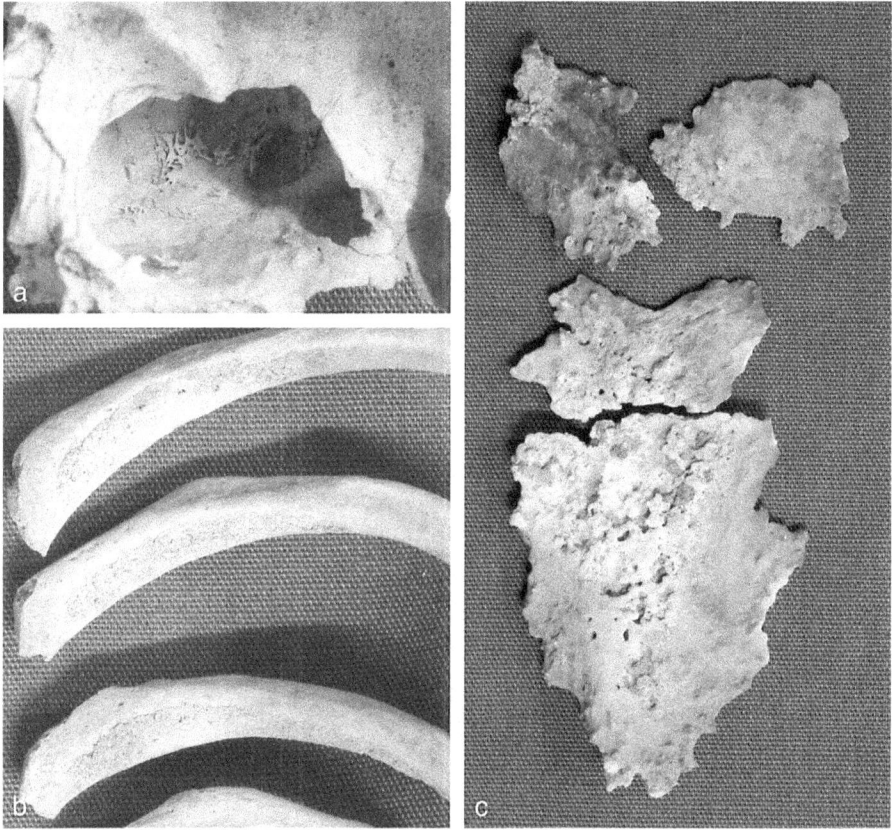

Figure 4.4. Examples of osseous lesions caused by respiratory disease: (a) indicative of chronic sinusitis, plaques of spiculated new bone on the floor of the left maxillary sinus of a twelve-year-old child (DCCXVIII); (b) fine deposits of active new bone on the visceral surface of the left ribs of an eleven-year-old child (CDXLII); (c) ossified lung tissue (pleura) found in the thorax of an early middle adult male (CCLXXXV). Photo by author.

families (Anonymous 1846). However, the proportion of Class 4 housing in Kilkenny was significantly lower than in the west of Ireland (Kennedy et al. 1999). Poor health related to poor housing was likely a much greater feature of the populace of western counties such as Cork, Kerry, Clare, Galway, and Mayo. As with tuberculosis and many other conditions, the skeletal manifestation of respiratory disease reflects a chronic or long-standing condition. The cases observed in the Kilkenny skeletons reveal that the poor often suffered from respiratory disease, corroborating

Table 4.2. Frequency and rate of individuals affected by chronic maxillary sinusitis by sex and age group, Kilkenny workhouse population

Age group	Males		Females		All[1]	
	n/total	%	n/total	%	n/total	%
1–5 years	--	--	--	--	2/164	1.22
6–12 years	--	--	--	--	6/124	4.84
13–17 years	--	--	--	--	2/36	5.56
18–25 years	1/16	6.25	1/16	6.25	1/16	6.25
26–35 years	2/32	6.25	2/32	6.25	2/32	6.25
36–45 years	13/65	20.00	13/65	20.00	13/65	20.00
≥ 46 years	3/27	11.11	3/27	11.11	3/27	11.11
>18 years	0/2	0.00	5/19	26.32	5/21	23.81
Total	19/142	13.38	14/121	11.57	43/588	7.31

[1] Includes unsexed adults.

Tighe's description of the local impoverished populace about four decades before the famine.

Forty-three individuals displayed osseous manifestations of maxillary sinusitis, an infection of the paranasal sinuses that may result in new bone formation of the sinus walls (Aufderheide and Rodríguez-Martín 1998, 257). When found skeletally in archaeological populations (figure 4.4a), it has generally been discussed as the result of poor ventilation, air pollution, and allergies (e.g., Merrett and Pfeiffer 2000; Roberts 2007). Although it was present in young children to older adults, the greatest frequencies were noted among late middle adults. The overall frequency for non-adults was 3 percent; among adults, in contrast, the frequency was 13 percent. Males were slightly more affected than females, but the difference between the sexes was not statistically significant (table 4.2). Two individuals displayed new bone formation on the medial surface of the nasal bones, an indication of inflammation of the mucous membrane (rhinitis). The skeleton of an early middle adult female (CLXXIX) displayed evidence of chronic maxillary sinusitis and general poor oral health. The lesion, which was located on the left section of the nasal cavity, consisted of proliferated porous bone. The second individual (CDXLVII), also a late middle adult female, displayed a porous and lytic lesion on the medial surface of the left wall of the nasal cavity. This individual also suffered from chronic maxillary sinusitis.

Osseous lesions due to pulmonary disease or infection are predominantly noted on the visceral surface of the ribs (facing the lungs) (figure 4.4b), and such lesions were present in 7 percent (60/822) of the Kilkenny workhouse population. It was manifested unilaterally in thirty-eight individuals (63.33 percent) and bilaterally in twenty-two individuals (36.67 percent). New bone formation on the visceral surfaces of the ribs is often reported in cases of pulmonary tuberculosis; for example, Kelley and Micozzi (1984) noted that 56 percent of the individuals in the Hamann-Todd Osteological Collection at the Cleveland Museum of Natural History, which consists of more than 3,000 skeletons of individuals of known identity and cause of death, displayed skeletal evidence of tuberculosis involving rib lesions. These were either in the form of diffuse new bone formation or osteolytic abscesses, predominantly located on left ribs. Ortner (2003, 247) argued that endemic tuberculosis is the most common cause for periosteal lesions on ribs, and a strong correlation between rib lesions and tuberculosis has been suggested in several other studies (e.g., Alfer 1891; Kelley and Micozzi 1984; Roberts 1999; Roberts et al. 1998; Roberts, Lucy, and Manchester 1994). Additional pulmonary disease processes—such as acute pneumonia and actinomycosis (a bacterial infection often affecting the nose and throat) (Molto 1990; Roberts, Lucy, and Manchester 1994)—can result in an inflammatory reaction on these rib surfaces, and a direct diagnosis of tuberculosis based on rib lesions alone is not possible (Mays, Fysh, and Taylor 2002; Rogers and Waldron 1989, 165). Of the skeletons diagnosed with tuberculosis, three displayed osseous changes to the ribs (XV, CXXXIX, CCCLXIV, and CCCXCVI). Rib lesions were most common in adult individuals (9.33 percent; 32/343), especially late middle adults. Non-adults were less affected (5.85 percent; 28/479), and the lowest rates were observed in neonates and infants (table 4.3).

Ossified plaques of lung tissue were found among the left ribs of the skeleton of an early middle adult male (CCLXXXV) (see figure 4.4c). The skeleton did not display any other evidence of pulmonary infection, despite the fact that the bones were very well preserved. As with rib lesions, this type of calcified tissue has often been discussed in conjunction with tuberculosis (Møller-Christensen 1958, 177–78), although it is not pathognomonic for the disease (Roberts and Buikstra 2003, 107).

Table 4.3. Frequency and rate of skeletons with periosteal rib lesions and tuberculous cases within this group, Kilkenny workhouse population

Age group	Rib lesions		Tuberculous	
	n/total	%	n	%
~ birth	1/31	3.23	0	0.00
0–1 years	2/60	3.33	0	0.00
1–5 years	8/210	3.81	1	12.50
6–12 years	11/137	8.03	0	0.00
13–17 years	6/41	14.63	0	0.00
18–25 years	4/35	11.43	1	25.00
26–35 years	9/94	9.57	1	11.11
36–45 years	15/144	10.42	0	0.00
≥ 46 years	3/59	5.08	0	0.00
>18 years	1/11	9.09	0	0.00
Total	60/822	7.30	3	5.00

Osteomyelitis

Osteomyelitis was diagnosed in nine skeletons of three non-adults and six adult individuals (figure 4.5). Among the latter, four could be sexed as males and one as female. The bones of the lower extremity were most commonly affected, especially the femora. Osteomyelitis, an infection of the bone marrow and surrounding bone, is usually the result of pyogenic bacteria. It is manifested in three main ways: directly through trauma or surgical wounds (acute osteomyelitis), from soft tissue infections, or indirectly via the blood flow (hematogenous osteomyelitis) (Ortner 2003, 181). The infecting bacteria produce pus that eventually breaks through the bone via an opening—a so-called cloaca. Further bone destruction can also be evident in an infected element, but generally a considerable buildup of reactive new bone (involucrum) is also observed, as is dead bone tissue called sequestrum (Aufderheide and Rodríguez-Martín 1998, 172–81). Osteomyelitis can be an agonizing condition. In addition to considerable pain, typical symptoms include fever, irritability, fatigue and warmth, and swelling and redness of the affected area (Zeller 2008).

The initial cause of the infection in the diagnosed cases could generally not be determined because osteomyelitis is generally a nonspecific reaction to infection. However, the underlying cause of osteomyelitis in the Kilkenny skeletons was very clear in one case; this was evidently due to trauma to the left thigh in an older adult male individual (CCCXVIII)

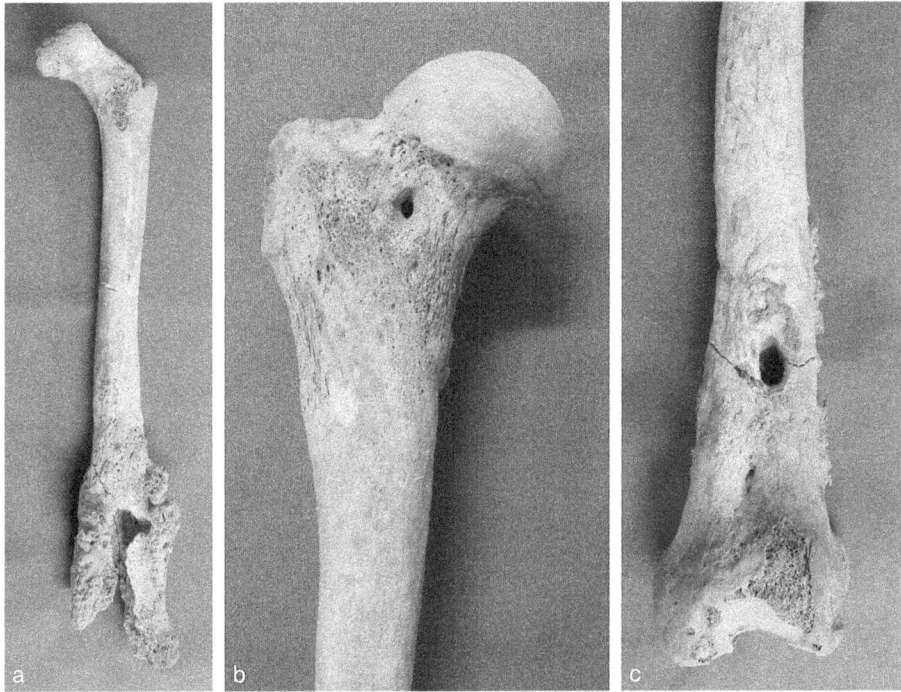

Figure 4.5. Three examples of severe osteomyelitic infections: (a) distal right femur of a twelve- to thirteen-year-old child (DCLIX); (b) proximal right femur of an early middle adult male (DCCXXXII); (c) left femur of an older adult male (CCCXVIII). Photo by author.

that manifested as a likely oblique fracture at the midshaft portion of the femur. There was also a case of severe osteomyelitis that had formed in the arm bones of the skeleton of a young child (CCCLXIV); these bone infections were probably related to tuberculosis (see figure 4.3c). Considering the historical context of the Kilkenny burials, however, the osteomyelitis observed may have been a consequence of typhoid fever. This is an alternative diagnosis for the condition in this child. It is even possible that the child suffered from both tuberculosis and typhoid fever. Typhoid osteomyelitis is reported in about 1 percent of infected individuals, and then it most frequently affected children. In those cases, the infection most commonly affected the lumbar spine, the ribs, and the tibiae (Adler 2000; Aufderheide and Rodríguez-Martín 1998; Veal 1939). Osteomyelitis can also occur with smallpox in children and is then most commonly manifested in the elbow, followed by the ankle and foot, the shoulders, the knees, the

Table 4.4. Crude prevalence rates of osteomyelitis, nineteenth-century skeletal populations

Population	n/total	%
Kilkenny Union Workhouse, Kilkenny	9/970	0.93
Hospital of the Assumption, Thurles	0/9	0.00
All Saints, Chelsea Old Church, London	0/198	0.00
Bow Baptist Church, London	5/416	1.20
Christ Church, Spitalfields, London	0/968	0.00
Cross Bones, London	1/148	0.68
St. Benet Sherehog, London	0/177	0.00
St. George's, London	0/111	0.00
St. Luke's, Islington, London	14/503	2.78
St. Mary and St. Michael, London	0/705	0.00
St. Marylebone Church, London	3/301	0.97
Sheen's Burial Ground, London	1/254	0.39
City Bunhill Burial Ground, London	1/239	0.42
St. Martin's, Birmingham	0/505	0.00
St. Peter's, Wolverhampton	0/150	0.00

hips, and the wrist and hand bones (Aufderheide and Rodríguez-Martín 1998, 207).

Despite potential associations of osteomyelitis with "famine diseases," there was not a particularly high prevalence rate of the disease in the Kilkenny workhouse population (table 4.4). Etiologies due to trauma and probable tuberculosis could be ascertained in two cases, and the remaining cases are nonspecific but may relate to typhoid fever. While typhoid fever was evidently one of the infectious diseases that caused much concern for the workhouse physicians, most people who died of this disease during the famine are unlikely to have lived long enough for osteomyelitis to develop in their skeletons. The historical records indicate that smallpox was present in the Kilkenny workhouse during the famine, but as none of the osteomyelitic lesions identified in the individuals from the mass burials displayed features that are characteristic of the disease, diagnosis was not possible from the skeletal remains.

Vitamin C Deficiency and Scurvy

Vitamin C can be stored in the human body for four to five months in adults. After being deprived of the vitamin for this period of time, scorbutic symptoms begin to appear (Stuart-Macadam 1989, 219–20). The historical record from the Great Famine is consistent with this progression. By the end of 1845, medical professionals had noticed the first cases of scurvy. One of the early accounts mentioned people suffering from the disease in Naas, County Kildare. They were described as suffering from "rose-coloured patches" that would have been due to ecchymoses (bruises), severe bone pain, and swollen muscles "so acute that the patients [winced] on the slightest pressure" (Crawford 1988, 286). This account vividly illustrates the pain associated with scurvy. This develops early and often results in a pseudoparalysis. Other consequences include spongy and bleeding gums (gingivitis) that often result in tooth loss, swelling of the lower extremities, and discharges of blood from body cavities (perifollicular hemorrhages) (Sullivan 1903, 235–36). Additional symptoms, such as alternatively feeling hot and cold, vertigo, faintness, profuse sweating, hemorrhagic spots in the eyes, abnormal dryness of the skin (xerosis), hyperkeratosis, bent and coiled body hairs, and impaired wound healing are also reported (Hirschmann and Raugi 1999; Hodges et al. 1969).

The nature of the disease is dependent on the age of the affected individual. Infantile scurvy is particularly prevalent between six and twelve months of age. Before the studies of Thomas Barlow (1845–1945) in the late nineteenth century, the disease was often misdiagnosed as rickets (Steinbock 1976, 254). Barlow's identification of diagnostic criteria, which included extreme pain and tenderness of the limbs due to subperiosteal hemorrhage, meant that the disease was more frequently diagnosed and reported. The main cause of infantile scurvy in the nineteenth century was evidently a lack of fresh vegetables in the diet, but another cause was the increasing practice of heating milk. Proprietary foods, which became commonly used by well-to-do families during this period, also had a negative impact on infant health, and infantile scurvy came to be recognized as a disease of families of the middle and higher socioeconomic strata of society (Rajakumar 2001). Scurvy is more likely to appear in infants who are weaned, although a child who is breastfed by a severely malnourished mother who is deprived of Vitamin C will also become deficient (Brickley and Ives 2008, 45). Scurvy can also develop in infants who are fed on cow's milk alone (Wing and Brown 1979, 39).

Skeletally, scurvy is most noticeable and specific in non-adult individuals. Most cases of osseous changes due to Vitamin C deficiency in infants are related to vascular responses to hemorrhages, which usually appear because of minor trauma and mechanical strains that result in porous and

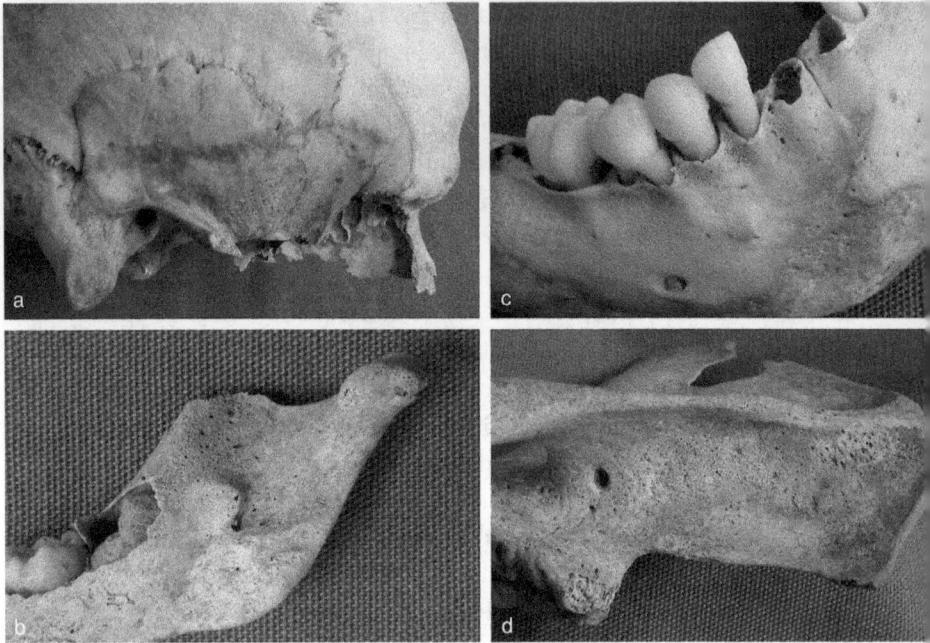

Figure 4.6. Scorbutic lesions indicative of Vitamin C deficiency: (a) porotic lesions on the right greater wing of the sphenoid bone in the skull of a late middle adult male (DIV); (b) porous new bone formation on the medial surface of the right half of the mandible of a one- to two-year-old child (CXCVI); (c) abnormal porosity at the alveolar margin of a five- to six-year-old child (DII); (d) new bone formation on the supraspinous area of the right scapula of a seven- to eight-year-old-child (CXIII). Photo by author.

hypertrophic bone formation at the affected areas (Ortner, Kimmerle, and Diez 1999). The typical lesions attributed to scurvy include porous new bone formation and porotic pitting of the greater wings of the sphenoid in the areas of the temples on the skull (figure 4.6a), porosity of the orbital roofs of the eye sockets, porous lesions of the posterior portion of the maxillae, internal porosity of the zygoma, porosity and hyperostosis at the infraorbital foramina on the maxillae, porosity of the palatal processes, and porous lesions on the medial surface at the coronoid processes (figure 4.6b). As bleeding gums are a clinical trait of scurvy, abnormal porosity at the sockets of the teeth (alveoli) is a common observation in skeletal remains (figure 4.6c). Other traits are less specific and may occur in other metabolic disorders such as anemia (see below). Less specific traits are also observed; these include general fractures in the skeleton due to a weakened bone structure, transverse fractures and dislocations of the osteochondral junction of the ribs, and apposition of proliferated new bone on the scapulae (figure 4.6d) and long bones (Brickley and Ives 2006, 2008; Ortner 2003).

Radiological studies of modern population adults suffering from severe Vitamin C deficiency have identified generalized spinal osteoporosis and an uneven lack of density and exaggeration of trabecular bone in long bones (Joffe 1961). Similar changes have been observed in experiments and radiological studies of guinea pigs deprived of Vitamin C. In such cases, the skeletal reaction to active scurvy took the form of microfractures and diaphyseal damage of long bones, resulting in overlapping epiphyses and bow-leggedness, diaphyseal thickening due to a periosteal reaction in animals that are partially deficient (Murray and Kodicek 1949a, 1949b). The latter is a reflection of the fact that Vitamin C is a requirement for osteoid formation (Bourne 1943). New bone growth relating to scurvy will be evident only if the vitamin has been reintroduced into the diet after a period of deficiency or at least is present in a small amount (Bourne 1942; Brickley and Ives 2008, 56). It is thus a reflection of the disease during its convalescence stage or after it has been cured.

As the majority of the skeletal indicators of scurvy are generally nonspecific, a three-scale diagnostic approach was used for the Kilkenny workhouse population. From these classifications, scurvy could confidently be diagnosed in 156 skeletons, a probable diagnosis was given to 138 skeletons, and a possible diagnosis was given to 205 skeletons (see Geber and Murphy 2012). In collation, this gave an overall prevalence rate of 52 percent (499/964) of all assessable skeletons. Considering that the diagnosis in this population was conducted solely macroscopically, the frequency constitutes an exceptionally high prevalence rate of the disease, even if only the most confident diagnoses are taken into account (see Brickley and Ives 2008, table A1). Even higher rates are observed in certain age groups (figure 4.7). The highest prevalence was noted in young children to adolescents; for this group, the total frequency of scurvy was 66–68 percent ($\bar{x}$ = 66.89 percent). Among the adults, the rates ranged from 31 percent in young adults to 49 percent in older adults ($\bar{x}$ = 40.91 percent). The lowest frequencies in this population were noted in neonatal and infant skeletons, for whom the range was 19–21 percent ($\bar{x}$ = 19.69 percent).

Among the adults, males were 1.7 times more frequently diagnosed with scurvy than females. This difference was statistically significant in

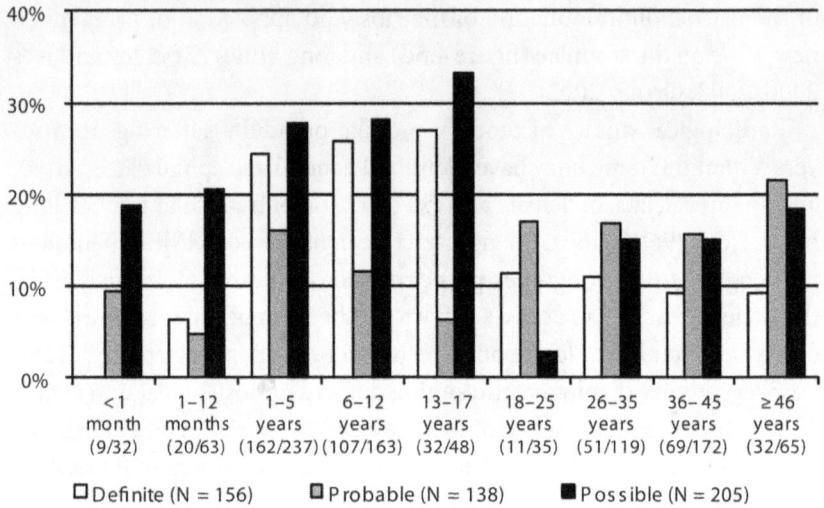

Figure 4.7. Frequency of skeletons displaying evidence of scurvy by age groups and diagnostic reliance scale categories.

the overall adult population and was more age-specific among the early middle adults and older adults (table 4.5). The largest difference was noted among the older adults, for whom more than three times as many males as females displayed scorbutic skeletal lesions. This discrepancy is probably a reflection of the difference in biological metabolism and the daily Vitamin C intake requirement between the sexes (Basu and Schorah 1982). This may indicate that the daily food ration supplied to the adult males in the workhouse was inadequate in terms of nutritional requirements. There is also a great likelihood that this sex difference is a reflection of an overall sex bias during the famine. Males may have suffered a proportionally greater loss of required nutritional intake during periods of food scarcity. The prevalence of scurvy in the Kilkenny workhouse population is exceptionally high in comparison with other nineteenth-century populations (table 4.6) and is clearly a direct reflection of the impact of the famine on the health of these people. It is clear that the prevalence rate of diagnosed cases of scurvy in archaeological populations is an underestimation, as it will only be detectable in individuals who developed skeletal lesions; the true rates of the disease are likely to have been much higher than what can be discerned from paleopathological diagnoses. The extreme rates noted in the Kilkenny skeletons reveal that this population suffered the disease to a degree that was very uncommon at the time and

Table 4.5. Frequency and rate of scurvy in adults by sex and age group, Kilkenny workhouse population

Age group	Male		Female		χ^2	df	p
	n/total	%	n/total	%			
18–25 years	8/18	44.44	3/17	17.65	2.913	1	.088
26–35 years	26/45	57.78	25/73	34.25	6.281	1	.012
36–45 years	43/94	45.74	25/74	33.78	2.459	1	.117
≥ 46 years	28/44	63.64	4/20	20.00	10.473	1	.001
Total[1]	107/210	50.94	58/196	29.59	19.175	1	< .001

[1] Includes generically aged adults (>18 years).

that it must have been a significant feature of the experience of famine for these people and probably also for those who survived it.

It is essential to consider the fact that scurvy will only be evident in the skeleton once Vitamin C has been reintroduced to the diet, particularly when interpreting the prevalence rate of the skeletal markers of the disease. The skeletons with identified traits associated with scurvy in the Kilkenny population are likely to reflect individuals who had been deprived of Vitamin C due to the potato blight but were provided some access to the vitamin through the workhouse diet. It could also be the case

Table 4.6. Frequency and rate of scurvy, nineteenth-century skeletal populations

Population	n/total	%
Kilkenny Union Workhouse, Kilkenny	499/964	51.76
All Saints, Chelsea Old Church, London	1/198	0.51
Bow Baptist Church, London	15/416	3.61
Christ Church Spitalfields, London	0/968	0.00
Cross Bones, London	0/148	0.00
New Bunhill Fields Burial Ground, London	0/514	0.00
St. Benet Sherehog, London	0/230	0.00
St. George's, London	0/111	0.00
St. Luke's, London	3/241	1.24
St. Mary and St. Michael, London	42/705	5.96
St. Marylebone Church, London	4/301	1.33
St. Pancras, London	0/715	0.00
Sheen's Burial Ground, London	1/254	0.39
City Bunhill Burial Ground, London	0/239	0.00
St. Martin's, Birmingham	6/505	1.19
St. Peter's, Wolverhampton	1/150	0.67

that these scorbutic skeletons may have been of individuals who had lived for a longer time in the workhouse prior to death than those who did not display evidence of the disease. The nonscorbutic skeletons could thus have been individuals who died before any bone remodeling and osseous changes had begun, even though they were probably given some access to Vitamin C when they entered the institution.

Was Scurvy Misdiagnosed by the Workhouse Physicians?

Considering the very high prevalence rate of scurvy, there is a noteworthy absence of any references to the disease in minute books or newspaper articles that reported on the weekly meetings of the Kilkenny Board of Guardians. None of the surviving medical reports by the workhouse physicians include any mention of the disease, yet there are strong reasons to believe that misdiagnoses were made. In 1846, severely ill patients in the Ballymore Eustace Dispensary in Naas, County Kildare, initially were described as suffering from "a peculiar form" of gastroenteritis before an alternative diagnosis of scurvy was made (Crawford 1988, 286). The same general lack of knowledge of the nature of the disease was evident in England at the same time. An 1849 article by Dr. John Barrett, senior surgeon to the Bath Western Dispensary, about the widespread occurrence of scurvy in the area of Bath in Somerset in 1847 expressed concern that many medical officers at the union workhouses in the vicinity had difficulty diagnosing scurvy and differentiating it from "purpura haemorrhagica" (Barrett 1849), a hemorrhagic condition affecting the skin that can be the result of various disorders that are not related to Vitamin C deficiency.

An article published by Dr. Lalor in the *Dublin Quarterly Journal of Medical Science* in 1848 should be read and understood in this context (Lalor 1848). Lalor described in great detail the nature and symptoms of an epidemic of what he diagnosed as "gastric fever"—a term that implies typhoid fever—in Kilkenny from the summer of 1844 to at least September 1847, when he submitted his article to the journal. From his text, it is clear that some of these symptoms are likely descriptions of scurvy. Beginning in the summer of 1845, he noted "purpuric eruption" in his patients. The condition became particularly frequent starting in September 1846. His further descriptions of these lesions suggest that they are scorbutic ecchymoses:

The order of frequency in which the skin of the different parts of the body was the seat of eruption, was pretty much as follows: the upper part of the chest, the inguinal regions, the back of the neck and throat, the abdomen, the flexures of the elbow-joints, the arms, forearms, legs, thighs, lumbar region, and lower part of chest. . . . The persistence of the spots after pressure by the finger was sufficient to distinguish them from the spots of typhus. (Lalor 1848, 16–17)

It is clear from this quote that Lalor had contemplated alternative diagnoses. In his description of the treatments he undertook, he also indirectly reveals that he had already discarded scurvy as a cause of the lesions:

Diluent drinks, and the abstraction of solid food, and of all external or internal irritants, formed the chief part of the general treatment. . . . Inflammatory complications were most safely and successfully treated by mercury, with opium and blisters; and the apparent analogy between this disease and scurvy should not deter us, in such complications, from the use of this medicine, which acted as favourably here as in idiopathic inflammations. (Lalor 1848, 19)

Lalor believed that the purpura he noted were associated with famine fever, which he would likely have been more familiar with. Considering the exceptionally high prevalence rate of scurvy identified in the skeletons from the Kilkenny Union Workhouse mass burials, it becomes clear that the workhouse physicians likely misdiagnosed presentations of scurvy during the famine. Whether this caused additional and unnecessary pain and deaths to those suffering from the disease is impossible to ascertain. The skeletal evidence indicates that most people had been given some access to Vitamin C prior to their death, most likely from the daily food rations provided by the workhouse. Lalor also mentioned that "habitual use of animal diet has been more or less preventive in gastro-purpuric" (1848, 29), which would suggest that workhouse inmates are unlikely to have died from scurvy, even though the disease is fatal if not treated. However, the age-at-death profiles reveal that scurvy significantly influenced the pattern of mortality (see below). A reduced immune defense due to inadequate intake of Vitamin C appears to have resulted in a high risk of acquiring an infectious disease that for many people led to death.

Rickets and Osteomalacia

Continuous deficiencies of Vitamin D, calcium, and phosphorus or an imbalance of the latter two minerals can result in rickets in non-adults and osteomalacia and osteoporosis in adults. The few dietary sources of Vitamin D include oily fish, egg yolks, butter, and liver (Insel et al. 2011, 410; Wing and Brown 1979, 61). However, humans can produce Vitamin D in vivo through ultraviolet radiation from natural sunlight via sterols in the skin (Holick and Adams 1998; Wing and Brown 1979, 39–40). As Vitamin D is fat soluble, dietary uptake is dependent on properly functioning fat absorption in the diet in general. In addition, Vitamin D on its own is required for dietary uptake of calcium and phosphorus and is essential for the adequate deposition of these minerals in the bone (Civitelli et al. 1998; Pitt 2002, 1905; Wing and Brown 1979, 39–40). Calcium and phosphorus, the most common minerals in the human body, are obtained from a variety of dietary sources such as dairy products, fish, meat, eggs, and nuts. Insufficient intake of these can also result in secondary rickets and osteomalacia, although this is considered to be very uncommon (Pitt 2002, 1915). Because of the increased requirements of calcium and Vitamin D during pregnancy and lactation, females are more likely to develop the disease than males during adulthood (Wing and Brown 1979, 40).

Deficiencies of Vitamin D, calcium, and phosphorus cause a disturbance in the normal osteoid mineralization process. To compensate for inadequate levels of serum calcium, the body withdraws calcium from the existing skeletal structure. When rickets is present, this results in a defective process of endochondral calcification in the growing skeleton; when osteomalacia is present, it causes an interruption of the bone remodeling process (Vaughan 1970, 240). Eventually, these conditions lead to swelling and an accumulation of unmineralized matrix, which is ultimately weakened through the weight of the body and causes bone deformities and fractures (Glorieux, Karsenty, and Thakker 1998, 765; Wing and Brown 1979, 39–40).

Rickets and osteomalacia were common diseases in the nineteenth century, especially in northern Europe and North America, because of urbanization, pollution, and indoor employment associated with the increasing industrialization (Steinbock 1993). Throughout much of the century, the role the environment played as a cause of the disease was little understood. An investigation in the 1880s of the prevalence of the

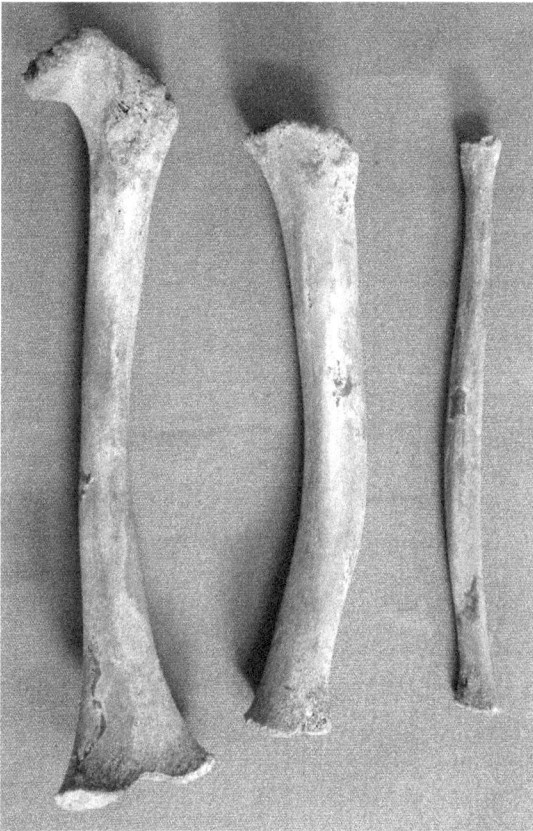

Figure 4.8. Indicative of rickets, curvature of the bones in the right lower extremity of a five-year-old child (DXL). Photo by author.

disease in Great Britain and Ireland by the British Medical Association revealed that rickets was less prevalent in rural districts but was very common in large industrial and urbanized areas. In Ireland, the disease was particularly observed in Dublin and Belfast, but across the rest of the country it was reported as relatively uncommon. A geographical exception was noted in the Blackwater Valley in the southern counties of Cork and Waterford, where coal was extensively mined (Owen 1889, 114). The prevalent theories in the nineteenth century about the cause of the disease identified factors such as infection, too much nutrition, poor nutrition, idleness, or inheritance (Holick and Adams 1998, 124). Cod liver oil, the most effective remedy, remained in widespread use well into the twentieth century (Holick and Adams 1998, 125; Park 1923; Pitt 2002, 1901–2).

Rickets were clearly manifested in twenty-two non-adult skeletons from the Kilkenny mass burials (figure 4.8). The majority of cases were

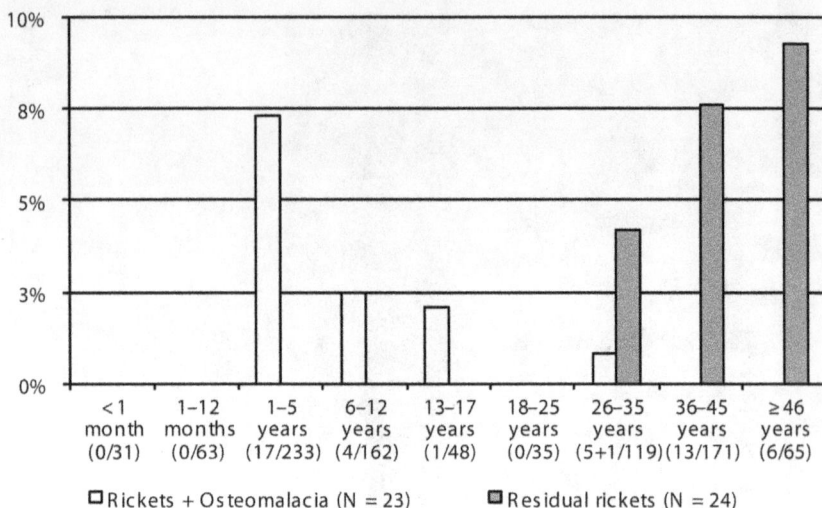

Figure 4.9. Frequency of rickets and osteomalacia by age group.

noticed in one- to five-year-old children. This possibly reflects the increased risk of developing rickets in the smallest children, who may have been cared for primarily indoors, especially if they were born in the workhouse. Of the older children and adolescents, approximately 2 percent displayed long-bone deformities indicative of rickets (figure 4.9). Residual rickets was identified in the skeletons of twenty-four adults (5.71 percent; 24/420); the highest prevalence rates were noted in the older age categories. The rates were slightly higher in males (6.67 percent; 14/210) than in females (5.13 percent; 10/195), although the difference was not statistically significant.[1] One case of osteomalacia was diagnosed in the skeleton of an early middle adult male (XC). He displayed diagnostic Looser zones fracture patterns at the lateral margin of the scapula, the pubic ramus, and one rib, although the latter may be the result of interpersonal violence, as this individual displayed additional fractures consistent with such a diagnosis (see chapter 3).

Concurring with the historical records, the Kilkenny skeletons reveal that rickets and osteomalacia were not unknown diseases for the poorer classes before the famine, even though the laboring agricultural population would have spent more time outdoors and hence would have been more exposed to sunlight than the more privileged classes. When the prevalence rate of rickets and osteomalacia in the Kilkenny skeletons is

Table 4.7. Frequency and rate of rickets/osteomalacia, nineteenth-century skeletal populations

Population	n/total	%
Kilkenny Union Workhouse, Kilkenny	47/957	4.91
Hospital of the Assumption, Thurles	0/9	0.00
All Saints, Chelsea Old Church, London	13/198	6.57
Bow Baptist Church, London	32/416	7.69
Christ Church Spitalfields, London	35/968	3.62
Cross Bones, London	10/148	6.76
New Bunhill Fields Burial Ground, London	20/514	3.89
St. Benet Sherehog, London	9/230	3.91
St. George's, London	1/111	0.90
St. Luke's, London	15/241	6.22
St. Mary and St. Michael, London	78/705	11.06
St. Marylebone Church, London	32/301	10.63
St. Pancras, London	20/715	2.80
Sheen's Burial Ground, London	14/254	5.51
City Bunhill Burial Ground, London	16/239	6.69
St. Martin's, Birmingham	45/505	8.91
St. Peter's, Wolverhampton	5/150	3.33

compared to that of other nineteenth-century skeletal populations, the frequency appears normal for the period and not particularly high or low (table 4.7). This would indicate that the factors that caused rickets in Kilkenny did not differ greatly from those elsewhere in Britain and Ireland. Interestingly, the prevalence of rickets in the London populations has a generally wide range, from less than 1 percent at St. George's to 11 percent at the Catholic Mission of St. Mary and St. Michael, suggesting that there is no clear definite correlation between rickets and urban living conditions, at least not when studied skeletally.

If these affected individuals from the workhouse burials were local to Kilkenny City, then the urban environment and medieval layout of the city, the industrial workplaces located nearby (see chapter 1), and an imbalance of calcium and phosphorus in the diet are all feasible reasons for the presence of the disease in this population. The disease causes dull and generalized bone pain that is often persistent and made worse by mechanical loading. In osteomalacia, it is often felt first in the lower back, later spreading to the pelvis, upper thighs, the upper back, and ribs. Muscle weakness also sets in that, together with the pain, often results in difficulties in walking (Parfitt 1998, 338–40; Wing and Brown 1979, 40). Even though the disease is unlikely to relate to famine-induced stress, these symptomatic consequences of the condition would have further debilitated those it afflicted while they struggled to survive the famine.

Porotic Hyperostosis and Cribra Orbitalia

Skeletal lesions indicative of iron deficiency anemia have traditionally been attributed to porotic hyperostosis and cribra orbitalia, although this has been debated extensively among paleopathologists (e.g., Aufderheide and Rodríguez-Martín 1998, 348–51; Ortner 2003, 102–5; Walker et al. 2009; Wapler et al. 2004). Both lesions reflect childhood conditions (Stuart-Macadam 1985, 1992) and when identified in adults they are generally healed conditions and therefore a reflection of a non-adult ailment rather than a disease experienced around the time of death. Porotic hyperostosis produces characteristic porotic lesions on the skull vault (figure 4.10a) due to expansion of the middle diploë layer that is caused by hyperactive bone marrow (Stuart-Macadam 1989, 214). It is particularly noted on the parietal bones and is usually bilateral. Cribra orbitalia is a similar lesion on the roof of the eye sockets (figure 4.10b–c). While the general consensus has often attributed porotic hyperostosis that exhibits an expanding diploë layer directly to iron deficiency anemia, cribra orbitalia is sometimes noted in association with other pathological conditions and metabolic disorders such as rickets, scurvy, hemangioma, and trauma (Brickley and Ives 2008, 3; Ortner, Kimmerle, and Diez 1999; Ortner and Mays 1998; Walker et al. 2009).

Walker et al. (2009) have contested iron deficiency as a likely etiology for these pathological changes. They have argued that it is physiologically impossible for iron deficiency anemia to cause marrow expansion because iron is required for the production of red blood cells and thus inevitably inhibits marrow hypertrophy. However, Oxenham and Cavill (2010) refute this argument. They point out that it is only anemia of chronic disease that is unable to trigger diploic expansion and not iron deficiency per se. Walker et al. argued that nutritional megaloblastic anemia, most commonly caused by Vitamin B12 deficiency, is the likely cause of these pathological changes. This vitamin is acquired from food of animal origin, and its metabolism in the human body provides a confident explanation for why active porotic hyperostosis and cribra orbitalia are primarily observed in non-adults. Although humans are able to store Vitamin B12

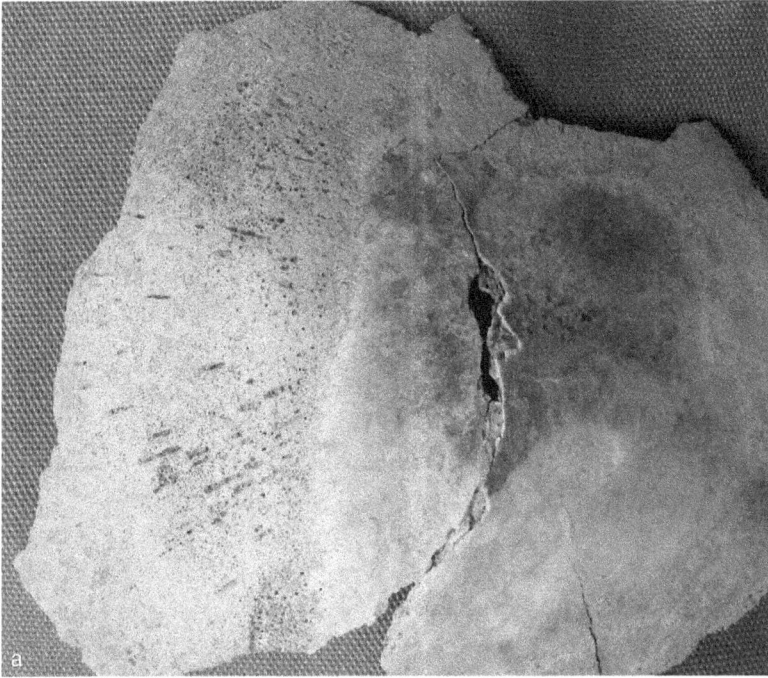

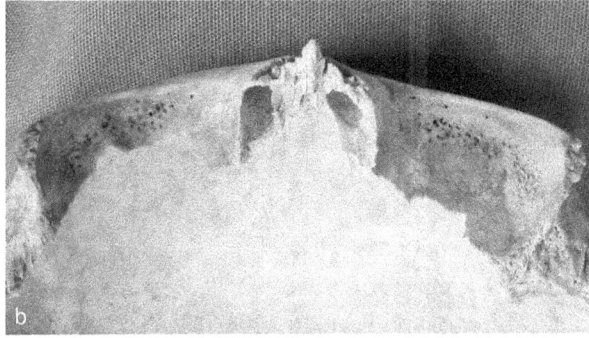

Figure 4.10. Examples of porotic hyperostosis and cribra orbitalia: (a) on a parietal bone of an infant child (CDXLI); (b) on the orbitae of a young child (XXXI); (c) on an early middle adult male (CMLXV). Photo by author.

in the liver, because infants have fewer reserves, they are more likely to develop symptoms in a period of deficiency. Taking the points of Oxenham and Cavill (2010) into consideration, both Vitamin B12 deficiency and iron deficiency anemia can be taken as plausible etiologies for these pathological changes in the Kilkenny Union Workhouse population.

Porotic hyperostosis of the cranial vault was recorded on a three-category scale (Stuart-Macadam 1985): light = scattered fine foramina; medium = large and small isolated foramina and foramina that have linked to form a trabecular structure; and severe = outgrowth in the trabecular structure from the normal contour of the outer bone table. The majority of the lesions were light (70.37 percent; 19/27), six cases were of medium development (22.22 percent), and only two were severe lesions (7.41 percent). The medium to severe lesions were identified only in non-adults, and all adults displayed only light porosities. This is a reflection of active lesions in non-adults and healed lesions in adults. Although iron deficiency anemia of the mother during pregnancy is known to increase the risk of premature births (Scholl 2005), the only neonatal case of porotic hyperostosis in the Kilkenny population was full term at the time of birth.

Cribra orbitalia in at least one eye socket was identified in 166 individuals out of 826, an overall prevalence rate of 20 percent. The prevalence rate was 25 percent (118/471) among non-adult individuals and 14 percent in adults (48/355). The highest frequencies were observed in skeletons of older children and adolescents (table 4.8). If we accept the iron deficiency hypothesis, this difference may reflect the facts that adolescents require a higher proportion of iron in the diet during the hormonal changes associated with puberty and that anemia is relatively common in girls after the onset of menstruation. A higher iron uptake is also required during childhood growth spurts (Bridges and Pearson 2008, 99). For all of these reasons, a diet inadequate in iron is expected to be visible particularly in the non-adult age groups. If these lesions were primarily caused by Vitamin B12 insufficiency, they may indicate that this proportion of the population was particularly prone to deficiencies because they were no longer breast fed and were not old enough to have built up a substantial reserve of Vitamin B12 in the liver.

The data also revealed a considerably higher frequency of cribra orbitalia in young children than in infants.[2] Studies have shown that late weaning after the sixth month has a significant risk of leading to the development of iron deficiency anemia in young children unless a complementary iron

le 4.8. Frequency and rate of porotic hyperostosis of the cranial vault and cribra
italia by age group, Kilkenny workhouse population

group	Porotic hyperostosis		Cribra orbitalia		Any	
	n/total	%	n/total	%	n/total	%
rth	1/28	3.57	0/25	0.00	1/29	3.45
years	3/59	5.08	1/55	1.82	4/61	6.56
years	5/221	2.26	48/209	22.97	52/226	23.01
2 years	4/145	2.76	55/140	39.29	57/147	38.78
17 years	1/45	2.22	14/42	33.33	15/46	32.61
25 years	2/33	6.06	10/33	30.30	12/33	36.36
35 years	6/106	5.66	17/104	16.35	21/107	19.63
45 years	4/156	2.56	15/151	9.93	20/161	12.42
5 years	1/63	1.59	6/62	9.68	7/64	10.94
years	0/6	0.00	0/5	0.00	0/8	0.00
al	27/862	3.13	166/826	20.10	189/882	21.43

source is present in the diet (Sultan and Zyberi 2003). The significant increase in the rate of cribra orbitalia between neonates/infants and young
children might therefore be a reflection of a late weaning practice in the
population. This would also suggest that young infants benefited from
being breastfed by their mothers, who would have had adequate Vitamin
B12 reserves in their bodies.

In general, females exhibited greater frequencies of both porotic hyperostosis of the cranial vault and cribra orbitalia than males, although the
difference was not statistically significant (table 4.9). Males were more frequently affected than females in the young adult age group, and it is possible that the non-adult age groups would have displayed a dominance of
boys if sexing of the juvenile skeletons were possible. It is known that male
infants have a higher rate of iron deficiency than females because they
have a faster growth rate and require a higher intake of dietary iron than
girls. A study of the prevalence rate of iron deficiency anemia in infants
in Rio de Janeiro revealed a 2.06 times greater risk of developing anemia
in boys than in girls (Alberico et al. 2003). Another study of Swedish and
Honduran infants at the age of nine months revealed that boys were ten
times more likely to be diagnosed with anemia than girls (Domellöf et al.
2002).

In comparison with contemporaneous populations, the frequency of
cribra orbitalia in the Kilkenny skeletons is high; it is surpassed only by
the frequency in the London populations buried at St. Benet Sherehog,

Table 4.9. Frequency and rate of porotic hyperostosis and cribra orbitalia in adults by sex and age group, Kilkenny workhouse population

	Male		Female		χ^2	df	p
	n/total	%	n/total	%			
POROTIC HYPEROSTOSIS							
18–25 years	1/17	5.88	1/16	6.25	.002	1	.965
26–35 years	3/42	7.14	3/63	4.76	.265	1	.607
36–45 years	2/84	2.38	2/69	2.90	.040	1	.842
≥ 46 years	0/43	0.00	1/19	5.26	2.300	1	.129
Total[1]	6/187	3.21	7/169	4.14	.220	1	.639
CRIBRA ORBITALIA							
18–25 years	6/17	35.29	4/16	25.00	.414	1	.520
26–35 years	3/42	7.14	14/61	22.95	4.510	1	.034
36–45 years	6/81	7.41	9/68	13.24	1.387	1	.239
≥ 46 years	4/41	9.76	2/20	10.00	.001	1	.976
Total[1]	19/181	10.50	29/169	17.16	3.278	1	.070
ANY							
18–25 years	7/17	41.18	5/16	31.25	.351	1	.554
26–35 years	6/43	13.95	15/63	23.81	1.563	1	.211
36–45 years	9/86	10.47	11/71	15.49	.884	1	.347
≥ 46 years	4/43	9.30	3/20	15.00	.449	1	.503
Total[1]	26/190	13.68	34/174	19.54	2.262	1	.133

[1] Includes generically aged adults (>18 years).

the Catholic Mission of St. Mary and St. Michael, and Bow Baptist Church (table 4.10). This could be because of a discrepancy because there is a disproportionally large number of non-adults in these populations and adults are more likely to display the lesion. But it may also be a direct reflection of the physiological stress the Kilkenny population experienced. Cribra orbitalia in the Kilkenny workhouse population also occurred in association with scorbutic lesions. Walker et al. (2009) argue that Vitamin C deficiency is likely to be a major causative agent for cribra orbitalia, and when that possibility is taken into consideration it seems most probable that the high frequencies of the pathological changes reflect the high rates of scurvy rather than iron deficiency anemia or Vitamin B12 deficiency in this population.

Table 4.10. Frequency and rate of cribra orbitalia, nineteenth-century skeletal populations

Population	n/total	%
Kilkenny Union Workhouse, Kilkenny	166/826	20.10
Hospital of the Assumption, Thurles	0/9	0.00
All Saints, Chelsea Old Church, London	18/198	9.09
Bow Baptist Church, London	93/416	22.36
Christ Church Spitalfields, London	141/968	14.57
Cross Bones, London	6/148	4.05
New Bunhill Fields Burial Ground, London	75/514	14.59
St. Benet Sherehog, London	25/98	25.51
St. George's, Bloomsbury, London	7/72	9.72
St. Luke's, Islington, London	23/241	9.54
St. Mary and St. Michael, London	250/705	35.46
St. Marylebone, London	13/301	4.32
St. Pancras, London	42/715	5.87
Sheen's Burial Ground, London	17/254	6.69
City Bunhill Burial Ground, London	12/239	5.02
St. Martin's, Birmingham	38/394	9.64
St. Peter's, Wolverhampton	8/81	9.88

Death by Famine

The number of deaths directly caused by conditions brought on by the blight and the famine in Ireland during the 1840s and early 1850s has been a divisive subject among historians. Estimates range from between 500,000 to 1.5 million deaths (Boyle and Ó Gráda 1986, 543). Ó Gráda and colleagues have done most of the recent work concerning the excessive deaths and mortality trends of the Great Famine. Their work is based on pre- and post-famine census data, which they have analyzed using a variety of statistical methods for the purpose of detecting famine-related deaths. This work has taken into account both natural deaths and population decline due to emigration and probably provides the most accurate estimations to date. Boyle and Ó Gráda (1986) estimate that over 1 million people died in Ireland as a direct consequence of famine between 1845 and 1852 (Boyle and Ó Gráda 1986). A different estimation by Cousens (1960, 1963), who used a similar statistical approach as Boyle and Ó Gráda (1986), gave a figure of 800,645 deaths, with an additional population loss of 967,908 individuals due to emigration.

Cousens estimated that 14,365 individuals died in County Kilkenny alone, of which 5,490 died in institutions such as the union workhouse, the fever hospital, and the jail. The excess mortality was just over 7 percent, according to Cousens. This number should be compared with the estimated rates of excess mortality of 15–17 percent that were seen in Counties Clare and Galway, and 13–15 percent in Counties Mayo, Kerry, and Cork. The lowest mortality rates are estimated from Counties Down and Kildare, where the estimated excess mortality was 3–5 percent. While the mortality rates fluctuated in most counties from year to year, especially in 1848 and 1849 when there was much regional variation, the excess mortality rate appears to have been relatively constant in County Kilkenny throughout the famine years (Cousens 1960, 1963). Joel Mokyr (1983) estimated that the excess mortality rate in County Kilkenny in 1846 to 1851 was 12.5 to 18.1 per 1,000 individuals. Of the twelve counties of Leinster, Kilkenny would then have experienced the sixth highest mortality in terms of the relative number of deaths (Mokyr 1983, table 9.2).

A minimum of 970 skeletons were identified in the mass burials at the Kilkenny workhouse. Of these, more than half (56.19 percent; 545/970) had died before the age of eighteen. Relatively few neonatal, adolescent, and young adult skeletons were present. Seventeen individuals were aged as late-term fetuses based on long-bone measurements, but as none of these could with confidence be observed as located in abdomens of females, they were most reasonably low birthweight newborns who died either during or immediately after birth. They were therefore considered neonates in this study. The majority of the adults were aged to the middle age category. Some thirty-two skeletons could not be aged more precisely than as adults (that is, more than eighteen years of age) (table 4.11). The small proportion of adolescents and young adults is interesting. This might be a reflection of the workhouse demographic profile, as this age group is likely to have constituted the most "able-bodied" proportion of the general population and therefore deemed "undeserving" of indoor relief. It is also clear that during catastrophic periods such as famines, these age groups are the most likely to survive (Margerison and Knüsel 2002, 140).

The human remains represent the minimum mortality among residents of the workhouse during a minimum period of three years and eight months. During this same period, based on evidence from the workhouse minute books, it is estimated that about 2,200 individuals died in the

Table 4.11. Age and sex profile of the Kilkenny Union Workhouse skeletal population

Age group	Male	Female	Indet.	All
Neonate (< 1 month)	--	--	32	32
Infant (1–12 months)	--	--	63	63
Young child (1–5 years)	--	--	239	239
Older child (6–12 years)	--	--	163	163
Adolescent (13–17 years)	4	3	41	48
Young adult (18–25 years)	18	17	0	35
Early middle adult (26–35 years)	46	74	1	121
Late middle adult (36–45 years)	94	74	4	172
Older adult (≥ 46 years)	44	20	1	65
Indet. adult (>18 years)	10	12	10	32
Total	216	200	554	970

Kilkenny Union (see figure 2.7). However, it is likely that many of these individuals died in the fever hospital and were interred in the intramural burial ground that was concurrently in use there. The archaeological excavation of the mass burial ground at the workhouse is also not fully complete, as disturbances were observed on the southern edge and the limit of the excavation did not fully encompass the northern and eastern extents of the cemetery. It is clear that the skeletal remains from the mass burials represent only a portion of the deaths that occurred in the workhouse. It is also reasonable to assume that some bodies were claimed by people outside the institution who had the ability and means to bury their relatives and friends in consecrated ground located elsewhere.

The question is whether the mortality profile—as indicated from the skeletons in the workhouse mass burials—is a valid representation of disease- and starvation-induced deaths in general during the famine or only of those that had taken place in the workhouses. It is also clear that a proportion of the inmates who died in the institution were not buried in the burial ground. The famine-induced mortality profile of the workhouses is also likely to have been different from what was occurring outside these institutions. Poor ventilation, leaking roofs, and overcrowding made these institutions vectors for the spread of infectious disease, and this influenced the mortality rates: the workhouses were perceived as death houses, and people did their utmost to avoid them. Also, individuals in the greatest and most desperate distress and in the poorest health were more likely to be admitted. It was these individuals who were most likely to die during the Great Famine. It has been estimated that about

200,000 people died as a consequence of famine-induced disease in Irish workhouses in the period 1846–1851 (Ó Gráda 2012). This accounts for about 20 percent of all who died during the famine.

Methodological issues are the greatest obstacle in any attempt to make a direct analogy between the death rates as indicated from the Kilkenny workhouse skeletal population and mortality data from historical sources. The error margins applicable to all osteological methods for estimating and determining age and sex from human skeletal remains have not always been adequately considered. Depending on skeletal preservation, sex can be confidently determined only for post-pubertal individuals (Sjøvold 1988); this is why no non-adult skeletons were sexed in this study. Age at death in the Kilkenny workhouse skeletons was estimated from stage of dental and skeletal development, from long-bone measurements in non-adult remains (Liversidge et al. 1998; Moorrees, Fanning, and Hunt 1963; Scheuer and Black 2000; Scheuer et al. 1980), from the morphology of the joint surface of the ribs and the hip bones, and from stage of sutural obliteration in the skulls of adults (Brooks and Suchey 1990; İşcan, Loth, and Wright 1984, 1985; Lovejoy et al. 1985; Meindl and Lovejoy 1985). Unfortunately, a systemic bias in the method of determining osteological age that can be very population specific means that there will always be a discrepancy between an individual's "biological age" and his or her true "chronological age" (see Cole et al. 1988; Introna and Campobasso 2006). It is anticipated that this deviation is present in the Kilkenny workhouse population, especially in the post-pubertal age groups. Overall, demographic data from archaeological samples are known to display higher mortality rates in young and middle adult individuals and relatively low levels of mortality in the older adult age category than we find in historical sources (Chamberlain 2006, 89–90). This is important to consider when interpreting paleodemographic data. Thus, it might not be accurate to perform direct comparisons with data derived from archaeological population groups and those obtained from historical sources. A study of the contrasts in the general trends in mortality models from both types of sample data is expected to be more valuable than the exact estimations themselves. Many of the mortality rates and much of the demographic information available for the period of the Great Famine are themselves estimations and are not based on clean empirical data.

Distributions of Skeletal Age at Death

For the purpose of assessing the mortality of the entire skeletal population from Kilkenny Union Workhouse, adult skeletons that could not be aged more precisely than as being over the age of eighteen were distributed in relative proportions to the age-group data of the rest of the adult population. The mortality profile—which was distributed through five-year age groups—indicated a significant mortality rate among non-adults, especially among children younger than ten; it was most noticeable in children aged less than five. The lowest level of mortality was observed in individuals aged between ten and thirty, after which mortality rates increased again (figure 4.11). Despite methodological issues, these data fit very well with Boyle and Ó Gráda's estimations that a higher prevalence of excess deaths occurred in the newborn to four-year age group and in individuals over the age of sixty during the Great Famine (Boyle and Ó Gráda 1986). It was not possible in this study to detect which individuals were older than sixty years, but these are likely to be included in the age categories over thirty years. This result would indicate that the skeletal profile of age

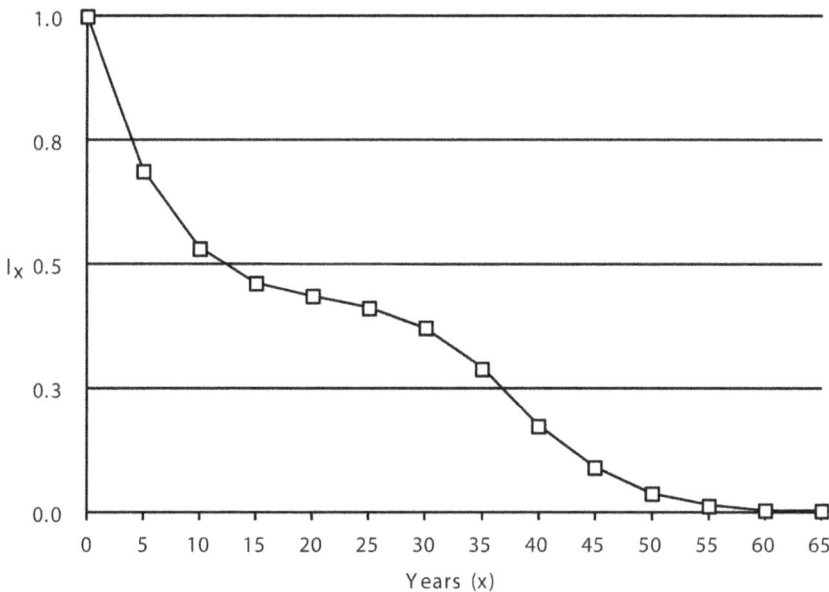

Figure 4.11. Expressed in a survivorship curve, mortality of the Kilkenny Union Workhouse skeletal population by five-year age groups.

at death in the Kilkenny workhouse population is a valid representation of famine-induced mortality.

A substantial proportion of the skeletons found in the mass burials were of infants and children, providing a stark reminder that the Great Famine was a catastrophe that particularly affected the young generation of Ireland. Many children would have resided in the workhouses of Ireland during the famine, either children from destitute families that were granted admission or orphan children who had no custodian. Children were also commonly abandoned in the workhouse, and the guardians made every attempt to relocate their parents so they could be forced to take economic responsibility for them. In many cases, parents feared that they would be deemed "undeserving" of indoor relief and that the Board of Guardians would have denied their children access. In that situation, the only way to secure the survival of their children would have been to abandon them. It was not uncommon for parents to abandon their children in the workhouse, emigrate to North America or elsewhere, and later send for them when they had enough money to do so.

Among the non-adults, the young child age category, that is, individuals between one and five years old, dominated the absolute mortality in the population. More precise age estimates revealed that infants and children aged less than two were at the most risk of dying (figure 4.12). The medical officers' report for January 1848 reflected on the particularly high mortality among the smallest children:

> Inspection of the infant children . . . at breakfast. . . . A great majority of them were fed by their parents with a portion of their own stir-about[3] only. . . . The feeding and general management of the infant children have been very defective at all times since the opening of the Workhouse. . . . The bad state of health of this class . . . was never more painfully exhibited than . . . by the great mortality amongst them, from febrile and other diseases. . . . The great number of deaths amongst the unhealthy children under ten years of age, which forms the largest portion of the present mortality. (*Kilkenny Journal* 1848b)

As is clear from this statement, the care of the smallest children in the workhouse was inadequate. Dr. Lalor reported on the neglect of a child in the workhouse in October 1848:

On my visit this morning I found a child of the name of Catherine Nowlan in Nurse Dawson's ward in a state of great filth having evidently been only half washed since her admission on yesterday. I should recommend that the Nurse of the Ward be fined for this neglect, and that Mrs. Hamilton states that she herself saw and permitted the child to be in this state: the neglect of a nurse sanctioned by the sufferance of the party over her becomes in my mind the fault of the latter party, and should be visited on the superior and not the inferior officer.[4]

These statements suggest that there may have been occasional abuses in terms of the care of the children in the workhouse and that some might have been subject to neglect. The workhouse physicians clearly connected this to the particularly high mortality of the youngest children. At the same time, human mortality naturally varies most greatly among infants (Weiss 1973, 26).

The burial and funerary treatment of deceased non-adults is perhaps the main archaeological source of insight into attitudes toward children in past societies (see Ingvarsson-Sundström 2008; Kraus 2006;

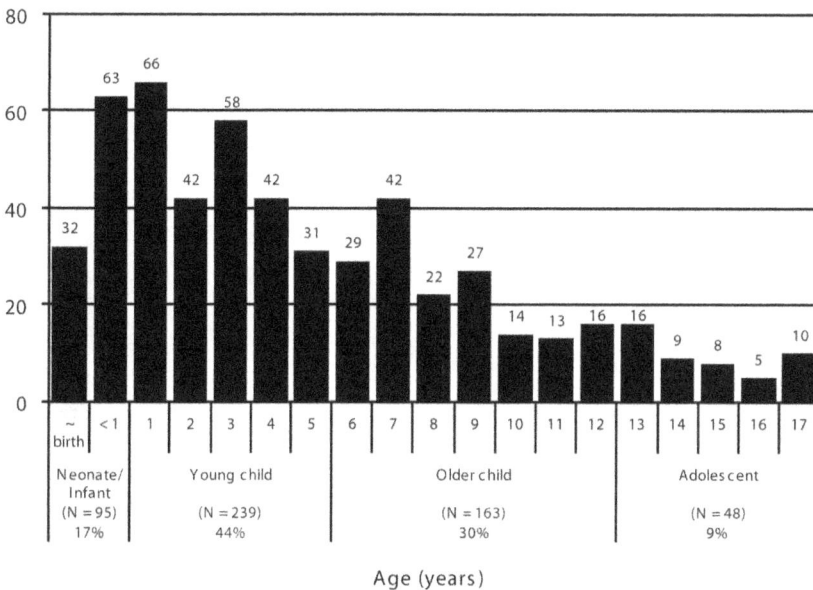

Figure 4.12. Number of individuals by skeletal age in the non-adult population.

Figure 4.13. Skeletons of two young children (DCII and DCIII) buried together in an adult coffin. Photo by Margaret Gowen & Co. Ltd.

Wilemann 2005, 71–93). The archaeological evidence from the Kilkenny Union Workhouse mass burial ground clearly indicates that children were buried with the same degree of respect and care as deceased adults. The placement of an infant child in the crook of the right arm of an adult female—presumably its mother—particularly reflects the sensitivity expressed in the interment of these smallest children (see figure 2.11). It is clear, however, that infant children placed in coffins with adults or, as in one case, two young children were placed in one adult coffin (figures 2.11 and 4.13) were mainly for economic reasons (see chapter 2).

A total of 200 females and 216 males could be osteologically sexed in the population. Seven of these were adolescents. The mean skeletal age at death of adult females was 36.5 years.[5] For adult males, it was 39.6 years,[6] a difference that was statistically significant when tested by age-group distribution;[7] females: median = 36.1 years, males: median = 40.3 years. There were more deceased females than males in the twenty-five to forty-five age groups; this was particularly evident in adults aged thirty to thirty-five years. This higher mortality proportion among females decreased after age forty-five, while it increased consistently in the male

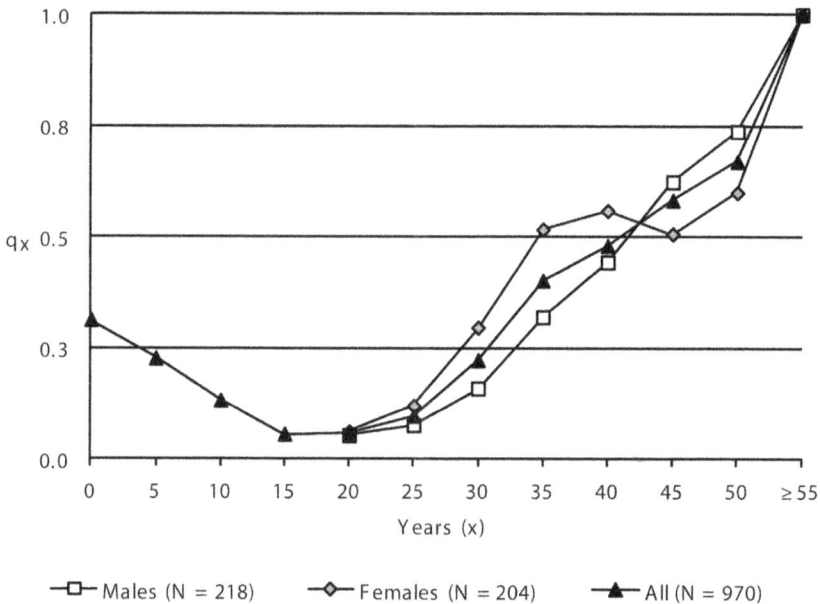

Figure 4.14. Probability of death rates in the population by five-year age groups and sex.

population (figure 4.14). A higher proportion of male deaths is consistent with the conclusions of Boyle and Ó Gráda, who estimated that about 1–2 percent more males than females died during the Great Famine (1986, table 8). Their conclusion is interesting, as it is identical to the difference noted in the mass burials from Kilkenny (see table 4.11). One must also consider the fact that several young female workhouse inmates from Kilkenny were transported to Australia during the famine (*Kilkenny Journal* 1849e), and this may have influenced the summary result from the osteological determination of age at death and sex in the adult skeletons.

Enamel Hypoplasia and Mortality Patterns

Enamel hypoplasia, an indicator of health in childhood, has been shown to correlate with mortality patterns later in life. It could be a reflection of a physiological change in early childhood that had a negative impact on the health of those who survived for the reminder of their lives. This suggestion is commonly referred to as the Barker hypothesis and is based on the initial observation of mortality patterns in English and Welsh populations in the 1920s and 1960s–1970s in an epidemiological study carried out by David Barker and Clive Osmond from the University of Southampton. They identified correlations in the same population between high infant mortality in the beginning of the twentieth century and death from coronary heart disease decades later (Barker and Osmond 1986). It is also possible that individuals displaying enamel hypoplasia had chronic poor health until their premature deaths.

Earlier mortality among individuals displaying enamel hypoplasia has been observed in several studies of skeletal populations (e.g., Armelagos et al. 2009; Cook and Buikstra 1979; Duray 1996). Armelagos et al. (2009) presented three possible causes for this pattern: that individuals displaying enamel hypoplasia have an underlying physiological frailty that remains throughout life; that enamel hypoplasia is an indirect reflection of sociocultural stratification and therefore reflects differential exposure and response to periods of stress of a proportion of a population; and that physiological stress in childhood resulting in enamel hypoplasia may have decreased the ability of affected individuals to respond to further stressors.

The mean skeletal age at death of individuals displaying enamel hypoplasia was twenty-five years.[8] Individuals with no enamel defects were, on average, aged twenty-one at the time of death.[9] This difference was statistically significant by age-group distribution.[10] The mortality curve, as illustrated in Figure 4.15, reveals that this difference was greatest among non-adults to early middle adults and less so in the late middle and older adult age categories. The difference contrasts with the findings observed in the skeletal studies of other archaeological populations (Armelagos et al. 2009; Cook and Buikstra 1979; Duray 1996). It suggests that in the Kilkenny workhouse population, individuals exposed to stress in childhood had a greater chance of surviving the famine for longer (Geber 2014). The great difference in the non-adult population probably reflects that the strongest children who most likely survived the famine were therefore most susceptible to the development of dental enamel defects. The finding supports the theory of the osteological paradox and is an important consideration when discussing the impact of famine in populations that died during a catastrophic event or period, as the inmates of the Kilkenny workhouse did (see Ortner 2003, 115).

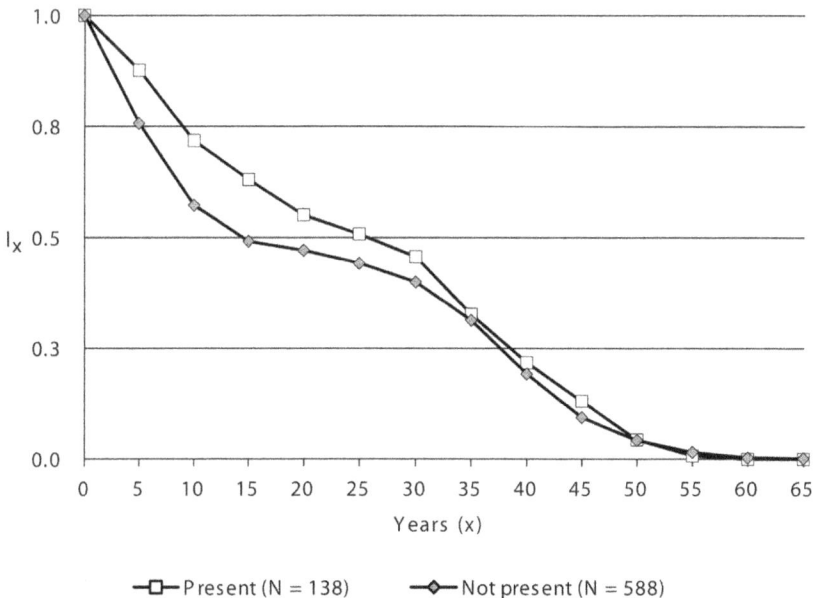

Figure 4.15. Mortality curves of the proportion of the population displaying dental enamel hypoplasia and those with no defects present.

Infectious Disease and Mortality

Infectious diseases have been the main cause of death in periods of famine both historically and in contemporary societies. In Ireland during the Great Famine, these were mainly epidemic typhus, typhoid fever, cholera, and tuberculosis. Only the latter is directly diagnosable in skeletal remains but was of a relatively low prevalence rate in the Kilkenny workhouse population. The reason for this is probably a reflection of the inability to survive the disease process long enough for any osseous manifestation to occur. For the purpose of assessing the influence of infectious disease on mortality in the population, all diagnosed cases of infectious disease such as pulmonary infection (rib lesions and maxillary sinusitis), tuberculosis, osteomyelitis, and syphilis were assessed both independently and as a collation (table 4.12). Cases of nonspecific new bone formation were excluded, as it seems most probable that these pathological changes are likely to be greatly influenced by metabolic conditions in the population and probably relate to scurvy in particular (see above). The results, when the whole population is taken into account, indicate that individuals with evidence of skeletal infection were generally nine years older than those with no evidence of infectious disease. This disparity was significant only among the non-adult proportion of the population, in which a difference of about three years was seen. Among the adults, the only noteworthy difference was observed in individuals with tuberculosis who were on an average eight years younger than those with no skeletal evidence of the disease when they died.

In the non-adult population, the differences were greatest in the diagnosed cases of pulmonary disease. These individuals were significantly older at the time of death than those who displayed no skeletal evidence of sinusitis or rib lesions. As previously discussed, the homes of the poor of County Kilkenny in the decades before the famine were described as being very poorly ventilated, and those who lived under such circumstances may have built up a stronger immune system that benefited the non-adult population when the famine occurred. This finding could be physical evidence that supports the observation during the 1840s that the relative mortality rate in Ireland was greater among individuals of higher socioeconomic standing, as they would not have been exposed to these diseases prior to the famine at the same rate as the lower classes (see chapter 2). Those at the higher end of the social scale had not built up

Table 4.12. Median and mean age at death (in years) of skeletons with evidence of infectious disease and chi-square test values by age category, Kilkenny workhouse population

	Present				Not present				χ^2	df	p
	Mdn	x̄	SD	n	Mdn	x̄	SD	n			
NON-ADULTS											
Sinusitis	11.50	10.09	5.09	9	4.50	5.66	4.48	357	5.408	4	.248
Rib lesions	7.75	7.80	5.34	28	3.50	4.88	4.39	451	9.597	4	.048
Tuberculosis	9.00	10.00	5.07	3	4.00	5.18	4.47	542	2.674	4	.614
Osteomyelitis	12.50	10.17	4.04	3	4.00	5.18	4.47	542	2.230	4	.693
Syphilis	1.80	1.80	– –	1	4.00	5.21	4.49	544	1.283	4	.864
Any	9.00	8.42	5.24	41	4.00	4.94	4.32	504	15.181	4	.004
ADULTS											
Sinusitis	39.75	39.33	7.32	34	38.27	38.06	8.48	225	3.106	3	.376
Rib lesions	37.00	36.73	7.82	31	38.52	38.44	8.64	301	1.646	3	.649
Tuberculosis	28.06	30.09	5.99	4	38.27	38.26	8.25	389	8.700	3	.034
Osteomyelitis	32.83	37.20	9.52	5	38.25	38.19	8.26	388	2.545	3	.467
Syphilis	31.71	31.71	8.54	2	38.27	38.21	8.26	391	4.781	3	.189
Any	38.35	37.87	7.81	66	38.24	38.24	8.37	327	1.349	3	.718
ALL											
Sinusitis	37.74	33.21	13.85	43	9.50	18.19	17.01	582	34.498	8	<.001
Rib lesions	24.27	23.00	16.04	59	9.00	18.31	17.66	752	13.440	8	.098
Tuberculosis	25.70	21.48	11.91	7	10.50	19.00	17.51	931	14.483	8	.070
Osteomyelitis	29.35	27.06	15.88	8	10.50	18.95	17.48	930	6.631	8	.577
Syphilis	25.67	21.74	18.29	3	11.00	19.01	17.48	935	9.088	8	.335
Any	30.29	26.59	15.96	107	9.00	18.04	17.43	831	31.736	8	<.001

resistance in their bodies to infectious disease to the same degree as the poor, and their risk of death became relatively greater. However, poverty would inevitably become the decisive factor in determining the chances of survival in Ireland from 1845 to 1852 (Ó Gráda 2012).

Metabolic Disease and Mortality

The mean age at death of individuals with skeletal evidence of metabolic disease was approximately four years less than in those with no skeletal evidence of nutritional deficiencies. This difference was statistically significant (table 4.13). Individuals who displayed porotic hyperostosis of the cranial vault and/or cribra orbitalia died at an age that was approximately three years younger than those who did not display these pathological changes. An opposite trend was observed in individuals exhibiting evidence of a rachitic disorder, from which it could be concluded that skeletons with no evidence of rickets were on an average five years younger when they died than those who were affected by the disease. This difference in average age at death between pathological and non-pathological skeletons was statistically significant and may suggest that individuals who were affected by poor health as children, as indicated by rickets, may have found it relatively easier to sustain the stresses of the famine.

The age distribution of skeletons displaying scorbutic lesions and those that did not differed significantly, suggesting that scurvy influenced the mortality in this population. The mean age at death of nonscorbutic skeletons was twenty-two, but for scorbutic skeletons it was only seventeen. This difference was statistically significant for the overall population. When the adults were analyzed separately, however, the results were not statistically significant. Among adult females, the mean skeletal age at death was thirty-seven years[11] in nonscorbutic skeletons and thirty-six years in scorbutic skeletons,[12] while for the males, the mean age at death of nonscorbutic skeletons was thirty-nine years[13] and the mean age at death of scorbutic skeletons was forty years.[14]

A different overall age distribution was further confirmed in a chi-square test,[15] although this was significant in non-adult age groups[16] and not for adults.[17] A disparity in the mortality profile of scorbutic and nonscorbutic skeletons is nonetheless evident, as is illustrated in the cumulative age-group distribution displayed in Figure 4.16. The highest risk of death, for individuals who displayed scorbutic skeletal lesions, occurred

Table 4.13. Median and mean age at death (in years) of skeletons with evidence of metabolic disease and chi-square test values by age group, Kilkenny workhouse population

	Present				Not present				χ^2	df	p
	Mdn	x̄	SD	n	Mdn	x̄	SD	n			
NON-ADULTS											
Porotic hyperostosis + cribra orbitalia	4.00	5.12	4.48	116	4.00	5.19	4.54	396	1.365	4	.850
Rickets	3.25	5.05	4.00	22	4.00	5.24	4.52	515	11.673	4	.020
Scurvy	4.50	5.67	4.38	330	3.00	4.51	4.57	213	44.610	4	< .001
Any	4.00	5.61	4.47	367	3.00	4.37	4.42	178	34.857	4	< .001
ADULTS											
Porotic hyperostosis + cribra orbitalia	39.91	39.63	7.69	70	37.93	37.93	8.54	280	1.931	3	.587
Rickets	43.40	41.93	7.63	24	37.97	37.98	8.28	365	4.036	3	.258
Scurvy	38.30	38.63	8.24	163	38.22	37.92	8.29	228	3.278	3	.351
Any	39.35	38.91	8.24	211	37.09	37.34	8.24	182	4.542	3	.209
ALL											
Porotic hyperostosis + cribra orbitalia	9.00	18.15	17.74	186	10.50	18.71	17.42	676	4.106	8	.847
Rickets	28.01	24.29	19.60	46	10.50	18.82	17.34	880	17.071	8	.029
Scurvy	8.00	16.57	16.62	493	22.91	21.78	18.02	441	79.092	8	< .001
Any	9.00	17.76	17.17	578	21.93	21.03	17.79	360	55.180	8	< .001

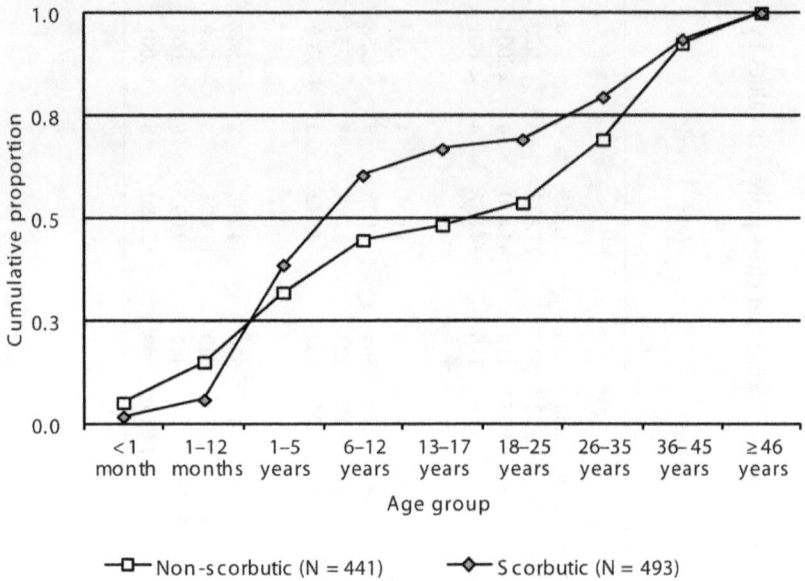

Figure 4.16. Cumulative age-group distribution of scorbutic and nonscorbutic skeletons.

between approximately six and twenty-five years of age. The greatest difference is noted within the adolescent population, in which a 19 percent higher mortality rate is noted for skeletons with scurvy. The trend differs for the neonatal and infant age groups, for whom greater frequencies of individuals were identified as nonscorbutic, but this may be another reflection of the osteological paradox; it is possible that many of the youngest members of the population who had scurvy died before skeletal lesions had time to develop.

As the skeletal manifestation of scurvy is believed to occur only if Vitamin C is reintroduced to the diet, it is not entirely possible to determine how scurvy influenced mortality among the Kilkenny workhouse inmates. If skeletons that displayed no lesions represent individuals who suffered from severe and active Vitamin C deficiency, the mortality curve suggests that they survived for longer than those who were recovering from the disease, which seems unlikely. If we take the historical research into account, it seems more feasible that the majority of inmates were deprived of Vitamin C before they entered the workhouse. Individuals who displayed scorbutic lesions were perhaps more likely to have been severe sufferers than those without lesions, and their relatively greater health impairment is then a probable factor in their death at an earlier age than other members of the workhouse population. However, this analysis of mortality patterns relating to scurvy is limited by the fact that the skeletal diagnosis of the disease is based on a pattern and distribution of lesions that differs between age groups and is inhibited by poor bone preservation and incomplete skeletons.

Dealing with the Famine: Bioarchaeological Insights

As the famine crisis escalated, the strain on the Irish workhouses became increasingly critical. Local relief committees struggled to raise enough funds from voluntary subscriptions to provide help to those in need, but as the crisis grew, these funds became inadequate. In the beginning of March 1847, the chairman of the Relief Committee in Kilkenny, Mayor Henry Potter, reported that his local committee was administering relief for nearly half the population of Kilkenny at an expense of almost £300 a week. However, the committee had been able to collect only £169.13.0 during the previous four weeks. Thirteen days later, the bank balance had been overdrawn by £50. Three weeks after that, the bank balance had been overdrawn by a total of £312.8.1, and the condition of the people was described as "deplorable in the extreme."[18] The atmosphere of despair among the inmates of the workhouse in Kilkenny is discernible in a January 1849 report in the *Kilkenny Journal* about a riot that occurred in one of the auxiliary workhouse buildings in the city:

> About 200 men rushed into the hall and refused to stir from the tables until they had disposed of what was intended as dinner both for themselves and those who were to succeed them. . . . The second batch . . . became clamorous, and the women . . . raised a shout and rushed towards the men's dining hall. . . . The police . . . soon arrived . . . but there was no occasion for their active interference, as the unruly inmates had no disposition to attack anything save the viands which formed an apology for a dinner. (*Kilkenny Journal* 1849a)

The eventual political decision to make the Poor Law and the workhouses completely responsible for administering and providing relief for the starving poor was likely one of the main causes of the mass deaths that occurred during the famine. The overcrowding in poor law institutions made it virtually impossible to prevent the spread of disease. In addition, the inadequate food rations provided—in terms of both quality and quantity—did little to strengthen the health of the inmates and may have indirectly caused further deaths. It is also clear that the efforts of physicians in Ireland during the famine saved countless people and that lives were in fact saved in the workhouses.

Attempting to Save Lives

Some of the attempts to keep people alive in the Kilkenny workhouse were physically apparent from the discovery of four amputations of the lower extremities of adult individuals that were found in the mass burials. Two cases were amputated limbs that were found on their own (figure 4.17), while the other two examples were placed in the coffins with the rest of the individuals, who clearly did not survive the procedures. Limb amputations were very risky in the mid-nineteenth century; the high mortality rate associated with such procedures was attributed to poor cleanliness and the lack of anesthesia (Robinson 1991). Amputations needed to be undertaken quickly and preferably in one single cut. The preferred procedure had evolved throughout the centuries. During the nineteenth century, so-called flap amputations were frequently performed. This technique involved using a portion of the soft tissue to cover the exposed flesh and bone. In the later part of the century, disarticulation rather than bone sectioning became common (Sachs, Bojunga, and Encke 1999). In this process, the diseased limb was separated from the rest of the body at a joint.

The skeleton of a young adult female (CLXXVIII) displayed an unhealed amputation of the right leg below the knee, just below the tibial tuberosity. The procedure was evidently completed in one attempt, starting at the medial surface of the tibia and continuing through to the dorsolateral margin. The amputated limb elements were severely osteoporotic. The considerable and localized osteoporosis suggests that the limb had been paralyzed for a very long time, and the fact that the affected limb was much shorter than its left-side counterpart (figure 4.18) may suggest that she was suffering from an underlying condition of poliomyelitis. This viral infection, which affects the central nervous system and the lower motor neurons of the spinal cord, causing muscle paralysis (Aufderheide and

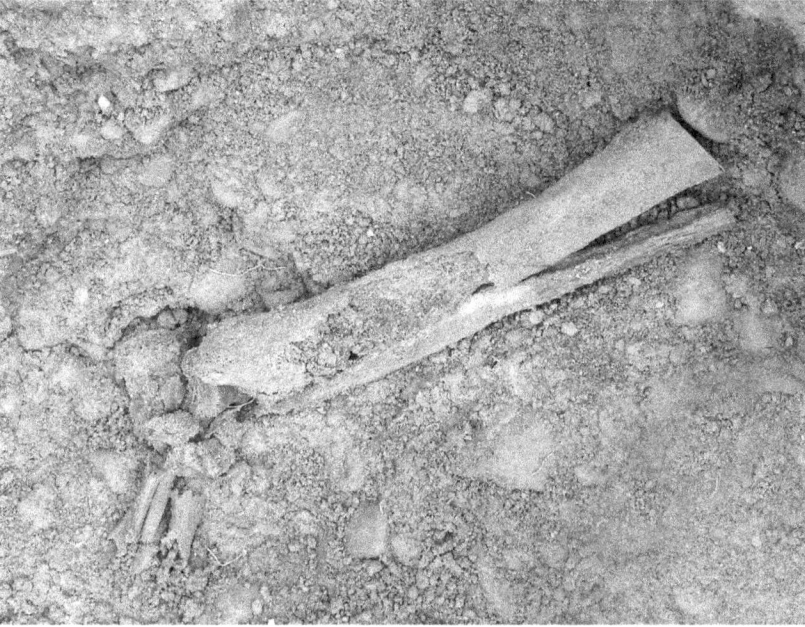

Figure 4.17. Amputated left leg of an adult individual (DCCCXXIII) as found in situ in the mass burial pit. Photo by Margaret Gowen & Co. Ltd.

Rodríguez-Martín 1998, 212), could in turn have exposed her to an infection of the lower extremity through trauma. Whether this infection was aggravated further in this individual due to deteriorating health caused by famine-induced stress is impossible to ascertain. No signs of healing were observed adjacent to the cut section, and it is most likely that she died during the procedure or immediately thereafter.

A second case of an unhealed amputation was observed in the skeleton of a young adult male (CCXXIV). The amputation, which involved the left lower extremity, was performed at the midshaft level of the femur. It was executed in a medial to lateral direction in two attempts; an initial shallow cut was located just above the completed section. The knee joint of the amputated limb was severely affected by considerable erosive arthropathy. The amputated limb was also osteopenic, which would suggest that he had suffered from the condition for quite some time before the procedure. No signs of healing were observed at the section point, and he may have died on the operating table.

Two cases of amputated limbs derived from adult individuals of unknown sex who may have survived. One of these was a right lower ex-

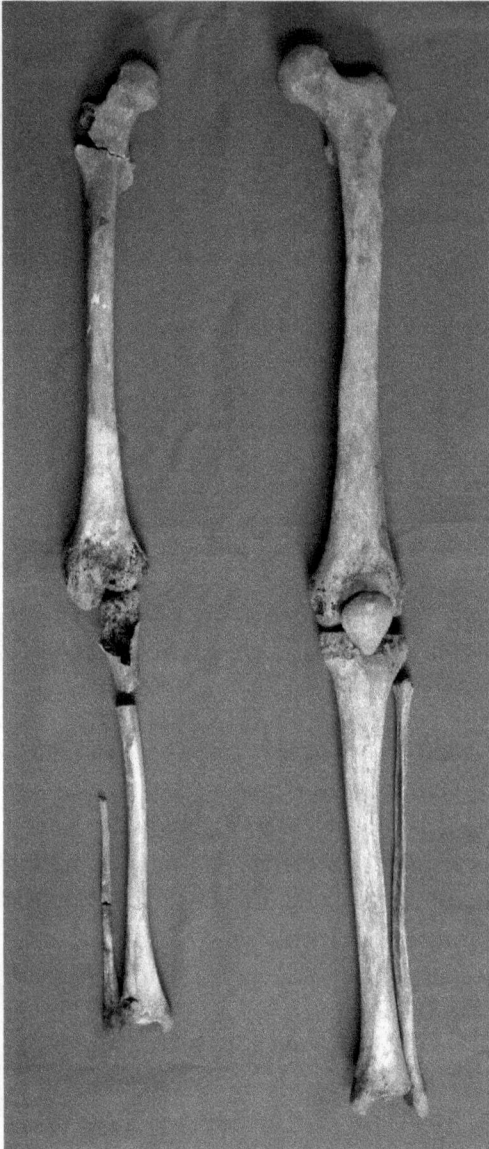

Figure 4.18. Lower extremities of a young adult female (CLXXVIII) displaying an amputation of the right leg. Photo by author.

tremity (DCCLXIII), on which the amputation was conducted at the level of the midshaft of the femur in a medial to lateral direction. No pathological changes were observed on the bones. The second case was a left leg (DCCCXXIII) amputated below the knee joint that was found at the bottom of a mass burial pit (see figure 4.17). Two attempts had been made to complete the section: one initial cut mark was localized just inferior to the completed attempt. This limb displayed an active infection indicated by dense nodules of new bone formed on the surfaces of the tibial shaft. The inferior portion of the bone was osteopenic and was probably affected by osteomyelitis (see above). The foot bones were extremely osteoporotic and fragile, and it is clear that this disease had been active and long-standing prior to the medical intervention.

Craniotomies: Autopsies or Dissections?

Perhaps one of the most intriguing discoveries made during the osteological analysis of the skeletons from the Kilkenny Union Workhouse mass burials was seven identified cases of craniotomy. These are postmortem procedures during which the top of the skull vault is sawed off transverse to expose the brain so it can be studied. Two of these cases had been aborted. The question is whether they were performed as autopsies for the purpose of determining the cause of death or as dissections for the purpose of anatomical study. Even though the Church had historically forbidden dissection, interest in human anatomy had increased since the fourteenth century. By the eighteenth century, dissection had become a legally accepted practice in most European countries (Grotta-Kurska 1974). In England, outmoded legislation from the sixteenth century was still in place in the early Victorian period. This early law stated that human dissections were to be performed on executed criminals only. Because of this association, dissection had become recognized as a further punishment to the deceased (Jones 1994, 103).

In the 1820s the uneven relationship between demand and supply of corpses for dissection had led to unlawful exhumations and an illegal trade in human bodies. Complete human corpses were exported from Dublin to the medical schools in London, since not enough bodies to meet the demand were obtainable from the London burial grounds (Goodman 1944, 808). This interest in the study of human anatomy by the Victorians was illustrated through the "Dublin mass corpse bequest" in late 1831; 400 people of good social standing expressed their will to donate their bodies for medical studies after their death (Richardson 1988, 167–68). Eventually, the Act for Regulating Schools of Anatomy was passed in 1832 after a period of debate in the British parliament in response to often dubious acts and malpractice by members of medical schools. The seventh clause of the law stipulated that unclaimed bodies were to be made accessible for anatomical dissections unless the subject had expressed in writing or in the presence of at least two witnesses that he or she would not want their body to be dissected or if a spouse or close relatives opposed it (Goodman 1944, 809).

Among ordinary people, the idea of autopsy or dissection was despised. But evidently postmortem examinations took place in the Kilkenny Union Workhouse before, during, and after the famine. The local attitude about these examinations was revealed in an article published in the *Kilkenny Journal* in August 1842. This particular case involved the corpse of an inmate named Anne O'Brien. After she died from dropsy, her body was examined by the medical officers of the workhouse. The rumor of the dissection had reached the general public, and someone removed the lid of the coffin when the body was taken to the local cemetery. What they saw was a naked and unshrouded body. This indecent treatment shocked those who saw the corpse, perhaps more than the autopsy itself. However, when the Board of Guardians questioned them, the medical officers argued that autopsy "was necessary to save the living" and that the procedure had been a "post-mortem examination" rather than a dissection. They also stated that the law was on their side and the guardians could not prevent them from continuing the practice (*Kilkenny Journal* 1842e). The story of this event was also published in the weekly edition of the *Dublin Medical Press* (Anonymous 1842), which focused on the right of the physicians to undertake the autopsy, and the matter was eventually resolved.

The cases identified in the Kilkenny Union Workhouse mass burials were seemingly craniotomies only (figures 4.19–22) and were performed on five females (LIII, CLXVII, CCCXVII, DCXCIII and CMXXV) and two males (XXIII and DCCXLV). The dominance of females is interesting, as it may reflect a bias in access to legally obtainable corpses for dissection at the time. Male corpses were probably more obtainable from the prison, at least in Kilkenny, while female corpses might have been easier to access from the workhouse. All of the females were also relatively short in stature, ranging from 147 cm (4' 10") to 158 cm (5' 2½"); their average height was only 152 cm (5' 0"). There was also a lack of any noteworthy pathological changes in their skeletons, which poses further questions about the underlying reason why these craniotomies were undertaken. The workhouse medical officers evidently performed postmortem examinations for the purpose of examining and describing the nature of the diseases to which inmates had succumbed. Dr. Lalor in his article on the

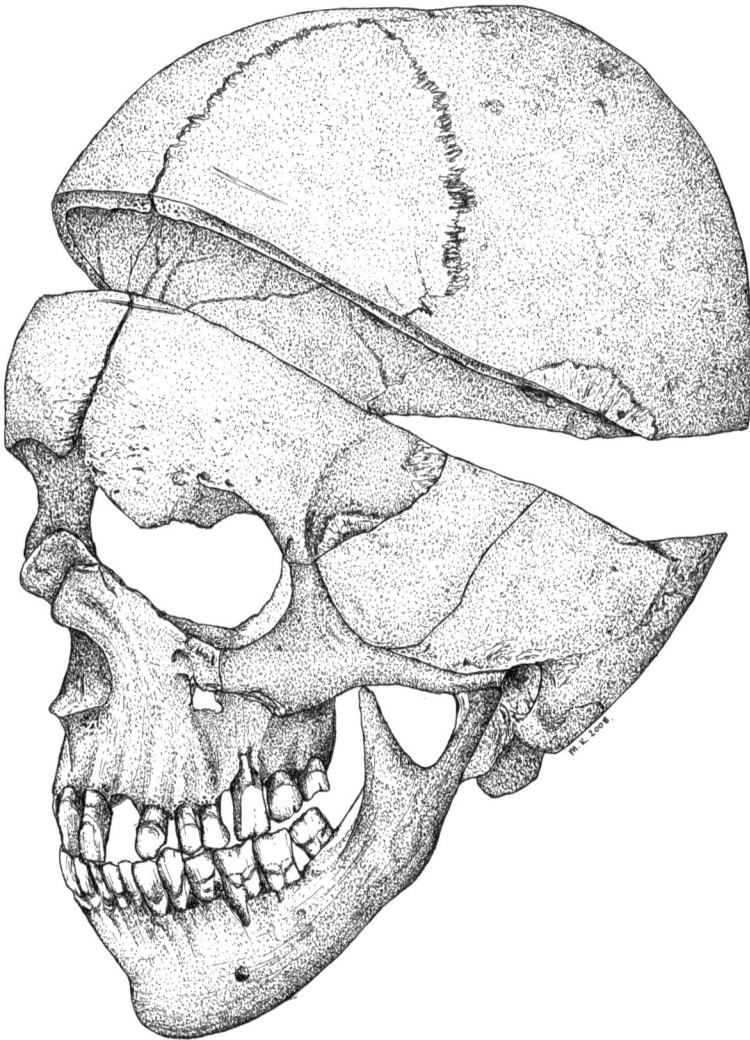

Figure 4.19. Complete craniotomy of the skull of an early middle adult male (DC-CXLV). Illustration by Małgorzata Kryczka.

treatment of patients at the fever hospital (Lalor 1848) mentioned having performed craniotomies, although these individuals are most likely to have been buried in the mass burials that were simultaneously being made on those premises and not at the workhouse. The cholera epidemic that reached Kilkenny in 1849 (see chapter 2) may have been another mass

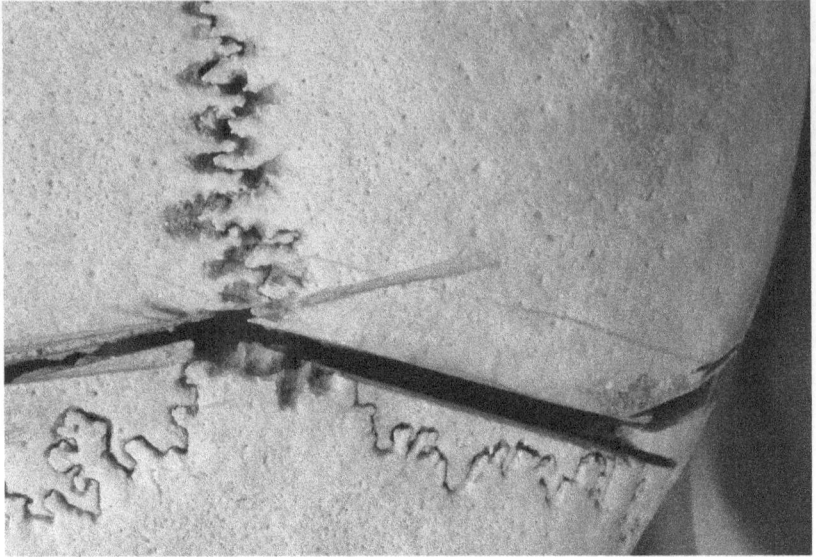

Figure 4.20. Saw marks on the posterior aspect of the skull from the craniotomy of a young adult female (DCXCIII). Photo by author.

death event that caused concern and, in the opinion of the workhouse physicians, warranted postmortem examinations of its victims.

Two of the craniotomies, in a male (XXIII) and female (CCCXVII) skeleton, were aborted attempts. The male skeleton was that of a late middle adult individual who displayed considerable degenerative joint disease and osteomyelitis. He was also one of the tallest individuals in the population, with an estimated living stature of 180 cm (5' 11"). The general coarse facial features (figure 4.21) and robustness of his skeleton indicate that he may have suffered from acromegaly, a hormonal disorder that is more commonly known as gigantism (see Aufderheide and Rodríguez-Martín 1998, 327–28; Ortner 2003, 420–23). However, not enough diagnostic traits were present to confirm such a diagnosis. The female case was an early middle adult (figure 4.22) with a stature of only 147 cm (4' 10"); she was the third shortest individual in the entire population. This raises the question of whether particular corpses were selected for dissection primarily for reasons of curiosity. It does not explain, however, why these two cases were never completed. Perhaps was there a moment of ethical hesitation by the medical officers. Perhaps were there no strong clinical

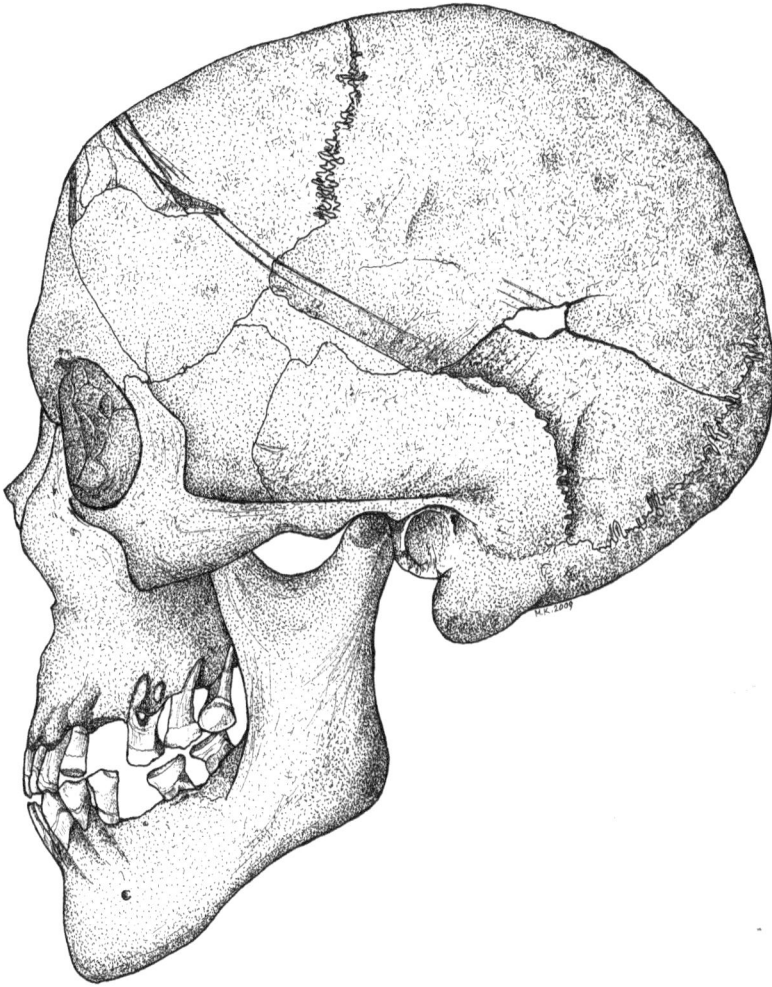

Figure 4.21. Skull of a late middle adult male displaying an incomplete craniotomy on the left side of the skull (XXIII). The elongated facial features of his cranium suggest that he may have suffered from acromegaly. Illustration by Małgorzata Kryczka.

arguments to support the performance of the procedures. Or perhaps others prevented the physicians from completing the dissections.

All examples of complete craniotomies displayed virtually no skeletal pathological changes. Considering the high frequencies of pathology in the population, this fact raises further questions about why these

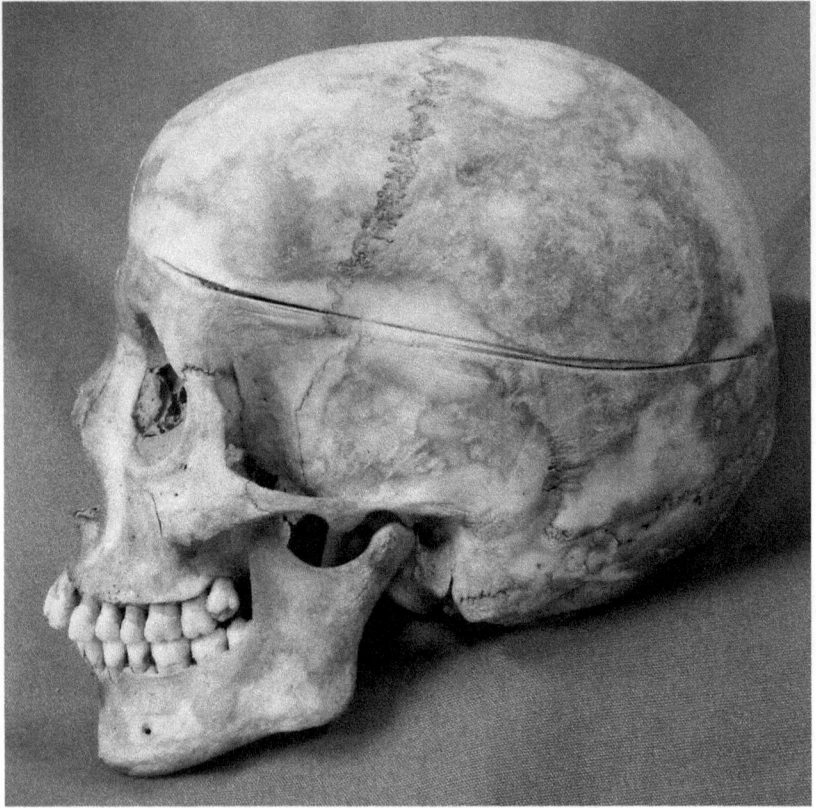

Figure 4.22. Incomplete craniotomy of the skull of an early middle adult female (CCCXVII). Photo by author.

particular individuals were craniotomized. While they could have died of infectious diseases with no skeletal manifestation, such as famine fever, dysentery, or cholera, the clear difference between these and others—and the fact that the majority are female—suggests that a selection of particular individuals was made and that autopsy may not have been the only reason for these craniotomies.

5

The Bioarchaeology of the Human Experience of Famine and Disaster

Shedding New Light on the Realities of the Great Irish Famine

Perhaps the poor children presented the most piteous and heartrending spectacle. Many were too weak to stand, their little limbs attenuated,—except where the frightful swellings had taken the place of previous emaciation,—beyond the *power of volition when moved*. Every infantile expression entirely departed; and in some, reason and intelligence had evidently flown. Many were *remnants of families*, crowded together in one cabin; orphaned little relatives taken in by the equally destitute, and even strangers, for these poor people are kind to one another to the end. In one cabin was a sister, just dying, lying by the side of her little brother, just dead.

William Bennett, *Narrative of a Recent Journey of Six Weeks to Ireland* (1847)

Opinion about when the Great Famine ended has varied throughout the historiography of the period. Initially, most historians marked 1848 as the final year of the famine, which is when the last occurrence of the blight took place. Whether the years of the blight should define the period of the Great Famine is, however, debatable. Much of the human suffering that followed the blight was due to an inadequate response by the government and was greatly influenced by economic, social, and political factors. Also, the first deaths caused by famine did not occur until 1846, and they continued on a significant scale long after the blight had disappeared. The nature, progression, and consequences of the famine also varied throughout Ireland; the worst scenes generally took place in the west (Kennedy et al. 1999). This means that the period of the famine in Ireland needs to be defined on a regional or sometimes even local level.

In 1849, Scottish writer and social commentator Thomas Carlyle (1795–1881) made a trip through Ireland. In July he reached Kilkenny, and on the eleventh day of that month he visited the union workhouse. He noted in his travel diary:

Workhouse; huge chaos, *ordered* "as one could";—O'S.,[1] poor light little Corker (he is from Cork, and a really active creature), proved to be the best of all the "orderers," I saw in Ireland in this office; but his establishment, the first I had ever seen, quite shocked me. Huge arrangements for eating, baking, stacks of Indian meal stirabout; 1000 or 2000 great hulks of men lying piled up within brick walls, in such a country, in such a day! Did a *greater* violence to the law of nature ever before present itself to sight, if one had an eye to see it? (Carlyle 1882, 83–84)

Seemingly, the situation in 1849 was still very difficult in Kilkenny. Although nationwide most of the potato harvest was healthy and the worst of the famine was over by the end of the year, a large proportion of the population of Ireland, about 14 percent, was still completely dependent on poor relief during 1849–1850 (Boyce 2005, 114; Kinealy 2006, 265, 270). Many poor law unions continued to suffer an immense economic burden due to high debt payments, and this resulted in a lack of funds for ordinary poor relief (Dunn 1992; Kinealy 2006, 271). The British government was still forced to provide relief for the poorest unions, most of which were located in the west of Ireland. Virtually no blight was seen in the 1852 potato harvest, and by the end of that year only 115,805 people in Ireland were receiving some form of poor relief (Kinealy 2006, 294). Thus, 1852 is probably the most suitable year to mark the end of the famine.

Kilkenny's Workhouse Dead: Who Were They?

Poverty and destitution were endemic in Ireland in the middle of the nineteenth century. Despite this, the life experience of the poor in Ireland is scantily understood. While many of the historical sources give a vivid and colorful description of the condition of these people, it is usually only in the folklore that their own voices can be heard. When the Irish Folklore Commission (Coimisiún Béaloideasa Éireann) was established in 1935 (Almqvist 1979), it was essentially too late to collect first-hand recollections of the famine years. Instead, the stories passed on to the children and grandchildren of the survivors of the period that were recorded (Lysaght 1996; Ó Gráda 2001; Quinlan 1996). Even though there is considerable historical value in oral tradition (see Fisher 2004; Nakagawa 2007; Rosenberg 1987), it was not possible for the folklorists to ask those who had experienced it direct questions about the famine. When considered in this context, the value of the human remains from the Kilkenny Union Workhouse mass burials as direct testimony from those who did not survive cannot be overemphasized.

The workhouses of Ireland were established to provide effective relief to the poor and destitute living within the borders of their respective poor law unions. In reality, these borders were permeable (Kinealy 2006, 338). For instance, from time to time the Kilkenny workhouse gave "strollers" from counties as far as Galway, Monaghan, Clare, and Tipperary temporary shelter for a night or two (*Kilkenny Journal* 1850e). Even before the famine, vagrants were occasionally admitted to the workhouse temporarily. For example, two brothers from Clonmel in County Tipperary, John and Patrick Saul, aged fifteen and thirteen, were temporarily admitted to the Kilkenny Union Workhouse in June 1842. Their parents had abandoned them in Dublin and had left for Australia. After that, the two brothers made their way back to Clonmel on foot, a distance of about 100 miles (*Kilkenny Journal* 1842d). When they reached Kilkenny, they had about thirty miles left to walk.

During the height of the famine, there were newspaper reports about nonlocal paupers from far western counties such as Clare and Limerick who had set up camps in various locations throughout the city (Geber 2012). Between October 1846 and January 1847, the Board of Guardians provided outdoor relief—which at times they did illegally (Patterson 1996)—and this might have spurred a further influx of people from areas assigned to poor law unions or in other counties. In the decades after the famine, American, French, and Chinese citizens were registered as indoor relief recipients in the Kilkenny Union, and foreign nationals might very well have been receiving relief in the workhouse during the famine years.[2] The individuals buried in the workhouse grounds in Kilkenny from 1847 to 1851 are therefore likely to have included both local residents and people from other counties. The fact that they were interred in the burial ground suggests that these were people who had no relatives or friends who were financially able to claim their bodies and provide them with a "proper" and "decent" burial in a consecrated cemetery.

While osteological and paleopathological analyses of these remains have focused on a population study, each analyzed skeleton from the

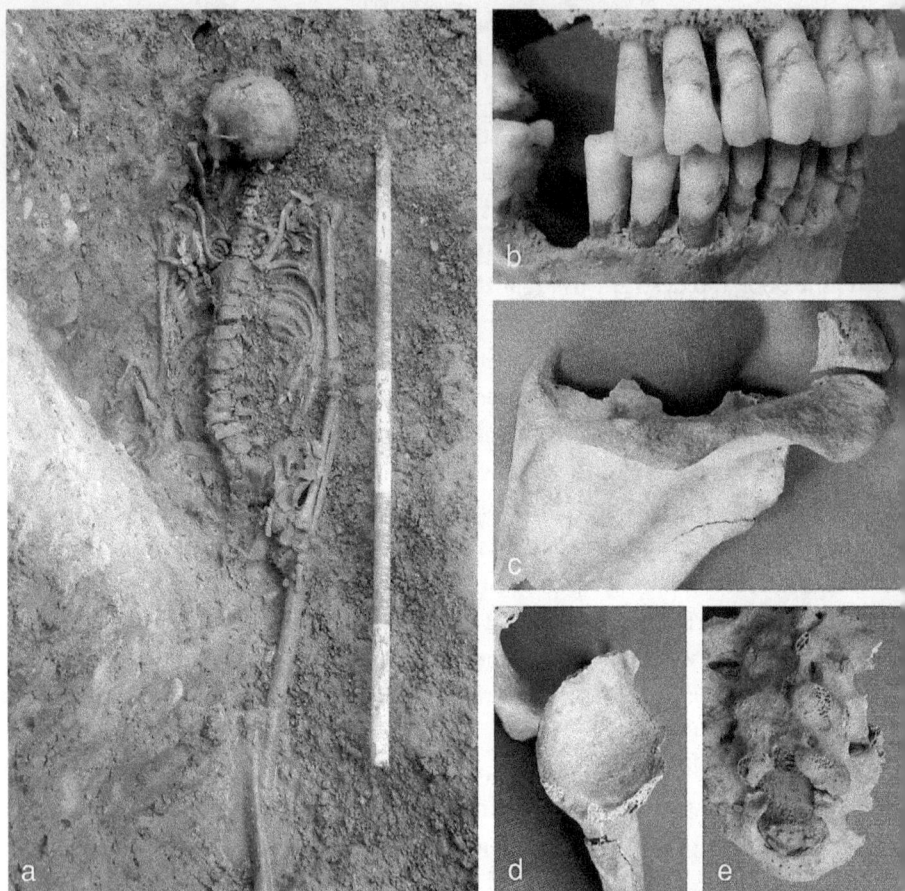

Figure 5.1. Skeletal remains of an older adult male (DCCLXV): (a) position of skeleton in the burial pit; (b) extramasticatory notches on anterior teeth; (c) *os acromiale* of the right shoulder; (d) degeneration of the right shoulder joint; (e) dislocated coccyx fused to the sacrum. Photo by Margaret Gowen & Co. Ltd. and author.

Kilkenny mass burials provides insight into one life, highlighting the individuality of the experience of the famine. This small-scale insight into life experiences was not the primary objective of the microarchaeological approach Fahlander and Cornell promoted (see chapter 1), but it has considerable value in bioarchaeological studies that consider cultural and historical contexts. One noteworthy example of such a so-called osteobiography could be interpreted from the remains of one older adult male (DCCLXV) (figure 5.1a). His skeleton revealed a mid-occlusal narrow notch present on the right maxillary and mandibular first incisors and canine teeth (figure 5.1b); he had a right unilateral *os acromiale* (figure 5.1c), a trait that indicates repetitive stress of the shoulder muscles; he suffered from degenerative joint disease, including osteoarthritis of his spine and considerable degeneration of his shoulders, particularly the right (figure 5.1d); and his coccyx was dislocated and had fused with the sacrum in an anterior angle (figure 5.1e). These skeletal changes could reflect a physical activity pattern associated with the work of a tailor or weaver, and he may have been employed in the Kilkenny textile industry, which collapsed in the decade before the famine (see chapter 2). The notches on his front teeth could have been damaged from using them as tools to hold pins during work, and his joint ailments in the back and the right shoulder and the dislocated coccyx may have occurred from weaving or sewing while sitting cross-legged in the tailor's position. His skeleton clearly illustrated the individuality revealed in the mass burials from the Kilkenny workhouse, and it provides a good example of how bioarchaeological studies of human remains offer unique insights into life experiences.

Factors Contributing to Institutionalization

Although poverty would have been the primary reason people sought and were granted indoor relief, the bioarchaeological evidence provides some additional insights into the physical state of the workhouse inmates. As poor health was generally accepted as a circumstance that rendered applicants "deserving" of relief according to the Poor Law, it must have been a contributing factor in some cases. The paleopathological evidence is limited by the small number of diseases that are potentially manifested skeletally and by the fact that these are usually visible only when they have reached a chronic state. Despite these limitations, the Kilkenny skeletons displayed an exceptionally high prevalence of pathological changes due to metabolic disease.

This evidence suggests the dire health conditions many would have experienced as they approached the workhouse for help. The skeletal evidence thus corroborates historical accounts from across Ireland. In March 1849, the poor law inspector for Gort Union Workhouse in County Galway wrote a letter to Sir Charles Trevelyan that he enclosed in an official report from the Famine Relief Commission. In it, he stated:

The fact is, the applicants of relief will not enter the workhouse until disease, engendered by long continued privation, has made such inroads into their constitution, that they may fairly be said to be admitted in a moribund state. This is particularly the case with the children and younger branches of the families. (Irish Poor Law Commissioners 1849)

The bioarchaeological evidence from the Kilkenny mass burials has revealed how a physical disability was likely another factor that contributed to an individual's chance of being granted indoor relief. This was particularly evident in cases involving females. One individual may have suffered from rheumatoid arthritis that could have limited her physical abilities. A second female suffered from a severe deformity of her spine due to tuberculosis, and another female likely had paralysis in her limbs that may have been caused by poliomyelitis. Among the males, the most severe case involved a late middle adult who suffered from a severe stage of tertiary syphilis that had probably made him blind and caused him to suffer from madness, a common consequence of a horrid disease that was incurable at the time. Other individuals presented evidence of long-standing bone infections that likely reduced their chances of surviving the famine. Each of these individuals was likely admitted to the workhouse on the basis of physical disability.

Age was clearly a determining factor when the Board of Guardians assessed applications for indoor relief. This consideration is probably why the Kilkenny mass burials included such a high proportion of children. The more elderly individuals in the group may also have been deemed deserving of relief because of their age. Gender was likely another determining factor; the minutes of a weekly Board of Guardians meeting in July 1850 stated that "the females in the house are now, and have always been, about 2 to 1" (*Kilkenny Journal* 1850f). However, a substantial gender bias was not evident from those interred in the workhouse mass burials. This may suggest that gender was a factor in determining which bodies were claimed by friends and relatives outside the institution and that males were more likely to be completely on their own at the stage when they applied for indoor relief, although this seems unlikely.

Consequences of Institutionalization

The mortality pattern as suggested from the bioarchaeological remains at Kilkenny indicates that the presence of underlying health conditions before an individual entered the institution influenced the likelihood of surviving. The main cause of death was infectious disease, and a feasible scenario is that many of the severely malnourished inmates acquired infectious diseases when they entered the workhouse that ultimately caused their premature demise. These would be diseases such as cholera, typhoid fever, typhus, and tuberculosis. The skeletons from the mass burials at the Kilkenny Union Workhouse represent only approximately 1 per mille of the estimated total number of people who died as a result of disease and starvation in Ireland from 1845 to 1852 and about 7 percent of the total number of people who died in County Kilkenny. They might have been considered fortunate because they were able to access indoor relief, but it was well known at the time that, for many, death would be the inevitable consequence of institutionalization during the famine.

Once in the institution, inmates had access to the infirmary and medical treatment, and both the historical and bioarchaeological evidence give indications of how the workhouse medical officers did their utmost to save lives. The skeletal evidence of these efforts includes the four cases of amputations identified in the mass burials. In two of these cases, it can be determined with certainty that the patients did not survive. The workhouse physicians also undertook autopsies and possibly dissections of some of the deceased, perhaps in an effort to try to understand what caused the mass deaths in the institution so they could combat famine-related health challenges more effectively.

The Archaeology of Mass Deaths: Famine Materialities in Context

While the realities of the Great Famine are difficult to comprehend today, the archaeological remains of the period provide insight that perhaps makes it easier to grasp what happened and how events and actions were played out. The mass burials at Kilkenny Union Workhouse provide a snapshot of some of the worst and most critical years of the catastrophe and insight into both the disease and deaths and the management of the crisis. When archaeologists first discovered the mass burials, the physical reality of the famine became very apparent. In addition to the large number of people interred in the mass burials, the mass burials in the unconsecrated ground of the workhouse are evidence of how desperate the situation was. The rate of mortality fluctuated, and it is evident that some weeks were more critical than others: some pits would have been completely full of coffins while others were backfilled when they were still half-empty. Even in such desperate conditions, though, burials appear to have been conducted in a structured and organized manner.

The mass burials would have been dug every week, in plain view of the workhouse inmates. The further the crisis progressed, the larger the cemetery became. The fact that one mass burial pit was found to be empty indicates how those in charge of the institution planned ahead. The inmates would also have seen with their own eyes the deaths of fellow inmates in the house, witnessed the process of the removal of bodies from the house or infirmary to the death house, and then the final transport along the cinder path that was discovered during the archaeological excavation to the northeast corner of the workhouse grounds where the mass burials took place. This would have involved physical work, which may well have been primarily conducted by the most able-bodied inmates. In a literal sense, some individuals in the workhouse might have dug their own graves.

Another important component of the story of these people is the intentional placement of inanimate objects in the coffins with some of the deceased. These objects indicate an emotional connection between the person who laid them in the coffin and the person lying therein. While this comfort may have been entirely personal, it was a function of the social and cultural fabric of the collective traditions of these people. Further evidence of the care and treatment of the dead is the fact that all individuals seem to have been interred in coffins, except for possibly one adult male individual who suffered from advanced stages of tertiary syphilis (see chapter 3). Even though burial took place in unconsecrated ground, the notion of a coffined burial was very important and was likely to have provided a sense of comfort to some. The coffins were stacked on top of each other and bodies were not haphazardly thrown into the pits, as would have been the case if the "sliding coffin" had been in use. The care that was taken when the dead were placed in their coffins was reflected in the case of an infant child that had been placed in the crook of the arm of its presumed mother. It is clear that these people were given a certain degree of dignity and respect in death.

The microperspective of the famine as seen in the archaeological remains from the Kilkenny workhouse provides insight into an otherwise poorly understood past. Because the extreme conditions in the west of Ireland during the famine were very well described at the time, a rather misleading general impression has perhaps prevailed about the nature of the famine in the east. Although the famine was indeed much worse in the west of Ireland, that does not mean that the conditions people experienced in the eastern counties were in any way more bearable or less harsh. The archaeology of the mass burials in Kilkenny highlights that the condition in the workhouse in Kilkenny was just as bad as in many other such institutions in Ireland during the famine. The Great Famine is also a good example of how both microarchaeology and microhistory can help broaden perspectives derived from perceptions of a period that are generic and perhaps too selective. Using several types of evidence in dialogue helps us tell a more complete story of those who died.

Several historical archaeologists (e.g., Beaudry 2011) point to the value of implementing the microperspective. This approach has primarily been used in single case studies. One such example is the famine-related study that Orser undertook at Ballykilcline townland in County Roscommon which was depopulated of its tenant farmers during the famine in 1848. Orser recognized the broad social structure in which this townland population acted. However, his interpretative basis remained conventional in the sense that he sought and requested further archaeological investigations to generate enough data to form a representative sample (Orser 2006b). Orser's studies of the famine period have been groundbreaking, and he has successfully demonstrated that the material culture of the poor is very present in the archaeological record and that this constitutes a wealth of information about the Great Famine (Orser 1996). In the late 1990s, historian Mary Daly responded to Orser's original study of the Gorttoose landscape (see chapter 1) with pessimism about what archaeological research could contribute to studies of the Great Famine. She asked whether material culture on an excavated site that had been in use not only during the famine but also before and after could reveal anything about the period. Her answer was "probably nothing" (Daly 1997, 600). However, the recent *Atlas of the Great Irish Famine* (Crowley, Smyth, and Murphy 2012) has demonstrated that famine studies today are much more interdisciplinary and contemplate more diverse sources of information pertaining to this period. Archaeology is dependent on context, and this is something that can often be provided through consideration of historical sources. But there is also much value in archaeological remains for historical research, particularly when discussing landscapes, material culture, and social relations. This is still an unexplored aspect of research into the Great Irish Famine that holds considerable potential.

The Human Experience of the Great Irish Famine

The numerous illustrations of the suffering in Ireland in English newspapers such as the *London Illustrated News* are well known (see Crawford 1994; Gray 1993; Kissane 1995). These were produced in a particular cultural and ideological setting and they have a historical value in themselves. With the exception of the politically charged and demeaning caricatures that were mainly produced in the satire magazine *Punch*, one can discern a romanticized, almost biblical, symbolism in many of these newspaper illustrations. Even though they were likely very shocking to view in their time, their imagery does not carry the same emotive charge today. The archaeology of Kilkenny Union Workhouse has provided a unique new depiction of the famine that has provided further insights into the reality of the period. This relates not only to the visual imagery of the skeletal remains of the victims but also to the way men, women, and children experienced the famine; how mass burials were excavated; how the corpses were prepared and placed in coffins and how coffins were interred; how the burial ground was managed; and how those in charge planned for further deaths. At the same time, it is important to put what we have learned from these remains in social and historical context so we can fully understand what this knowledge tells us. Each individual buried in the mass burials was subjected to policies that were the products of Victorian social ideology. The admission process of the workhouse—which each individual would have gone through—involved an assessment of each individual case by the guardians, who operated within the constraints of the Poor Law. The people who sought entry into the workhouse were often in a situation of utmost desperation.

The demeaning social attitudes toward the poor were never entirely uncontested. Historical sources from the period reveal that there were moral and ethical doubts about the treatment of the poor and about the burials that took place at the Kilkenny workhouse. The valiant efforts of workhouse medical officers to provide treatment and care to the sick and poor is also evident and must be acknowledged. In many nations and communities across the world, charities and other organizations (both those with a clear connection to Ireland and those from various non-Irish cultural and spiritual backgrounds) did their utmost to help those who suffered in Ireland. At the time, this relief effort was unprecedented in scale. In her book *Charity and the Great Hunger in Ireland*, Christine Kinealy gives several examples of how many of the poor in Britain contributed to this effort. One example is the money inmates at the Pentonville Female Penitentiary in London donated. These women undoubtedly suffered greatly from institutionalized hardships themselves, but they somehow managed to raise £1.1.0 to aid the Irish poor (Kinealy 2013, 219–20).

Each person had their own individual experience of the famine. This is perhaps a notion that has been forgotten when the consequences of the crisis are presented using statistics that quantify general trends. For each person, the experience of Ireland's Great Hunger depended on social class, heritage, gender, age, and location (Ó Gráda 2001). Health status and physical and mental strength determined how an individual fared in the crisis, not just hunger and bodily weakness. The entire sensory experience of the period is noteworthy; in addition to the biologically and culturally conditioned aspects of emotions, people also perceived the famine through the senses of sight, smell, sound, and touch (see Nyberg 2010; Tarlow 1999). For example, the location of the cemeteries used in Kilkenny during the early years of the famine reveals that it must have been a common and nearly constant sight to see coffins being transported from the workhouse to the burial ground through the city. This fact may also explain why reports in local newspapers of burials of workhouse paupers virtually stopped when the intramural burial ground was in use: the mass deaths in the workhouse were no longer as visible to those who were more fortunate and better off. Contemporary reports of the blight during the famine years also refer to its stench, which reportedly was perceptible all over the countryside (Donnelly 2001, 57) and would have been a constant reminder of the crisis. The sounds related to the famine would also have been part of people's experiences. These included the cries of the numerous vagrant beggars, perhaps the sound of the carts that transported coffins or bare corpses to their final resting place, or the sound of shovels digging graves and hammers building coffins. Finally, the experience of touch is represented by the physical actions of digging graves, preparing corpses for burial, or treating the sick and the dying.

The main disease that was diagnosed skeletally in this population that was a clear indicator of the famine was scurvy, or Vitamin C deficiency. It was observed in more than half of all individuals. Because the skeletal markers of the disease are apparent only when Vitamin C becomes part of the diet once again, it can be claimed with a great degree of certainty that the vast majority—if not all—would have suffered from this extremely painful disease during the famine. The excruciating agony and other clinical traits associated with the disease could have been one of the reasons why people saw no other choice than to ultimately resort to the workhouse. The pain associated with scurvy—which is clearly described in medical reports from this time and is verified in contemporary clinical literature—gives an insight into the probable physical and mental exhaustion many people would have felt during this period. However, the direct cause of death for these people would most likely have been infectious disease, primarily typhus. The paleopathological evidence suggests that metabolic disease and malnutrition had an indirect influence on mortality by causing a reduction in health that made people more susceptible to infectious disease with fatal results.

The skeletal analysis of the Kilkenny workhouse population has also indicated that individuals who had previously suffered physiological stress—as indicated by permanent markers of enamel hypoplasia in their dentitions—had a greater chance of longer survival. This indicates that those who had been strong enough to survive earlier calamities and food shortages fared better during the Great Famine crisis, though ultimately to no avail as they also eventually became victims.

The majority of those buried in the mass burials were non-adults, and it is reasonable to assume that a significant proportion of them were orphans. It is not possible to ascertain how many children entered the workhouse on their own and died anonymous and lonely deaths there. A similar situation might have been the case for many of the oldest members of the population. These individuals clearly did not have any children or other relatives nearby who had the means to care for them outside the workhouse walls. Perhaps this was because they were among the hundreds of thousands of individuals who emigrated. The other adults represented in the burials may have been the parents of some of the children.

A scenario where virtually complete families vanished in the workhouse is not unlikely. These families would not have had any surviving offspring who would have been able to pass on the memory and awareness of their deaths.

The Aftermath: An Archaeology of Silence?

Five additional burials were identified in the burial ground that were stratigraphically positioned above the mass burial pits and therefore clearly postdated the mass interments of 1847–1851: an older child (IV), two early middle adult females (I and VI), and one older adult male (III). These individuals were buried in single and very shallow grave cuts, with two burials that appear to be contemporaneous. All of these graves date to the second half of the nineteenth century (O'Meara 2010). Many of the bones in these skeletons were not level when they were found in the ground, an indication that these burials must have taken place before the coffins in the mass burial pit had completed the process of collapse.

It is not clear why these individuals were not buried in the designated workhouse cemetery, but it seems likely that social or religious factors were involved. In October 1853, the Kilkenny newspapers reported concerns regarding the practice of burying both Protestants (described as "pollutants") and Catholics in the same burial ground, as this prevented the burial ground from being properly consecrated by the Catholic clergy. The Board of Guardians responded by looking for a separate burial place for Protestant inmates (*Kilkenny Journal* 1853). This objection raises interesting questions about the ethical and religious concerns related to workhouse burials after the famine. It can be assumed that both Protestant and Catholic inmates were interred in workhouse mass burials, although this does not seem to have been mentioned in any local newspapers or discussed during the meetings of the Board of Guardians during the famine years. This seemingly new objection might be part of the communal religious revivals known to have taken place in Ireland in the years immediately after the famine (see Larkin and Freudenberger 1998; Parsons 1988) that unconsciously may have compensated for the ethical concessions made during the period. Perhaps there was a need to make a clear statement about burial practices of the workhouse inmates when the crisis was over. Regardless of what the social or religious context for these burials was, the location of graves on top of the mass burial ground indicates that at the time these individuals were interred, there was still an awareness of the mass burials that had taken place in the grounds of the workhouse during the famine a few decades earlier. We do not know when this knowledge was completely forgotten and lost.

The archaeological evidence from the Kilkenny Union Workhouse revealed that after these last intramural burials, a thick layer of sterile soil was placed on top of the burial ground (O'Meara 2010). The area was later used as the workhouse garden, and eventually the awareness of the fact that the most northeastern part of the workhouse grounds was a mass burial ground during the famine was forgotten. This raises the question of whether this was the result of an intentional desire to forget the burials and what took place there during the late 1840s and early 1850s. In the context of the usual Irish wakes and funerary traditions, there was a genuine sense of humiliation associated with the prospect of being buried in a workhouse coffin. When the further insult of being interred in unconsecrated ground within the walls of the workhouse was added, it might have been too painful for surviving friends and families to remember that during the famine they had not been able to claim and bury the bodies of their deceased relatives and friends. Recollecting and discussing these burials may have been a constant reminder of personal shame, of a failure to ensure that family members who died during the famine did not receive the respectful treatment that was the cultural and religious norm (see Quinlan 1996, 84).

Ó Gráda (2001) has discussed this possible denial of famine memories. He notes the scarcity of recorded recollections from workhouses, even though it is clear that a large proportion of those who survived would have experienced indoor relief during the famine. In fact, Ó Gráda makes the point that none of the recollections pertaining to workhouses during the famine that can be found in the archives of the Irish Folklore Commission give a notion of "having been there." His explanation for this silence is the social shame associated with the workhouse (2001, 135). There appears to have been some element of denial in post-famine Ireland. This is a feature of the psychological defense mechanism humans invoke when dealing with post-traumatic stress (see Siegel 1997) and is therefore not unexpected. This reaction was observed among some survivors of the Holocaust in Europe during World War II that has continued to this day. These Holocaust survivors (and even their children) have often suffered considerably from psychological problems, and the relative suicide rate among them is high (see Barak 2007; Barak et al. 2005; Lester 2005). Whether this was also the case in post-famine Ireland is not known. As Irish society so clearly valued community in the nineteenth century, the actions people had to take at the expense of others may have resulted in a sense of guilt for having survived and for failing to help those who did not. This shame and guilt may have stayed with the survivors for a long time afterward.

6

Conclusion

The Irish Famine of 1846 killed more than 1,000,000 people, but it killed poor devils only.

Karl Marx, *Capital: A Critique of Political Economy* (1867)

The Great Famine had a great impact on the course of the history of Ireland. It has remained controversial to this day and has been the subject of a scholarly debate that occasionally has been politically charged. The discovery and subsequent archaeological excavation of a previously unknown mass burial ground at the former union workhouse in Kilkenny City has provided a unique opportunity to study the impact of the famine on those who did not survive. This has been possible to do from both an individual and population level perspective. Another unique characteristic of this archaeological population is the fact that it represents a contemporaneous group of individuals; all were interred in a period of only forty-three months, and they can be historically contextualized with certainty as having suffered from the famine prior to death. The discovery is of international significance: at the time of writing, the remains constitute the second largest nineteenth-century skeletal population from a mass burial context ever to have been archaeologically excavated in Europe. It is surpassed only by the famous Napoleonic mass burial site outside Vilnius in Lithuania dating to 1812 (Signoli et al. 2004) and is thus one of the largest archaeological mass burial sites in the world. The biocultural analysis of the human remains from the mass burials has recognized the life experience of the poorer and destitute social classes in Victorian Ireland, who were treated in a rather demeaning and condescending manner by their contemporaries. These "paupers" are usually described only as a collective in the surviving historical sources. As many of them were illiterate, they generally left no written record behind. Relatively little is known about these people, but archaeology and bioarchaeology provide methods of studying them through the physical remains that are often the only surviving testimonies of their existence and the lives they lived. This research has revealed that the experience of poverty in County Kilkenny (and most likely Ireland in general) during the mid-nineteenth century involved poor dental health, joint disease and pain, and exposure to trauma, accidents, and violence. Most differences between the sexes in the frequency of diagnosed diseases and pathological changes were not statistically significant, but the overall pattern suggests that males were exposed to factors more likely to generate pain in the arms, while women were particularly affected by pain in their hands. This is likely to reflect differential and socially determined labor tasks based on gender. The frequencies were not substantially different from those of contemporaneous populations from the same social group and higher social groups. The stature of the adult proportion of the Kilkenny workhouse population was similar to that of higher-class populations, and poverty as a single factor does not appear to have been a cause for excessive stunting. This finding conforms to the results obtained from osteological and paleopathological analyses of nineteenth-century skeletal populations elsewhere and accentuates the notion that health and socioeconomic background were not necessarily correlated during this period.

The Kilkenny population exhibited a very high frequency of lesions indicative of Vitamin C deficiency or scurvy. The disease appears to have influenced the mortality of this population but is unlikely to have been a primary cause of death in the institution. Individuals who had survived previous episodes of stress appear to have fared better during the famine crisis. Mortality was exceptionally high among children, although the underlying demography of the workhouse institution is likely to distort the data. Among the adults, males appear to have been more severely affected by both disease and famine-induced deaths than females.

The archaeological and osteological evidence also reveals that genuine efforts were made to keep people alive. Examples of amputations and craniotomies illustrate aspects of nineteenth-century medicine and medical science in Ireland. Evidence of autopsies/dissections, trephinations, and amputations have frequently been encountered in postmedieval cemeteries in Britain (Mitchell 2011) and Ireland (e.g., Buckley and Ó Donnabháin 1992; Geber 2009; Murphy 2011). Medical officers amputated limbs—probably with only limited resources—in presumably desperate attempts to keep people alive. In at least two cases, they failed. The histori-cal sources also give weight to the notion that workhouse physicians did everything in their power to battle the spread of infectious disease, know-ing that it would not be contained in the workhouse and would therefore pose a great threat to the general population of Kilkenny. This may be one of the reasons why craniotomies were performed in the institution. These procedures took place in the workhouse at the surgery on the ground floor (see figure 2.3). Considering the fact that the house was so over-crowded with people, it seems unlikely that inmates were unaware that these procedures took place. Both dissection and autopsy were despised practices that had been seen as a means of further punishment of crimi-nals in death for centuries. The knowledge that one's poverty and lack of social standing might make one subject to such an act may have caused further distress and worry.

Evidence from the burials shows that workhouse officials made efforts to give individuals the most respectful treatment in death the situation allowed. This included, for example, making sure that each individual was provided with a shroud and coffin as part of their burial. This evidence provides new insight into how the dead were treated during the Great Famine. This archaeological evidence that the deceased were treated with dignity and care challenges the general conception that people were thrown haphazardly in large burial pits. This is an interesting topic that may be investigated further through study of the surviving archival re-cords from other union workhouses, hospitals, and similar institutions in Ireland and through the use of nonintrusive ground-penetrating radar (Ruffell et al. 2009) at known mass burial grounds for famine victims.

The individuals buried anonymously in the Kilkenny mass burial pits lived a life full of hardship. Their struggle for existence culminated in the Great Famine, during which they ultimately perished. These individu-als made the desperate decision to seek help from a despised and much-feared institution. This notion provides an indirect insight into the physi-cal suffering these people must have sustained. About 1 million people perished as a consequence of famine in Ireland between 1845 and 1852. The workhouse inmates interred in the Kilkenny mass burials would have remained an anonymous statistic if it had not been for the archaeological discovery of their remains. Through the archaeological excavation and the bioarchaeological study of their remains, the existence of these people has been fully acknowledged. Their story—what they went through and how they eventually died—has been told and will provide a constant reminder of what the reality was like for thousands of people in Ireland during the period that later came to be referred to as the Great Famine.

Epilogue

The management of the Kilkenny Union Workhouse was taken over by the Sisters of Mercy in 1875. The Irish workhouse system was phased out in the early 1920s following the establishment of the Irish Free State, and the first Dáil Éireann (the lower house of the Irish Parliament) declared that "the Irish Republic fully realises the necessity of abolishing the present odious, degrading and foreign poor law system and substituting therefor a sympathetic native scheme for the care of the nation's aged and infirm, who shall not be regarded as a burden but rather entitled to the nation's gratitude and consideration" (Houses of the Oireachtas 1919). From the early 1920s, the workhouse buildings in Kilkenny functioned as the Kilkenny Central Hospital. After 1942, the complex was used as a depot by the Kilkenny County Council, and since 2007 the surviving structures have been incorporated into the MacDonagh Junction Shopping Centre complex (Geber 2011).

Figure 6.1. Reburial ceremony at the famine memorial garden by Hebron Road in Kilkenny, 19 May 2010. Photo by author.

Following the osteological and paleopathological analysis, the skeletal remains were finally reinterred in a crypt at a purpose-built famine memorial garden adjacent to the old workhouse (figure 6.1). A multidenominational ceremony that included St. John's Catholic Church, the Church of Ireland, Kilkenny Presbyterian Church, and Kilkenny Methodist Church took place in May 2010 and was attended by the mayor of Kilkenny and representatives of Kilkenny County Council, a military color party from the James Stephens Military Barracks, and ordinary citizens and members of the general public (Geber 2010). The remains of the people who died under horrendous circumstances were awarded a final respectful acknowledgment in death, something that was denied to them when they were originally buried 160 years ago. *Suaimhneas síoraí dá n-anamnacha.*

Appendix

Summary Catalog of the Human Skeletons from the Kilkenny Union Workhouse Mass Burial Ground

Abbreviations

Compl. = Percentage complete

Age group: N = neonate (< 1 month); I = infant (1–12 months); YC = young
child (1–5 years); OC = older child (6–12 years); Adol. = adolescent
(13–17 years); YA= young adult (18–25 years); EMA = early middle adult
(26–35 years); LMA = late middle adult (36–45 years); OA = older adult
(≥46 years); ?A = indeterminable adult (>18 years)

Sex: F = female; M = male; ? = unsexed

Dental disease: c = caries; cl = calculus; eh = enamel hypoplasia; pl = periapical lesion; pd = periodontal disease; amtl = antemortem tooth loss

Joint disease: oa = osteoarthritis; sdjd = spinal degenerative joint disease;
dish = diffuse idiopathic skeletal hyperostosis; ra? = possible rheumatoid
arthritis

Metabolic disease: sc = scurvy; sc? = probable scurvy; sc?? = possible scurvy;
co = cribra orbitalia; ph = porotic hyperostosis; r = rickets;
om = osteomalacia

Infectious disease: tb = tuberculosis; om = osteomyelitis; pm? = possible
poliomyelitis; rl = rib lesions; si = sinusitis; sy = syphilis

Other: tr = trauma; od = osteochrondritis dissecans; sfc = slipped femoral
capital epiphysis; am = amputation; cr = craniotomy; cp = clay pipe facet;
n.a. = not available (no bones/teeth available or no methods available)

Id no.	Compl.	Age group	Sex	Stature (cm)	Pathology and skeletal markers				
					Dental	Joint	Metabolic	Infectious	O
I	75	EMA	F	n.a.	cl				
II	90	EMA	M	166	c, cl, eh, amtl				
III	20	OA	M	168					
IV	10	OC	?	n.a.	n.a.				
V	90	EMA	M	171	cl, pl		sc?		
VI	85	EMA	F	158	n.a.			om	
VII	75	EMA	F	163	n.a.		sc?		
VIII	95	Adol.	?	n.a.	cl, eh		sc??		
IX	90	OC	?	n.a.	eh		sc??, r		
X	90	N	?	n.a.	n.a.				
XI	95	OC	?	n.a.	cl		sc, co		
XII	90	OC	?	n.a.	cl, eh		sc?		
XIII	98	EMA	M	159	c, cl, pd, amtl	oa, sdjd			
XIV	95	YA	F	159	c, cl, pl, pd, amtl	oa			
XV	98	OC	?	n.a.			sc, co	tb	
XVI	98	LMA	M	169	c, cl, amtl		sc??		c)
XVII	98	LMA	M	164	c, cl, pl, pd		sc??		
XVIII	95	YC	?	n.a.					
XIX	98	YC	?	n.a.	c		sc		
XX	95	LMA	F	166	c, cl, eh, amtl	oa, sdjd			
XXI	95	LMA	M	176	c, cl, pl, amtl	oa, sdjd	sc?	rl	c)
XXII	45	I	?	n.a.	n.a.				
XXIII	98	LMA	M	180	c, cl, eh, amtl		sc??		c)
XXIV	90	YC	?	n.a.	cl		sc, co		
XXV	95	YC	?	n.a.			sc??, co		
XXVI	98	OA	M	174	c, cl, pd	oa, sdjd	sc??	rl	c)
XXVII	90	OA	F	n.a.	cl, pd, amtl	oa, sdjd			o
XXVIII	95	OC	?	n.a.			sc		
XXIX	90	YC	?	n.a.	cl		sc??, co		
XXX	90	OC	?	n.a.	cl, eh				

d no.	Compl.	Age group	Sex	Stature (cm)	Pathology and skeletal markers				
					Dental	Joint	Metabolic	Infectious	Other
XXXI	90	YC	?	n.a.	cl, eh		sc??, co		
XXXII	95	EMA	F	158	cl, amtl			si	
XXXIII	95	OC	?	n.a.	c				
XXXIV	95	OC	?	n.a.	cl		sc??, co		
XXXV	95	EMA	F	154	c, cl, pd, amtl		sc		
XXXVI	95	YC	?	n.a.	n.a.		sc??		
XXXVII	85	YC	?	n.a.	n.a.		sc?, co		
XXXVIII	98	OA	M	163	c, cl, pd	oa, sdjd		si	cp, tr
XXXIX	85	I	?	n.a.	n.a.				
XL	90	YC	?	n.a.	n.a.		r		tr
XLI	85	YC	?	n.a.	n.a.				
XLII	90	YC	?	n.a.	n.a.		sc??, co		
XLIII	98	Adol.	?	n.a.	cl, eh		sc		
XLIV	95	YC	?	n.a.			sc		
XLV	30	OC	?	n.a.	n.a.		sc??	rl	
XLVI	85	YC	?	n.a.	n.a.		sc??, co		
XLVII	90	YC	?	n.a.	n.a.		sc??, co		
XLVIII	95	LMA	F	160	c, cl, pl, pd, amtl	oa, sdjd			cp, tr
XLIX	90	YC	?	n.a.			sc, co		
L	65	N	?	n.a.	n.a.				
LI	90	N	?	n.a.	n.a.		sc?		
LII	85	YC	?	n.a.			sc		
LIII	98	YA	F	158	cl				cr, tr
LIV	90	YC	?	n.a.			sc??		
LV	35	YC	?	n.a.	n.a.				
LVI	90	LMA	F	156	cl, pd	sdjd	sc?		tr
LVII	95	I	?	n.a.	n.a.				
LVIII	95	OC	?	n.a.			sc, co		
LIX	90	YC	?	n.a.	n.a.		sc, co		
LX	95	OA	M	180	c, cl, eh, pl, pd, amtl	oa, sdjd	sc??, co		
LXI	90	LMA	M	165	c, cl, eh, pd	sdjd	co		cp, tr
LXII	90	YC	?	n.a.	n.a.		sc		
LXIII	90	YC	?	n.a.	eh				
LXIV	50	?A	F	n.a.	cl, eh, pd, amtl	oa			cp

Id no.	Compl.	Age group	Sex	Stature (cm)	Pathology and skeletal markers				
					Dental	Joint	Metabolic	Infectious	Oth
LXV	90	OC	?	n.a.	cl				
LXVI	85	YC	?	n.a.	n.a.				
LXVII	98	OA	M	174	c, cl, pd, amtl	oa, sdjd	sc?, r		cp,
LXVIII	95	YC	?	n.a.			sc??		
LXIX	85	YC	?	n.a.			sc??, co		
LXX	10	YC	?	n.a.	n.a.				
LXXI	20	YC	?	n.a.					
LXXII	80	I	?	n.a.	n.a.				
LXXIII	98	EMA	F	161	c, cl, pl, amtl		sc?		
LXXIV	9	YC	?	n.a.					
LXXV	95	LMA	F	170	c, cl, pl, pd	oa, sdjd	sc?		cp,
LXXVI	95	OC	?	n.a.	c		sc??, co		
LXXVII	95	OC	?	n.a.	cl		sc??, co	si	
LXXVIII	95	YC	?	n.a.			sc??		
LXXIX	95	OA	F	163	c, cl, pd, amtl	oa, sdjd	co, r		cp,
LXXX	50	OA	M	160	c, cl, eh, pd, amtl	oa	sc?, co, r		c)
LXXXI	98	EMA	F	164	c, cl	oa	sc??		c)
LXXXII	65	I	?	n.a.	n.a.				
LXXXIII	90	YC	?	n.a.			sc??, co		
LXXXIV	20	N	?	n.a.	n.a.				
LXXXV	95	LMA	M	174	c, cl, pl, pd, amtl	sdjd	sc?		c)
LXXXVI	80	YC	?	n.a.			sc??, co		
LXXXVII	95	YA	F	161	cl, eh, amtl				
LXXXVIII	40	OC	?	n.a.	n.a.				
LXXXIX	70	YC	?	n.a.	n.a.				
XC	98	EMA	M	172	c, cl, pl, pd, amtl	oa, sdjd	om		t
XCI	90	OA	M	170	pd, amtl	oa, sdjd	sc??		t
XCII	98	LMA	F	151	cl, pd, amtl				
XCIII	95	LMA	M	180	c, cl, pl, pd, amtl	sdjd			t

no.	Compl.	Age group	Sex	Stature (cm)	Dental	Joint	Metabolic	Infectious	Other
CIV	95	OA	F	158	cl, pl, pd, amtl	oa, sdjd	ph		
CV	85	YC	?	n.a.			sc?, co		
CVI	95	OC	?	n.a.	cl		sc		cp
CVII	95	LMA	F	157	c, cl, pl, pd, amtl	oa, sdjd			cp
CVIII	80	YC	?	n.a.					
CIX	8	YC	?	n.a.	n.a.				
	95	YC	?	n.a.			sc		
I	90	YC	?	n.a.			sc?		
II	85	YC	?	n.a.	eh		sc??		
III	90	YC	?	n.a.			sc??, co		
V	70	EMA	F	n.a.	cl		sc??		
V	98	EMA	F	164	c, cl, pl, pd, amtl	oa, sdjd			tr
VI	98	OC	?	n.a.	cl		sc?		
VII	95	OC	?	n.a.			sc?, co		
VIII	98	OA	M	176	c, cl, pl, pd, amtl	oa, sdjd	co, r	rl	tr
X	90	LMA	M	171	cl, eh	oa, sdjd			cp, tr
X	85	EMA	M	165	n.a.				
XI	35	Adol.	?	n.a.	n.a.				
XII	85	YC	?	n.a.			sc??, co		
XIII	95	OC	?	n.a.	cl		sc?	rl	
XIV	95	LMA	M	174	c, cl, pd, amtl	oa			tr
XV	75	I	?	n.a.	n.a.				
XVI	98	EMA	M	159	c, cl		co		
XVII	95	LMA	F	154	pd, amtl	oa, sdjd			od, tr
XVIII	95	EMA	F	159	c, cl, pl, pd, amtl				
XIX	90	YC	?	n.a.			sc		
XX	80	YC	?	n.a.			sc		
XXI	90	OC	?	n.a.	eh		sc?		
XXII	90	EMA	F	155	c, cl, pd, amtl	oa, sdjd			cp
XXIII	75	YC	?	n.a.					

Id no.	Compl.	Age group	Sex	Stature (cm)	Dental	Joint	Metabolic	Infectious	Ot[h]
CXXIV	60	YC	?	n.a.					
CXXV	85	YC	?	n.a.			sc		
CXXVI	90	EMA	F	159	c, cl, eh, pd		r		
CXXVII	85	EMA	M	167	c, cl		sc??		
CXXVIII	98	LMA	M	170	c, cl, pd, amtl	oa			cp
CXXIX	85	OA	F	165	c, cl, eh, pd, amtl	oa, sdjd	co, r		c
CXXX	85	YC	?	n.a.					
CXXXI	95	OC	?	n.a.			sc??, co		
CXXXII	98	OC	?	n.a.					
CXXXIII	95	LMA	F	163	c, cl, eh, amtl	sdjd		si	c
CXXXIV	75	OC	?	n.a.			sc, co		
CXXXV	95	YC	?	n.a.			sc, ph		
CXXXVI	95	Adol.	?	n.a.	c, cl, eh		sc??, co	rl	
CXXXVII	75	YC	?	n.a.					
CXXXVIII	90	YA	F	161			co		
CXXXIX	95	YA	M	172	c, cl			tb, rl	
CXL	20	OC	?	n.a.	n.a.				
CXLI	95	OA	M	n.a.	c, cl, pd, amtl	oa, sdjd	sc?		cp
CXLII	85	YC	?	n.a.					
CXLIII	65	I	?	n.a.	n.a.				
CXLIV	85	LMA	M	171	pd, amtl	oa, sdjd	sc?, r		
CXLV	65	YC	?	n.a.	n.a.		sc??		
CXLVI	15	I	?	n.a.	n.a.				
CXLVII	90	N	?	n.a.	n.a.				
CXLVIII	90	LMA	F	162	c, cl, pl, pd, amtl	oa, sdjd	sc?		
CXLIX	80	I	?	n.a.	n.a.				
CL	65	I	?	n.a.	n.a.				
CLI	98	YC	?	n.a.	cl		sc		
CLII	95	OC	?	n.a.	cl		sc, co		
CLIII	90	Adol.	?	n.a.	cl, eh		sc?	rl	
CLIV	90	OC	?	n.a.	cl		sc??, co	si	t
CLV	98	YA	F	159	cl				
CLVI	10	I	?	n.a.	n.a.				

no.	Compl.	Age group	Sex	Stature (cm)	Pathology and skeletal markers				
					Dental	Joint	Metabolic	Infectious	Other
VII	90	OA	F	162	c, cl, eh, pd, amtl	oa, sdjd			cp
VIII	98	LMA	F	158	c, cl, pd, amtl				tr
IX	95	Adol.	?	n.a.	cl		sc??		tr
X	95	OC	?	n.a.	c		sc		
XI	80	N	?	n.a.	n.a.		sc??		
XII	98	LMA	F	160	c, pd, amtl	oa, sdjd	r		cp, tr
XIII	90	YC	?	n.a.			sc??		
XIV	90	N	?	n.a.	n.a.				
XV	90	YC	?	n.a.			sc		
XVI	95	OC	?	n.a.			sc, co		
XVII	98	EMA	F	153	cl, eh		co		cr
XVIII	20	YC	?	n.a.	n.a.				
XIX	85	YC	?	n.a.	eh				
XX	85	YC	?	n.a.	pl		sc??		
XXI	90	YC	?	n.a.			sc??		
XXII	98	EMA	M	171	c, cl	sdjd			
XXIII	90	OC	?	n.a.	eh		sc, r		
XXIV	95	LMA	F	154	c, cl, eh, pd, amtl				
XXV	90	EMA	M	167	c, cl, pd, amtl	sdjd	sc?		tr
XXVI	90	I	?	n.a.	n.a.		sc		
XXVII	90	I	?	n.a.	n.a.				
XXVIII	90	YA	F	158	cl, eh	oa		pm?	am
XXIX	95	EMA	F	151	c, cl, pl, pd, amtl	oa	sc??	si	cp
XXX	90	OC	?	n.a.	c, pd		sc?		
XXXI	45	YC	?	n.a.			sc??, co		
XXXII	90	LMA	M	162	cl		sc?		
XXXIII	90	LMA	M	176	c, cl, pd, amtl		sc??		cp
XXXIV	90	YC	?	n.a.	c		sc?		
XXXV	90	YC	?	n.a.	eh		r		
XXXVI	20	?A	M	177	n.a.		sc?		tr
XXXVII	90	YC	?	n.a.			sc		
XXXVIII	65	YC	?	n.a.	n.a.		sc?		
XXXIX	95	N	?	n.a.	n.a.				

Id no.	Compl.	Age group	Sex	Stature (cm)	Pathology and skeletal markers				
					Dental	Joint	Metabolic	Infectious	O⁙
CXC	98	LMA	F	157	c, cl, pd, amtl	oa, sdjd	sc??		cp
CXCI	98	LMA	F	146	cl, pl, pd, amtl	sdjd	sc		
CXCII	85	YC	?	n.a.			sc??		
CXCIII	85	YC	?	n.a.			sc		
CXCIV	95	EMA	F	156	c, cl, amtl				
CXCV	98	LMA	M	177	c, cl, pl, pd, amtl	oa, sdjd	sc		cp
CXCVI	90	YC	?	n.a.			sc		
CXCVII	85	YC	?	n.a.			sc?, co, ph		
CXCVIII	20	I	?	n.a.	n.a.				
CXCIX	98	EMA	F	153	c, cl, eh			om	
CC	80	LMA	M	166	c, cl, pl, amtl	oa, sdjd, dish	sc??	rl	cp
CCI	95	YC	?	n.a.			sc		
CCII	80	YC	?	n.a.	n.a.		sc??		
CCIII	95	YC	?	n.a.			sc??		
CCIV	95	YC	?	n.a.	cl		sc?		
CCV	95	EMA	F	n.a.	c, cl, pl, pd, amtl	sdjd			
CCVI	40	LMA	M	169	c, cl, pd, amtl		sc?		
CCVII	98	Adol.	?	n.a.			sc		
CCVIII	85	YC	?	n.a.					
CCIX	95	YC	?	n.a.			sc	si	
CCX	95	LMA	M	168	c, cl, pd, amtl		sc?		cp
CCXI	95	YC	?	n.a.			sc?, co		
CCXIII	95	Adol.	?	n.a.			sc??, co		
CCXIV	90	OC	?	n.a.	cl		sc, co		
CCXV	98	YA	M	172	cl, eh		sc?, co		
CCXVI	98	LMA	M	176	c, cl, pl, pd, amtl	sdjd	sc??, co		
CCXVII	40	OA	M	n.a.	c, cl, pd	sdjd	sc		
CCXVIII	98	EMA	F	157	c, cl, pl		sc??	rl, si	
CCXIX	98	LMA	M	175	c, pd, amtl	sdjd	sc		cp
CCXX	90	OA	F	156	c, cl, eh, pd, amtl	sdjd	sc?		

no.	Compl.	Age group	Sex	Stature (cm)	Dental	Joint	Metabolic	Infectious	Other
CXXI	98	LMA	M	171	pd, amtl	oa, sdjd	sc??		
CXXII	95	EMA	F	159	c, cl, pd, amtl				
CXXIII	95	OC	?	n.a.	cl				
CXXIV	95	YA	M	179	c, cl, eh	oa			am
CXXV	98	LMA	F	164	c, cl, amtl	oa			
CXXVI	95	LMA	F	155	cl, pd, amtl	oa, sdjd			cp
CXXVII	98	OA	M	169	c, cl, pd, amtl	oa, sdjd	sc??		cp
CXXVIII	85	YC	?	n.a.			sc?		
CXXIX	90	YC	?	n.a.			sc??		
CXXX	75	OC	?	n.a.	c		sc??		
CXXXI	90	YC	?	n.a.			sc		
CXXXII	90	YC	?	n.a.					
CXXXIII	98	LMA	M	169	c, cl, eh, pd	oa, sdjd	sc??, r	om, si	cp, tr
CXXXIV	95	EMA	F	159	c, cl, pd	sdjd	r		cp
CXXXV	95	OC	?	n.a.	cl		sc	rl	
CXXXVI	95	I	?	n.a.	n.a.				
CXXXVII	80	Adol.	?	n.a.	eh				
CXXXVIII	90	YC	?	n.a.	eh		sc?, co, r		
CXXXIX	95	YC	?	n.a.					
CXL	30	I	?	n.a.	n.a.			si	
CXLI	90	LMA	M	174	c, cl, pd, amtl	sdjd	sc??		cp, tr
CXLII	80	I	?	n.a.	n.a.				
CXLIII	95	Adol.	?	n.a.	cl, pd		sc, co		
CXLIV	90	YC	?	n.a.	c, pl				
CXLV	40	EMA	F	153	cl		sc??	si	
CXLVI	98	EMA	F	163	c, cl, eh		sc		
CXLVII	90	I	?	n.a.			sc		
CXLVIII	95	LMA	F	163	cl	sdjd	sc?		cp, tr
CXLIX	85	YC	?	n.a.			sc??, co		
CL	85	YC	?	n.a.	c		sc??		
CLI	98	OC	?	n.a.	cl		sc, co	rl	
CLII	65	LMA	M	174	cl, pd, amtl	oa, sdjd			

Id no.	Compl.	Age group	Sex	Stature (cm)	Dental	Joint	Metabolic	Infectious	Oth
CCLIII	95	OC	?	n.a.	cl				
CCLIV	85	N	?	n.a.	n.a.		sc?		
CCLV	90	LMA	M	164	c, cl, pl, pd	sdjd			cp,
CCLVI	85	I	?	n.a.	n.a.		sc??		
CCLVII	85	LMA	M	175	n.a.	oa, sdjd		rl	tr
CCLVIII	90	OC	?	n.a.	c, cl		sc		
CCLIX	10	YC	?	n.a.	n.a.		sc??		
CCLX	5	YC	?	n.a.	n.a.				
CCLXI	95	LMA	F	153	c, cl, pl, pd, amtl	oa, sdjd	sc?	si	tr
CCLXII	90	YC	?	n.a.			sc		
CCLXIII	65	LMA	M	172	amtl	sdjd	sc?		tr
CCLXIV	5	I	?	n.a.	n.a.				
CCLXV	85	YC	?	n.a.			sc		
CCLXVI	85	OC	?	n.a.	cl		sc??		
CCLXVII	90	EMA	M	170	c, cl, eh, pd, amtl		sc	rl, si	cp
CCLXVIII	90	OA	M	174	c, cl, pd, amtl	oa, sdjd	sc	si	cp
CCLXIX	95	YA	F	157	cl		sc??		tr
CCLXX	95	LMA	F	156	c, cl, pd	oa, sdjd	co		tr
CCLXXI	95	LMA	M	168	c, cl, pd, amtl	oa	sc?		cp
CCLXXII	80	N	?	n.a.	n.a.				
CCLXXIII	85	OC	?	n.a.	cl		sc??, co	si	
CCLXXIV	90	LMA	F	163	c, pd, amtl	oa, sdjd	sc?, co		
CCLXXV	75	YC	?	n.a.					
CCLXXVI	85	OC	?	n.a.			sc??, co		
CCLXXVII	85	I	?	n.a.	n.a.				
CCLXXVIII	75	I	?	n.a.	n.a.				
CCLXXIX	95	YA	M	166	c, cl, eh				cp
CCLXXX	95	YC	?	n.a.			sc, r		
CCLXXXI	95	YC	?	n.a.			sc??, co	rl	
CCLXXXII	98	LMA	M	179	c, cl, pl, pd, amtl	oa, sdjd	sc?		cp,

no.	Compl.	Age group	Sex	Stature (cm)	Pathology and skeletal markers				
					Dental	Joint	Metabolic	Infectious	Other
CLXXXIII	95	OC	?	n.a.			sc??, co		
CLXXXIV	95	YA	M	165	c, cl	oa	co		
CLXXXV	98	EMA	M	179	c, cl, pl, pd, amtl	oa	sc		cp, tr
CLXXXVI	95	LMA	M	174	c, cl		sc??, r	rl	
CLXXXVII	35	OA	M	n.a.	c, cl, eh, pd, amtl		sc??		cp
CLXXXVIII	98	EMA	M	163	c, cl, eh	sdjd	sc?	rl	
CLXXXIX	98	EMA	F	166	c, cl		co		
CXC	98	YA	M	171	c, cl			rl	
CXCI	60	YC	?	n.a.					
CXCII	85	YC	?	n.a.			sc		
CXCIII	90	OC	?	n.a.	cl, eh				
CXCIV	95	I	?	n.a.	n.a.		sc		
CXCV	85	I	?	n.a.	n.a.				
CXCVI	85	YC	?	n.a.			sc, ph		
CXCVII	90	EMA	F	157	c, cl, amtl	oa, sdjd	co		
CXCVIII	95	OA	M	176	c, cl, eh, pl, pd, amtl	oa, sdjd			cp, tr
CXCIX	98	EMA	M	163	c, cl, pd	oa	sc?	si	cp
CC	85	OC	?	n.a.	c		sc??, co		
CCI	80	YC	?	n.a.	n.a.		sc, co		
CCII	95	I	?	n.a.	n.a.				
CCIII	80	?A	M	171	c, pd, amtl	oa, sdjd			cp
CCIV	95	EMA	F	158	c, pd, amtl	oa, sdjd			
CCV	90	YC	?	n.a.			sc?		
CCVI	85	YC	?	n.a.			sc??, co		
CCVII	98	LMA	F	160	c, cl, pl, pd		sc??, ph		cp
CCVIII	98	YA	M	164	cl		sc		cp
CCIX	65	LMA	M	170	n.a.	oa			
CCX	90	YC	?	n.a.	c		sc		
CCXI	95	OC	?	n.a.	c		sc		
CCXII	85	N	?	n.a.	n.a.				
CCXIII	95	N	?	n.a.	n.a.				

Id no.	Compl.	Age group	Sex	Stature (cm)	Pathology and skeletal markers				
					Dental	Joint	Metabolic	Infectious	Ot
CCCXIV	98	EMA	F	155	cl, eh, pd		sc?		t
CCCXV	80	LMA	M	170	c, cl, pl, amtl	oa		rl	
CCCXVI	95	LMA	M	178	c, cl, pl, pd, amtl	oa, sdjd, dish	sc??	rl	c
CCCXVII	95	EMA	F	147	c, cl		co		cr,
CCCXVIII	98	OA	M	171	c, cl, pl, pd, amtl	sdjd	sc??	om	cp
CCCXIX	90	EMA	M	174	cl	sdjd	sc?, r	rl	
CCCXX	98	EMA	F	160	cl, eh		sc?, co, ph		
CCCXXI	98	EMA	F	146	c, cl, eh, pl, pd, amtl	oa	sc	rl	t
CCCXXII	95	LMA	M	174	c, cl, pd	oa	ph		
CCCXXIII	95	YC	?	n.a.			sc??, co		
CCCXXIV	80	I	?	n.a.	n.a.				
CCCXXV	98	LMA	F	148	c, cl, eh, pd, amtl	sdjd	r		
CCCXXVI	30	N	?	n.a.	n.a.				
CCCXXVII	90	OC	?	n.a.					
CCCXXVIII	90	I	?	n.a.	n.a.				
CCCXXIX	85	I	?	n.a.	n.a.				
CCCXXX	95	LMA	F	168	c, cl, pd	oa			cp
CCCXXXI	95	OA	M	n.a.	pl, pd, amtl	oa, sdjd	sc		
CCCXXXII	85	I	?	n.a.	n.a.				
CCCXXXIII	85	LMA	M	177	c, cl, pd	oa, sdjd	r		cp
CCCXXXIV	98	LMA	F	160	c, cl, pl, pd, amtl	sdjd	sc	si	
CCCXXXV	15	YC	?	n.a.	n.a.				
CCCXXXVI	90	YC	?	n.a.			sc??		
CCCXXXVII	90	N	?	n.a.	n.a.				
CCCXXXVIII	80	OC	?	n.a.					
CCCXXXIX	95	I	?	n.a.	n.a.				
CCCXL	90	EMA	M	166	c, cl, pd				

no.	Compl.	Age group	Sex	Stature (cm)	Pathology and skeletal markers				
					Dental	Joint	Metabolic	Infectious	Other
CXLI	98	OC	?	n.a.	cl				
CXLII	95	LMA	M	174	c, cl, pl, pd, amtl	oa, sdjd	sc	rl, si	tr
CXLIII	95	YA	M	165	cl		co		
CXLIV	80	YC	?	n.a.			sc??		
CXLV	90	OC	?	n.a.			sc??		
CXLVI	95	LMA	M	168	cl, pl, pd	sdjd			
CXLVII	95	EMA	M	177	c, cl, pd		sc??		cp
CXLVIII	90	YC	?	n.a.			sc		
CXLIX	80	YC	?	n.a.			sc??		
CL	95	OC	?	n.a.	c		sc	rl	
CLI	98	YC	?	n.a.	cl		sc		
CLII	98	OA	M	172	c, cl, pd, amtl	oa, sdjd	sc?		cp, tr
CLIII	60	YC	?	n.a.					
CLIV	98	OC	?	n.a.			sc?		
CLV	98	Adol.	M	n.a.	eh		sc		cp
CLVI	95	EMA	F	158	cl		sc?		tr
CLVII	50	I	?	n.a.	n.a.		sc??		
CLVIII	95	Adol.	?	n.a.	cl		sc?		
CLIX	90	OC	?	n.a.	cl				
CLX	30	N	?	n.a.	n.a.		sc?		
CLXI	95	Adol.	?	n.a.	cl		sc	rl	
CLXII	90	YC	?	n.a.	n.a.		sc??		
CLXIII	90	YC	?	n.a.			sc, co		
CLXIV	98	YC	?	n.a.			sc	tb, om, rl	
CLXV	98	OA	M	180	c, amtl	oa, sdjd	sc?		tr
CLXVI	95	EMA	M	169	c, cl, pd				cp
CLXVII	95	EMA	F	151	c, cl, pl, pd, amtl	oa			
CLXVIII	95	OC	?	n.a.	c		sc??		
CLXIX	95	YC	?	n.a.	eh				
CLXX	85	YA	M	172	c, cl				
CLXXI	50	I	?	n.a.	n.a.				
CLXXII	98	OC	?	n.a.	eh		sc?, co		

Id no.	Compl.	Age group	Sex	Stature (cm)	Pathology and skeletal markers				
					Dental	Joint	Metabolic	Infectious	O
CCCLXXIII	95	Adol.	?	n.a.	cl		sc		od
CCCLXXIV	45	YC	?	n.a.					
CCCLXXV	95	OC	?	n.a.	eh		sc??, co		
CCCLXXVI	90	OC	?	n.a.					
CCCLXXVII	90	OC	?	n.a.	cl		sc, co		
CCCLXXVIII	98	OA	M	183	c, cl, pd, amtl	oa, sdjd			
CCCLXXIX	98	OA	F	166	c, cl, pd, amtl	oa, sdjd	sc?		
CCCLXXX	90	OC	?	n.a.	cl		sc??		
CCCLXXXI	90	YC	?	n.a.			sc??, co		
CCCLXXXII	80	YC	?	n.a.			sc		
CCCLXXXIII	85	I	?	n.a.	n.a.		sc??		
CCCLXXXIV	90	Adol.	?	n.a.			sc?	rl, si	
CCCLXXXV	90	LMA	F	n.a.	c, cl, eh, pd amtl			rl	
CCCLXXXVI	75	YC	?	n.a.					
CCCLXXXVII	95	LMA	M	168	c, cl, amtl	sdjd			
CCCLXXXVIII	95	OC	?	n.a.			sc, co		
CCCLXXXIX	80	YC	?	n.a.	n.a.				
CCCXC	98	YA	F	161	cl				
CCCXCI	80	I	?	n.a.	n.a.		sc??		
CCCXCII	40	I	?	n.a.	n.a.				
CCCXCIII	95	LMA	F	n.a.	c, cl, pd, amtl	oa, sdjd, ra?	sc??	rl	
CCCXCIV	95	OA	F	n.a.	amtl	oa, sdjd			
CCCXCV	90	LMA	F	n.a.	c, pl, pd, amtl	oa, sdjd		si	
CCCXCVI	98	EMA	M	164	cl	oa, sdjd	sc?	tb, rl	
CCCXCVII	95	YC	?	n.a.			sc?		
CCCXCVIII	98	LMA	M	177	c, cl, pd	oa, sdjd			
CCCXCIX	98	YA	M	174	cl	oa	co		

no.	Compl.	Age group	Sex	Stature (cm)	Dental	Joint	Metabolic	Infectious	Other
					Pathology and skeletal markers				
D	95	LMA	M	167	c, cl, pl, pd		r		cp, tr
DI	98	EMA	M	164	c, cl	oa	sc??	om	cp
DII	85	YC	?	n.a.	eh				
DIII	90	OC	?	n.a.					
DIV	95	OA	F	162	c, cl, eh, pd, amtl	oa		si	tr
DV	90	LMA	F	151	c, cl, pd, amtl	sdjd			tr
DVI	95	LMA	M	167	amtl	oa, sdjd			
DVII	95	LMA	F	161	c, cl, eh, pd, amtl	oa, sdjd	sc	si	cp
DVIII	95	EMA	F	150	cl, pd				tr
DIX	85	Adol.	?	n.a.	eh		sc??, co		
DX	95	YA	M	164	c, cl		sc?		
DXI	98	OC	?	n.a.			sc		
DXII	98	LMA	F	156	cl				cp
DXIII	90	N	?	n.a.	n.a.				
DXIV	35	I	?	n.a.	n.a.		sc??		
DXV	95	OA	M	167	c, cl, pl, pd	oa, sdjd			cp, tr
DXVI	95	YA	M	167	cl		sc?, co	rl	
DXVII	98	YA	M	169	c, cl, pd		ph		
DXVIII	95	YC	?	n.a.			sc		
DXIX	95	YC	?	n.a.	eh		sc, co		
DXX	98	YC	?	n.a.			sc?, co		
DXXI	95	OC	?	n.a.	cl				
DXXII	98	OA	M	179	c, cl, pl, pd, amtl	oa, sdjd	sc?		cp
DXXIII	95	Adol.	?	n.a.	cl, eh		sc??, co		
DXXIV	95	OA	M	175	c, cl, eh, pl, pd, amtl	oa, sdjd	sc??, co		cp, tr
DXXV	95	LMA	M	177	cl, eh	oa			cp, tr
DXXVI	20	?A	M	177	n.a.		sc?		
DXXVII	98	EMA	F	153	c, cl, eh, pd, amtl	oa			
DXXVIII	95	LMA	F	164	c, cl, eh, pd, amtl	sdjd	co, r		

Id no.	Compl.	Age group	Sex	Stature (cm)	Pathology and skeletal markers				
					Dental	Joint	Metabolic	Infectious	Otl
CDXXIX	95	YA	F	163	cl, amtl		co		
CDXXX	95	OA	F	156	c, cl, pl, pd, amtl	sdjd			c]
CDXXXI	95	Adol.	F	n.a.	cl			rl	t
CDXXXII	85	LMA	F	151	c, cl	sdjd	sc??		c]
CDXXXIII	95	EMA	F	169	c, cl		sc	si	
CDXXXIV	98	OC	?	n.a.					
CDXXXV	65	YC	?	n.a.			r		
CDXXXVI	90	OC	?	n.a.	c				
CDXXXVII	98	YA	M	164	cl, pl		sc	rl, si	
CDXXXVIII	95	YA	M	169	c, cl, pl, amtl		sc?		
CDXXXIX	98	LMA	F	152	c, cl, eh, pl, amtl	sdjd	sc?		
CDXL	95	OA	M	177	c, cl, pd	oa, sdjd	sc??		
CDXLI	30	I	?	n.a.	n.a.		sc??, ph		
CDXLII	95	OC	?	n.a.			sc, co	rl	
CDXLIII	90	EMA	F	159	cl, pl, amtl	sdjd		si	c]
CDXLIV	95	OC	?	n.a.	eh		sc, co		
CDXLV	90	YC	?	n.a.			sc		
CDXLVI	98	LMA	M	164	c, cl, eh, pl	oa, sdjd	sc	si	t
CDXLVII	98	LMA	F	156	c, cl, eh	sdjd	sc	rl, si	
CDXLVIII	98	EMA	M	168	c, cl		sc??		c]
CDXLIX	98	EMA	M	178	cl		sc??	si	c]
CDL	15	N	?	n.a.	n.a.				
CDLI	98	LMA	F	163	c, cl, eh, pd			rl	
CDLII	90	OA	M	168	amtl	oa, sdjd	sc?		t
CDLIII	95	Adol.	?	n.a.	cl		sc??		o
CDLIV	90	YC	?	n.a.			sc??		
CDLV	95	Adol.	?	n.a.	cl, eh		sc??, co		
CDLVI	98	OA	F	n.a.	c, pd, amtl	oa, sdjd			c]
CDLVII	45	N	?	n.a.	n.a.		sc??, ph		
CDLVIII	90	YC	?	n.a.	eh		sc?		

no.	Compl.	Age group	Sex	Stature (cm)	Pathology and skeletal markers				
					Dental	Joint	Metabolic	Infectious	Other
⊃LIX	95	LMA	M	168	c, cl, eh, pl, amtl	oa, sdjd	sc		sfc, tr
⊃LX	85	YC	?	n.a.		n.a.			
⊃LXI	90	YC	?	n.a.			sc??		
⊃LXII	95	EMA	M	171	c, cl, eh, pl, pd, amtl		sc??, ph, r		cp, tr
⊃LXIII	30	N	?	n.a.		n.a.			
⊃LXIV	95	Adol.	?	n.a.	c, eh		sc, ph, r		
⊃LXV	80	I	?	n.a.		n.a.			
⊃LXVI	98	EMA	M	178	c, cl, eh, pl, pd, amtl	oa	sc??		cp
⊃LXVII	98	OA	M	173	c, cl, pl, pd, amtl	oa, sdjd, dish	r	si	cp, tr
⊃LXVIII	95	OA	M	180	c, cl, pl, pd, amtl	oa, sdjd	sc?		tr
⊃LXIX	98	EMA	F	149	c, cl	oa, sdjd	sc?		cp
⊃LXX	98	LMA	F	163	c, cl, pl, pd, amtl	oa, sdjd	co		
⊃LXXI	90	LMA	F	166	pd, amtl	oa, sdjd	sc?		tr
⊃LXXII	95	OC	?	n.a.	c, cl		sc?		
⊃LXXIII	95	OA	M	174	c, cl, eh, amtl	sdjd	sc??		
⊃LXXIV	95	EMA	F	163	cl, eh				cp
⊃LXXV	98	LMA	M	171	c, cl, pl, pd, amtl	oa, sdjd			cp
⊃LXXVI	90	OA	F	159	cl, amtl		sc??		
⊃LXXVII	85	LMA	M	178	cl, pd			si	cp, tr
⊃LXXVIII	95	LMA	M	162	c, cl, eh, pd, amtl	oa, sdjd	sc, co		
⊃LXXIX	95	OC	?	n.a.			sc??, co		
⊃LXXX	90	EMA	M	174	cl, pd		sc??	si	cp, tr
⊃LXXXI	95	OC	?	n.a.			sc?		
⊃LXXXII	90	OC	?	n.a.					
⊃LXXXIII	85	YC	?	n.a.	c, cl				
⊃LXXXIV	90	OC	?	n.a.	cl				

Id no.	Compl.	Age group	Sex	Stature (cm)	Pathology and skeletal markers				
					Dental	Joint	Metabolic	Infectious	Ot
CDLXXXV	90	OC	?						
CDLXXXVI	98	OA	M	175	c, cl, pd, amtl	oa	sc?		
CDLXXXVII	98	LMA	M	168	c, cl, pd, amtl	oa, sdjd	sc??	rl, si	t
CDLXXXVIII	85	LMA	F	156	c, cl, pd		co		
CDLXXXIX	95	EMA	M	174	c, eh, amtl		sc?	rl	
CDXC	90	OC	?	n.a.	cl, eh		sc, co	rl	
CDXCI	98	EMA	F	163	cl	sdjd	co		t
CDXCII	90	OC	?	n.a.	c		sc, co		
CDXCIII	95	OC	?	n.a.			sc??, co		
CDXCIV	85	YC	?	n.a.	cl				
CDXCV	98	YA	F	148	cl, eh, amtl	oa		sy	
CDXCVI	98	Adol.	F	n.a.	cl	oa	sc??, co		
CDXCVII	80	OA	F	n.a.	c, cl, pl, pd, amtl	oa, sdjd			
CDXCVIII	95	OC	?	n.a.	c		sc??		
CDXCIX	85	LMA	F	152	c, cl, pl, pd, amtl	oa, sdjd			o
D	95	OC	?	n.a.				si	
DI	95	YC	?	n.a.			sc?		
DII	95	YC	?	n.a.			sc, co		
DIII	95	EMA	M	167	c, cl, pd, amtl		sc?		c
DIV	98	LMA	M	174	c, cl, eh, pd, amtl	oa, sdjd	r		cp
DV	30	I	?	n.a.	n.a.				
DVI	95	OC	?	n.a.			sc??		
DVII	90	YC	?	n.a.	eh				
DVIII	95	YA	M	169	cl, eh		co		
DIX	90	YC	?	n.a.	eh		sc??, r		
DX	95	OC	?	n.a.	cl		sc, co		
DXI	75	OA	M	n.a.	pd, amtl	oa, sdjd	co		
DXII	95	OA	M	182	c, cl, eh, pl, pd, amtl	sdjd	sc		od
DXIII	90	Adol.	?	n.a.	c, cl				
DXIV	35	OC	?	n.a.	cl				

no.	Compl.	Age group	Sex	Stature (cm)	Dental	Joint	Metabolic	Infectious	Other
XV	80	EMA	F	159	c, cl, pl, pd, amtl	oa, sdjd			cp
XVI	20	Adol.	?	n.a.	n.a.				od
XVII	20	?A	?	n.a.	c, cl		sc??		
XVIII	95	OC	?	n.a.	cl		sc		
XIX	20	I	?	n.a.	n.a.				
XX	98	LMA	F	157	c, cl, eh, pl, amtl	sdjd	co	si	cp, tr
XXI	98	EMA	M	161	c, cl, pl, amtl				tr
XXII	85	I	?	n.a.	n.a.				
XXIII	80	YC	?	n.a.			sc, co		
XXIV	80	YC	?	n.a.			sc		
XXV	90	OC	?	n.a.					
XXVI	95	Adol.	?	n.a.	cl		sc, co		tr
XXVII	90	LMA	F	159	c, cl, amtl	oa, sdjd			
XXVIII	95	YC	?	n.a.	cl		sc		
XXIX	95	OA	M	167	pd, amtl	oa	sc?		cp, tr
XXX	95	Adol.	?	n.a.	cl		sc, co	si	
XXXI	95	LMA	M	168	pd, amtl	oa, sdjd	sc?	si	
XXXII	98	YC	?	n.a.			sc??, co		tr
XXXIII	95	LMA	M	174	c, cl, eh, pl, pd	oa, sdjd	sc	si	tr
XXXIV	95	OC	?	n.a.	cl		sc?, co		
XXXV	90	YC	?	n.a.			sc		
XXXVI	98	YC	?	n.a.			sc??, r		
XXXVII	90	YC	?	n.a.			sc		
XXXVIII	98	Adol.	?	n.a.	cl, eh				
XXXIX	95	OC	?	n.a.					
XL	95	YC	?	n.a.	cl, eh		sc?, r		
XLI	90	YC	?	n.a.	eh		sc, r	sy	
XLII	90	OC	?	n.a.			sc?, co		
XLIII	95	LMA	F	154	cl, pd, amtl	sdjd	sc??		cp
XLIV	90	YC	?	n.a.	c		sc??, r		
XLV	95	OC	?	n.a.	eh		sc??, co		

Id no.	Compl.	Age group	Sex	Stature (cm)	Pathology and skeletal markers				
					Dental	Joint	Metabolic	Infectious	O⟩
DXLVI	30	?A	F	n.a.	amtl				
DXLVII	95	LMA	M	175	cl, pl, pd, amtl	oa			cp
DXLVIII	90	OC	?	n.a.			sc??, co, ph		
DXLIX	85	YC	?	n.a.			sc??, co		
DL	80	YC	?	n.a.	n.a.		sc??		
DLI	98	LMA	F	160	c, cl, pl, pd, amtl	oa, sdjd	co		
DLII	30	I	?	n.a.	n.a.				
DLIII	98	OC	?	n.a.	cl, eh				
DLIV	98	OA	M	174	c, cl, pd, amtl	sdjd	sc?		cp
DLV	95	LMA	M	173	cl, eh, pd, amtl	oa, sdjd			•
DLVI	95	YA	F	149	cl		co		
DLVII	95	LMA	F	160	c, cl, pl, amtl	oa, sdjd		tb	
DLVIII	90	YC	?	n.a.					
DLIX	98	EMA	F	160	cl, pd, amtl		sc?		
DLX	98	YA	M	171	cl	oa	sc		cp
DLXI	90	YC	?	n.a.			sc??	rl	
DLXII	80	YC	?	n.a.	n.a.		sc??		
DLXIII	98	OC	?	n.a.			sc		
DLXIV	95	YA	F	162	c, cl, amtl			tb	
DLXV	90	YC	?	n.a.				rl	
DLXVI	80	YC	?	n.a.			sc?		
DLXVII	95	YC	?	n.a.	n.a.		sc?, co		
DLXVIII	90	I	?	n.a.	n.a.		sc?, ph		
DLXIX	90	OC	?	n.a.	c		sc, co		
DLXX	90	YC	?	n.a.			sc??		
DLXXI	90	OC	?	n.a.			sc??		
DLXXII	98	LMA	F	171	c, cl, pl, pd, amtl	oa, sdjd	sc		
DLXXIII	90	YC	?	n.a.			sc?		
DLXXIV	95	LMA	M	172	c, cl, eh, pd, amtl	oa, sdjd			
DLXXV	95	OA	F	158	c, cl, eh, pl, amtl	oa, sdjd			
DLXXVI	95	EMA	F	151	cl, pl, amtl		co		c⟩

no.	Compl.	Age group	Sex	Stature (cm)	Dental	Joint	Metabolic	Infectious	Other
LXXVII	98	OA	M	180	cl, pd, amtl	oa, sdjd	sc??		cp
LXXVIII	95	YC	?	n.a.					
LXXIX	98	YC	?	n.a.					
LXXX	85	YC	?	n.a.			sc??		
LXXXI	95	OC	?	n.a.	cl, eh				
LXXXII	98	YA	F	158	cl, pd		co		
LXXXIII	98	LMA	F	166	c, cl, amtl	oa, sdjd	sc?		cp
LXXXIV	90	YC	?	n.a.					
LXXXV	90	YC	?	n.a.			sc?		
LXXXVI	80	YC	?	n.a.	c, cl		sc, r		
LXXXVII	98	EMA	M	166	cl, pl, amtl	oa			cp
LXXXVIII	90	OC	?	n.a.					
LXXXIX	95	Adol.	?	n.a.	cl				
XC	95	YC	?	n.a.	c, eh		sc, co		
XCI	98	Adol.	M	n.a.	c, eh		sc??		
XCII	25	I	?	n.a.	n.a.				
XCIII	90	YC	?	n.a.			sc?		
XCIV	90	I	?	n.a.	n.a.			rl	
XCV	85	OA	F	154	cl, pd, amtl	oa, sdjd			
XCVI	95	OC	?	n.a.	eh		sc?, co		
XCVII	98	LMA	M	183	cl, pd	sdjd	sc?, co		cp
XCVIII	90	EMA	M	167	c, cl, pd		sc		cp
XCIX	20	YC	?	n.a.	n.a.		sc??		
C	85	YC	?	n.a.			sc		
CI	98	LMA	F	164	c, cl, pd, amtl	sdjd			cp
CII	95	YC	?	n.a.			sc??, co		
CIII	95	YC	?	n.a.			sc?		
CIV	90	LMA	F	161	c, cl, amtl	sdjd			
CV	95	LMA	F	163	c, cl				
CVI	95	OC	?	n.a.			sc??, co		
CVII	25	?A	F	179	n.a.				
CVIII	95	OA	M	168	c, pl, pd, amtl	sdjd, dish	sc		cp, tr

Id no.	Compl.	Age group	Sex	Stature (cm)	Dental	Joint	Metabolic	Infectious	Oth
							Pathology and skeletal markers		
DCIX	98	OC	?	n.a.	cl				tr
DCX	90	OC	?	n.a.			sc, co		
DCXI	95	LMA	M	172	c, cl, eh, pd	sdjd	sc?	si, sy	cp,
DCXII	90	OC	?	n.a.	cl, eh		sc		
DCXIII	95	LMA	F	155	c, cl, amtl	oa			tr
DCXIV	95	Adol.	?	n.a.			sc??, co		
DCXV	95	LMA	F	158	c, cl, eh, pd, amtl	sdjd			tr
DCXVI	95	OC	?	n.a.	c		sc?, co		
DCXVII	85	YC	?	n.a.			sc?		
DCXVIII	98	LMA	M	168	c, cl, pd, amtl	oa, sdjd	sc?		cp
DCXIX	95	OC	?	n.a.	cl			rl	
DCXX	95	LMA	M	179	c, cl, pd, amtl	oa	sc, r		o
DCXXI	90	YC	?	n.a.			sc??		
DCXXII	30	EMA	F	n.a.	n.a.		sc??		
DCXXIII	40	EMA	F	171	n.a.		sc??		tr
DCXXIV	98	OC	?	n.a.	c		sc??, co, r	om	
DCXXV	80	I	?	n.a.	n.a.		sc??		
DCXXVI	98	OC	?	n.a.			sc		
DCXXVII	95	EMA	F	152	c, cl, amtl				tr
DCXXVIII	90	YC	?	n.a.			sc??		
DCXXIX	95	EMA	F	158	c, cl, pd, amtl		co		
DCXXX	95	YC	?	n.a.	c		sc, co		
DCXXXI	95	LMA	F	n.a.	c, cl, pd, amtl		r		
DCXXXII	90	YC	?	n.a.			r		
DCXXXIII	95	YC	?	n.a.					
DCXXXIV	75	YC	?	n.a.	n.a.		sc, co		
DCXXXV	85	OA	F	168	cl, amtl	oa, sdjd			
DCXXXVI	95	OC	?	n.a.			sc, co		
DCXXXVII	90	OC	?	n.a.	c		sc?	rl	
DCXXXVIII	85	N	?	n.a.	n.a.		sc??		
DCXXXIX	85	I	?	n.a.	n.a.		sc??		
DCXL	85	I	?	n.a.	n.a.		sc??		

no.	Compl.	Age group	Sex	Stature (cm)	Dental	Joint	Metabolic	Infectious	Other
CXLI	95	LMA	F	156	c, cl, pl, pd, amtl	oa, sdjd	sc, co	rl	tr
CXLII	40	YC	?	n.a.	n.a.				
CXLIII	90	YC	?	n.a.					
CXLIV	80	YC	?	n.a.					
CXLV	95	YC	?	n.a.			sc		
CXLVI	98	LMA	M	169	c, cl, pd		co	si	cp
CXLVII	90	YC	?	n.a.					
CXLVIII	90	OC	?	n.a.					
CXLIX	98	EMA	F	161	c, cl, eh, amtl	oa, sdjd	sc?, co		
CL	98	EMA	F	156	cl				
CLI	85	OC	?	n.a.	c				
CLII	60	YC	?	n.a.	c		sc??		
CLIII	90	OC	?	n.a.	c, cl		sc?, co		
CLIV	90	YC	?	n.a.					
CLV	98	EMA	F	160	c, cl, eh, pl, amtl		sc, r		
CLVI	95	OC	?	n.a.	c, cl, eh		sc?		
CLVII	40	N	?	n.a.	n.a.				
CLVIII	95	OC	?	n.a.	c, cl		sc, co		
CLIX	95	OC	?	n.a.			sc, co	om	
CLX	40	LMA	F	n.a.	c, cl, amtl		r		
CLXI	85	OA	F	158	c, cl, pl, pd, amtl	oa, sdjd			tr
CLXII	85	YC	?	n.a.					
CLXIII	65	YC	?	n.a.			sc?		
CLXIV	95	OC	?	n.a.					
CLXV	98	LMA	M	164	c, cl, pd, amtl	oa			
CLXVI	95	OC	?	n.a.	cl, eh				
CLXVII	15	?A	M	n.a.	n.a.				
CLXVIII	75	YC	?	n.a.	n.a.		sc??, r		
CLXIX	95	Adol.	?	n.a.	cl		sc		
CLXX	95	OC	?	n.a.	c, cl		sc??, co	rl	
CLXXI	98	YA	F	162	cl		sc		
CLXXII	35	N	?	n.a.	n.a.		sc??		

Id no.	Compl.	Age group	Sex	Stature (cm)	Dental	Joint	Metabolic	Infectious	Oth
DCLXXIII	98	Adol.	?	n.a.	c, cl				
DCLXXIV	80	YC	?	n.a.	n.a.				
DCLXXV	85	OC	?	n.a.			sc		
DCLXXVI	80	YC	?	n.a.	n.a.		sc?		
DCLXXVII	90	YC	?	n.a.	n.a.		sc??		
DCLXXVIII	80	OA	M	175	c, cl, pl, amtl	oa, sdjd	sc??		
DCLXXIX	95	OC	?	n.a.	eh		sc, co		
DCLXXX	95	YC	?	n.a.					
DCLXXXI	98	YA	F	153	cl, pd				
DCLXXXII	98	EMA	M	177	cl		sc		
DCLXXXIII	98	LMA	M	173	c, cl, pd			rl	t
DCLXXXIV	75	YC	?	n.a.			sc		
DCLXXXV	98	LMA	F	158	c, cl, pd, amtl	oa, sdjd			t
DCLXXXVI	98	OC	?	n.a.			sc		
DCLXXXVII	95	OC	?	n.a.	cl				
DCLXXXVIII	65	LMA	F	n.a.	c, cl, pd, amtl				
DCLXXXIX	95	LMA	F	164	c, cl, pl, pd, amtl		sc		
DCXC	60	LMA	F	159	amtl	sdjd			
DCXCI	90	YC	?	n.a.			sc		
DCXCII	65	N	?	n.a.	n.a.		sc??		
DCXCIII	95	YA	F	151	cl, eh, pl		ph		
DCXCIV	75	YC	?	n.a.			r		
DCXCV	95	EMA	F	155	c, cl, pl, pd, amtl	oa	sc, co		
DCXCVI	95	YC	?	n.a.			sc?	pm?	
DCXCVII	98	LMA	F	156	c, cl, pl, pd	oa, sdjd			
DCXCVIII	60	OC	?	n.a.	c, cl		r	rl	
DCXCIX	85	YC	?	n.a.	eh		sc		
DCC	70	N	?	n.a.	n.a.				
DCCI	75	I	?	n.a.	n.a.		sc?		
DCCII	95	Adol.	?	n.a.	cl, eh		sc??, co		
DCCIII	95	EMA	F	155	c, cl, eh, pl		co		

no.	Compl.	Age group	Sex	Stature (cm)	Pathology and skeletal markers				
					Dental	Joint	Metabolic	Infectious	Other
CCIV	80	N	?	n.a.	n.a.				
CCV	30	I	?	n.a.	n.a.		sc??		
CCVI	30	YC	?	n.a.	n.a.				
CCVII	95	Adol.	?	n.a.			sc??		
CCVIII	90	OC	?	n.a.	eh				
CCIX	80	YC	?	n.a.			sc		
CCX	75	YC	?	n.a.	n.a.		sc, co		
CCXI	95	LMA	M	165	c, cl, pd, amtl	sdjd	r	si	cp, tr
CCXII	10	YC	?	n.a.					
CCXIII	85	EMA	F	160	amtl	oa, sdjd			tr
CCXIV	85	I	?	n.a.	n.a.		sc??, ph		
CCXV	95	OC	?	n.a.	cl				
CCXVI	65	YC	?	n.a.	n.a.		sc??		
CCXVII	85	YC	?	n.a.			sc?		
CCXVIII	98	OC	?	n.a.				si	
CCXIX	90	OC	?	n.a.			sc		
CCXX	30	I	?	n.a.	n.a.		sc		
CCXXI	40	N	?	n.a.	n.a.				
CCXXII	90	OA	M	169	c, cl, pl, amtl	sdjd			cp, tr
CCXXIII	80	YC	?	n.a.			r		
CCXXIV	80	I	?	n.a.	n.a.				
CCXXV	90	OC	?	n.a.	cl, eh		sc??		
CCXXVI	98	OA	M	176	c, cl, eh, pl, pd, amtl	sdjd			cp, tr
CCXXVII	90	EMA	F	162	c, eh, pd, amtl	oa, sdjd	sc?		
CCXXVIII	75	YC	?	n.a.			sc?, co		
CCXXIX	85	EMA	F	165	c, cl, pd, amtl		ph		tr
CCXXX	80	YC	?	n.a.			r		
CCXXXI	90	YC	?	n.a.			sc??		
CCXXXII	98	EMA	M	179	cl		sc??	om	
CCXXXIII	90	OA	M	163	c, cl, pd, amtl	oa, sdjd			cp
CCXXXIV	90	N	?	n.a.	n.a.		sc??		

Id no.	Compl.	Age group	Sex	Stature (cm)	Pathology and skeletal markers				
					Dental	Joint	Metabolic	Infectious	Ot
DCCXXXV	90	OC	?	n.a.	cl		sc??, co		
DCCXXXVI	95	LMA	M	174	c, cl, pd, amtl	sdjd		si	cp
DCCXXXVII	95	LMA	M	168	c, cl	sdjd			
DCCXXXVIII	90	Adol.	?	n.a.	cl		sc??, co		
DCCXXXIX	98	LMA	M	169	c, cl, eh, pd	sdjd	sc??		
DCCXL	90	YC	?	n.a.	eh		sc?, co	rl	
DCCXLI	90	YC	?	n.a.	eh		sc?, co		
DCCXLII	90	OC	?	n.a.	cl		sc??, co		
DCCXLIII	95	YC	?	n.a.			sc??, co		
DCCXLIV	98	LMA	M	174	c, cl, eh, pl, pd, amtl	sdjd			
DCCXLV	65	EMA	M	180	c, cl	oa	sc, co		
DCCXLVI	90	I	?	n.a.	n.a.		sc??		
DCCXLVII	35	EMA	F	161	c, cl				
DCCXLVIII	95	LMA	F	148	cl		sc?		
DCCXLIX	70	YC	?	n.a.	n.a.			rl	
DCCL	35	OC	?	n.a.	cl		sc??		
DCCLI	75	Adol.	?	n.a.	cl, eh		sc, co		
DCCLII	85	YC	?	n.a.			sc?, co, r		
DCCLIII	85	OC	?	n.a.					
DCCLIV	90	OC	?	n.a.	cl		sc, co		
DCCLV	90	YC	?	n.a.	n.a.		sc??		
DCCLVI	85	OC	?	n.a.	eh		sc?, ph		
DCCLVII	85	LMA	F	152	cl, pd				
DCCLVIII	90	LMA	M	180	c, cl, pl, amtl	oa, sdjd	sc??		sf
DCCLIX	95	I	?	n.a.	n.a.				
DCCLX	98	Adol.	M	n.a.	c, cl, pl		sc		
DCCLXI	80	YC	?	n.a.	n.a.				
DCCLXII	40	LMA	F	n.a.	c, pd, amtl	oa, sdjd			
DCCLXIII	15	?A	?	n.a.	n.a.		sc?		
DCCLXIV	95	LMA	M	165	c, cl		sc?, co		
DCCLXV	70	OA	M	178	c, cl, pl, pd, amtl	oa, sdjd			c
DCCLXVI	15	YA	F	n.a.	n.a.		sc?		
DCCLXVII	80	YC	?	n.a.	n.a.		sc?		

no.	Compl.	Age group	Sex	Stature (cm)	Dental	Joint	Metabolic	Infectious	Other
CCLXVIII	80	N	?	n.a.	n.a.				
CCLXIX	95	?A	F	157	amtl	oa, sdjd			
CCLXX	95	OC	?	n.a.			sc??, co		
CCLXXI	95	EMA	M	171	c, cl, pd, amtl	sdjd			cp, tr
CCLXXII	90	LMA	F	157	c, cl, eh, pd, amtl	oa, sdjd			
CCLXXIII	10	I	?	n.a.	n.a.				
CCLXXIV	90	OC	?	n.a.			sc??, co		
CCLXXV	90	YC	?	n.a.					
CCLXXVI	45	YA	M	174	n.a.		sc?		
CCLXXVII	90	Adol.	?	n.a.	cl, eh				
CCLXXVIII	90	Adol.	F	n.a.	c, cl	oa	sc??	tb	
CCLXXIX	20	YC	?	n.a.	n.a.				
CCLXXX	85	YC	?	n.a.			sc?		
CCLXXXI	80	OC	?	n.a.	n.a.				
CCLXXXII	50	EMA	F	158	n.a.	sdjd			tr
CCLXXXIII	98	EMA	M	182	c, cl		sc, ph		cp, tr
CCLXXXIV	95	OC	?	n.a.	cl				
CCLXXXV	90	LMA	M	168	cl, pd, amtl	sdjd	sc		cp, tr
CCLXXXVI	90	OC	?	n.a.	cl		sc??		
CCLXXXVII	95	LMA	M	163	c, cl, pd, amtl	sdjd			tr
CCLXXXVIII	90	LMA	M	176	c, cl, pd, amtl	oa, sdjd, dish			cp
CCLXXXIX	95	LMA	F	155	cl, amtl	oa, sdjd			
CCXC	95	EMA	M	171	c, cl, eh, amtl		sc?		tr
CCXCI	80	YC	?	n.a.	n.a.		sc?, co		
CCXCII	80	N	?	n.a.	n.a.				
CCXCIII	70	Adol.	?	n.a.			sc??		
CCXCIV	60	YC	?	n.a.					
CCXCV	95	OA	M	175	c, pd, amtl	oa, sdjd			sfc

Id no.	Compl.	Age group	Sex	Stature (cm)	Dental	Joint	Metabolic	Infectious	Oth
DCCXCVI	95	EMA	F	170	c, cl, pd, amtl	oa, sdjd	sc??		o(
DCCXCVII	80	LMA	M	n.a.	c, cl, pd, amtl	oa, sdjd			c|
DCCXCVIII	20	YC	?	n.a.			sc?		
DCCXCIX	80	LMA	F	155	c, cl, pd, amtl	oa, sdjd	sc??		cp,
DCCC	95	LMA	F	166	c, cl, pl, pd, amtl	oa, sdjd	sc?, ph		
DCCCI	98	Adol.	?	n.a.	cl				
DCCCII	98	EMA	F	168	c, cl, pd, amtl	oa	sc??, co, ph		o(
DCCCIII	20	I	?	n.a.	n.a.				
DCCCIV	80	OA	M	168	c, cl, pd	oa, sdjd			
DCCCV	90	OA	M	171	c, cl, pd	sdjd	sc?		t|
DCCCVI	90	I	?	n.a.	n.a.			rl	
DCCCVII	95	Adol.	M	n.a.	cl, pd				
DCCCVIII	98	EMA	M	166	c, cl	oa	sc		cp,
DCCCIX	90	I	?	n.a.	n.a.		sc??		
DCCCX	90	YC	?	n.a.					
DCCCXI	90	YC	?	n.a.	cl		sc??		
DCCCXII	80	YC	?	n.a.	n.a.		sc?		
DCCCXIII	90	YC	?	n.a.	cl		sc??, co		
DCCCXIV	90	OA	?	n.a.	c, cl, pl, pd, amtl	oa, sdjd			cp,
DCCCXV	95	EMA	F	156	c, cl, pd				
DCCCXVI	25	?A	F	151	c, cl, eh, pl, pd, amtl				
DCCCXVII	80	YC	?	n.a.	n.a.		sc?		
DCCCXVIII	98	EMA	F	155	c, cl, eh, pd, amtl				
DCCCXIX	70	OC	?	n.a.	cl		sc?, co, ph		
DCCCXX	45	YC	?	n.a.	n.a.		sc??	rl	
DCCCXXI	55	YC	?	n.a.			sc		
DCCCXXII	90	OC	?	n.a.			sc		
DCCCXXIII	10	?A	?	n.a.	n.a.		sc?	om, rl	a|
DCCCXXIV	65	YC	?	n.a.	eh		sc??		

no.	Compl.	Age group	Sex	Stature (cm)	Pathology and skeletal markers				
					Dental	Joint	Metabolic	Infectious	Other
CCCXXV	80	OC	?	n.a.			sc??, co		
CCCXXVI	95	LMA	M	171	c, cl, pl, pd, amtl	sdjd	sc?		cp
CCCXXVII	98	LMA	F	155	c, cl, pl, amtl		sc??		
CCCXXVIII	95	LMA	M	167	cl				cp
CCCXXIX	95	EMA	F	155	cl, eh		co	rl	cp
CCCXXX	90	Adol.	?	n.a.	c, cl		sc, co	rl	
CCCXXXI	90	YC	?	n.a.			sc	rl	
CCCXXXII	95	OA	F	n.a.	c, cl, amtl	oa, sdjd	sc	rl	
CCCXXXIII	80	I	?	n.a.	eh		sc?, co		
CCCXXXIV	90	OC	?	n.a.			sc??		
CCCXXXV	90	LMA	M	183	c, cl, pl	oa, sdjd	sc?		
CCCXXXVI	95	Adol.	?	n.a.	cl				
CCCXXXVII	20	Adol.	?	n.a.					
CCCXXXVIII	95	LMA	M	169	c, pl, amtl	oa, sdjd	ph		tr
CCCXXXIX	95	N	?	n.a.	n.a.			rl	
CCCXL	40	LMA	M	n.a.	c, cl, pd, amtl				
CCCXLI	30	EMA	M	n.a.	cl	sdjd	ph		
CCCXLII	75	LMA	M	175	pl, amtl	sdjd	sc??		
CCCXLIII	95	OC	?	n.a.			sc, ph		
CCCXLIV	85	EMA	F	164	c, cl, eh, amtl			rl	
CCCXLV	60	I	?	n.a.	n.a.				
CCCXLVI	60	N	?	n.a.	n.a.				
CCCXLVII	95	YC	?	n.a.			sc		
CCCXLVIII	90	OC	?	n.a.	c, cl, eh		sc??, co		
CCCXLIX	80	N	?	n.a.	n.a.				
CCCL	30	EMA	F	n.a.	amtl				
CCCLI	85	YC	?	n.a.					
CCCLII	40	EMA	F	163	eh				
CCCLIII	30	OC	?	n.a.	n.a.		sc??		
CCCLIV	80	LMA	F	152	c, cl, eh, amtl				

Id no.	Compl.	Age group	Sex	Stature (cm)	Dental	Joint	Metabolic	Infectious	Ot
DCCCLV	90	EMA	M	166	c, cl				
DCCCLVI	70	OA	F	n.a.	c, cl, amtl				
DCCCLVII	7	LMA	F	n.a.	n.a.				
DCCCLVIII	5	EMA	M	n.a.	n.a.				
DCCCLIX	30	YC	?	n.a.	n.a.				
DCCCLX	5	I	?	n.a.	n.a.				
DCCCLXI	55	YC	?	n.a.	cl				
DCCCLXII	30	?A	M	167	cl, pd				c
DCCCLXIII	5	?A	?	n.a.	n.a.				
DCCCLXIV	20	LMA	M	n.a.	c, cl, pd, amtl			sc??	c
DCCCLXV	25	LMA	M	n.a.	c, cl, pd, amtl	oa			
DCCCLXVI	25	?A	F	n.a.	c, amtl			sc?	
DCCCLXVII	55	LMA	M	156	cl, amtl				
DCCCLXVIII	55	LMA	M	170	n.a.				
DCCCLXIX	40	LMA	F	n.a.	n.a.				
DCCCLXX	30	LMA	F	165	c, cl, amtl	oa			
DCCCLXXI	20	?A	M	172	amtl				
DCCCLXXII	60	OC	?	n.a.				sc??	
DCCCLXXIII	55	YC	?	n.a.	n.a.			sc?, co	
DCCCLXXIV	50	YC	?	n.a.	cl				
DCCCLXXV	35	OC	?	n.a.					
DCCCLXXVI	35	OC	?	n.a.					
DCCCLXXVII	20	OC	?	n.a.	eh			sc??	
DCCCLXXVIII	5	OC	?	n.a.					
DCCCLXXIX	20	YC	?	n.a.	n.a.				
DCCCLXXX	10	I	?	n.a.	n.a.				
DCCCLXXXI	65	LMA	M	176	c, cl, pd				
DCCCLXXXII	80	Adol.	?	n.a.	cl				
DCCCLXXXIII	15	?A	F	154	n.a.				
DCCCLXXXIV	75	LMA	M	n.a.	c, cl, pd, amtl				c
DCCCLXXXV	45	LMA	M	168	cl				c
DCCCLXXXVI	20	?A	M	165	n.a.				
DCCCLXXXVII	20	EMA	F	155	n.a.				
DCCCLXXXVIII	15	?A	F	157	cl	oa			
DCCCLXXXIX	40	EMA	F	152	n.a.	oa, sdjd		sc?	

no.	Compl.	Age group	Sex	Stature (cm)	Pathology and skeletal markers				
					Dental	Joint	Metabolic	Infectious	Other
ƆCCXC	40	EMA	M	n.a.	c, cl, pd, amtl	oa			
ƆCCXCI	15	YC	?	n.a.	n.a.				
ƆCCXCII	20	Adol.	?	n.a.	n.a.			sc??	
ƆCCXCIII	20	OC	?	n.a.	n.a.				
ƆCCXCIV	75	EMA	M	175	cl, eh, pd				cp
ƆCCXCV	70	OA	F	154	cl, amtl				
ƆCCXCVI	40	?A	F	n.a.	n.a.				
ƆCCXCVII	40	LMA	M	n.a.	pl, amtl				
ƆCCXCVIII	20	?A	F	n.a.	n.a.				
ƆCCXCIX	10	?A	M	n.a.	n.a.				
ⱯI	15	LMA	M	n.a.	n.a.				
ⱯII	15	LMA	F	n.a.	n.a.	oa			
ⱯIII	10	LMA	M	n.a.	n.a.			sc??	
ⱯIIII	5	?A	?	n.a.	n.a.	sdjd			
ⱯIV	5	?A	M	n.a.	c, pl, pd, amtl				
ⱯV	75	OC	?	n.a.				sc??, co	
ⱯVI	70	Adol.	?	n.a.	eh				
ⱯVII	75	OC	?	n.a.					
ⱯVIII	25	OC	?	n.a.	n.a.				
ⱯIX	15	YC	?	n.a.				sc??, co	
ⱯX	20	OC	?	n.a.	n.a.				
ⱯXI	40	EMA	M	172	n.a.				
ⱯXII	20	EMA	F	151	cl	sdjd			
ⱯXIII	20	EMA	F	150	n.a.				
ⱯXIV	15	LMA	F	160	n.a.	sdjd			
ⱯXV	15	LMA	M	173	c, cl, amtl				cp
ⱯXVI	15	EMA	F	156	cl				
ⱯXVII	10	EMA	F	154	n.a.				
ⱯXVIII	10	EMA	F	n.a.					
ⱯXIX	15	OC	?	n.a.					
ⱯXX	7	YC	?	n.a.	n.a.				
ⱯXXI	45	OC	?	n.a.	cl				tr
ⱯXXII	15	OC	?	n.a.	eh			sc??	
ⱯXXIII	7	YC	?	n.a.	c			sc	
ⱯXXIV	20	OC	?	n.a.					

Id no.	Compl.	Age group	Sex	Stature (cm)	Dental	Joint	Metabolic	Infectious	O
CMXXV	85	EMA	F	152	c, eh				•
CMXXVI	65	OC	?	n.a.	n.a.				
CMXXVII	20	OC	?	n.a.	eh		sc		
CMXXVIII	30	OC	?	n.a.					
CMXXIX	30	OC	?	n.a.	n.a.				
CMXXX	8	OC	?	n.a.	n.a.		sc??, co		
CMXXXI	75	LMA	F	155	cl	sdjd			
CMXXXII	75	OA	M	175	pd, amtl				•
CMXXXIII	40	EMA	F	n.a.	n.a.				
CMXXXIV	75	LMA	M	174	c, pd, amtl	sdjd			
CMXXXV	70	LMA	M	n.a.	cl, pd, amtl				
CMXXXVI	60	EMA	M	n.a.	c, cl				
CMXXXVII	30	EMA	?	n.a.	cl, amtl				
CMXXXVIII	20	LMA	?	n.a.	n.a.				
CMXXXIX	15	?A	?	n.a.	n.a.				
CMXL	20	?A	?	n.a.	n.a.				
CMXLI	20	?A	?	n.a.	n.a.				
CMXLII	75	LMA	M	181	c, cl, amtl	oa, sdjd		si	cp
CMXLIII	75	EMA	F	n.a.	cl, amtl				
CMXLIV	75	EMA	F	n.a.	c, cl	sdjd			
CMXLV	50	LMA	?	170	cl, amtl		sc??		
CMXLVI	50	LMA	M	179	cl, pd, amtl		sc??		•
CMXLVII	35	OA	M	173	c, cl, pd				•
CMXLVIII	25	?A	F	n.a.	amtl				
CMXLIX	40	OC	?	n.a.	c, pd		sc??		
CML	25	OC	?	n.a.	cl		sc??		
CMLI	50	YC	?	n.a.	n.a.				
CMLII	50	YC	?	n.a.	n.a.		sc		
CMLIII	25	OC	?	n.a.			sc??		
CMLIV	15	YC	?	n.a.	n.a.				
CMLV	5	YC	?	n.a.	n.a.		sc??, ph		
CMLVI	20	YC	?	n.a.	n.a.		sc??		
CMLVII	10	YC	?	n.a.	n.a.				
CMLVIII	5	YC	?	n.a.	n.a.				

no.	Compl.	Age group	Sex	Stature (cm)	Pathology and skeletal markers				
					Dental	Joint	Metabolic	Infectious	Other
MLIX	15	OA	M	n.a.	c, cl, pl	oa, sdjd			cp
MLX	15	LMA	M	n.a.	c, cl, pd, amtl				cp
MLXI	15	EMA	F	n.a.	c, cl, amtl				
MLXII	10	EMA	F	n.a.	c, cl, amtl			co	
MLXIII	10	EMA	M	n.a.	c, cl, pd, amtl				
MLXIV	10	LMA	?	n.a.	c, cl, pl	sdjd			
MLXV	7	EMA	M	n.a.	amtl	oa		co	
MLXVI	7	LMA	?	n.a.	amtl				
MLXVII	5	?A	?	n.a.	c, pl, amtl				
MLXVIII	5	?A	?	n.a.	cl				
MLXIX	40	OC	?	n.a.				sc	
MLXX	5	OC	?	n.a.	eh				
MLXXI	50	EMA	M	170	c, cl, pl, amtl	oa, sdjd		sc?	tr
MLXXII	15	?A	M	n.a.	n.a.				
MLXXIII	35	LMA	M	171	n.a.	sdjd			tr
MLXXIV	25	?A	F	174	n.a.	sdjd			
MLXXV	65	Adol.	?	n.a.	cl, eh				
MLXXVI	60	YC	?	n.a.					

Notes

Chapter 1. Setting the Stage for a Bioarchaeology of the Great Irish Famine

1. The term microarchaeology is occasionally used for microscopic analyses in archaeological sciences (e.g., Weiner 2010).

Chapter 2. "An entire nation of paupers": Contextualizing Poverty and Famine in Mid-Nineteenth-Century Ireland and Kilkenny

1. Kilkenny Board of Guardians Minutes, 17 June 1847, 12/7K, Kilkenny County Library.

2. The human skeletons from the Kilkenny mass burials were assessed for evidence of animal gnaw marks on the bones. No such evidence was found.

3. Kilkenny Board of Guardians Minutes, 4 March 1847, 12/7K, Kilkenny County Library.

4. During the same period when the mass burials were undertaken within the grounds of the workhouse, an unknown number of deceased were interred on the grounds of the Fever Hospital. The exact location of these burials at the time of this writing was unknown.

5. Kilkenny Board of Guardians Minutes, 13 March 1851, 17/10K, Kilkenny County Library.

6. Ibid., 8 and 22 April 1847, 12/7K, Kilkenny County Library.

7. Ibid., 25 March and 25 June 1846, 10/6K, Kilkenny County Library.

8. Ibid., 25 March 1847, 12/7K, Kilkenny County Library.

9. Ibid., 14 March 1848, 13/8K, Kilkenny County Library.

10. Ibid., 15 April 1847, 12/7K, Kilkenny County Library.

11. Ibid., 15 May 1847, 12/7K, Kilkenny County Library.

12. Ibid., 17 June 1847, 12/7K, Kilkenny County Library.

13. Ibid., 26 May 1846, 10/6K, Kilkenny County Library.

Chapter 3. A Life Endured in Poverty: A Social Bioarchaeology of the "Deserving Poor"

1. $\chi^2(6) = 361.828, p < .001$.
2. $\chi^2(6) = 363.599, p < .001$.
3. $\chi^2(6) = 289.160, p < .001$.

4. $U = 3341.000$, $Z = -.159$, $p = .874$.

5. $\chi^2(1) = 11.982$, $p = .001$.

6. $U = 12,648.00$, $Z = -.679$, $p = .497$.

7. $U = 12,250.00$, $Z = -.534$, $p = .593$.

8. $\chi^2(1) = 3.745$, $p = .053$.

9. $\chi^2(1) = 6.066$, $p = .014$.

10. $\chi^2(6) = 49.200$, $p < .001$.

11. $\chi^2(1) = 3.037$, $p = .081$.

12. $\chi^2(3) = 57.154$, $p < .001$.

13. $\chi^2(1) = 3.947$, $p = .047$.

14. $\chi^2(1) = 4.884$, $p = .027$.

15. $\chi^2(1) = 0.927$, $p = .336$.

16. $\chi^2(1) = 32.106$, $p < .001$.

17. $\chi^2(3) = 16.769$, $p = .001$) and $\chi^2(3) = 13.821$, $p = .003$), respectively.

18. $\chi^2(3) = 34.050$, $p < .001$.

19. $\chi^2(1) = .863$, $p = .353$.

20. $\chi^2(1) = .899$, $p = .343$.

21. $\chi^2(1) = 7.350$, $p = .007$.

22. $\chi^2(1) = .000$, $p = .990$.

23. $N = 152$, $p = .012$.

24. $\chi^2(1) = .488$, $p = .485$.

25. $\chi^2(1) = 1.521$, $p = .217$.

26. $\chi^2(3) = 16.923$, $p = .001$.

27. $\chi^2(3) = 108.026$, $p < .001$.

28. $U = 5727.500$, $Z = -2.566$, $p = .010$.

29. $U = 7399.000$, $Z = -2.295$, $p = .022$.

30. $\chi^2(3) = 36.639$, $p < .001$.

31. The term "codfish vertebra" refers to the general appearance of a vertebra that displays a biconcave appearance typical of fish vertebrae due to poor mineralization and compression.

32. $\chi^2(3) = 23.754$, $p < .001$.

33. $\chi^2(1) = 1.402$, $p = .236$.

34. $\chi^2(1) = 10.673$, $p = .001$.

35. $\chi^2(1) = 1.089$, $p = .297$.

36. $\chi^2(1) = 6.946$, $p = .008$.

37. $\chi^2(1) = 8.781$, $p = .003$.

38. $\chi^2(1) = 6.852$, $p = .009$.

39. $\chi^2(1) = .231$, $p = .631$.

40. $\chi^2(1) = 3.879$, $p = .049$.

41. $\chi^2(1) = 1.674$, $p = .196$.

Chapter 4. Institutionalization as the Last Resort: Famine Diseases, Mortality, and Medical Interventions

1. $\chi^2(1) = .445, p = .505$.
2. $\chi^2(1) = 12.883, p < .001$.
3. A gruel of Indian meal (maize) or oatmeal.
4. Kilkenny Board of Guardians Minutes, 17 October 1848, 13/8K, Kilkenny County Library.
5. SD = 7.75, n = 185.
6. SD = 8.36, n = 202.
7. $\chi^2(3) = 17.229, p = 0.001$.
8. SD = 16.15; n = 138.
9. SD = 17.32; n = 588.
10. $\chi^2(7) = 24.448, p = .001$. Present: median = 23.4 years; not present: median = 14.0 years.
11. SD = 8.14; n = 127.
12. SD = 6.84; n = 57.
13. SD = 7.98; n = 96.
14. SD = 7.98; n = 105.
15. $\chi^2(8) = 79.092, p < 0.001$.
16. $\chi^2(4) = 44.610, p < .001$.
17. $\chi^2(3) = 3.278, p = .351$.
18. Henry Potter to Commissary General Sir Randolf I. Routh, Commissariat Relief Office, Dublin, 4 March 1847, 17 March 1847, and 8 April 1847, Famine Relief Commission Incoming Letters, RLFC3/2/14/49, National Archives of Ireland, Dublin.

Chapter 5. The Bioarchaeology of the Human Experience of Famine and Disaster: Shedding New Light on the Realities of the Great Irish Famine

1. Mark S. O'Shaughnessy, Esq., vice-guardian of the Kilkenny Poor Law Union.
2. Kilkenny Board of Guardians Minutes, 2 August 1883, 51/40K, Kilkenny County Library.

References

Adams, Josephine, and Kevin Colls
2007 *"Out of Darkness, Cometh Light." Life and Death in Nineteenth-Century Wolver-hampton: Excavation of the Overflow Burial Ground of St Peter's Collegiate Church, Wolverhampton. 2001–2002.* BAR British Series 442. Archaeopress, Oxford.

Adler, Claus-Peter
2000 *Bone Diseases: Macroscopic, Histological, and Radiological Diagnosis of Structural Changes in the Skeleton.* Springer, Berlin.

Aladel, Jean Marie
1880 *The Miraculous Medal: Its Origin, History, Circulation, Results.* H. L. Kilner and Co., Philadelphia.

Alberico, Ana Paula Mena, Glória Valeria da Veiga, Miriam Ribeiro Baião, Marta Maria Antonieta de Souza Santos, Sônia Buongermino de Souza, and Sophia Cornbluth Szarfarc
2003 Iron Deficiency Anaemia in Infants Attended at Municipal Primary Health Care Centres in Rio de Janeiro-Brazil. *Nutrition and Food Science* 33(2):50–55.

Alfer, Karl Leopold
1891 Die Häufigkeit der Knochen und Gelenktuberkulose in Beziehung auf Alter, Ge-schlecht, Stand und Erblichkeit. *Beiträge zur Klinischen Chirurgie* 8(2):277–290.

Almqvist, Bo
1979 *The Irish Folklore Commission: Achievement and Legacy.* Folklore Studies Pamphlets 3. Comhairle Bhéaloideas Éireann, Dublin.

Alter, George, Muriel Neven, and Michel Oris
2004 Stature in Transition: A Micro-Level Study from Nineteenth-Century Belgium. *Social Science History* 28(2):231–247.

Alvarez, Jose O., and Juan M. Navia
1989 Nutritional Status, Tooth Eruption, and Dental Caries: A Review. *The American Journal of Clinical Nutrition* 49(3):417–426.

Ambrose, Nicola L., Fiona Keogan, J. P. O'Callaghan, and Paul G. O'Connell
2010 Obesity and Disability in the Symptomatic Irish Knee Osteoarthritis Population. *Irish Journal of Medical Science* 179(2):265–268.

Anonymous
1842 Post-Mortem Examinations in the Kilkenny Workhouse. *Dublin Medical Press* 8(189):110–111.

1846 *The Parliamentary Gazetteer of Ireland, Adapted to the New Poor-Law, Franchise, Municipal and Ecclesiastical Arrangements, and Compiled with a Special Reference to the Lines of Railroad and Canal communications, as Existing in 1844–45.* Volume II. A. Fullarton and Co., Dublin.

1849 Report upon the Recent Epidemic Fever in Ireland. *Dublin Quarterly Journal of Medical Science* 7(2):340–404.

1896 Social Status of the British Medical Profession. *The Journal of the American Medical Association* 27(17):920.

1953 Hunger Oedema. *Acta Psychiatrica Scandinavica* 28(S83):93–112.

Arabaolaza, Iraia, Paola Ponce, and Anthea Boylston

2007 Skeletal Analysis. In *"Out of Darkness, Cometh Light": Life and Death in Nineteenth-Century Wolverhampton. Excavation of the Overflow Burial Ground of St Peter's Collegiate Church, Wolverhampton 2001–2002,* edited by Josephine Adams and Kevin Colls, pp. 39–69. BAR British Series 442. Archaeopress, Oxford.

Arcini, Caroline

1999 *Health and Disease in Early Lund: Osteo-Pathologic Studies of 3,305 Individuals Buried in the Cemetery Area of Lund, 990–1536.* Lund University, Lund.

Armelagos, George J., Alan H. Goodman, Kristin N. Harper, and Michael L. Blakey

2009 Enamel Hypoplasia and Early Mortality: Bioarchaeological Support for the Barker Hypothesis. *Evolutionary Anthropology* 18(6):261–271.

Armelagos, George J., and Dennis P. van Gerven

2003 A Century of Skeletal Biology and Paleopathology: Contrasts, Contradictions and Conflicts. *American Anthropologist* 105(1):53–64.

Arosarena, Oneida A., Travis A. Fritsch, Yichung Hsueh, Behrad Aynehchi, and Richard Haug

2009 Maxillofacial Injuries and Violence against Women. *Archives of Facial Plastic Surgery* 11(1):48–52.

Aufderheide, Arthur C., and Conrado Rodríguez-Martín

1998 *The Cambridge Encyclopedia of Human Paleopathology.* Cambridge University Press, Cambridge.

Bagge, Elisabeth, Anders Bjelle, Staffan Edén, and Alvar Svanborg

1991 Osteoarthritis in the Elderly: Clinical and Radiological Findings in 79- and 85-Year-Olds. *Annals of the Rheumatic Diseases* 50(8):535–539.

Bailey, Craig

2006 Micro-Credit, Misappropriation and Morality: British Responses to Irish Distress, 1822–1831. *Continuity and Change* 21(3):455–474.

Barak, Yoram

2007 The Aging of Holocaust Survivors: Myth and Reality Concerning Suicide. *Medicine and the Holocaust* 9(3):196–198.

Barak, Yoram, Dov Aizenberg, Henry Szor, Marnina Swartz, Rachel Maor, and Haim Y. Knobler

2005 Increased Risk of Attempted Suicide among Aging Holocaust Survivors. *American Journal of Geriatric Psychiatry* 13(8):701–704.

Barker, David J., and Clive Osmond
1986 Infant Mortality, Childhood Nutrition, and Ischaemic Heart Disease in England and Wales. *The Lancet* 327(8489):1077–1081.
Barrett, John
1849 Observations on Scurvy as It Was Developed in Bath and Its Neighbourhood, in the Spring of 1847. *Provincial Medical and Surgical Journal* 13(6):148–153.
Bartlett, John G.
2004 Bioterrorism. In *Infectious Diseases*, edited by Sherwood L. Gorbach, John G. Bartlett, and Neil R. Blacklow, pp. 116–125. Lippincott Williams and Wilkins, Philadelphia.
Bartoletti, Susan Campbell
2001 *Black Potatoes: The Story of the Great Irish Famine, 1845–1850.* Houghton Mifflin Harcourt, New York.
Basker, Robin M., and John C. Davenport
2002 *Prosthetic Treatment of the Edentulous Patient.* 4th ed. Blackwell Munksgaard, Oxford.
Bassett, George Henry
1884 *Kilkenny City and County Guide and Directory: A Book for Manufacturers, Merchants, Traders, Land-Owners, Farmers, Tourists, Anglers, and Sportsmen Generally.* Sealy, Bryers and Walker, Dublin.
Basu, Tapan Kumar, and Chris J. Schorah
1982 *Vitamin C in Health and Disease.* AVI Publishing Company, London.
Beaudry, Mary C.
2011 Stitching Women's Lives: Interpreting the Artifacts of Sewing and Needlework. In *Interpreting the Early Modern World: Transatlantic Perspectives*, edited by Mary C. Beaudry and James Symonds, pp. 145–159. Springer, London.
Beinert, Wolfgang
1992 Rosenkranz. In *Evangelisches Kirchenlexikon: Internationale Theologische Enzyklopädie*, Vol. 3, 1718–1719. Vandenhoeck and Ruprecht, Göttingen.
Bekvalac, Jelena, and Tania Kausmally
2008 Life and Death in Chelsea. In *Late 17th- to 19th-Century Burial and Earlier Occupation at All Saints, Chelsea Old Church, Royal Borough of Kensington and Chelsea*, edited by Robert Cowie, Jelena Bekvalac, and Tania Kausmally, pp. 40–59. Molas Archaeology Studies Series 18. Museum of London Archaeology Service, London.
Bennett, William
1847 *Narrative of a Recent Journey of Six Weeks in Ireland, in Connexion with the Subject of Supplying Small Seed to some Remoter Districts: with Current Observations on the Depressed Circumstances of the People, and the Means Presented for the Permanent Improvement of their Social Condition.* Charles Gilpin, London.
Bindon, Jim
2007 Biocultural Linkages: Cultural Consensus, Cultural Consonance, and Human Biological Research. *Collegium Antropologicum* 31(1):3–10.
Binford, Lewis R.
1962 Archaeology as Anthropology. *American Antiquity* 28(2):217–225.

Binford, Sally R., and Lewis R. Binford
1968 *New Perspectives in Archaeology*. Aldine Publishing Company, Chicago.
Birkett, David A.
1983 Non-Specific Infections. In *Disease in Ancient Man*, edited by Gerald D. Hart, pp. 99–105. Clarke Irwin, Toronto.
Birthistle, Dorcas
1964 Alms Houses of Kilkenny. *Old Kilkenny Review* 16:61–63.
Boston, Ceridwen, Angela Boyle, John Gill, and Annsofie Witkin
2009 *"In the Vaults Beneath": Archaeological Recording at St. George's Church, Bloomsbury*. Oxford Archaeology Monograph 8. Oxford Archaeology, Oxford.
Bourke, P. M. Austin
1968 The Use of the Potato Crop in Pre-Famine Ireland. *Journal of the Statistical and Social Inquiry Society of Ireland* 11(6):72–96.
Bourne, Geoffrey H.
1942 The Effect of Graded Doses of Vitamin C upon the Regeneration of Bone in Guinea Pigs on a Scorbutic Diet. *Journal of Physiology* 101(3):327–336.
1943 Some Experiments on the Possible Relationship between Vitamin C, and Calcification. *Journal of Physiology* 102(3):319–328.
Boyce, David George
2005 *Nineteenth-Century Ireland: The Search for Stability*. New Gill History of Ireland 5. Gill and Macmillan, Dublin.
Boyle, Angela, Ceridwen Boston, and Annsofie Witkin
2005 The Archaeological Experience at St Luke's Church, Old Street, Islington. Unpublished report, Oxford Archaeology, Oxford.
Boyle, Phelim P., and Cormac Ó Gráda
1986 Fertility Trends, Excess Mortality, and the Great Irish Famine. *Demography* 23(4):543–562.
Bradley, John
2000 *Irish Historic Towns Atlas: Kilkenny*. Royal Irish Academy, Dublin.
Brandt, Allan M.
1993 Sexually Transmitted Diseases. In *Companion Encyclopedia of the History of Medicine*, edited by William F. Bynum and Roy Porter, Vol. 1, pp. 562–584. Routledge, London.
Brickley, Megan
2004 The Skeletons. Appendix in Daniel Lewis and P. J. Pikes, The Tanyard and Quaker Burial Ground, Bromyard, Herefordshire: Archaeological Excavation and Monitoring. Unpublished report, Archenfield Archaeology Ltd., Fownhope.
Brickley, Megan, Helena Berry, Gaynor Western, Annete Hancocks, and Michael Richards
2006 The People: Physical Anthropology. In *St. Martin's Uncovered: Investigations in the Churchyard of St. Martin's-in-the-Bull Ring, Birmingham, 2001*, edited by Megan Brickley, Simon Buteux, Josephine Adams, and Richard Cherrington, pp. 90–151. Oxbow, Oxford.

Brickley, Megan, and Rachel Ives
2006 Skeletal Manifestations of Infantile Scurvy. *American Journal of Physical Anthropology* 129(2):163–172.
2008 *The Bioarchaeology of Metabolic Bone Disease.* Academic Press, Amsterdam.
Brickley, Megan, Adrian Miles, and Hilary Stainer
1999 *The Cross Bones Burial Ground, Redcross Way, Southwark London. Archaeological Excavations (1991–1998) for the London Underground Limited Jubilee Line Extension Project.* MOLAS Monograph 3. Museum of London, London.
Bridges, Kenneth R., and Howard A. Pearson
2008 *Anemias and Other Red Blood Cell Disorders.* The McGraw-Hill Companies, New York.
Bridges, Patricia S.
1994 Vertebral Arthritis and Physical Activities in the Prehistoric Southeastern United States. *American Journal of Physical Anthropology* 93(1):83–93.
Brooks, Sheilagh, and Judy M. Suchey
1990 Skeletal Age Determination Based on the Os Pubis: A Comparison of the Acsádi-Nemeskéri and Suchey-Brooks Methods. *Human Evolution* 5(3):227–238.
Brothwell, Don
1961 The Palaeopathology of Early British Man: An Essay on the Problems of Diagnosis and Analysis. *The Journal of the Royal Anthropological Institute of Great Britain and Ireland* 91(2):318–344.
1981 *Digging Up Bones.* 3rd ed. Cornell University Press, Ithaca, New York.
Buckley, Laureen, and Barra Ó Donnabháin
1992 Trephination: Early Cranial Surgery in Ireland. *Archaeology Ireland* 6(4):10–12.
Buikstra, Jane E.
1977 Biocultural Dimensions of Archeological Study: A Regional Perspective. In *Biocultural Adaptation in Prehistoric America,* edited by Robert L. Blakely, pp. 67–84. University of Georgia Press, Athens.
Buikstra, Jane E., and Lane E. Beck
2006 *Bioarchaeology: The Contextual Analysis of Human Remains.* Academic Press, London.
Burchiel, Kim J.
2002 *Surgical Management of Pain.* Thieme Medical Publishers, Inc., New York.
Buzon, Michele R., Phillip L. Walker, Francine Drayer Verhagen, and Susan L. Kerr
2005 Health and Disease in Nineteenth-Century San Francisco: Skeletal Evidence from a Forgotten Cemetery. *Historical Archaeology* 39(2):1–15.
Cammisa, Mario, Antonio De Serio, and Giuseppe Guglielmi
1998 Diffuse Idiopathic Skeletal Hyperostosis. *European Journal of Radiology* 27(1):7–11.
Carlyle, Thomas
1882 *Reminiscences of My Irish Journey in 1849.* Sampson Low, Marston, Searle, and Rivington, London.
Carman, H. Frank
1937 Symptoms of Early Tuberculosis. *Chest* 3(7):13–30.

Carpenter, Kenneth J.
1986 *The History of Scurvy and Vitamin C*. Cambridge University Press, Cambridge.

Carrigan, William
1905 *The History and Antiquities of the Diocese of Ossory*. Sealy, Bryers and Walkers, Dublin.

Chamberlain, Andrew
2006 *Demography in Archaeology*. Cambridge Manuals in Archaeology. Cambridge University Press, Cambridge.

Civitelli, Roberto, Konstantinos Ziambaras, and Rattana Leelawattana
1998 Pathophysiology of Calcium, Phosphate, and Magnesium Absorption. In *Metabolic Bone Disease and Clinically Related Disorders*, edited by Louis V. Avioli and Stephen K. Krane, pp. 165–205. Academic Press, London.

Coaccioli, Stefano, Giuseppe Fatati, L. Di Cato, D. Marioli, E. Patucchi, C. Pizzuti, M. Ponteggia, and Adolfo Puxeddu
2000 Diffuse Idiopathic Skeletal Hyperostosis in Diabetes Mellitus, Impaired Glucose Tolerance and Obesity. *Panminerva Medica* 42(4):247–251.

Coggon, David, Isabel Reading, Peter Croft, Magnus McLaren, David Barrett, and Cyrus Cooper
2001 Knee Osteoarthritis and Obesity. *International Journal of Obesity and Related Metabolic Disorders* 25(5):622–627.

Cohen, Marilyn
2002 Toward an Historical Ethnography of the Great Irish Famine: The Parish of Tullylish, County Down, 1841–1851. In *Locating Capitalism in Time and Space: Global Restructurings, Politics, and Identity*, edited by David Nugent, pp. 113–136. Stanford University Press, Stanford, California.

Cole, A. J. L., L. Webb, and T. J. Cole
1988 Bone Age Estimation: A Comparison of Methods. *The British Journal of Radiology* 61(728):683–686.

Connell, Brian, and Adrian Miles
2010 *The City Bunhill Burial Ground, Golden Lane, London: Excavations at South Islington Schools, 2006*. MOLA Archaeology Studies Series 21. Museum of London Archaeology, London.

Connolly, Sean J.
2001 *Priests and People in Pre-Famine Ireland, 1780–1845*. Four Courts History Classics. Four Courts Press Ltd., Dublin.

Cook, Della Collins, and Jane E. Buikstra
1979 Health and Differential Survival in Prehistoric Populations: Prenatal Dental Defects. *American Journal of Physical Anthropology* 51(4):649–664.

Cook, Gordon C.
2004 Scurvy in the British Mercantile Marine in the 19th Century, and the Contribution of the Seamen's Hospital Society. *Postgraduate Medical Journal* 80(942):224–229.

Cornell, Per, and Fredrik Fahlander
2002a Microarchaeology, Materiality and Social Practice. *Current Swedish Archaeology* 10:21–38.

2002b *Social praktik och stumma monument: Introduktion till mikroarkeologi.* Gotark Serie 46. Institutionen för arkeologi, Göteborgs universitet, Göteborg.

2007 Encounters—Materialities—Confrontations: An Introduction. In *Encounters— Materialities—Confrontations: Archaeologies of Social Space and Interaction*, edited by Per Cornell and Fredrik Fahlander, pp. 1–14. Cambridge Scholars Press, Newcastle.

Cousens, Stuart H.

1960 Regional Death Rates in Ireland during the Great Famine, from 1846 to 1851. *Population Studies* 14(1):55–74.

1963 The Regional Variation in Mortality during the Great Irish Famine. *Proceedings of the Royal Irish Academy* 63C:127–148.

Cowie, Robert, Jelena Bekvalac, and Tania Kausmally

2008 *Late 17th- to 19th-Century Burial and Earlier Occupation at All Saints, Chelsea Old Church, Royal Borough of Kensington and Chelsea.* Museum of London Archaeology Service, London.

Crawford, E. Margaret

1988 Scurvy in Ireland during the Great Famine. *The Society for the Social History of Medicine* 1(33):281–300.

1994 The Great Irish Famine 1845–49: Image versus Reality. In *Ireland: Art into History*, edited by Raymond Gillespie and Brian P. Kennedy, pp. 75–88. Town House, Dublin.

1995 Food and Famine. In *The Great Irish Famine*, edited by Cathal Póirtéir, 60–73. Radio Telefís Éireann/Mercier Press, Dublin.

Crotty, Margaret

1996 Kilkenny Board of Guardians 1839–1923. Unpublished dissertation, Kilkenny.

Crowley, John, William J. Smyth, and Mike Murphy (editors)

2012 *Atlas of the Great Irish Famine, 1845–52.* Cork University Press, Cork.

Csonka, George W., and John K. Oates

1990 Syphilis. In *Sexually Transmitted Diseases: A Textbook of Genitourinary Medicine*, edited by George W. Csonka and John K. Oates, pp. 227–276. Baillière Tindall, London.

Cullen, Louis Michael

1990 The Social and Economic Evolution of Kilkenny in the Seventeenth and Eighteenth Centuries. In *Kilkenny: History and Society. Interdisciplinary Essays on the History of an Irish County*, edited by William Nolan and Kevin Whelan, pp. 273–288. Geography Publications, Dublin.

Curran, John Oliver

1847 Observations on Scurvy as It Has Lately Appeared throughout Ireland, and in Several Parts of Great Britain. *Dublin Quarterly Journal of Medical Science* 4(1):83–134.

Curtin, Philip D.

1990 *The Rise and Fall of the Plantation Complex: Essays in Atlantic History.* Cambridge University Press, Cambridge.

Cusack, James William, and William Stokes

1848 On the Mortality of Medical Practitioners in Ireland: Second Article. *Dublin Journal of Medical Science* 5:111–128.

Cush, John J., Arthur Kavanaugh, and C. Michael Stein
2005 *Rheumatology: Diagnosis and Therapeutics*. Lippincott Williams and Wilkins, Philadelphia.
"D."
1838 On the Agriculture of the County of Kilkenny. *The Quarterly Journal of Agriculture* 9:475–495.
Daly, Mary E.
1986 *The Famine in Ireland*. Historical Association of Ireland, Dublin.
1997 Review article: Historians and the Famine: A Beleaguered Species? *Irish Historical Studies* 30(120):591–601.
Daryl, Philippe
1888 *Ireland's Disease: Notes and Impressions*. George Routledge and Sons, London.
Davis, Graham
1997 The Historiography of the Irish Famine. In *The Meaning of the Famine*, edited by Patrick O'Sullivan, pp. 15–39. Vol. 6 of *The Irish World Wide: History, Heritage, Identity*. Leicester University Press, London.
Davis, Maradee A., Walter H. Ettinger, John M. Neuhaus, Sangsook A. Cho, and Walter W. Hauck
1989 The Association of Knee Injury and Obesity with Unilateral and Bilateral Osteoarthritis of the Knee. *American Journal of Epidemiology* 130(2):278–288.
de Beaumont, Gustave
2006 [1839] *Ireland: Social, Political, and Religious*. Translated by W. C. Taylor, The Belknap Press of Harvard University Press, London.
de Pablo, Paola, Thomas Dietrich, and Timothy E. McAlindon
2008 Association of Periodontal Disease and Tooth Loss with Rheumatoid Arthritis in the US Population. *Journal of Rheumatology* 35(1):70–76.
de Tocqueville, Alexis
1997 [1835] *Alexis de Tocqueville's Memoir on Pauperism*. Translated by Seymour Drescher. Rediscovered Riches 2. Civitas, London.
Dias, George, and Nancy Tayles
1997 "Abscess Cavity"—A Misnomer. *International Journal of Osteoarchaeology* 7(5):548–554.
Dickson, David
2012 1740–41 Famine. In *Atlas of the Great Irish Famine 1845–52*, edited by John Crowley, William J. Smyth, and Mike Murphy, pp. 23–27. Cork University Press, Cork.
Dieppe, Paul, Louise Loe, Lee Shepstone, and Iain Watt
2006 What "Skeletal Paleopathology" Can Teach Us about Arthritis: The Contributions of the Late Dr. Juliet Rogers. *Reumatismo* 58(2):79–84.
Dirvin, Joseph I.
1969 Miraculous Medal. In *New Catholic Encyclopedia*, Vol. 9, 894–895. McGraw-Hill Book Company, New York.
Doherty, Michael, and Bryan Preston
1989 Primary Osteoarthritis in the Elbow. *Annals of the Rheumatic Diseases* 48(9):743–747.

Domellöf, Magnus, Bo Lönnerdal, Kathryn G. Dewey, Roberta J. Cohen, L. Landa Rivera, and Olle Hernell
2002 Sex Differences in Iron Status during Infancy. *Pediatrics* 110(3):545–552.
Donnelly, James S.
2001 *The Great Irish Potato Famine*. Sutton Publishing, Stroud.
Doyle, Niamh
2010 Report on the Clay Pipe from McDonagh Junction Famine Burial Ground. Appendix in Brenda O'Meara, McDonagh Junction, Hebron Road, Final report on the Findings from the Excavation of a Famine Burial Ground. Unpublished report, Margaret Gowen and Co. Ltd., Dublin.
Driscoll, Stephen T.
2002 *Excavations at Glasgow Cathedral, 1988–1997*. The Society for Medieval Archaeology Monograph 18. Maney Publishing, Leeds.
Driver, Felix
1993 *Power and Pauperism: The Workhouse System, 1834–1884*. Cambridge Studies in Historical Geography. Cambridge University Press, Cambridge.
Dunn, Joseph (director)
1992 *When Ireland Starved*. DVD. Presented by Peter Kelly. Radharc Films, Dublin.
Duray, Stephen M.
1996 Dental Indicators of Stress and Reduced Age at Death in Prehistoric Native Americans. *American Journal of Physical Anthropology* 99(2):275–286.
Eberle, John
1831 *A Treatise on the Practice of Medicine*. Vol. 2. John Grigg, Philadelphia.
Egan, Patrick McEgan
1884 *The Illustrated Guide to the City and County of Kilkenny*. P. M. Egan's Printing and Publishing Works,
Fahlander, Fredrik
2001 *Archaeology as Science Fiction: A Microarchaeology of the Unknown*. University of Göteborg, Department of Archaeology, Göteborg.
2003 *The Materiality of Serial Practice: A Microarchaeology of Burial*. Gotarc Series B, no. 23. University of Göteborg, Department of Archaeology, Göteborg.
Farrar, W. Edmund
1992 The Gastrointestinal Tract. In *Infectious Diseases: Text and Color Atlas*, edited by W. Edmund Farrar, James W. Wood, John A. Innes, and Hugh Tubbs, pp. 41–50. Gower Medical Publishing, London.
Favret, Amy C.
2006 Archaeological Investigations of Unmarked Graves at Eastern State Hospital Lexington, Fayette County, Kentucky. Unpublished report, Kentucky Archaeological Survey, Lexington.
Featherstone, John D. B.
2000 The Science and Practice of Caries Prevention. *The Journal of the American Dental Association* 131(7):887–899.

Feldman, Victor B., and Frank Astri
2001 An Atypical Clay Shoveler's Fracture: A Case Report. *Journal of the Canadian Chiropractic Association* 45(4):213–220.

Fewer, Thomas G.
1997 The Archaeology of the Great Famine: Time for a Beginning? *Group for the Study of Irish Historic Settlement Newsletter* 8:8–13.

Fibiger, Linda
2002 Report on Human Skeletal Remains from Creagh Junction, Ballinasloe, County Galway. Unpublished report for Moore Group Ltd., Galway.
2003 Report on the Human Remains from Our Lady's Hospital, Manorhamilton, Co. Leitrim (Excavation No. 01E0720 Ext.). Unpublished report for Moore Group Ltd., Galway.
2010 Report on the Human Skeletal Remains from the Hospital of the Assumption, Thurles, Co. Tipperary. Appendix in Bruce Sutton, Archaeological Excavation Report, Hospital of the Assumption, Thurles, Co. Tipperary. Eachtra Journal 5. Eachtra Archaeological Projects, Innishannon.

Fibiger, Linda, and Christopher J. Knüsel
2005 Prevalence Rates of Spondylolysis in British Skeletal Populations. *International Journal of Osteoarchaeology* 15(3):164–174.

Fisher, Robert C.
2004 "The Grandmother's Story": Oral Tradition, Family Memory, and a Mysterious Manuscript. *Archivaria* 57:107–130.

Floud, Roderick, Kenneth Wachter, and Annabel Gregory
1990 *Height, Health and History: Nutritional Status in the United Kingdom, 1750–1980.* Cambridge University Press, Cambridge.

Freund, Peter E. S.
1988 Bringing Society into the Body: Understanding Socialized Human Nature. *Theory and Society* 17(6):839–864.

Froggatt, Peter
1999 Medicine in Ulster in Relation to the Great Famine and "the Troubles." *British Medical Journal* 319:1636–1639.

Geber, Jonny
2009 Ormond Quay: Human Bone Report. Unpublished report, Margaret Gowen and Co. Ltd., Dublin.
2010 Report on the Re-Interment of Archaeological Human Remains from Kilkenny Union Workhouse (MacDonagh Junction: 05E0435) into a Purpose Built Crypt at the Famine Memorial Garden at MacDonagh Junction, Kilkenny. Unpublished report, Margaret Gowen and Co. Ltd., Dublin.
2011 Osteoarchaeological and Archaeological Insights into the Deaths and Intramural Mass Burials at the Kilkenny Union Workhouse between 1847–51 during the Great Famine. *Old Kilkenny Review* 63:64–75.
2012 Burying the Famine Dead: Kilkenny Union Workhouse. In *Atlas of the Great Irish Famine 1845–52*, edited by John Crowley, William J. Smyth, and Mike Murphy, pp. 341–348. Cork University Press, Cork.

2013 Painful Ailments, Trauma and Violent Deaths at Owenbristy, Co. Galway: Physical Pain Interpreted from Human Skeletal Remains. In *Futures and Pasts: Proceedings of a Public Seminar on Archaeological Discoveries on National Road Schemes, August 2012*, edited by Bernice Kelly, Niall Roycroft and Michael Stanley, pp. 51–61. National Roads Authority, Dublin.

2014 Skeletal Manifestations of Stress in Child Victims of the Great Irish Famine (1845–1852): Prevalence of Enamel Hypoplasia, Harris Lines, and Growth Retardation. *American Journal of Physical Anthropology* 155(1):149–161.

Geber, Jonny, and Eileen Murphy

2012 Scurvy in the Great Irish Famine: Evidence of Vitamin C Deficiency from a Mid-19th Century Skeletal Population. *American Journal of Physical Anthropology* 148(4):512–524.

Geissler, Catherine A., and John F. Bates

1984 The Nutritional Effects of Tooth Loss. *The American Journal of Clinical Nutrition* 39(3):478–489.

Giuffra, Valentina, Sara Giusiani, Antonio Fornaciari, Natale Villari, Angelica Vitiello, and Gino Fornaciari

2010 Diffuse Idiopathic Skeletal Hyperostosis in the Medici, Grand Dukes of Florence (XVI Century). *European Spine Journal* 19(S2):103–107.

Gjestland, Trygve

1955 The Oslo Study of Untreated Syphilis: An Epidemiological Investigation of the Natural Course of the Syphilitic Infection Based upon a Re-Study of the Boeck-Bruusgaard Material. *Acta Dermato-Venereologica* 35(S34):1–368.

Glorieux, Francis H., Gerard Karsenty, and Rajesh V. Thakker

1998 Metabolic Bone Disease in Children. In *Metabolic Bone Disease and Clinically Related Disorders*, edited by Louis V. Avioli and Stephen K. Krane, pp. 759–783. Academic Press, London.

Goldring, Steven R., and Richard P. Polisson

1998 Bone Disease in Rheumatological Disorders. In *Metabolic Bone Disease and Clinically Related Disorders*, edited by Louis V. Avioli and Stephen K. Krane, pp. 621–635. Academic Press, London.

Goodman, Neville M.

1944 The Supply of Bodies for Dissection: A Historical Review. *British Medical Journal* 2(4381):807–811.

Gray, Peter

1993 Punch and the Great Famine. *History Ireland* 1(2):26–33.

1995 Ideology and the Famine. In *The Great Irish Famine*, edited by Cathal Póirtéir, pp. 86–103. Radio Telefís Éireann/Mercier Press, Dublin.

1999 *Famine, Land and Politics: British Government and Irish Society 1843–50*. Irish Academic Press, Dublin.

2009 *The Making of the Irish Poor Law, 1815–43*. Manchester University Press, Manchester.

2012 British Relief Measures. In *Atlas of the Great Irish Famine, 1845–52*, edited by John

Crowley, William J. Smyth, and Mike Murphy, pp. 75–84. Cork University Press, Cork.

Green, Edward Rodney Richey

1956 Agriculture. In *The Great Famine: Studies in Irish History, 1845–52*, edited by R. Dudley Edwards and Gerald R. Williams, pp. 89–128. The Lilliput Press, Dublin.

Grenby, Trevor H.

1997 Summary of the Dental Effects of Starch. *International Journal of Food Sciences and Nutrition* 48(6):411–416.

Griffiths, Anthony Royston Grant

1970 The Irish Board of Works in the Famine Years. *The Historical Journal* 13(4):634–652.

Grotta-Kurska, Daniel

1974 Introduction. In *Gray's Anatomy (1901 ed.)*, edited by T. Pickering Pick and R. Howden, pp. 1–2. Running Press Book Publishers, Philadelphia.

Hackett, Cecil John

1975 An Introduction to Diagnostic Criteria of Syphilis, Treponarid and Yaws (Treponematosis) in Dry Bones, and Some Implications. *Virchows Archive A: Pathological Anatomy and Histology* 368(3):229–241.

Haines, Robin

2004 *Charles Trevelyan and the Great Irish Famine*. Four Courts Press, Dublin.

Hall, Reginald Dalton McKellar

1940 Clay-Shoveler's Fracture. *The Journal of Bone and Joint Surgery* 22(1):63–75.

Halpin, Thomas B.

1989 A Brief History of the Brewing Industry in Kilkenny. *Old Kilkenny Review* 4(1):583–591.

Hardy, Anne

1988 Urban Famine or Urban Crisis? Typhus in the Victorian City. *Medical History* 32(4):401–425.

Henderson, Michael, Adrian Miles, Don Walker, Brian Connell, and Robin Wroe-Brown

2013 *"He Being Dead Yet Speaketh": Excavations at Three Post-Medieval Burial Grounds in Tower Hamlets, East London, 2004–10*. MOLA Monograph 64. Museum of London, London.

Hershkovitz, Israel, Charles M. Greenwald, Bruce Latimer, Lyman M. Jellema, Susanne Wish-Baratz, Vered Eshed, Olivier Dutour, and Bruce M. Rothschild

2002 Serpens Endocrania Symmetrica (SEM): A New Term and a Possible Clue for Identifying Intrathoracic Disease in Skeletal Populations. *American Journal of Physical Anthropology* 118(3):201–216.

Heuzé, Yann, and José Braga

2008 Application of Non-Adult Bayesian Dental Age Assessment Methods to Skeletal Remains: The Spitalfields Collection. *Journal of Archaeological Science* 35(2):368–375.

Heyck, Thomas William

2008 *The Peoples of the British Isles: A New History*. Vol. 2, *From 1688 to 1870*. 3rd ed. Lyceum Books, Chicago.

Higgins, Rosanne L., Michael R. Haines, Lorena Walsh, and Joyce E. Sirianni

2002 The Poor in the Mid-Nineteenth-Century Northeastern United States: Evidence from the Monroe County Almshouse, Rochester, New York. In *The Backbone of History: Health and Nutrition in the Western Hemisphere*, edited by Richard H. Steckel and Jerome C. Rose, pp. 162–184. Cambridge University Press, Cambridge.

Hillson, Simon

1996 *Dental Anthropology*. Cambridge University Press, Cambridge.

2001 Recording Dental Caries in Archaeological Human Remains. *International Journal of Osteoarchaeology* 11(4):249–289.

2005 *Teeth*. 2nd ed. Cambridge Manuals in Archaeology. Cambridge University Press, Cambridge.

Hillson, Simon, Caroline Gribson, and Sandra Bond

1998 Dental Defects of Congenital Syphilis. *American Journal of Physical Anthropology* 107(1):25–40.

Hinnebussch, William A.

1969 Rosary. In *New Catholic Encyclopedia*, Vol. 12, 667–670. McGraw-Hill Book Company, New York.

Hirschmann, Jan V., and Gregory J. Raugi

1999 Adult Scurvy. *Journal of the American Academy of Dermatology* 41(6):895–906.

His Majesty's Commissioners for Enquiring into the Condition of the Poorer Classes in Ireland

1835 *Selection of Parochial Examinations Relative to the Destitute Classes in Ireland*. Milliken and Son, Dublin.

Hodges, Robert E., Eugene M. Baker, James Hood, Howerde E. Sauberlich, and Steven C. March

1969 Experimental Scurvy in Man. *The American Journal of Clinical Nutrition* 22(5):535–548.

Holick, Michael F., and John S. Adams

1998 Vitamin D Metabolism and Biological Function. In *Metabolic Bone Disease and Clinically Related Disorders*, edited by Louis V. Avioli and Stephen K. Krane, pp. 124–164. Academic Press, London.

Horning, Audrey

2007 Materiality and Mutable Landscapes: Rethinking Seasonality and Marginality in Rural Ireland. *International Journal of Historical Archaeology* 11(4):358–378.

Hough, Aubrey J., Jr.

2007 Pathology of Osteoarthritis. In *Osteoarthritis: Diagnosis and Medical/Surgical Management*, edited by Roland W. Moskowitz, Roy D. Altman, Marc C. Hochberg, Joseph A. Buckwalter, and Victor M. Goldberg, pp. 51–72. 4th ed. Lippincott Williams and Wilkins, Philadelphia.

Houses of the Oireachtas

1919 Democratic Programme. *Dáil Éireann Debate* F(1): 21 January.

Inglis, Henry D.

1835 *Ireland in 1834: A Journey throughout Ireland, during the Spring, Summer, and Autumn of 1834*. Whittaker and Co., London.

Ingvarsson-Sundström, Anne

2008 *Children Lost and Found: A Bioarchaeological Study of Middle Helladic Children in*

Asine with a Comparison to Lerna. Asine III Supplementary Studies on the Swedish Excavations 1922–1930. Svenska Institutet i Athen, Stockholm.

Insel, Paul, Don Ross, Kimberley McMahon, and Melissa Bernstein
2011 *Nutrition.* 4th ed. Iones and Bartlett Publishers, London.

Introna, Francesco, and Carlo P. Campobasso
2006 Biological vs. Legal Age of Living Individuals. In *Forensic Anthropology and Medicine: Complementary Sciences from Recovery to Cause of Death,* edited by Aurore Schmitt, Eugénia Cunha, and João Pinheiro, pp. 57–82. Humana Press, Totowa, New Jersey.

Inwood, Kris, and Evan Roberts
2010 Longitudinal Studies of Human Growth and Health: A Review of Recent Historical Research. *Journal of Economic Surveys* 24(5):801–840.

Irish Poor Law Commissioners
1849 *Papers Relating to the Aid Afforded to the Distressed Unions in the West of Ireland.* Her Majesty's Stationary Office, London.

İşcan, Mehmet Yaşar, Susan R. Loth, and Ronald K. Wright
1984 Metamorphosis at the Sternal Rib End: A New Method to Estimate Age at Death in White Males. *American Journal of Physical Anthropology* 65(2):147–156.
1985 Age Estimation from the Rib by Phase Analysis: White Females. *Journal of Forensic Sciences* 30(3):853–863.

Issa, Sakeba N., and Leena Sharma
2005 Osteoarthritis. In *Menopause, Postmenopause and Aging,* edited by Louis Keith, pp. 68–77. Royal Society of Medicine Press Ltd., London.

Jackson, Robert Wyse
1974 *The Story of Kilkenny.* Mercier Press, Dublin.

Jalland, Pat
1996 *Death in the Victorian Family.* Oxford University Press, Oxford.

Jankauskas, Rimantas
2003 The Incidence of Diffuse Idiopathic Skeletal Hyperostosis and Social Status Correlations in Lithuanian Skeletal Materials. *International Journal of Osteoarchaeology* 13(5):289–293.

Jelliffe, Derrick B., and E. F. Patrice Jelliffe
1971 The Effects of Starvation on the Function of the Family and of Society. In *Famine: A Symposium Dealing with Nutrition and Relief Operations in Times of Disasters,* edited by Gunnar Blix, Yngve Hofvander, and Bo Conradsson Vahlquist, pp. 54–63. Swedish Nutrition Foundation, Uppsala.

Joffe, Norman
1961 Some Radiological Aspects of Scurvy in the Adult. *British Journal of Radiology* 34(403):429–437.

Jones, D. Gareth
1994 Use of Bequeathed and Unclaimed Bodies in the Dissecting Room. *Clinical Anatomy* 7(2):102–107.

Jordan, Thomas E.
2003 Two Thomases: Dublin Castle and the Quality of Life in Victorian Ireland. *Social Indicators Research* 64(2):257–291.

Jurmain, Robert
1999 *Stories from the Skeleton: Behavioral Reconstruction in Human Osteology.* Gordon and Breach Publishers, Amsterdam.

Kalm, Leah M., and Richard D. Semba
2005 They Starved So that Others be Better Fed: Remembering Ancel Keys and the Minnesota Experiment. *The Journal of Nutrition* 135(6):1347–1352.

Kaprio, Jaakko, Urho M. Kujala, Leena Peltonen, and Markku Koskenvuo
1996 Genetic Liability to Osteoarthritis May Be Greater in Women Than Men. *British Medical Journal* 313(7051):232.

Keenan, Desmond
2000 *Pre-Famine Ireland: Social Structure.* Xlibris Corporation, Philadelphia.

Kelley, Marc A., and Marc S. Micozzi
1984 Rib Lesions in Chronic Pulmonary Tuberculosis. *American Journal of Physical Anthropology* 65(4):381–386.

Keneally, Thomas
2012 The Great Famine and Australia. In *Atlas of the Great Irish Famine, 1845–52*, edited by John Crowley, William J. Smyth, and Mike Murphy, pp. 550–560. Cork University Press, Cork.

Kennedy, Arthur Colville, David Anthony Smith, G. Grey, M. K. Jasani, and William Watson Buchanan
1975 Osteoporosis in patients with rheumatoid arthritis. *Annals of the Rheumatic Diseases* 34(6):542–543.

Kennedy, Líam, Paul S. Ell, E. Margaret Crawford, and Leslie A. Clarkson
1999 *Mapping the Great Irish Famine.* Four Courts Press, Dublin.

Kerr, Neill Watson
1994 Prevalence and Natural History of Periodontal Disease in a London, Spitalfields, Population (1645–1852 AD). *Archives of Human Biology* 39(7):581–588.

Keys, Ancel, Josef Brožek, Austin Henschel, Olaf Mickelsen, and Henry Longstreet Taylor
1950 *The Biology of Human Starvation.* University of Minnesota Press, Minneapolis.

Kilkenny Journal
1842a Kilkenny Board of Guardians. 22 March.
1842b Kilkenny Board of Guardians. 23 April.
1842c Kilkenny Board of Guardians. 11 June.
1842d Kilkenny Board of Guardians. 25 June.
1842e Kilkenny Union Workhouse—Dissection—Indecent Exposure of a Dead Body. 6 August.
1844a St. Patrick's Church-Yard. 27 January.
1844b Kilkenny Board of Guardians 22 February.
1844c Kilkenny Board of Guardians. 20 March.
1844d Kilkenny Board of Guardians. 30 March.
1844e Kilkenny Board of Guardians. 22 May.
1844f Kilkenny Board of Guardians. 22 June.
1844g Kilkenny Board of Guardians. 3 August.

1845a Kilkenny Board of Guardians. 15 January.
1845b Kilkenny Board of Guardians. 15 February.
1845c Kilkenny Board of Guardians. 28 June.
1845d Kilkenny Board of Guardians. 22 October.
1846a Kilkenny Board of Guardians. 6 June.
1846b Kilkenny Board of Guardians. 28 March.
1847a Kilkenny Board of Guardians. 5 January.
1847b Kilkenny Board of Guardians. 20 March.
1847c Kilkenny Board of Guardians. 27 March.
1847d Kilkenny Board of Guardians. 17 April.
1847e Kilkenny Board of Guardians. 8 May.
1847f Kilkenny Board of Guardians. 24 July.
1847g Kilkenny Board of Guardians. 14 August.
1847h Kilkenny Board of Guardians. 30 October.
1847i Kilkenny Board of Guardians. 25 December.
1848a Board of Guardians. 1 January.
1848b Board of Guardians. 29 January.
1848c Board of Guardians. 11 March.
1848d Board of Guardians. 17 June.
1849a Riot in the Workhouse. 24 January.
1849b Board of Guardians. 10 February.
1849c Board of Guardians. 17 March.
1849d Board of Guardians. 13 June.
1849e Kilkenny Board of Guardians. 13 June.
1849f Intramural Burial—Kilkenny. 25 August.
1849g To the Editor of Kilkenny Journal. 25 August.
1850a Kilkenny Union: Pauper Misconduct. 16 February.
1850b Letter from Thomas Ryan. 16 February.
1850c Kilkenny Union. 23 February.
1850d Kilkenny Union. 2 March.
1850e Kilkenny Union: Nightly Lodgers. 13 March.
1850f Kilkenny Union. 6 July.
1850g Kilkenny Union. 10 July.
1850h Kilkenny Union. 17 August.
1853 Kilkenny Board of Guardians. 22 October.
Kilkenny Moderator
1851 Kilkenny Union. 8 March.
Killeen, John
1995 *The Famine Decade: Contemporary Accounts 1841–1851.* Blackstaff Press, Belfast.
Kinealy, Christine
1995 The Role of the Poor Law during the Famine. In *The Great Irish Famine*, edited by Cathal Póirtéir, pp. 104–122. Radio Telefís Éireann/Mercier Press, Dublin.
2005 Was Ireland a Colony? The Evidence of the Great Famine. In *Was Ireland a Colony? Economics, Politics and Culture in Nineteenth-Century Ireland*, edited by Terrence McDonough, pp. 48–65. Irish Academic Press, Dublin.

2006 *This Great Calamity: The Irish Famine 1845–52.* 2nd ed. Gill and Macmillan, Dublin.
2013 *Charity and the Great Hunger in Ireland.* Bloomsbury, London.
Kiss, Csaba, M. Szilágyi, A. Paksy, and Gyula Poór
2002 Risk Factors for Diffuse Idiopathic Skeletal Hyperostosis: A Case-Control Study. *Rheumatology* 41(1):27–30.
Kissane, Noel
1995 *The Irish Famine: A Documentary History.* National Library of Ireland, Dublin.
Kjellström, Anna
2010 Tracing Pain: Identifying Suffering in Skeletal Remains. In *Making Sense of Things: Archaeologies of Sensory Perception,* edited by Fredrik Fahlander and Anna Kjellström, pp. 51–67. Stockholm Studies in Archaeology. Stockholm University, Stockholm.
Knüsel, Christopher J.
2000 Bone Adaptation and Its Relationship to Physical Activity in the Past. In *Human Osteology in Archaeology and Forensic Science,* edited by Margaret Cox and Simon Mays, pp. 381–401. Cambridge University Press, Cambridge.
Knüsel, Christopher J., Sonia Göggel, and David Lucy
1997 Comparative Degenerative Joint Disease of the Vertebral Column in the Medieval Monastic Cemetery of the Gilbertine Priory of St. Andrew, Fishergate, York, England. *American Journal of Physical Anthropology* 103(4):481–495.
Kobelt, Gisela
2009 The Social and Economic Impact of Rheumatoid Arthritis. In *Rheumatoid Arthritis,* edited by Marc C. Hochberg, Alan J. Silman, Josef S. Smolen, Michael E. Weinblatt, and Michael H. Weisman, pp. 83–89. Mosby Elsevier, Philadelphia.
Komlos, John
1998 Shrinking in a Growing Economy? The Mystery of Physical Stature during the Industrial Revolution. *The Journal of Economic History* 58(3):779–802.
Koval, Kenneth J., and Joseph D. Zuckerman
2002 *Handbook of Fractures.* 2nd ed. Lippincott Williams and Wilkins, Philadelphia.
Kraus, Barbara
2006 *Befund Kind: Überlegungen zu archäologischen und anthropologischen Untersuchungen von Kinderbestattungen.* Archäologische Berichte 19. Deutsche Gesellschaft für Ur- und Frühgeschichte e.V., Bonn.
LaFond, Rebecca E., and Sheila A. Lukehart
2006 Biological Basis for Syphilis. *Clinical Microbiology Reviews* 19(1):29–49.
Lalor, Joseph
1848 Observations on the Late Epidemic Fever. *Dublin Quarterly Journal of Medical Science* 5(9):12–30.
Lantzsch, Jana, and Klaus Schuster
2009 Socioeconomic Status and Physical Stature in 19th-Century Bavaria. *Economics and Human Biology* 7(1):46–54.
Larkin, Emmet, and Herman Freudenberger
1998 *A Redemptorist Missionary in Ireland 1851–1854: Memoirs by Joseph Prost, C. Ss. R.* Cork University Press, Cork.

Larsen, Clark Spencer (editor)

1990 *The Archaeology of Mission Santa Catalina de Guale: 2. Biocultural Interpretations of a Population in Transition*. American Museum of Natural History, New York.

1997 *Bioarchaeology: Interpreting Behavior from the Human Skeleton*. Cambridge University Press, Cambridge.

2000 *Skeletons in Our Closet: Revealing Our Past through Bioarchaeology*. Princeton University Press, Princeton, New Jersey.

Latour, Bruno

2005 *Reassembling the Social: An Introduction to Actor-Network-Theory*. Oxford University Press, Oxford.

Law, Edward J.

1996 Cholera in Kilkenny, 1832–33. *Old Kilkenny Review* 48:117–122.

Laxton, Edward

1996 *The Famine Ships: The Irish Exodus to America 1846–51*. Bloomsbury, London.

Lengel, Edward G.

2002 *The Irish through British Eyes: Perceptions of Ireland in the Famine Era*. Praeger, London.

Lester, Charles W., and Harry L. Shapiro

1968 Vertebral Arch Defects in the Lumbar Vertebrae of Pre-Historic American Eskimos: A Study of Skeletons in the American Museum of Natural History, Chiefly from Point Hope, Alaska. *American Journal of Physical Anthropology* 28(1):43–47.

Lester, David

2005 *Suicide and the Holocaust*. Nova Science Publishers, Inc., New York.

Lewis, Mary E.

2004 Endocranial Lesions in Non-Adult Skeletons: Understanding Their Aetiology. *International Journal of Osteoarchaeology* 14(2):82–97.

Lewis, Mary E., and Charlotte Roberts

1997 Growing Pains: The Interpretation of Stress Indicators. *International Journal of Osteoarchaeology* 7(6):581–586.

Lewis, Samuel

1837 *A Topographical Dictionary of Ireland*. S. Lewis and Co., London.

Lind, James

1753 *A Treatise of the Scurvy*. Sands, Murray and Cochran, Edinburgh.

Lingström, Peter, Jörgen Holm, Dowen Birkhed, and Inger Björck

1989 Effects on Variously Processed Starch on pH of Human Dental Plaque. *Scandinavian Journal of Dental Research* 97(5):392–400.

Lingström, Peter, Johannes van Houte, and S. Kashket

2000 Food Starches and Dental Caries. *Critical Reviews in Oral Biology and Medicine* 11(3):366–380.

Little, Barbara J.

2007 *Historical Archaeology: Why the Past Matters*. Left Coast Press, Walnut Creek.

Liversidge, Helen M., Berthold Herdeg, and Friedrich W. Rösing

1998 Dental Age Estimation of Non-Adults. A Review of Methods and Principles. In

Dental Anthropology. Fundamentals, Limits and Prospects, edited by Kurt W. Alt, Friedrich W. Rösing, and Maria Teschler-Nicola, pp. 419–442. Springer, Vienna.

Liversidge, Helen M., and Theya I. Molleson

1995 Spitalfields Children: The Influence of Rickets on Dental Formation in Early Childhood. *Bone* 16(6):693.

1999 Deciduous Tooth Size and Morphogenetic Fields in Children from Christ Church, Spitalfields. *Archives of Human Biology* 44(1):7–13.

Locker-Lampson, Godrey

1907 *A Consideration of the State of Ireland in the Nineteenth Century*. Archibald Constable and Co. Ltd., London.

Lorentz, Kirsi

2008 From Bodies to Bones and Back: Theory and Human Bioarchaeology. In *Between Biology and Culture*, edited by Holger Schutkowski, pp. 273–303. Cambridge University Press, Cambridge.

Loth, Susan R.

1995 Age Assessment of the Spitalfields Cemetery Population by Rib Phase Analysis. *American Journal of Human Biology* 7(4):465–471.

Lough, Thomas

1896 *England's Wealth: Ireland's Poverty*. T. Fisher Unwin, London.

Lovejoy, C. Owen, Richard S. Meindl, Thomas R. Pryzbeck, and Robert P. Mensforth

1985 Chronological Metamorphosis of the Auricular Surface of the Ilium: A New Method for the Determination of Adult Skeletal Age at Death. *American Journal of Physical Anthropology* 68(1):15–28.

Lovell, Nancy C.

1997 Trauma Analysis in Paleopathology. *Yearbook of Physical Anthropology* 104(S25):139–170.

Lowe, J., E. Libson, I. Ziv, Meir Nyska, Yizhar Floman, R. A. Bloom, and G. C. Robin

1987 Spondylolysis in the Upper Lumbar Spine: A Study of 32 Patients. *The Journal of Bone and Joint Surgery* 69(4):582–586.

Lynch, Linda G.

2001 Osteo-Archaeological Report on Human Skeletal Remains Excavated at St. John the Baptist, John Street, Sligo Town. Licence No. 01E0207. Unpublished report for Aegis Archaeology Ltd., Limerick.

2002 Osteo-Archaeological Report on Human Skeletal Remains Excavated at Our Lady's Hospital, Manorhamilton, County Letrim. Licence No. 01E0720. Unpublished report for Aegis Archaeology Ltd., Limerick.

2004 Osteo-Archaeological Report on Human Skeletal Remains Excavated at Shandon Court Hotel, Cork City. Licence No. 01E0529. Unpublished report for Aegis Archaeology Ltd., Limerick.

Lysaght, Patricia

1996 Perspectives on Women during the Great Irish Famine from the Oral Tradition. *Béaloideas* 64:63–130.

Maat, George J. R.

1990 Growth Changes in Bones: A Means of Assessing Health Status and the Relative

Position of Secular Growth Shift in Stature. In *Populations of the Nordic Countries: Human Population Biology from the Present to the Mesolithic*, edited by Elisabeth Iregren and Rune Liljekvist, pp. 88–93. Institute of Archaeology Report Series. University of Lund, Lund.

MacArthur, William P.

1951 A Medical Survey of the Irish Famine of 1846: A Robert Campbell Memorial Oration. *Ulster Medical Journal* 20(1):1–15.

1956 Medical History of the Famine. In *The Great Famine: Studies in Irish History, 1845–52*, edited by R. Dudley Edwards and T. Desmond Williams, pp. 261–315. Lilliput Press, Dublin.

MacLennan, William J.

2003 Stature in Scotland over the Centuries. *The Journal of the Royal College of Physicians of Edinburgh* 33(1):46–53.

Mahfoud, Philomena

2009 Kilkenny in the 1840s: The Guardians and the Poor Workhouse. Unpublished BA dissertation, Open Education Unit, Dublin City University, Dublin.

Mahoney, James.

1847 Sketches in the West of Ireland. *The Illustrated London News*, 13 February.

Malone, David G., John R. Caruso, and Nevan G. Baldwin

1999 Degenerative and Noninfectious Inflammatory Disease. In *The Thoracic Spine*, edited by Edward C. Benzel and Charles Blair Stillerman, pp. 597–606. Quality Medical Publishing, St. Louis, Mo.

Manek, Nisha J., Deborah Hart, Timothy D. Spector, and Alexander J. MacGregor

2003 The Association of Body Mass Index and Osteoarthritis of the Knee Joint. *Arthritis and Rheumatism* 48(4):1024–1029.

Margerison, Beverley J., and Christopher J. Knüsel

2002 Paleodemographic Comparison of a Catastrophic and an Attritional Death Assemblage. *American Journal of Physical Anthropology* 119(2):134–142.

May, Trevor

2003 *The Victorian Workhouse*. Shire Publications Ltd., Princes Risborough.

Mays, Simon

2010 *The Archaeology of Human Bones*. 2nd ed. Routledge, Abingdon.

Mays, Simon, Edward Fysh, and G. Michael Taylor

2002 Investigation of the Link between Visceral Surface Rib Lesions and Tuberculosis in a Medieval Skeletal Series from England Using Ancient DNA. *American Journal of Physical Anthropology* 119(1):27–36.

Mays, Simon, G. Michael Taylor, Anthony J. Legge, Douglas B. Young, and Gordon Turner-Walker

2001 Paleopathological and Biomolecular Study of Tuberculosis in a Medieval Skeletal Collection from England. *American Journal of Physical Anthropology* 114(4):298–311.

McCorkle, William W., Jr.

2010 *Ritualizing the Disposal of the Deceased: From Corpse to Concept*. Peter Lang Publishing, New York.

McDowell, Robert B.

1956 Ireland on the Eve of the Famine. In *The Great Famine: Studies in Irish History, 1845–52*, edited by R. Dudley Edwards and T. Desmond Williams, pp. 3–86. Lilliput Press, Dublin.

1986 The Age of the United Irishmen: Revolution and the Union, 1794–1800. In *Eighteenth-Century Ireland, 1691–1800*, edited by T. W. Moody and W. E. Vaughan, pp. 339–373. Oxford University Press, Oxford.

McEvoy, Frank

1981 Kilkenny Races. *Old Kilkenny Review* 2(3):208–212.

McGowan, Mark G.

2012a Black '47 and Toronto, Canada. In *Atlas of the Great Irish Famine, 1845–52*, edited by John Crowley, William J. Smyth, and Mike Murphy, pp. 525–531. Cork University Press, Cork.

2012b Grosse Île, Quebec. In *Atlas of the Great Irish Famine, 1845–52*, edited by John Crowley, William J. Smyth, and Mike Murphy, pp. 532–535. Cork University Press, Cork.

McHugh, Roger J.

1956 The Famine in Irish Oral Tradition. In *The Great Famine: Studies in Irish History, 1845–52*, edited by R. Dubley Edwards and T. Desmond Williams, pp. 389–436. Lilliput Press, Dublin.

McKee, James

2006 Archaeological Excavation Report: For the Development at the Old Donard School Site, Edenderry Road, Banbridge, Co. Down. Unpublished report, Archaeological Development Services, Belfast.

McKeogh, Tadhg K.

1996 Dr. Joseph Lalor (1811–1886): "A Credit to Ireland." *Old Kilkenny Review* 48:9–19.

Meindl, Richard S., and C. Owen Lovejoy

1985 Ectocranial Suture Closure: A Revised Method for the Determination of Skeletal Age at Death Based on the Lateral-Anterior Sutures. *American Journal of Physical Anthropology* 68(1):57–66.

Merbs, Charles F.

1983 *Patterns of Activity-Induced Pathology in a Canadian Inuit Population*. Mercury Series 119. National Museums of Canada, Ottawa.

Merrett, Deborah C., and Susan Pfeiffer

2000 Maxillary Sinusitis as an Indicator of Respiratory Health in Past Populations. *American Journal of Physical Anthropology* 111(3):301–318.

Miedany, Yasser M., el, G. Wassif, and Mohammed el Baddini

2000 Diffuse Idiopathic Skeletal Hyperostosis (DISH): Is It of Vascular Aetiology? *Clinical and Experimental Rheumatology* 18(2):193–200.

Miles, Adrian, and Brian Connell

2012 *New Bunhill Fields Burial Ground, Southwark: Excavations at Globe Academy, 2008*. MOLA Archaeology Studies Series 24. Museum of London, London.

Miles, Adrian, Natasha Powers, Robin Wroe-Brown, and Don Walker

2008 *St Marylebone Church and Burial Ground in the 18th and 19th Centuries: Excava-*

tions at St Marylebone School, 1992 and 2004–6. MOLAS Monograph 46. Museum of London Archaeological Service, London.

Miles, Adrian, William White, and Danae Tankard

2008 *Burial at the Site of the Parish Church of St. Benet Sherehog Before and After the Great Fire. Excavations at 1 Poultry, City of London.* MOLAS Monograph 39. Museum of London Archaeological Service, London.

Mitchel, John

1876 *The Last Conquest of Ireland (Perhaps).* Cameron, Ferguson, Glasgow. Available at LibraryIreland.com.

Mitchell, Piers D. (editor)

2011 *Anatomical Dissection in Enlightenment Britain and Beyond: Autopsy, Pathology and Display.* Ashgate Publishing, Aldershot.

Mokyr, Joel

1983 *Why Ireland Starved: A Quantitative and Analytical History of the Irish Economy, 1800–1850.* Routledge, London.

Mokyr, Joel, and Cormac Ó Gráda

1988 Poor and Getting Poorer? Living Standards in Ireland before the Famine. *Economic History Review* 41(2):209–235.

1994 The Heights of the British and Irish c. 1800–1815: Evidence from Recruits to the East India Company's Army. In *Stature, Living Standards, and Economic Development: Essays in Anthropometric History,* edited by John Komlos, pp. 39–59. University of Chicago Press, Chicago.

1999 Famine Disease and Famine Mortality: Lessons from the Irish Experience. University College Dublin Centre for Economic Research Working Paper 12. University College Dublin, Dublin.

Møller-Christensen, Vilhelm

1958 *Bogen om Æbenholt kloster.* Dansk Videnskabs Forlag, Copenhagen.

Molleson, Theya I., Margaret Cox, Harry Arthur Waldron, and David K. Whittaker

1993 *The Spitalfields Project.* Vol. 2, *The Anthropology: The Middling Sort.* CBA Research Report 86. Council for British Archaeology, York.

Molto, J. E.

1990 Differential Diagnosis of Rib Lesions: A Case Study from Middle Woodland Southern Ontario circa 230 A.D. *American Journal of Physical Anthropology* 83(4):439–447.

Mooney, James

1888 The Funeral Customs of Ireland. *Proceedings of the American Philosophical Society* 25(128):243–296.

Moorrees, Coenraad F. A., Elizabeth A. Fanning, and Edward E. Hunt Jr.

1963 Age Variation of Formation Stages for Ten Permanent Teeth. *Journal of Dental Research* 42(6):1490–1502.

Morash, Chris, and Richard Hayes (editors)

1996 *"Fearful Realities": New Perspectives on the Famine.* Irish Academic Press, Dublin.

Morgan, Oliver

2004 Infectious Disease Risks from Dead Bodies Following Natural Disasters. *Pan American Journal of Public Health* 15(5):307–312.

Moskowitz, Roland W., Roy D. Altman, Marc C. Hochberg, Joseph A. Buckwalter, and Victor M. Goldberg
2007 *Osteoarthritis: Diagnosis and Medical/Surgical Management*. Lippincott Williams and Wilkins, Philadelphia.

Muir, Edward
1991 Introduction: Observing Trifles. In *Microhistory and the Lost Peoples of Europe*, edited by Edward Muir and Guido Ruggiero, pp. vii–xxviii. Johns Hopkins University Press, London.

Mulhern, Philip F.
1969 Medals, Religious. In *New Catholic Encyclopedia*, Vol. 9, pp. 547–549. McGraw-Hill Book Company, New York.

Murphy, Claire
2011 What Can an Osteological Investigation Reveal about Medical Education in Eighteenth-Century Dublin? *Archaeology Ireland* 25(3):30–34.

Murphy, Eileen, Yuri K. Chistov, Richard Hopkins, Paul Rutland, and G. Michael Taylor
2009 Tuberculosis among Iron Age Individuals from Tyva, South Siberia: Palaeopathological and Biomolecular Findings. *Journal of Archaeological Science* 36(9):2029–2038.

Murray, Elizabeth A., and Anthony J. Perzigian
1995 A Glimpse of Early-Nineteenth-Century Cincinnati as Viewed from Potter's Field: An Exercise in Problem Solving. In *Bodies of Evidence: Reconstructing History through Skeletal Analysis*, edited by Anne L. Grauer, pp. 173–184. Wiley-Liss, New York.

Murray, Patrick Desmond Fitzgerald, and Egon Kodicek
1949a Bones, Muscles and Vitamin C: II. Partial Deficiencies of Vitamin C and Mid-Diaphyseal Thickenings of the Tibia and Fibula in Guinea Pigs. *Journal of Anatomy* 83(3):205–223.
1949b Bones, Muscles and Vitamin C: III. Repair of the Effects of Total Deprivation of Vitamin C at the Proximal Ends of the Tibia and Fibula in Guinea Pigs. *Journal of Anatomy* 83(4):285–295.

Murray, Ronald O.
1965 The Aetiology of Primary Osteoarthritis of the Hip. *British Journal of Radiology* 38(455):810–824.

Nakagawa, Satoru
2007 Accord or Discord: Returning to Oral Traditions? *The Canadian Journal of Native Studies* 27(2):451–477.

Neely, William G.
1989 *Kilkenny: An Urban History, 1391–1843*. The Institute of Irish Studies, Queen's University Belfast, Belfast.

Nic Eoin, Máirín
1990 Irish Language and Literature in County Kilkenny in the Nineteenth Century. In *Kilkenny: History and Society. Interdisciplinary Essays on the History of an Irish County*, edited by William Nolan and Kevin Whelan, pp. 465–480. Geography Publications, Dublin.

Nyberg, Jenny
2010 A Peaceful Sleep and Heavenly Celebration for the Pure and Innocent: The Sensory Experience of Death during the Long Eighteenth Century. In *Making Sense of Things: Archaeologies of Sensory Perception*, edited by Fredrik Fahlander and Anna Kjellström, pp. 15–33. Stockholm Studies in Archaeology 53. Department of Archaeology and Classical Studies, Stockholm University, Stockholm.

Ó Bolbuidhir, Liam
2006 The Military in Kilkenny 1800–1870. *Old Kilkenny Review* 58:139–151.

Ó Ciosáin, Niall
1998 Boccoughs and God's Poor: Deserving and Undeserving Poor in Irish Popular Culture. In *Ideology and Ireland in the Nineteenth Century*, edited by Tadhg Foley and Seán Ryder, pp. 93–99. Four Courts Press, Dublin.

Ó Drisceoil, Cóilín
2005 *Archaeological Assessment of Workhouse Burial Site, MacDonagh Junction Development, Kilkenny*. Unpublished report, Kilkenny Archaeology, Kilkenny.

Ó Gráda, Cormac
1991 The Heights of Clonmel Prisoners 1845–49: Some Dietary Implications. *Irish Economic and Social History* 18:24–33.

1993 *Ireland before and after the Famine. Explorations in Economic History, 1800–1925*. Manchester University Press, New York.

1999 *Black '47 and Beyond: The Great Irish Famine in History, Economy, and Memory*. Princeton University Press, Princeton, New Jersey.

2001 Famine, Trauma and Memory. *Béaloideas* 69:121–143.

2006 Ireland's Great Famine. In *Ireland's Great Famine: Interdisciplinary Perspectives*, edited by Cormac Ó Gráda, pp. 7–23. University College Dublin Press, Dublin.

2012 Mortality and the Great Famine. In *Atlas of the Great Irish Famine, 1845–52*, edited by John Crowley, William J. Smyth, and Mike Murphy, pp. 170–179. Cork University Press, Cork.

Ó Súilleabháin, Seán
1969 *Irish Wake Amusements*. Mercier Press, Cork.

Ó Tuathaigh, Gearóid
2007 *Ireland before the Famine: 1798–1848*. Gill and Macmillan, Dublin.

O'Boyle, Edward J.
2005 Classical Economics and the Great Irish Famine: A Study in Limits. *Forum for Social Economics* 35(2):21–53.

O'Connor, John
1995 *The Workhouses of Ireland: The Fate of Ireland's Poor*. Anvil Books, Dublin.

O'Donnell, Lorna
2010 Report on the Charcoal and Wood from the Cremation Deposit and Nineteenth Century Coffins. Appendix in Brenda O'Meara, McDonagh Junction, Hebron Road, Kilkenny. Final Report on the Findings from the Excavation of a Famine Burial Ground. Unpublished report, Margaret Gowen and Co. Ltd., Dublin.

O'Meara, Brenda
2010 McDonagh Junction, Hebron Road, Kilkenny. Final Report on the Findings from

the Excavation of a Famine Burial Ground. Unpublished report, Margaret Gowen and Co. Ltd., Dublin.

O'Neill, Thomas P.

1956 The Organisation and Administration of Relief, 1845–52. In *The Great Famine: Studies in Irish History, 1845–52*, edited by R. Dudley Edwards and Gerald R. Williams, pp. 209–259. Lilliput Press, Dublin.

1958 The Famine in Kilkenny. *Old Kilkenny Review* 10:1–5.

O'Rourke, John

1902 *The History of the Great Irish Famine of 1847, with Notices of Earlier Irish Famines.* 3rd ed. J. Duffy and Co., Dublin.

O'Sullivan, Patrick

1997 Introduction to Volume 6: The Meaning of the Famine. In *The Meaning of the Famine*, edited by Patrick O'Sullivan, pp. 1–14. Vol. 6 of The Irish World Wide. Leicester University Press, London.

Orser, Charles E., Jr.

1996 Can There Be an Archaeology of the Great Famine? In *"Fearful Realities": New Perspectives on the Famine*, edited by Chris Morash and Richard Hayes, pp. 77–89. Irish Academic Press, Blackrock.

1997 Archaeology and Nineteenth-Century Rural Life in County Roscommon. *Archaeology Ireland* 11(1):14–17.

2006a Discovering Our Recent Pasts: Historical Archaeology and Early Nineteenth-Century Rural Ireland. In *Unearthing Hidden Ireland: Historical Archaeology at Ballykilcline, County Roscommon*, edited by Charles E. Orser Jr., pp. 1–17. Wordwell, Bray.

2006b Seeking Hidden Ireland: History, Meaning and Material Culture. In *Unearthing Hidden Ireland: Historical Archaeology at Ballykilcline, County Roscommon*, edited by Charles E. Orser Jr., pp. 217–228. Wordwell, Bray.

Ortner, Donald J.

2003 *Identification of Pathological Conditions in Human Skeletal Remains.* 2nd ed. Academic Press, Amsterdam.

Ortner, Donald J., Erin H. Kimmerle, and Melanie Diez

1999 Evidence of Scurvy in Subadults from Archaeological Sites in Peru. *American Journal of Physical Anthropology* 108(3):321–331.

Ortner, Donald J., and Simon Mays

1998 Dry-Bone Manifestations of Rickets in Infancy and Early Childhood. *International Journal of Osteoarchaeology* 8(1):45–55.

Owen, Isambard

1889 Reports of the Collective Investigation Committee of the British Medical Association: Geographical Distribution of Rickets, Acute and Subacute Rheumatism, Chorea, Cancer and Urinary Calculus in the British Isles. *The British Medical Journal* 1(1464):113–116.

Oxenham, Marc Fredrick, and Ivor Cavill

2010 Porotic Hyperostosis and Cribra Orbitalia: The Erythropoietic Response to Iron-Deficiency Anaemia. *Anthropological Science* 118(3):199–200.

Parascandola, John
2008 *Sex, Sin, and Science: A History of Syphilis in America*. Praeger Publishers, Westport.

Parfitt, A. Michael
1998 Osteomalacia and Related Disorders. In *Metabolic Bone Disease and Clinically Related Diseases*, edited by Louis V. Avioli and Stephen K. Krane, pp. 327–386. Academic Press, London.

Park, Edwards A.
1923 The Etiology of Rickets. *Physiological Reviews* 3(1):106–163.

Parsons, Gerald
1988 Irish Disestablishment. In *Religion in Victorian Britain: Controversies*, edited by Gerald Parsons, pp. 124–146. Manchester University Press, Manchester.

Patterson, Tony
1996 Illegal Outdoor Relief in Kilkenny Workhouse. *Old Kilkenny Review* 48:23–37.
1997 Famine fever in Kilkenny. *Old Kilkenny Review* 49:74–88.
1998 Robert Cane and Young Ireland. *Old Kilkenny Review* 50:67–82.

Paz, Denis G.
1992 *Popular Anti-Catholicism in Mid-Victorian England*. Stanford University Press, Stanford, California.

Pearson, Osbjorn M., and Daniel E. Lieberman
2004 The Aging of Wolff's "Law": Ontogeny and Responses to Mechanical Loading in Cortical Bone. *Yearbook of Physical Anthropology* 47(S39):63–99.

Peltonen, Matti
2001 Clues, Margins, and Monads: The Micro-Macro Link in Historical Research. *History and Theory* 40(3):347–359.

Pitt, Michael J.
2002 Rickets and Osteomalacia. In *Diagnosis of Bone and Joint Disorders*, edited by Donald Resnick, pp. 1901–1945. W. B. Saunders, Philadelphia.

Pizzutillo, Peter
1992 Slipped Capital Femoral Epiphysis. In *The Hip*, edited by Richard A. Balderston, Richard H. Rothman, Robert E. Booth, and William J. Hozack, pp. 152–160. Lea and Febiger, Philadelphia.

Plumptre, Anne
1817 *Narrative of a Residence in Ireland during the Summer of 1814, and That of 1815*. Henry Colburn, London.

Porteus, Sarah
2006 Human Skeletal Report on the Remains from Edenderry Road, Banbridge. Co. Down, AE/05/148. Appendix in James McKee, Archaeological Excavation Report. For the Development at the Old Donard School site, Edenderry Road, Banbridge, Co. Down. Unpublished report, Archaeological Development Services, Belfast.

Powell, Malachy
1965 The Workhouses of Ireland. *University Review* 3(7):3–16.

Powell, Mary Lucas
1988 *Status and Health in Prehistory: A Case Study of the Moundville Chiefdom*. Smithsonian Institution Press, Washington.

Powers, Natasha
2011 Health and Disease: Osteological Evidence. In *St Pancras Burial Ground: Excavations for St. Pancras International, the London Terminus of High Speed 1, 2002–3*, edited by Phillip A. Emery and Kevin Wooldridge, pp. 127–153. Gifford, London.

Quétel, Claude
1990 *History of Syphilis*. Translated by Judith Braddock and Brian Pike. Polity Press, Cambridge.

Quinlan, Carmel
1996 "A Punishment from God": The Famine in the Centenary Folklore Questionnaire. *The Irish Review* 19:68–86.

Radin, Eric L., Igor L. Paul, and Robert M. Rose
1972 Role of Mechanical Factors in Pathogenesis of Primary Osteoarthritis. *The Lancet* 1(7749):519–522.

Raftery, Walter
1995 Wilkinson the Workhouse Builder, 1839–54. *Galway Roots* 3:127–139.

Rajakumar, Kumaravel
2001 Infantile Scurvy: A Historical Perspective. *Pediatrics* 108(4):1–3.

Rauh, Günter, B. Stiefenhofen, H. Dörfler, G. Lohmöller, D. Hahn, and N. Zöllner
1990 Knochenschmerzen im Erwachsenenalter als Erstsymptom einer Syphilis connata tarda. *Deutsche Medizinische Wochenschrift* 115(14):534–538.

Reader, William Joseph
1966 *Professional Men: The Rise of the Professional Classes in Nineteenth-Century England*. Weidenfeld and Nicolson, London.

Reed, William
1866 *The History of Sugar and Sugar-Yielding Plants, Together with an Epitome of Every Notable Process of Sugar Extraction, and Manufacture, from the Earliest Times to the Present*. Longman, Green, and Co., London.

Reichart, Peter A., and Hans Peter Philipsen
2000 *Oral Pathology*. George Thieme Verlag, Stuttgart.

Resnick, Donald, and Thomas G. Goergen
2002 Physical Injury: Concepts and Terminology. In *Diagnosis of Bone and Joint Disorders*, edited by Donald Resnick, pp. 2627–2782. W. B. Saunders, Philadelphia.

Resnick, Donald, Stephen R. Shaul, and Jon M. Robins
1976 Diffuse Idiopathic Skeletal Hyperostosis (DISH): Forestier's Disease with Extraspinal Manifestations. *Radiology* 115(3):513–524.

Richards, N. David
1968 Dentistry in England in the 1840s: The First Indications of a Movement towards Professionalization. *Medical History* 12(2):137–152.

Richardson, Ruth
1988 *Death, Dissection and the Destitute*. Phoenix Press, London.

Roberts, Charlotte
1999 Rib Lesions and Tuberculosis: The Current State of Play. In *Tuberculosis: Past and Present*, edited by György Pálfi, Olivier Dutour, J. Deák, and I. Hutás, pp. 311–316. Golden Book Publishers, Budapest.

2007 A Bioarchaeological Study of Maxillary Sinusitis. *American Journal of Physical Anthropology* 133(2):792–807.

Roberts, Charlotte, Anthea Boylston, Laureen Buckley, Andrew C. Chamberlain, and Eileen Murphy
1998 Rib Lesions and Tuberculosis: The Palaeopathological Evidence. *Tubercle and Lung Disease* 79(1):55–60.

Roberts, Charlotte, and Jane E. Buikstra
2003 *The Bioarchaeology of Tuberculosis: A Global View on a Reemerging Disease.* University Press of Florida, Gainesville.

Roberts, Charlotte, and Margaret Cox
2003 *Health and Disease in Britain.* Sutton Publishing, Stroud.

Roberts, Charlotte, David Lucy, and Keith Manchester
1994 Inflammatory Lesions of the Ribs: An Analysis of the Terry Collection. *American Journal of Physical Anthropology* 95(2):169–182.

Roberts, Charlotte, and Keith Manchester
2005 *The Archaeology of Disease.* 3rd ed. Sutton Publishing, Stroud.

Robertson, David Hunter Henderson, Alexander McMillan, and H. Young
1989 *Clinical Practice in Sexually Transmissible Diseases.* Churchill Livingstone, New York.

Robins, Joseph
1995 *The Miasma: Epidemic and Panic in Nineteenth-Century Ireland.* Institute of Public Administration, Dublin.

Robinson, Kingsley P.
1991 Historical Aspects of Amputation. *Annals of the Royal College of Surgeons of England* 73(3):134–136.

Rogers, Juliet
2000 The Palaeopathology of Joint Disease. In *Human Osteology in Archaeology and Forensic Science*, edited by Margaret Cox and Simon Mays, pp. 163–182. Cambridge University Press, Cambridge.

Rogers, Juliet, and Tony Waldron
1989 Infections in Palaeopathology: The Basis of Classification According to Most Probable Cause. *Journal of Archaeological Science* 16(6):611–625.
1995 *A Field Guide to Joint Disease in Archaeology.* John Wiley and Sons, Chichester.

Rogers, Juliet, Tony Waldron, Paul Dieppe, and Iain Watt
1987 Arthropathies in Palaeopathology: The Basis of Classification According to Most Probable Cause. *Journal of Archaeological Science* 14(2):179–193.

Rogers, Tom, Linda Fibiger, Linda G. Lynch, and Declan Moore
2006 Two Glimpses of Nineteenth-Century Institutional Burial Practice in Ireland: A Report on the Excavation of Burials from Manorhamilton Workhouse, Co. Leitrim, and St. Brigid's Hospital, Ballinasloe, Co. Galway. *The Journal of Irish Archaeology* 15:93–104.

Rosenberg, Bruce A.
1987 The Complexity of Oral Tradition. *Oral Tradition* 2(1):73–90.

Rösing, Friedrich W.
1988 Körperhöhenrekonstruktion aus Skelettmaßen. In *Wesen und Methoden der Anthropologie. 1 Teil. Wissenschaftstheorie, Geschichte, morphologische Methoden*, edited by Rainer Knußmann, pp. 586–600. Gustav Fischer Verlag, Stuttgart.

Ruffell, Alastair, Alan Mccabe, Colm Donnelly, and Brian Sloan
2009 Location and Assessment of an Historic (150–60 Years Old) Mass Grave Using Geographic and Ground Penetrating Radar Investigation, NW Ireland. *Journal of Forensic Science* 54(2):383–394.

Sachs, Michael, Jörg Bojunga, and Albrecht Encke
1999 Historical Evolution of Limb Amputation. *World Journal of Surgery* 23(10):1088–1093.

Sager, Philip
1969 *Spondylosis Cervicalis. A Pathological and Osteoarchaeological Study of Osteochondrosis Intervertebralis Cervicalis, Arthrosis Uncovertebralis, and Spondylarthrosis Cervicalis*. Munksgaard, Copenhagen.

Salo, Wilmar L., Arthur C. Aufderheide, Jane Buikstra, and Todd A. Holcomb
1994 Identification of Mycobacterium Tuberculosis DNA in a Pre-Columbian Peruvian Mummy. *Proceedings of the National Academy of Sciences of the United States of America* 91(6):2091–2094.

Sandmeier, Robert H.
2000 Osteoarthritis and Exercise: Does Increased Activity Wear Out Joints? *The Permanente Journal* 4(4):26–28.

Sartre, Jean-Paul
1976 [1960] *Critique of Dialectical Reason*. Translated by Alan Sheridan-Smith. NLB, London.

Saunders, Shelley R., Carol De Vito, and M. Anne Katzenberg
1997 Dental Caries in Nineteenth-Century Upper Canada. *American Journal of Physical Anthropology* 104(1):71–87.

Scheuer, J. Louise, and Sue Black
2000 *Developmental Juvenile Osteology*. Academic Press, London.

Scheuer, J. Louise, Jonathan H. Musgrave, and S. P. Evans
1980 The Estimation of Late Fetal and Perinatal Age from Limb Bone Length by Linear and Logarithmic Regression. *Annals of Human Biology* 7(3):257–265.

Scholl, Theresa O.
2005 Iron Status during Pregnancy: Setting the Stage for Mother and Infant. *American Journal of Clinical Nutrition* S81:1218–1222.

Schwartz, Jeffrey H.
1995 *Skeleton Keys: An Introduction to Human Skeletal Morphology, Development, and Analysis*. Oxford University Press, Oxford.

Scully, Siobhán
2010 Report on the Personal Possessions, Metal Finds and Coffin Nails from McDonagh Junction Famine Burial Ground. Appendix in Brenda O'Meara, McDonagh Junction, Hebron Road, Kilkenny. Final Report on the Findings from the Excavation of a Famine Burial Ground. Unpublished report, Margaret Gowen and Co. Ltd., Dublin.

Selwitz, Robert H., Amid I. Ismail, and Nigel B. Pitts
2007 Dental Caries. *The Lancet* 369(9555):51–59.

Sexton, Regina
2012 Diet in Pre-Famine Ireland. In *Atlas of the Great Irish Famine 1845–52*, edited by John Crowley, William J. Smyth, and Mike Murphy, pp. 41–43. Cork University Press, Cork.

Shrout, Anelise H.
2012 The Famine and New York City. In *Atlas of the Great Irish Famine, 1845–52*, edited by John Crowley, William J. Smyth, and Mike Murphy, pp. 536–546. Cork University Press, Cork.

Siegel, Daniel J.
1997 Memory and Trauma. In *Psychological Trauma: A Developmental Approach*, edited by Dora Black, Martin Newman, Jean Harris-Hendriks, and Gillian Mezey, pp. 44–53. Gaskell, London.

Signoli, Michel, Yann Ardagna, Pascal Adalian, William Devriendt, Loïc Lalys, Catherine Rigeade, Thierry Vette, Albinas Kuncevicius, Justina Poskiene, Arunas Barkus, Zydruné Palubeckaité, Antanas Garmus, Virgilijus Pugaciauskas, Rimantas Jankauskas, and Olivier Dutour
2004 Discovery of a Mass Grave of Napoleonic Period in Lithuania (1812, Vilnius). *Comptes Rendus Palevol* 3(3):219–227.

Sjøvold, Torstein
1988 Geschlechtsdiagnose am Skelett. In *Wesen und Methoden der Anthropologie. 1 Teil. Wissenschaftstheorie, Geschichte, morphologische Methoden*, edited by Rainer Knußmann, pp. 444–480. Gustav Fischer Verlag, Stuttgart.
1990 Estimation of Stature from Long Bones Utilizing the Line of Organic Correlation. *Human Evolution* 5(5):431–447.

Snodgrass, J. Josh
2004 Sex Differences and Aging of the Vertebral Column. *Journal of Forensic Science* 49(3):1–6.

Sofaer, Joanna R.
2006 *The Body as Material Culture: A Theoretical Osteoarchaeology*. Topics in Contemporary Archaeology. Cambridge University Press, Cambridge.

Somerville, Alexander
1994 *Letters from Ireland during the Famine of 1847*. Irish Academic Press, Dublin.

Spector, Tim D., Flavia Cicuttini, Juliet Baker, and John Loughlin
1996 Genetic Influences on Osteoarthritis in Women: A Twin Study. *British Medical Journal* 312(7036):940.

Stanley, William
1833 *Commentaries on Ireland*. Richard Milliken and Son, Dublin.

Start, Helen, and Lucy Kirk
1998 "The Bodies of Friends"—The Osteological Analysis of a Quaker Burial Ground. In *Grave Concerns: Death and Burial in England 1700 to 1850*, edited by Margaret Cox, pp. 167–177. CBA Research Report. Council for British Archaeology, York.

Steckel, Richard H.

1995 Stature and the Standard of Living. *Journal of Economic Literature* 33(4):1903–1940.

Steinbock, R. Ted

1976 *Paleopathological Diagnosis and Interpretation*. Charles C. Thomas, Springfield.

1993 Rickets and Osteomalacia. In *The Cambridge World History of Human Disease*, edited by Kenneth F. Kiple, pp. 978–980. Cambridge University Press, Cambridge.

Stuart-Macadam, Patricia L.

1985 Porotic Hyperostosis: Representative of a Childhood Condition. *American Journal of Physical Anthropology* 66(4):391–398.

1989 Nutritional Deficiency Diseases: A Survey of Scurvy, Rickets, and Iron-Deficiency Anemia. In *Reconstruction of Life from the Skeleton*, edited by Mehmet Yaşar İşcan and Kenneth A. R. Kennedy, pp. 201–222. Alan R. Liss, Inc., New York.

1992 Porotic Hyperostosis: A New Perspective. *American Journal of Physical Anthropology* 87(1):39–47.

Sullivan, William Norbert

1903 Diseases of Infancy Due to Faulty Nutrition: Infantile Rhachitis, Infantile Scorbutus and Infantile Atrophy. *California State Journal of Medicine* 1(8):234–236.

Sultan, Ali N., and Rukhsana Wamiq Zyberi

2003 Late Weaning: The Most Significant Risk Factor in the Development of Iron Deficiency Anaemia at 1–2 years of Age. *Journal of Ayub Medical College, Abbottabad* 15(2):3–7.

Sutton, Bruce

2010 Archaeological Excavation Report, Hospital of the Assumption, Thurles, Co. Tipperary, Eachtra Journal 5. Eachtra Archaeological Projects, Innishannon.

Tainter, Joseph A.

1980 Behavior and Status in a Middle Woodland Mortuary Population from the Illinois Valley. *American Antiquity* 45(2):308–313.

Tarlow, Sarah

1999 *Bereavement and Commemoration: An Archaeology of Mortality*. Blackwell Publishers Ltd., Oxford.

Tedberg, Annabel, and Joan E. Hodgman

1973 Congenital Syphilis in Newborn. *California Medicine* 118(4):5–10.

Tighe, William

1802 *Statistical Observations Relative to the County of Kilkenny Made in the Years 1800 and 1801*. Graisberry and Campbell, Dublin.

Tilley, Lorna, and Marc Fredrick Oxenham

2011 Survival Against the Odds: Modeling the Social Implications of Care Provision to Seriously Disabled Individuals. *International Journal of Paleopathology* 1(1):35–42.

Tóibín, Colm, and Diarmaid Ferriter

2001 *The Irish Famine: A Documentary*. Profile Books Ltd., London.

Trotter, Mildred, and Goldine C. Gleser

1952 Estimation of Stature from Long Bones of American Whites and Negroes. *American Journal of Physical Anthropology* 10(4):463–514.

1958 A Re-Evaluation of Estimation of Stature Based on Measurements of Stature Taken during Life and of Long Bones after Death. *American Journal of Physical Anthropology* 16(1):79–123.

Tubbs, Hugh
1992 Systemic Infections. In *Infectious Diseases: Text and Color Atlas*, edited by W. Edmund Farrar, Martin J. Wood, John A. Innes, and Hugh Tubbs, 13–26. Gower Medical Publishing, London.

Vanhaute, Eric, Richard Paping, and Cormac Ó Gráda
2007 The European Subsistence Crisis of 1845–1850: A Comparative Perspective. In *When the Potato Failed: Causes and Effects of the "Last" European Subsistance Crisis, 1845–1850*, edited by Cormac Ó Gráda, Richard Paping, and Eric Vanhaute, pp. 15–40. Brepols Publishers, Turnhout.

Vaughan, Janet M.
1970 *The Physiology of Bone*. Clarendon Press, Oxford.

Veal, Ross J.
1939 Typhoid and Paratyphoid Osteomyelitis. *The American Journal of Surgery* 43(2):594–597.

Verlaan, Jorrit Jan, F. Cumhur Öner, and George J. R. Maat
2007 Diffuse Idiopathic Skeletal Hyperostosis in Ancient Clergymen. *European Spine Journal* 16(8):1129–1135.

Waldron, Harry Arthur
1993 The Health of the Adults. In *The Spitalfields Project*. Vol. 2, *The Anthropology: The Middling Sort*, edited by Theya Molleson, Margaret Cox, Harry Arthur Waldron, and David K. Whittaker, pp. 67–91. CBA Research Report 86. Council for British Archaeology, York.

Waldron, Harry Arthur, and Margaret Cox
1989 Occupational Arthropathy: Evidence from the Past. *British Journal of Industrial Medicine* 46(6):420–422.

Waldron, Tony
2007 *St. Peter's, Barton-upon-Humber, Lincolnshire: A Parish Church and Its Community*. Vol. 2, *The Human Remains*. Oxbow Books, Oxbow.

Walker, Don, and Michael Henderson
2010 Smoking and Health in London's East End in the First Half of the 19th Century. *Post-Medieval Archaeology* 44(1):209–222.

Walker, Phillip L.
1997 Wife Beating, Boxing, and Broken Noses: Skeletal Evidence for the Cultural Patterning of Violence. In *Troubled Times: Violence and Warfare in the Past*, edited by Debra L. Martin and David W. Frayer, pp. 145–180. Gordon and Breach Publishers, Amsterdam.

Walker, Phillip L., Rhonda R. Bathurst, Rebecca Richman, Thor Gjerdrum, and Valerie A. Andrushko
2009 The Cause of Porotic Hyperostosis and Cribra Orbitalia: A Reappraisal of the Iron-Deficiency-Anemia Hypothesis. *American Journal of Physical Anthropology* 139(2):109–125.

Walsh, Pat
1966 Kilkenny in the 19th Century. *Old Kilkenny Review* 19:52–58.
Walsh, Walter
2008 *Kilkenny: The Struggle for the Land 1850–1882.* Walsh Books, Kilkenny.
Wapler, Ulrike, Eric Crubézy, and Michael Schultz
2004 Is Cribra Orbitalia Synonymous with Anemia? Analysis and Interpretation of Cranial Pathology in Sudan. *American Journal of Physical Anthropology* 123(4):333–339.
Waterlow, John C.
1992 *Protein-Energy Malnutrition.* Edward Arnold, London.
Weiner, Stephen
2010 *Microarchaeology: Beyond the Visible Archaeological Record.* Cambridge University Press, Cambridge.
Weiss, Elizabeth
2006 Osteoarthritis and Body Mass. *Journal of Archaeological Science* 33(5):690–695.
Weiss, Elizabeth, and Robert Jurmain
2007 Osteoarthritis Revisited: A Contemporary Review of Aetiology. *International Journal of Osteoarchaeology* 17(5):437–450.
Weiss, Kenneth M.
1973 Demographic Models for Anthropology. *American Antiquity* 38(2):1–186.
Welinder, Stig
1992 *Det arkeologiska perspektivet.* Från Forntid och Medeltid 9. Almqvist and Wiksell International, Lund.
Wells, Lawrence H.
1969 Stature in Earlier Races of Mankind. In *Science in Archaeology. A Survey of Progress and Research*, edited by Don Brothwell and Eric Higgs, pp. 453–467. Praeger Publishers, New York.
Wesolowski, Veronica
2006 Caries Prevalence in Skeletal Series: Is It Possible to Compare? *Memórias do Instituto Oswaldo Cruz* 101(2):139–145.
Weston, Darlene A.
2012 Nonspecific Infection in Paleopathology. In *A Companion to Paleopathology*, edited by Anne L. Grauer, pp. 492–512. Blackwell Publishing Ltd., Chicester.
Whelan, Kevin
2004 The Revisionist Debate in Ireland. *Boundary 2* 31(1):179–205.
White, William
2008 The Human Skeletal Remains from the Burial Ground of St. Benet Sherehog. In *Burial at the Site of the Parish Church of St. Benet Sherehog Before and After the Great Fire: Excavations at 1 Poultry, City of London*, edited by Adrian Miles, William White, and Danae Tankard, pp. 70–92. MOLAS Monograph 39. Museum of London Archaeology Service, London.
2011 Burial and Population: Osteological Evidence. In *St. Pancras Burial Ground: Excavations for St. Pancras International, the London Terminus of High Speed 1, 2002–3*, edited by Phillip A. Emery and Kevin Wooldridge, pp. 112–117. Gifford, London.

Whitman, Steven, Rochelle Coonley-Hoganson, and Bindu I. Desai
1984 Comparative Head Trauma Experiences in Two Socioeconomically Different Chicago-Area Communities: A Population Study. *American Journal of Epidemiology* 119(4):570–580.

Whittaker, David K.
1993 Oral Health. In *The Spitalfields Project*. Vol. 2, *The Anthropology: The Middling Sort*, edited by Theya Molleson, Margaret Cox, Harry Arthur Waldron, and David K. Whittaker, pp. 49–65. CBA Research Report 86. Council for British Archaeology, York.

Whittaker, David K., S. Griffiths, A. Robson, P. Roger-Davies, G. Thomas, and Theya I. Molleson
1990 Continuing Tooth Eruption and Alveolar Crest Height in an Eighteenth-Century Population from Spitalfields, East London. *Archives of Oral Biology* 35(2):81–85.

Whittaker, David K., J. W. Jones, P. W. Edwards, and Theya I. Molleson
1990 Studies on the Temporomandibular Joints of an Eighteenth-Century London Population (Spitalfields). *Journal of Oral Rehabilitation* 17(1):89–97.

Wilbur, Alicia K., Amy Walker Farnbach, Kelly J. Knudson, and Jane E. Buikstra
2008 Diet, Tuberculosis, and the Paleopathological Record. *Current Anthropology* 46(6):963–991.

Wilemann, Julie
2005 *Hide and Seek: The Archaeology of Childhood*. Tempus Publishing Limited, Stroud.

Willey, Gordon R., and Philip Phillips
1958 *Method and Theory in American Archaeology*. University of Chicago Press, Chicago.

Wilson, Andrew Norman
2003 *The Victorians*. Arrow Books, London.

Wing, Elizabeth S., and Antoinette B. Brown
1979 *Paleonutrition: Method and Theory in Prehistoric Foodways*. Academic Press, New York.

Wolff, Julius
1892 *Das Gesetz der Transformation der Knochen*. Hirschwald, Berlin.

Wood, James W., George R. Milner, Henry C. Harpending, and Kenneth M. Weiss
1992 The Osteological Paradox: Problems of Inferring Prehistoric Health from Skeletal Samples. *Current Anthropology* 33(4):343–370.

Woodham-Smith, Cecil
1964 *The Great Hunger: Ireland 1845–1849*. Penguin Books, London.

Woods, Charles R.
2005 Syphilis in Children: Congenital and Acquired. *Seminars in Pediatric Infectious Diseases* 16(4):245–257.

Woods, Colin G.
1994 Metabolic Bone Diseases. In *Diseases of Bones and Joints: Cell Biology, Mechanisms, Pathology*, edited by Jonathan R. Salisbury, Colin G. Woods, and Paul D. Byers, pp. 236–285. Chapman and Hall Medical, London.

Woods, Robert
1996 Physician, Heal Thyself: The Health and Mortality of Victorian Doctors. *Social History of Medicine* 9(1):1–30.

Woolfe, Jennifer A.
1987 *The Potato in the Human Diet*. Cambridge University Press, Cambridge.
Young, Kristin, John H. Relethford, and Michael H. Crawford
2008 Postfamine Stature and Socioeconomic Status in Ireland. *American Journal of Human Biology* 20(6):726–731.
Zadoks, Jan C.
2008 The Potato Murrain on the European Continent and the Revolutions of 1848. *Potato Research* 51(1):5–45.
Zeller, John L.
2008 Osteomyelitis. *The Journal of the American Medical Association* 299(7):858.
Zhou, Liming, and Robert S. Corruccini
1998 Enamel Hypoplasias Related to Famine Stress in Living Chinese. *American Journal of Human Biology* 10(6):723–733.

Index

Jonny Geber is a lecturer in biological anthropology at the University of Otago, New Zealand. His particular research interests include social bio-archaeology and the osteoarchaeology and burial archaeology of Ireland.

Bones of Complexity: Bioarchaeological Case Studies of Social Organization and Skeletal Biology, edited by Haagen D. Klaus, Amanda R. Harvey, and Mark N. Cohen (2017)

A World View of Bioculturally Modified Teeth, edited by Scott E. Burnett and Joel D. Irish (2017)

Children and Childhood in Bioarchaeology, edited by Patrick Beauchesne and Sabrina C. Agarwal (2018)

Bioarchaeology of Pre-Columbian Mesoamerica: An Interdisciplinary Approach, edited by Cathy Willermet and Andrea Cucina (2018)

www.ingramcontent.com/pod-product-compliance
Lightning Source LLC
Chambersburg PA
CBHW020525270326
41927CB00006B/454